THE YALE-HOOVER SERIES ON STALIN, STALINISM, AND THE COLD WAR

MASTER OF THE HOUSE

STALIN AND HIS INNER CIRCLE

OLEG V. KHLEVNIUK

Translated by Nora Seligman Favorov

Hoover Institution
Stanford University
Stanford, California

Yale University Press

New Haven and London

Set in Sabon type by The Composing Room of Michigan, Inc., Grand Rapids, Michigan.
Printed in the United States of America by Thomson-Shore, Inc., Dexter, Michigan.

Library of Congress Cataloging-in-Publication Data
Khlevniuk, Oleg V.
    Master of the house : Stalin and his inner circle / Oleg V. Khlevniuk ; translated by
Nora Seligman Favorov.
        p. cm.— (Yale-Hoover Series on Stalin, Stalinism, and the Cold War)
    Includes bibliographical references and index.
    ISBN 978-0-300-11066-1 (alk. paper)
    1. Soviet Union—Politics and government—1917–1936. I. Title.
    DK266.K456 2008
    947.084′2—dc22
    2008017715

A catalogue record for this book is available from the British Library.

This paper meets the requirements of ANSI/NISO Z39.48-1992 (Permanence of Paper).
It contains 30 percent postconsumer waste (PCW) and is certified by the Forest Stewardship
Council (FSC).

10 9 8 7 6 5 4 3 2 1

Contents

Acknowledgments

This book has taken shape over fifteen years of research in the archives of the Soviet government and the administrative structures of the Soviet Communist Party. Every time a new body of previously top secret archival material was opened to researchers, work on this manuscript entered a new stage. This publication represents the culmination of this work, and I am extremely pleased that it will be part of a new series, the Yale-Hoover Series on Stalin, Stalinism, and the Cold War, being launched by two leading institutions in the study of Soviet archives—Stanford University's Hoover Institution on War, Revolution and Peace, whose director is John Raisian, and Yale University Press, whose director is John Donatich. I am also grateful to the series editors, Jonathan Brent and Paul Gregory, for their advice and assistance in bringing this book to fruition. I wish as well to express my thanks to the Hoover Institution for its support of the latest phase of my work, including its sponsorship with the Russian State Archive of Social and Political History (RGASPI) of the publication of Politburo stenograms by the Russian Political Encyclopedia (ROSSPEN). These stenograms are an important new source that has illuminated questions addressed in this book.

Let me turn to the more distant origins of this publication. Since 1992, under the auspices of two projects—Decision-Making Mechanisms within the Stalinist Command Economy in the 1930s and the series Documents of Soviet History—I have been investigating the archives of the Politburo and the Council of People's Commissars, which were opened to researchers in the former Central Party Archive (now RGASPI) and the Central State Archive of the October Revolution and the Supreme Organs of State Power of the USSR (now the State Archive of the Russian Federation—GARF). This research led to several articles and a collection entitled *Stalinskoe politburo v 30-e gody* (Stalin's Politburo in the 1930s) (Moscow: AIRO-XX, 1995). Even more than these (undoubtedly important) publications, I value the personal and scholarly relationships I developed over the course of this work. Thanks to these relationships, for many years now I have considered myself a member of two extraordinarily interesting teams. The first is the Birmingham University team headed by R. W. Davies. The members of this team—Arfon Rees, the late Derek Watson, Melanie Ilič, Mark Harrison, Stephen Wheatcroft—have become valued colleagues. I have derived great pleasure and benefit from the discussions we shared concerning the problems of Soviet history of the 1930s. My participation in the second team came about thanks to the involvement of Andrea Graziosi and Moshe Lewin in the Documents of Soviet History series, which is supported by the Istituto Italiano per gli Studi Filosofici. It has provided me with invaluable experience in the study and publication of archival materials. Suffice it to say that over the course of fifteen years' work on this project, thirteen collections of documents have been published, many of which are directly tied to the political history of the Soviet Union.

My first monograph dealing with the highest echelons of power in the Soviet Union of the 1930s was devoted to the conflict between Stalin and his close comrade-in-arms Grigory "Sergo" Ordzhonikidze. The book was first published in Russian and has come out in an English-language edition thanks to the efforts of Donald J. Raleigh (Oleg V. Khlevniuk, *In Stalin's Shadow: The Career of "Sergo" Ordzhonikidze* [New York: M. E. Sharpe, 1995]).

Nicolas Werth proposed writing a book about Stalin's Politburo for his series of Soviet historical studies (O. Khlevniouk, *Le Cercle du Kremlin. Staline et le Bureau politique dans les années 1930: Les jeux du pouvoir* [Paris, Seuil, 1996]). Also in 1996, an expanded and revised Russian version of this book was put out by the publisher ROSSPEN under the title *Politbiuro. Mekhanizmy politicheskoi vlasti v 1930-e gody* (The Politburo: Mechanisms of political power in the 1930s). Markus Wehner, Reinhard Müller, and the scholars and directors of the Hamburg Institute of Social Research arranged to have my work published in German translation. For this edition (Oleg W. Chlewnjuk, *Das Politbüro. Mechanismen der politischen Macht in der Sowjetunion der dreißiger Jahre,* Hamburger Edition [Hamburg: Hamburg Institute of Social Research, 1998]) I again revised and expanded the manuscript. This additional work on the book was necessitated by rapid growth in the historiography of the Soviet period and by the constant emergence of documents that shed light on the subject, primarily from the Presidential Archive of the Russian Federation (APRF). The book you now hold in your hands is substantially different from the previous versions in terms of its sources. While I was researching it the opportunity arose to work with exceptionally important archival documents (primarily from Stalin's personal papers) that were moved from APRF to RGASPI in recent years, as well as a number of other sources from Politburo thematic folders, which continue to be held by APRF.

Several recent projects greatly influenced the writing of this book. First among them is the collaboration between the Hoover Institution and RGASPI, which culminated in the publication of a three-volume collection of Politburo stenograms (*Stenograms of the TsK RKP[b]-VKP[b] Politburo Meetings, 1923–1938* [Moscow: ROSSPEN, 2007]), which facilitates further study into the period. The driving force behind this project was Paul Gregory. The second project that should be mentioned was carried out by my friend Yoram Gorlizki and me and was devoted to the highest bodies of Stalinist power during their heyday (Yoram Gorlizki and Oleg Khlevniuk, *Cold Peace: Stalin and the Soviet Ruling Circle, 1945–1953* [New York: Oxford University Press, 2004]). This project provided new opportunities for a comparative study of the development of the Soviet system and, consequently, for a better understanding of each development stage. Yoram proved to be a patient and wise coauthor who not only bravely endured my shortcomings but took upon himself the main burden of preparing the book. Third, together with Viktor Danilov and Aleksandr Vatlin, I edited five volumes of Central Committee plenum stenograms for 1928–1929 (*Kak lomali nep. Stenogrammy plenumov TsK VKP[b] 1928–1929 gg.* [How NEP was broken: TsK VKP(b) plenum stenograms, 1928–1929] [Moscow: MDF,

2000]). This provided valuable experience researching new sources that illuminate the period of struggle between Stalin and the "rightists." Unfortunately, the death of Viktor Danilov prevented us from carrying out other endeavors and deprived us of a wise and experienced colleague.

Collaboration and communication with my fellow historians have had an incalculable impact on my work. Although I will not be able to name them all, I would nonetheless like to express my sincere gratitude to Golfo Alexopoulos, Jörg Baberowski, Dietrich Beyrau, Alain Blum, Yves Cohen, Marta Craveri, Benno Ennker, Antonio Gargano, Klaus Gestwa, Arch Getty, Julie Hessler, Jana Howlett, Vladimir Kozlov, Hiroaki Kuromiya, Terry Martin, Jan Plamper, Silvio Pons, Andrea Romano, Robert Service, David Shearer, Peter Solomon, Ronald Suny, Takeshi Tomita, Valery Vasiliev, Lynne Viola, Haruki Wada, Amir Weiner, Viktor Zaslavsky, and Elena Zubkova. I am particularly thankful for my interactions with Sheila Fitzpatrick, who has now been supporting my efforts for twenty years.

Spending, as I do, a significant portion of my time in archives, I have developed many valued relationships there with true friends, colleagues, and coauthors. At RGASPI I have been fortunate to work with M. S. Astakhova, G. V. Gorskaya, E. E. Kirillova, L. P. Kosheleva, L. N. Malashenko, and L. A. Rogovaya. Our congenial and highly professional team has prepared quite a few collections of documents. Efforts at GARF would not be possible without the constant support and valuable guidance of G. A. Kuznetsova, D. N. Nokhotovich, S. V. Somonova, and T. Yu. Zhukova.

Many important documentary publications and monographs would never have seen the light of day had Jonathan Brent not overcome a multitude of problems and obstacles to launch the Annals of Communism series at Yale University Press in the early 1990s. It is largely thanks to Jonathan Brent and Vadim Staklo that this series has achieved the recognition it deserves. Within Russia, books from this series are known not only to specialists familiar with the original English-language publications but also to a broader audience, reading Russian-language editions put out by ROSSPEN under the stewardship of A. K. Sorokin. I am pleased to have my name on the covers of three books in the Annals of Communism series and excited that the endeavor begun with this series will expand into new projects, including the joint undertaking of the Hoover Institution and Yale University Press to publish

The Yale-Hoover Series on Stalin, Stalinism, and the Cold War, the significance of which cannot be overstated. I am grateful to Paul Gregory, who not only selected my book for publication under the auspices of this project but undertook the challenging task of editing it.

It was a pleasure working with Nora Favorov, who not only translated the book into English but was its highly professional, good-natured, and patient critic. I am grateful to Mary Pasti of Yale University Press for the skill and effort she put into editing the book.

As always, I wish to express particular gratitude to my wife and daughter.

Introduction

In December 1929, Joseph Stalin wrote to his closest comrade-in-arms, Viacheslav Mikhailovich Molotov, who was on vacation in the south. "Hello, Viacheslav. Of course I got your first letter. I know you are cursing me in your heart for my silence. I can't deny that you are fully within your rights to do so. But try to see things my way: I'm terribly overloaded and there's no time to sleep (literally!). Soon I will write a proper letter [. . .]. Once again: I promise to write a proper letter. Warm regards."[1] A few years later, Stalin fundamentally changed his relationship with Molotov. In 1937 and 1938, Stalin ordered that Molotov's assistants be arrested. Molotov's people were no safer than those working for other members of the Politburo, many of whose aides were swept away in the Great Terror. In 1939 the NKVD fabricated a case against Molotov's wife (although her arrest would not come until later). Molotov himself was subject to numerous demeaning attacks, and in May 1941 he was removed from the post of chairman of the Council of People's Commissars in disgrace. On 6 December 1945, Stalin, who was away on vacation, wrote the following to Lavrenty Beria, Georgy Malenkov, and Anastas Mikoyan: "I have become convinced that Molotov does not hold the interests of our state and the prestige of our government in very high regard—all he cares about is popularity in certain foreign circles. I can no longer consider such a comrade to be my first deputy." As a final humiliating blow he added, "I am sending this cipher to you three only. I didn't send it to Molotov since I don't have faith in the trustworthiness of certain of his close associates. I am asking you to summon Molotov and read him my telegram in its entirety, but don't give him a copy of it."[2] Molotov's response was humbly repentant. "I will try to earn your trust through my deeds. For any honorable Bolshevik, your trust represents the trust of the Party, which is dearer to me than life itself."[3] Nevertheless, Molotov continued to be subjected to indignity. Under pressure from Stalin, Molotov divorced his wife, who was arrested in 1949. In October 1952, just a few months before he died, Stalin made Molotov the target of a sharp public rebuke during a plenary session of the Central Committee of the Communist Party and then removed him almost entirely from government affairs.[4]

Unlike many other high-ranking members of the Soviet leadership, not to mention millions of Soviet government officials and ordinary citizens, Molotov survived the terror. But although his life was spared, he still had to pay a price for his role in helping Stalin defeat the oppositionists in the Politburo in the 1920s, for his long years of friendship with Stalin, for his past "oligarchic" independence, and for the fact that Stalin had once felt compelled to offer excuses for not writing to him.

The evolving relationship between Stalin and Molotov reflected changes at the highest echelons of power in the Soviet Union, changes that I investigate in this book. In short, I address the interrelated processes that led to the breakdown of the oligarchic collective leadership of the Politburo and the consolidation of Stalin's dictatorship. This outcome, which not only proved tragic for old Bolsheviks and the Soviet *nomenklatura* but also had an enormous impact on the fate of the entire country undoubtedly had historic antecedents and identifiable causes. Many prefer to believe that Stalin's dictatorship was inevitable, either because "that's all you can expect from Russia/the Bolsheviks" or because that is what the underlying ideology of state ownership and administrative planning give rise to. Both this thesis and its antithesis (that chance played an important role in Stalin's takeover of power) belong to a realm of history where we will never have clear-cut answers. Which side we come down on is largely a matter of our "historical faith" or our political inclinations. But for the historian, it seems to me, the concept of the "iron march of history" is, at the very least, uninspiring. Chronicler of the inevitable—why would anyone who has read and analyzed tens of thousands of pages of the most diverse documents, who has learned the fates of faceless millions, not to mention hundreds of flesh-and-blood individuals, many of whom desperately fought for their interests and ideals—why would such a person agree with such a characterization? The idea of inevitability comes when we try to arrange history into some kind of orderly progression. Specific knowledge complicates the picture, revealing the diversity of factors involved in any human endeavor, the complex interplay between historical traditions and the logic governing events as they unfold, between political conflict at the top and social pressures at the bottom, and, in the end, the role of chance.

This work presents and synthesizes evidence about the change in models of power at the highest political levels in the Soviet Union that took place between the late 1920s and the early 1940s. The gradual consolidation of Stalin's dictatorship that characterized this period went through several stages. Each chapter of this book is devoted to one of these stages.

The main result of the struggle at the highest levels of the party that took place in the 1920s between Lenin's heirs was the gradual Stalinization of the Politburo. The essence of this Stalinization was Stalin's ascent to dominance within a system of collective leadership that nonetheless remained primarily oligarchic in nature. The Politburo's acceptance and implementation of the political course that Stalin was advocating—accelerated industrialization and forced mass collectivization—can be seen as the culmination of this process. But although Stalin may have dominated the Politburo, it was several years before he achieved dictatorial powers. Victory over Aleksei Rykov, Nikolai Bukharin, and Mikhail Tomsky in 1928 and 1929, which was vital to Stalinization at the highest levels, demanded significant effort on the part of Stalin and his supporters.[5] Furthermore, the growing crisis that came out of the policy of accelerated economic reorganization forced Stalin to act with more restraint than would have been expected from an absolute victor. Evidence of this can be found in behind-the-scenes actions taken against the rightists and certain thoroughly loyal members of the Politburo, as well as the confrontation between Stalin's Politburo and Rykov's Council of People's Commissars in 1930, discussed in the first chapter of this book.

At the end of 1930 a resolution to the problem of the rightists (or,

rather, the problem of Rykov) meant that the Politburo leadership of
Stalin, Rykov, and Bukharin was replaced by Stalin's sole leadership, albeit leadership that still bore many of the hallmarks of oligarchy. This
was an important step on the road to consolidating his one-man dictatorship, but it still did not constitute such a dictatorship.[6] The early
1930s was a transitional period, and historians have come up with several theories to explain it. I will talk about them in the order in which
they emerged.

The first theory asserts that policy at the highest levels of the Soviet
leadership during this period was shaped by a confrontation between
two factions—the "radicals" and the "moderates." At this point Stalin
still lacked the strength to consolidate his dictatorship, and, according
to this version, the outcome of the confrontation finally tilted the scales
in his favor. This theory had its origin in the 1930s. By then, news of
conflict at the top and of clashes between proponents of harsher and
more moderate lines had already appeared in the foreign press. These
political rumors were lent credence by an article entitled "How the
Moscow Trial Was Prepared: Letter of an Old Bolshevik," published in
Sotsialistichesky vestnik (Socialist herald).[7] The article, which detailed
evidence of a standoff within Stalin's Politburo, was published anony-
mously. Years later, the well-known historian Boris Nikolaevsky acknowledged his authorship and revealed that in "Letter of an Old Bolshevik" he had relied on the testimony of Nikolai Bukharin, with
whom he met in Paris in 1936.[8] The article contained truly sensational
allegations. Nikolaevsky described a battle for influence over Stalin between proponents of a policy of moderation and a gradual diminution
of the terror, headed by Sergei Kirov, who had the support of the influential Soviet writer Maxim Gorky, and their opponents, led by Lazar
Kaganovich and Nikolai Yezhov. After Kirov's death, the last two tri-
umphed.

For many years, there was no way to verify the authenticity of Nikolaevsky's account through archival sources, but as soon as Bukharin's
widow, Anna Larina, was able to publish her memoirs, she categorically
denied that Bukharin had given any information to Nikolaevsky.[9] Her
denial was received skeptically.[10] In any event, over subsequent decades, Nikolaevsky's work exerted tremendous influence both over
scholarly literature and textbooks and over the testimony of individual
eyewitnesses, who used the appealing idea of factions within the Polit-

buro for their own purposes. Such, for example, was the case with former NKVD general Alexander Orlov, who constructed his well-known but absolutely inauthentic book around Nikolaevsky's account.[11]

Nikolaevsky's version of events was further bolstered by official Soviet propaganda during the years of Khrushchev's thaw. The cornerstone of Nikita Khrushchev's de-Stalinization was the sorting of Stalin's former comrades-in-arms into "bad" and "good." Beria, Malenkov, Molotov, Kaganovich, and Yezhov all fell into the first category. That left, for the second category, Khrushchev himself, Kliment Voroshilov, Mikoyan, Mikhail Kalinin, and Grigory "Sergo" Ordzhonikidze, as well as all of the Politburo members who had been repressed during the 1930s. The crimes of the former regime were attributed to Stalin's "bad" cohort (Stalin himself was often absolved of blame and labeled a victim of Politburo members' intrigues). At the same time, Khrushchev vaguely suggested that the "good" members of the Politburo had attempted to fight abuse of power, even during Stalin's lifetime. These ideas found their fullest expression in Khrushchev's speech to the 20th Party Congress and later in the memoirs of old Bolsheviks collected by dissident historians. New versions of events, countenanced from above, entered into circulation through a variety of channels. There were new accounts of meetings of high-level party functionaries, who purportedly were hatching plans during the 17th Party Congress to replace Stalin with Kirov as general secretary of the Central Committee; a new notion that Kirov was killed by order of Stalin, who saw in the Leningrad party secretary a political rival; a new version of the circumstances of Ordzhonikidze's death and allegations that it resulted from conflict with Stalin; and a new suggestion that Postyshev spoke out against repression during the February–March 1937 Central Committee plenum, among others.

None of these accounts were backed up with documentary evidence. Even Khrushchev, who had the entire party archive at his disposal, preferred to rely on the recollections of old Bolsheviks returning from the camps. This did not faze historians. The complete inaccessibility of Soviet archives and the lack of candidness, to put it mildly, of Soviet political leaders were both taken for granted. Given the unavailability of hard evidence, for many historians the slightest hint in a speech by Khrushchev or in the official Soviet press took on the weight of fact. As a result, every scrap of evidence that there was conflict within the Politburo was stitched together into a confused patchwork in which it was hard to distinguish rumor from hard fact or opportunistic falsification from mistaken recollection.

The testimonies of Nikolaevsky and other memoirists made the faction theory appealing, but the theory also fit with actual events in the early 1930s. Its appeal and fit notwithstanding, careful investigations of all available sources have allowed historians to identify apparent inconsistencies in economic, social, punitive, and foreign policy and to discern a circuitous path leading to Stalin's dictatorship, quite separate from factionalism.[12] Such scholarship has stood the test of time.

In addition to factions, historians took a growing interest in *vedomstvennost'*, the competing interests of government agencies within the Stalinist political system. Fruitful areas for investigation were the commissariats that drove the Soviet economy and the collective process of drafting plans for industrial production and capital investment.[13] The research spotlighted the role of the influential Politburo member Sergo Ordzhonikidze, who appeared to follow two opposing models of behavior during his tenure in different posts, depending on the interests of the particular institution he was currently representing—in the late 1920s he was chairman of the party's Central Control Commission, and starting in 1931, he became chairman of the Supreme Economic Council and then head of the People's Commissariat of Heavy Industry. Ordzhonikidze is also worthy of attention as the sole Politburo member to express his opposition to aspects of the incipient terror to Stalin. The confrontation with Stalin, which can be traced through numerous archival sources, ended in Ordzhonikidze's death.[14] Another active participant in inter-institutional conflicts was Viacheslav Molotov. As head of the government, he fought for overall state interests. Recent studies have made significant contributions to our understanding of Molotov's positions and the role of government structures.[15]

One of the objectives of research for this book was to gather archival evidence of clashes and disagreements within the Politburo and through this evidence to investigate political decision-making mechanisms in place during the early 1930s. Three of the chapters reflect the results of this effort, each covering a specific stage in the development of the USSR, periods when shifts in the "general line" provide a window onto the mechanisms of power. In chapter 2, I explore the crisis years of 1931–1933. At the same time that the Stalinist leadership was turning to terror, it was also making inconsistent attempts at reform. The swings between liberalization and terror, which had their origins in the Polit-buro, provide an opportunity to study the alignment of forces at the highest echelons of political power. In chapter 3, I examine evidence associated with the moderate policies undertaken in 1934 and explore the role played by Sergei Kirov in these initiatives. Changes to the makeup and activities of the Politburo, as well as political trends after Kirov's death (in 1935 and 1936), are addressed in chapter 4.

Although extensive evidence of discord within the Politburo exists, archival sources have yet to be found that would support the hypothesis that there was a clash between moderates and radicals. Almost all of the discord within the Politburo was generated by conflicting institutional interests. As a result, individual Politburo members on different occasions took stances that could be characterized as moderate or radical, depending on the circumstances. Furthermore, all of the most important political decisions previously attributed to one of the supposed factions turn out, upon closer examination, to be initiatives of Stalin. Although Politburo members may have enjoyed a certain independence in deciding many matters, primarily those of an operational nature, the historical record shows that Stalin tended to have the final word. As time went on, this tendency became more pronounced.

Even though these conclusions may lack a certain sensationalism, they are the conclusions that the evidence forces us to accept. It is possible that in the future some lucky historian will find hard evidence of a more dramatic struggle within the Politburo. Some may also be disappointed to read the conclusions drawn in chapter 5, in which I analyze how and why the party and government purges and large-scale repression of 1937–1938 were carried out. Over the past ten years, a vast number of documents have been discovered that advance our understanding of these exceptionally important events.[16] As far as the question of who was behind the Great Terror is concerned, we can now state with greater certainty what was clear to many observers and historians long before the archives became accessible: "The nature of the whole Purge depends in the last analysis on the personal and political drives of Stalin."[17] Correspondingly, it is argued in chapter 5 that theories about the elemental, spontaneous nature of the terror, about a loss of central control over the course of mass repression, and about the role of regional leaders in initiating the terror simply are not supported by the historical record.[18]

Now that we have access to essentially all of the key documents associated with the mass repression of 1937 and 1938, we have every reason to see the Great Terror as a series of centralized, planned mass operations that were conducted on the basis of Politburo decisions (that is, Stalin's decisions) aimed at destroying "anti-Soviet elements" and "counter-revolutionary national contingents." The objective, given growing international tensions and the threat of imminent war, was the liquidation of a "fifth column." This is why the majority of those arrested in 1937 and 1938 (at least 700,000 people) were shot. Executions on such a large scale had not been seen in the Soviet Union before, nor have they been since. The special role played by Stalin in orchestrating this eruption of terror is beyond doubt and is fully supported by documentary evidence. His role can be put even more starkly. Everything we know today about the preparations for and conduct of the large-scale operations of 1937 and 1938 supports the idea that without Stalin's orders, the Great Terror simply would not have taken place, and the mass repressions (which were characteristic of Stalin's regime overall) would have remained at the normal or slightly elevated level that was seen in the mid-1930s and again from 1939 until Stalin's death.[19] (Of course, what was normal under Stalin was exceptional by the international standards of the twentieth century.)

Of all the means of governing exercised by Stalin, terror was the simplest and easiest to apply. The organs of state security had a much easier time fulfilling and surpassing arrest and execution quotas than the industrial and agricultural commissariats had achieving their targets for construction, manufacturing, harvests, and animal husbandry. The most sophisticated propaganda was not able to instill in society a shared vision of where it was headed or destroy many traditions. Even after anti-religious campaigns had roiled the country for years, the 1937 census showed that only 43 percent of the adults in the population called themselves nonbelievers (even though, as the authorities understood, this figure was surely inflated by those reluctant to admit their religious feelings). Using terror, these "alien ideologies" could be destroyed by destroying their adherents—for example, priests and other religious practitioners. Some historians seem to have trouble imagining the ease with which the dictatorship carried out mass repression. The limited level of centralization and the absence of total state control in many areas of socioeconomic and political life—for example, the rather tenuous relationship between economic plans and the actual economy, the persistence of many elements of mass culture, the existence of family and professional relations, and the complex nature of interactions between the center and regional officials—are indisputable. But presuming that this imperfect control applied to every aspect of the Stalinist dictatorship distorts the true picture. The institutions of government responsible for carrying out state terror were the most centralized and totalitarian elements of the system.

The large-scale operations of 1937 and 1938 were a clear demonstration of the essence and capabilities of the Stalinist dictatorship, which achieved its full powers with the onset of the Great Terror. One decisive step along this path was the purge of high-level and mid-level party and state officials, carried out under Stalin's close supervision.[20] By physically destroying some members of the Politburo, promoting a new generation of functionaries in their place, and persecuting the close associates and relatives of his comrades-in-arms, Stalin achieved the total subjugation of the Politburo. The Politburo ceased to function as it had in the past. All important questions were decided by Stalin alone, who consulted with other Politburo members in small informal meetings on particular matters as he saw fit. The running of the country (primarily the economy) fell increasingly to the apparatus of the Council of People's Commissars. The organizational culmination of this process was Stalin's takeover of the chairmanship of the council and the restructuring of the system of supreme authority. The apparatuses of the Central Committee of the All-Union Communist Party (Bolshevik), or TsK VKP(b), and the Council of People's Commissars, which had been placed under the leadership of two of Stalin's newly promoted favorites, Georgy Malenkov and Nikolai Voznesensky, respectively, functioned as supercommissions, drafting resolutions to be approved by Stalin. Power became even more centralized. This period is examined in the book's final chapter.

Like any other scholarly investigation, this one was made possible by the availability of a substantial complex of sources, primarily archival. The study of archival sources and the collation of the information they contain with previously published materials was one of my main objectives in writing this book.

Among the most important archival sources are the protocols of Politburo meetings.[21] For the past fifteen years scholars have been able to study reference copies of protocols from the former Central Party Archive, now known as the Russian State Archive of Social and Political History (RGASPI; the protocols are in collection [fond]17, inventory [opis'] 3). These reference copies are typed folio-sized booklets, each of which contains the protocol of one Politburo meeting, with any meeting decisions approved through polling after the fact appended to them. Politburo resolutions voted on during the meeting are arranged by date and the order in which they were considered; each has its own number.[22] Some of the Politburo decisions were designated "special file" decisions, putting them in the highest classification of confidentiality. Such decisions were recorded in special meeting protocols that are also stored at RGASPI (f. 17, op. 162). Many of these resolutions, especially those concerned with the activities of the secret police and international issues, have been widely published.[23]

The original Politburo meeting protocols, which were moved to RGASPI (f. 17, op. 163) from the Presidential Archive of the Russian Federation (APRF), have undergone less scholarly study. The original protocols are the initial versions, often handwritten, of the typed reference copies of protocols. These original protocols provide additional opportunities for studying the decision-making process followed by the Politburo. From them, for example, we can determine what changes were made to a particular resolution, in whose hand it was written, how voting was conducted, and whether there even was a vote, among other things. They are also valuable for the background materials (memorandums, reports) on which were based the decisions that were often appended to them.

Most of the original background materials associated with Politburo decisions are not yet available to researchers, however. These documents currently make up most of the collection of APRF.[24] The Politburo materials held by APRF are organized along thematic lines, with files containing copies of Politburo decisions, background materials pertaining to the decisions, and informational sources (for example, secret police reports) related to particular issues. Despite the restricted access to APRF holdings, individual historians have studied materials from this archive in recent years and shared their findings with the scholarly community.[25] Some thematic files from APRF were used in researching this book.

Allowing scholars occasional peeks at Politburo documents held by

APRF is not sufficient to satisfy the requirements for complete historical understanding. The historical portion of APRF's holdings should be made available to researchers, although the prospects of this happening in Russia anytime soon do not look good. Still, historians should not view the inaccessibility of portions of the Politburo archives as an insurmountable obstacle. The body of documents accessible in other archives, along with the tremendous number of already published materials, allows the investigation of most problems of Soviet history. For example, copies of background materials on which Politburo decisions were based, the originals of which are in the closed thematic folders in APRF, can be found in open archives of the various government bodies from which these materials were sent to the Politburo. The most notable example of this is the bountiful archive of the Council of People's Commissars, which is stored in the State Archive of the Russian Federation (GARF, f. R-5446). The personal papers of individual Politburo members held by RGASPI—Stalin, Molotov, Mikoyan, Kaganovich, Voroshilov, Ordzhonikidze, Kuibyshev, Kirov, Kalinin, Zhdanov, and Andreev—are also extremely valuable.

One additional aspect of Politburo recordkeeping should be mentioned: the stenographic records of meetings. According to the rules governing Politburo procedures approved on 14 June 1923, the main delivered reports on questions being considered by the Politburo, supplementary reports by commissions, and the concluding remarks by those delivering reports were supposed to be included in the stenographic record of a meeting. Discussions of a given matter could be included in the record at members' discretion.[26] These guidelines were not followed. The number and length of Politburo meetings made it virtually impossible to record everything required by the rules. Certainly the growing secretiveness and closed nature of the Politburo also played a role here. The collection of original Politburo meeting protocols moved from APRF to RGASPI included twenty-eight stenograms of meetings from 1923 to 1929 and five from 1930 to 1938 (f. 17, op. 163).[27] An extensive search of the archives suggests that this collection of stenograms is probably almost complete. It has been possible thus far to identify only two stenograms, surviving as fragments, that were not included in this collection. These were stenograms of joint sessions of the Politburo and the presidium of the Central Control Commission on 30 January and 9 February 1929. It was at these sessions that the decisive confrontation between the Rykov, Bukharin, and Tomsky group and the Stalinist majority took place.[28]

Although the stenograms of Politburo meetings that we do have are not plentiful, they are exceptionally valuable sources for studying power at the top levels of the party. The stenogram of the 4 November 1930 session of the Politburo, which dealt with the Syrtsov-Lominadze affair, is, for example, one of the few sources to permit a rather complete understanding of this important episode in Soviet political history.

The rarity of stenographic records of Politburo meetings and meetings of other top party-state bodies severely limits opportunities for studying the logic of political decision making and the actions and positions of particular Soviet leaders. Matters are made worse by the paucity of memoirs in both numbers and content and the almost total absence of personal journals left by either Politburo members or their assistants. Beside the famous memoirs of Nikita Khrushchev and the recently published recollections of Anastas Mikoyan, we have the fairly interesting record of discussions that the poet Feliks Chuev had with both Viacheslav Molotov and Lazar Kaganovich.[29] Rumors that Kaganovich left several volumes of memoirs, supposedly written during the final years of his life, turned out to be greatly exaggerated. The recently released book of notes by Kaganovich amounts, with a few exceptions, to little more than a rehashing of the official *Short Course on the History of the VKP(b),* works by Stalin and Lenin, and stenograms of party congresses.[30]

At this point, the only thing we have to substitute for missing stenograms of Politburo meetings and the dearth of memoirs is the correspondence between members of the Soviet leadership. It sheds light on many unofficial aspects of how party and state structures conducted themselves and on the relationships between Politburo members, allowing us a window onto the conflicts that arose within the top Soviet leadership, among other things. Several thousand letters and telegrams exchanged by the country's leaders have been preserved among the personal papers of Politburo members. A significant portion of this correspondence from the 1930s has been published.[31]

Although the correspondence between Soviet leaders should be seen as an invaluable and unique historical resource, the shortcomings of this sort of document should be recognized. The main drawback is that these letters and telegrams were both fragmentary and intermittent.

Politburo members wrote to one another only when one of them was out of town on vacation. Whether or not letters were written often depended on the state of communications between Moscow and southern vacation spots, telephone lines in particular. It is a stroke of historical luck that during the early 1930s these phone lines were unreliable. "It's hard to talk on the telephone—you have to shout, you can barely hear, although sometimes you can hear pretty well," wrote Ordzhonikidze to his wife from the south in March 1933. "I'm writing this letter and sending it with Com. Ginzburg. I tried to call you on the telephone, but I couldn't get through." A statement made by Voroshilov in a letter to Stalin dated 21 June 1932 gives us some indication of what might have been the fate of written correspondence if Politburo members had had a decent telephone line at their disposal. "Too bad that in Sochi (I don't understand why) there is no *vertushka* connection [a government direct line]; then we could get in touch directly and not via letters."[32]

Improved telephone service may be one reason that we see almost no correspondence between Politburo members after 1936, although political factors were probably more important here than technical ones. Beginning in 1937, Stalin and, following his example, many other members of the Politburo stopped taking lengthy vacations in the south, limiting themselves to time off at their dachas outside Moscow. By the late 1930s things had changed radically, and Stalin no longer felt the need for extensive consultation with his comrades-in-arms, and they were even less inclined toward frank discussion. As a result, fewer and fewer sources shed light on the unofficial aspects of high-level Soviet politics of this and subsequent periods. Nevertheless, despite the many lacunae and the limited access to a number of archival collections, the sources that are available to historians of the Soviet period are extensive enough that it will take a great deal more time and effort to assimilate them. This book is just one step along that path.

Abbreviations

APRF	Presidential Archive of the Russian Federation
Com.	Comrade
GARF	State Archive of the Russian Federation
Gosplan	State Planning Commission
Komsomol	All-Union Leninist Youth League
NKVD	People's Commissariat of Internal Affairs
OGPU	Unified State Political Administration (state security)
ORPO	department of leading party organs [of the Central Committee of the VKP(b)]
RGASPI	Russian State Archive of Social and Political History
RSFSR	Russian Soviet Federated Socialist Republic
SNK, Sovnarkom	Council of People's Commissars
STO	Labor and Defense Council
TsK VKP(b)	Central Committee of the VKP(b)
TsKK	Central Control Commission [of the VKP(b)]
VKP(b)	All-Union Communist Party (Bolshevik)
VSNKh	Supreme Economic Council

Master of the House

1 The Stalinization of the Politburo
1928–1930

AFTER LENIN'S DEATH the most important outcome of the power struggle among Bolshevik leaders was the formation of a majority faction within the Politburo that went on to become the Stalinist faction. Once Stalin managed to eliminate almost all of the prominent revolutionary figures who had been a part of Lenin's circle, he became the strongest figure in the Politburo and began to set the "general line" the party would follow. This was the main sign of the Stalinization of the Politburo. While a number of the traditions and procedures of collective leadership remained in place, from this point forward the Politburo had a leader who was concentrating power in his own hands.

Although it is possible to point to milestones along the way, the Stalinization of the Politburo did not happen in a single step, nor was it predetermined. Even the defeat of the Rykov-Bukharin group in April 1929 was not a decisive victory for Stalin. Ensuring victory demanded further efforts to crush leaders of the "right deviation" and, most important, rightist ideology, which life's realities had led many Communists to embrace, whether or not they were consciously aware of it. That the fight was not yet over was confirmed by political events of 1930: new attacks against the rightists, fabricated cases against "terrorist organizations," the castigation of Sergei Syrtsov and Vissarion Lominadze, and reshufflings at the highest echelons of party and state power. The elimination end of July and the beginning of August but in October. In the middle of the conflicts, Molotov sent Stalin an anxious letter, on 4 July 1927. "The worst part of it is the situation within the 'semyorka.' On the opposition, on China, on ARK [Anglo-Russian Trade Union Committee], more or less clear divisions can already be seen, and a single vote will wind up being decisive [. . .]. I'm increasingly wondering whether you may need to come back to M[oscow] ahead of schedule. This may be undesirable from the point of view of your treatment, but you yourself see the situation [. . .]. The signs are bad, things may not hold. I haven't talked to anyone about this, but I feel things aren't going well."[3]

In 1927, Viacheslav Mikhailovich Molotov appeared generally to be Stalin's most reliable and absolute supporter in the Politburo. The son of a shop clerk in Vyatka Province, he had entered the party in 1906 at the age of sixteen. Molotov was a simple but hardworking Soviet functionary who in the 1920s held the important post of secretary of the Central Committee. That was when he made his political choice to cast his lot with Stalin. Molotov's unconditional loyalty was one of Stalin's greatest advantages in the struggle for power. This struggle erupted with new force in 1928, after the defeat of the united opposition of Trotsky and Zinoviev, when members of the Politburo lost the common enemy that had united them for several years.

Personal ambition and pretensions to leadership fueled this discord, but so did matters of principle. Facing serious economic difficulties in 1928, especially in the countryside, the Politburo embarked on a path of repressive—or, to use the contemporary name, emergency—measures, including the forced expropriation of grain from the peasants and the suppression of private merchants. At first there was no disagreement over this *chrezvychaishchina* (emergency regime) within the Politburo. But when the emergency measures not only exacerbated the situation but seemed poised to turn into a permanent policy, two groups within the party leadership came into conflict. The first, led by Stalin, insisted on continuing the emergency measures. The second, represented by Rykov, Bukharin, and Tomsky, demanded a retreat from the emergency regime, even at the risk of certain political and economic consequences.

During this final stage in the struggle for power, Stalin and his supporters had important advantages. They held key posts within the party apparatus. Their battle cries for an "offensive against the *kulaks*" and in

favor of forced industrialization struck a chord with a significant portion of party officials. But this did not mean that Stalin's victory was inevitable. Among mid-level functionaries, who constituted a majority in
the Central Committee and in the Politburo itself, the prevailing mood
favored unity. Almost everyone was worried about new clashes, not
only because a critical situation was developing in the country, creating
a growing threat to the regime itself, but also because conflict at the top
endangered the existing balance of power and undermined the system of
collective leadership that was advantageous for mid-level politicians. A
schism within the Politburo would force them to immediately take sides
and be drawn into the fight, placing their careers at risk if their side lost.

Those members of the Politburo who supported Stalin did not view
the Rykov-Bukharin group the same way they had viewed previous opposition forces, such as Trotsky and Zinoviev. Even during the bitter
conflict, Bukharin, Rykov, Tomsky, and Nikolai Uglanov tended to be
viewed as "one of us." The rightists were less inflexible and tried to act
within the framework of party legality, not making categorical demands
about Politburo staffing changes, which is why they were labeled a "deviation" rather than an "opposition." Before their fall, the rightists had
good personal relationships with many members of the Politburo, with
whom they had shared years of merciless struggle against a common enemy, the Trotsky-Zinoviev opposition.

All of these circumstances forced Stalin to act cautiously against the
Bukharin group in 1928 and at the beginning of 1929 and keep an eye
on the mood of his comrades-in-arms. We can see this in letters he wrote
to Molotov in August 1928. "I was at Sergo's. He's in a good mood.
He's standing firm and decisively supports the TsK line against the wa-
verers and vacillators. [. . .] It appears that Andreev visited Sergo and
talked to him. Sergo believes that Andreev firmly supports the TsK line.
Apparently Tomsky tried (at the plenum) to 'corrupt' him [. . .] but he
wasn't able to 'lure' Andreev." And, "Under no circumstances should
Tomsky (or anyone else) be allowed to 'turn' Kuibyshev or Mikoyan."[4]

This expression of confidence in Ordzhonikidze's firm stance was
probably calculated to encourage Molotov, but it did not reflect Ordzhonikidze's actual frame of mind, which was more complex. In a letter
to Stalin dated 18 August 1928, Ordzhonikidze himself demonstrated
an attitude that was fully "conciliatory." After informing Stalin about
his conversation with Bukharin, who had shared his concerns about the

current policy and assured Ordzhonikidze that he wanted to avoid a confrontation within the Politburo, Ordzhonikidze wrote, "Even now, in my opinion, he wants to restore good relations with you, but he doesn't know how. I think everything possible should be done to avoid losing him, and without him Al[eksei Rykov] will instantly stop his grumbling."[5] Based on the evidence, it appears that Ordzhonikidze had a sincere desire to preserve the status quo in the Politburo. Despite the obvious escalation of the situation, he wrote the following in a letter to Rykov in November 1928: "I am begging you to try to reconcile Bukharin and Stalin [. . .]. It is ridiculous, of course, to talk about 'replacing' you, or Bukharin or Tomsky. That would be crazy. It appears that the relationship between Stalin and Bukharin has significantly deteriorated, but we have to do everything we can to reconcile them. This is possible [. . .]. In general, Aleksei, we have to be incredibly careful in dealing with any issues that could trigger a 'fistfight.' The greatest restraint is needed to keep a fight from breaking out."[6]

Signs that many Politburo members still held the rightists in high regard were evident even after the Bukharin-Rykov-Tomsky group suffered their decisive defeat in April 1929. For example, in June 1929 the Politburo was deciding on a post for Bukharin, who had by then been replaced as editor of *Pravda*. Stalin insisted on appointing Bukharin people's commissar of education. This was an honorable but dangerous form of political exile for Bukharin. The post of education commissar looked like an important and prestigious party assignment. Stalin had proposed this solution, feigning impartiality and a readiness to reestablish a working relationship with Bukharin. In actuality, things were quite different. Maximally removed from real political power, the Education Commissariat was subject to constant attacks and criticism from party functionaries, the All-Union Leninist Youth League (Komsomol) leadership, labor unions, and other quarters. Nor was the situation within the commissariat simple. As education commissar, then, Bukharin would be drawn into a maelstrom of endless arguments, squabbles, and public censure, which would guarantee his being cut off from the center of political power. Understanding this, Bukharin resisted, and made an unexpected move—he asked to be given the unpretentious post of head of the Scientific-Technical Administration of the Supreme Economic Council. This demotion would have made Bukharin's disgrace and Stalin's true aspiration to drive him out of the party leadership more explicit. Unlike the post of education commissar, this post guaranteed a relatively peaceful and easy job and would have left Bukharin time to follow high-level policy decisions.

Despite Stalin's objections, the Politburo supported Bukharin. We know what happened from a letter dated 8 June 1929 from Voroshilov to Ordzhonikidze: "Bukharin begged everyone not to appoint him to the Commissariat of Education and proposed and then insisted on the job as administrator of science and technology. I supported him in that, as did several other people, and because we were a united majority, we pushed it through (against Koba [Stalin])."[7] Stalin had to deal with the possibility of such conflicts and the prevailing inclination toward solidarity. He acted carefully, publicly supporting unity while delivering stealthy blows behind the scenes. In the end, his ruthlessness, decisiveness, and cunning led to his victory, as did a number of serious political blunders on the part of the rightists, especially Bukharin. The entire sequence of intrigues and clashes within the Politburo and the party apparatus over the course of almost two years fully supports the arguments of historians who assert that Stalin achieved victory by playing the role of advocate of the golden mean, impressing others with his pragmatism and his "calm tone and quiet voice."[8]

There is reason to believe that Stalin gained the loyalty of some Politburo members through blackmail. The Ordzhonikidze archive includes pre-revolutionary police records, which he received in December 1928 and March 1929 (when he was serving as chairman of the Central Control Commission), indicating that Kalinin and Rudzutak gave candid testimony while in the custody of the tsarist police—testimony that enabled the police to make further arrests within underground revolutionary organizations.[9] Such materials could well have served as the basis for expulsion from the party or even arrest. It is probably not a coincidence that these documents surfaced at this decisive stage of the confrontation with the rightists.

Outplaying his opponents in political intrigue, Stalin transformed himself into Politburo leader. He no longer faced opposition from any in the first circle of Soviet leaders who had begun the fight over Lenin's legacy. The positions of rank-and-file members of the Politburo and the Central Committee, who were no longer able to maneuver between different centers of influence, were also seriously undermined. The former balance of power at the highest echelons of power had been destroyed.

Nonetheless, Stalin's own position could not be considered absolutely secure. His political future depended on the success of the program he had advocated throughout his march to victory. In 1928 and 1929 this had been the program of forced industrialization and the strong-arm amalgamation of peasants into kolkhozes.

Stalin's ultraleft policies plunged the country into what amounted to a state of civil war. A particularly critical situation developed in the countryside. The response there to forcible grain collection and collectivization, accompanied by mass arrests of peasants and the ruin of their farms, was violent protest. According to Unified State Political Administration (OGPU) figures for 1926–1927, those two years had seen a total of 63 riots in the countryside. The number rose to more than 1,300 (involving 244,000 participants) for the single year of 1929.[10] For the month of January 1930 alone, the number of riots slightly exceeded 400 (approximately 110,000 participants), in February it reached 1,066 (214,000 participants), and in March it reached 6,512 (1,400,000 participants).[11] The wave of rebellion in the countryside could be subdued only through harsh repression and political maneuvering. The frightened authorities promised to fix the "distortion of the party line in the kolkhoz movement." While uprisings on the scale seen in the countryside during the first months of 1930 did not recur after that time, the kolkhoz adventure undermined the productive capability of agricultural areas and led to "food difficulties" and famine throughout the country.

The other leg of Stalin's policy, forced industrialization, wreaked havoc from the start. The efforts were devastating and inefficient. As a result of ill-conceived expenditures of resources, many hundreds of millions of rubles went to construction projects that were never completed. Manufacturing facilities, especially those that were serving the needs of the population, cut back production owing to shortages of equipment and raw materials. The cost of production went up, and quality went way down. Like the agricultural sector of the economy, the industrial sector was gripped by crisis during the summer of 1930. One of the outcomes of this crisis was the breakdown of the monetary system and the complete bankruptcy of the government. The enormous budget deficit was covered through price increases, the introduction of compulsory loans, and, most important, the printing of paper rubles. Over the course of twenty-one months—from the autumn of 1928 until July

1930—1.6 billion rubles went into circulation, even though only 1.3 billion were supposed to be issued for the entire period of the First Five-Year Plan.[12] The fall in value of the ruble led to the hoarding of goods and the naturalization of barter. In open-air markets, peasants sold produce to city dwellers not for money but in exchange for soap, thread, sugar, textiles, footwear, and other everyday products. Since paper money was constantly dropping in value, the population amassed coins, which still contained some silver. The monetary system bifurcated, with prices depending on whether purchasers were using coins or paper money; in many places sellers refused to accept paper money. Vast sums of silver languished in money boxes. Despite the minting of new coins, mostly out of scarce imported silver, there were never enough in circulation. The country had a coin crisis.

The breakdown of agriculture, the channeling of tremendous resources into heavy industry, and the allocation of enormous amounts of food for export all led to a sharp drop in the standard of living. Even in large cities, which the government viewed as its main base and which were given distribution priority, huge lines formed for food, which was rationed. The price of food sold on the free market was out of the reach of the typical consumer.

Inevitably, the flip side of people's dissatisfaction with the government was an increase in the popularity of leaders of the right deviation, who had warned of the heavy price that would be paid for repression of the peasants and accelerated industrialization. The publication of an article by Stalin in March 1930 entitled "Dizzying Success"—in which he was forced, in light of pressures created by the peasant uprisings, to recognize that wholesale forcible collectivization had been a mistake—brought a wave of criticism down on him. An eyewitness of events, the trade union activist B. G. Kozelev, wrote in his diary on 14 March 1930: "At Mostrikotazh Factory no. 3 in Mos[cow], one worker gave a speech, stating, 'St[alin] wrote a correct article, but too late. Bukharin wrote the same thing half a year ago and now it's being done Bukharin's way. Ilyich [Lenin] was right in saying, 'Don't trust St[alin], he'll ruin you.'[13] Everyone there was so stunned by the unexpectedness of it that they didn't know how to react."[14] Such moods were widespread, and the country's top leadership undoubtedly knew it. In a letter to Ordzhonikidze dated 17 September 1930, for example, E. M. Yaroslavsky noted that "conversations with workers at meetings, their notes and questions, letters to the editors of *Pravda,* reports [*svodki*]—everything indicates a tremendous strain. Of course there is greater awareness; the enthusiasm of workers at the forefront, shock workers, is strong; the successes of workers at the forefront have been colossal. But there are many whose moods are not so good because of the supply situation. The mood has soured. You can hear workers reminiscing out loud about how things were three years ago, when you could buy as much *chow* as you wanted *freely.*"[15]

Under such circumstances, the predominant tools used in implementing the great leap leftward were violence and mass repression, as mandated by the general line. In 1930 more than 330,000 people were arrested and 208,000 convicted on the basis of cases initiated by the OGPU. Of those convicted, 20,000 were shot. This is approximately the same number convicted and shot based on cases brought by the All-Russian Extraordinary Commission for Combating Counterrevolution and Sabotage (VChK, better known as the Cheka) and the OGPU for the entire nine-year period of 1921–1929. More than 550,000 kulaks were sent into exile in 1930.[16] The prevalence of rightist tendencies within the party was the main reason for the party purge conducted around that time. From 1929 through 1931 approximately 250,000 people were expelled from the Communist Party, a significant proportion of whom were paying the price of involvement in the right deviation with their party membership cards.[17]

Despite Stalin's commitment to violence as the primary method for solving the multiplying problems, occasionally he would retreat and take a more roundabout approach. It is evident, for example, that he was careful in shaping the new system of relationships within the Politburo. Even though political victory over the rightists had been achieved by April 1929, Bukharin, Tomsky, and Rykov were removed from the Politburo gradually and with a degree of caution. Bukharin was removed from the Politburo in November 1929. Tomsky was not elected to a new Politburo term after the 16th Party Congress in July 1930. Rykov was included in the newly constituted Politburo and remained there for several more months, until December 1930. But Stalin was not able to permit himself too much caution. Policy failures strengthened the position of the rightists. Circumstances could be envisioned that might lead to a shifting of power within the leadership. This would have been all the more natural as Rykov continued to hold key posts within the party-state apparatus. The Rykov factor and the fate of the chairmanship of the Council of People's Commissars (SNK) were among the most significant political problems facing Stalin at this stage.

Aleksei Ivanovich Rykov was one of the oldest and most distinguished members of the party, which he had joined in 1898 at the age of seventeen. Abandoning his study of law at Kazan University, he became a professional underground revolutionary. He took part in the revolution of 1905–1907 and was repeatedly arrested and exiled. During the first Soviet government, Rykov held the post of people's commissar of internal affairs. In the Civil War he was in charge of managing the economy and supplying the Red Army. In his Civil War work Rykov, as one scholar noted, "appears to us more as a practical man, carefully studying what was going on around him, not giving in to extremism, ready to compromise."[18]

After Lenin's death, Rykov replaced him as chairman of the Council of People's Commissars. As head of the government, Rykov held significant power. It was difficult for Stalin to control the council, especially since traditions established in the 1920s gave the organs of government a great deal of independence. That Rykov was an ethnic Russian with a peasant background (and therefore a more fitting leader for peasant Russia than were Stalin and his Caucasian comrades-in-arms) contributed to his stature.

Having more experience and self-restraint, Rykov did not commit the sorts of naive political blunders that, for example, Bukharin had. Despite his political defeat in April 1929, Rykov tried to conduct himself with dignity, albeit circumspectly. He condemned his own past mistakes in speeches at various party meetings but made an effort to save political face, never crossing a certain line. He tried to maintain good relations with Stalin's numerous commissars and managed to steer clear of conflict by resisting obvious pressure from the Central Committee apparatus. But whenever possible, he showed his mettle, asserting his rights as head of state.

In early February 1930, for example, the Central Committee's Organizational Bureau (Orgburo) decided to dismiss an employee of the Council of People's Commissars. When Rykov received a document that included this decision, he sent an official letter to the Central Committee secretary, A. P. Smirnov, stating, "I will not dispute this decision, but I urge you in the future to dismiss SNK employees with my knowledge or the knowledge of my deputies."[19] Two months later, on 3 April 1930, Rykov reacted strongly to a proposal by Smirnov, who was overseeing the Central Committee department of agitation and mass campaigns, that a special committee be established for printing and publishing. "In connection with your letter [. . .] concerning the Committee on Publishing Issues, I am expressing (along with the SNK) my categorical opposition to the establishment of such a committee within the Sovnarkom [SNK] of the Union of the USSR. The Sovnarkom can render a determination about the allotment of paper for various users in the course of its normal functioning, just as this is done in regard to the distribution of construction and other such materials, without the creation of a special Committee."[20]

Rykov's behavior at a conference of the Ural Province party organization in Sverdlovsk in June 1930, to which he (as a member of the Politburo) had been sent to present a report on the eve of the upcoming party congress, provides a clear picture of his position. The leadership of the Ural Province committee had arranged for a display of public criticism of Rykov for his "rightist errors" to take place at the conference, possibly on its own initiative but more likely on orders from Moscow. Several specially rehearsed orators made speeches featuring harsh allegations and calls for "repentance" from Rykov. He, however, rebuffed them. In his closing remarks on 4 June he said, "I am here to speak on behalf of the Politburo, and the report I delivered was delivered by me as a member of the Politburo, empowered to defend the TsK line at your conference. [. . .] Speeches by several orators sounded as if they were made not in response to a report by a member of the Politburo, an official Politburo speaker, but in response to a report simply made by Rykov, who, during a particular period [. . .] had a disagreement with the TsK majority and the majority within the Politburo."[21] One delegate to the conference, who had demanded an accounting of Rykov's work and his repentance, was the object of a particularly harsh rebuke.

> Com. Rumiantsev, and he is not a rank-and-file member of the party, should weigh his words. We are members of the ruling party. I am chairman of the Sovnarkom of the [Soviet] Union, a member of the Politburo, and if after my statement that I voted for the resolutions and took part in the drafting of some of them [. . .] if after seven months of political, economic, and council work [. . .] a person comes here and asks me, "How do you feel about the general line of the party?" then there is only

one thing I can say in response: I absolutely do not understand what basis there could be for such a question. The danger is absolutely clear to me. Because the very fact that I am being addressed as if I were the leader of some sort of splinter group [. . .] suggests to the party the certainty that such a splinter group, created within the party with my participation, exists. Why sow such doubts? [. . .] And if someone incorrectly states such things, he is inflicting a severe blow to the unity of the party. [. . .] Therefore I must demand an explanation of why, on the basis of what findings, Com. Rumiantsev is able to present me with questions as if he is talking to the leader of some existing organization.[22]

Having demonstrated his resoluteness and confidence, Rykov drew an appropriate reaction from the auditorium. His speech was repeatedly interrupted by applause and ended, according to the stenographic record, "with a lengthy and thunderous ovation," as befitted a speech by one of the leaders of the party.

To ensure that such scenes were not repeated, sowing confusion among party officials, Stalin had to remove Rykov from the highest post in the government. But as usual in such situations, Stalin did not rush headlong to do so.

NEW ATTACKS AGAINST THE RIGHTISTS

There is substantial evidence that Stalin began working on a solution to the problem of the rightists, including the replacement of Rykov, immediately after the 16th Party Congress. Initially his attack centered on the Conference of Deputies, which was made up of the chairman of the Council of People's Commissars and the Labor and Defense Council (STO)—Rykov—and his deputies.

The USSR constitution did not provide for the creation of a Conference of Deputies. Rykov and his deputies at the Council of People's Commissars created this working government body in January 1926, and a decision of the Politburo legalized it in May 1926. The conference was established to develop operating plans for the Council of People's Commissars and the Labor and Defense Council, put together agendas for their meetings, and review "administrative issues that do not need to be submitted to the SNK and STO."[23] Over time, the Conference of Deputies became quite influential. Convening weekly in the meeting hall of the two composite councils, it dealt expeditiously with many important issues. In addition to Rykov and his deputies, the Conference of Deputies came to include the heads of key government agencies: the chairman of the Council of People's Commissars of the Russian Soviet Federated Socialist Republic (RSFSR), the people's commissars of finance, agriculture, commerce, and transport, and the chairmen of the Supreme Economic Council, State Planning Commission (Gosplan), and Gosbank. Formally, Stalin, Kalinin, Molotov, and Voroshilov were all members of the conference. All administrative orders coming out of the conference regarding the admission of new members, the drafting of agendas, and such were issued by Rykov personally.[24]

On several occasions during the summer and fall of 1930, Stalin managed to overturn decisions by the Conference of Deputies related to a variety of questions. One of the most contentious issues was the coin shortage.

The breakdown of the financial system and the disappearance of metal coins from circulation was both a serious economic problem and a serious political problem, prompting widespread discontent. The heads of the Finance Commissariat and Gosbank proposed increasing the release of coins into circulation. In February 1930, N. P. Briukhanov, the finance commissar, warned the Council of People's Commissars of the difficulties surrounding the minting of silver coins and the need to purchase imported silver. He proposed producing coins out of nickel rather than silver. At the time, these measures were rejected.[25] However, the worsening financial crisis necessitated a return to this question in the summer of 1930. On 18 July, on Briukhanov's initiative, the Conference of Deputies adopted a decision to accelerate the minting of bronze coins and to submit a proposal to the Politburo to approve additional expenditures for the purchase of silver overseas, for which an additional four million rubles were to be allocated. The conference also assigned the OGPU the task of organizing a "decisive fight against the malevolent hoarding of and speculation on silver coins."[26]

Stalin decided to use the situation to his own advantage. He suddenly showed a keen interest in the coin problem and took matters into his own hands. First, Stalin condemned the proposal to mint additional coins from imported silver. On 20 July 1930 the Politburo overturned the proposal that had come out of the Conference of Deputies.[27] The only methods that would now be applied to the problem were repressive ones. At the end of July, a campaign was launched in the Soviet press tying the coin crisis to an underhanded plot by the class enemy. Newspapers featured stories of numerous arrests of coin speculators and the employees of commercial establishments, banks, and other institutions assisting them.[28] On 2 August 1930, Stalin sent the OGPU chairman, Viacheslav Menzhinsky, the following inquiry: "Can you send a memo on the results of the struggle (through [O]GPU channels) against the small-change speculators (how much silver was confiscated and for which period; what institutions are most involved in this; the role of foreign countries and their agents; how many people have been arrested, what sort of people, and so on). Report also on your thoughts about what measures to take for further struggle."[29] The inquiry was answered within a few days. On 9 August, once he had familiarized himself with the issue and learned that only 280,000 rubles in change had been confiscated, Stalin sent Menzhinsky a written reprimand for his poor performance.[30]

Stalin spelled out a more detailed characterization of the problem, as he understood it, in a letter to Molotov. He wrote that the situation taking shape was the consequence of mistakes by Yury Piatakov, head of Gosbank, and Briukhanov, head of the Finance Commissariat, who had allowed themselves to be controlled by "specialist-wreckers" from these organs of government. "It is thus important to a) fundamentally purge the Finance and Gosbank bureaucracy, despite the wails of dubious Communists like Briukhanov-Piatakov; b) definitely shoot two or three dozen wreckers from these apparatuses, including several dozen common cashiers; c) continue OGPU operations throughout the USSR that are aimed at seizing small change (silver)."[31] Soon afterward, on 20 August 1930, the Politburo assigned the OGPU to "apply stronger measures in the fight against speculators and those concealing stashes of coins, including those within Soviet-cooperative enterprises."[32] On 15 October 1930 the Politburo relieved Piatakov and Briukhanov of their duties.[33]

In taking control of the campaign against coin speculators, Stalin was pursuing a number of goals. First, he was yet again accusing Rykov and his apparatus of being incompetent. Second, he was demonstrating his own decisiveness and effectiveness. Third, he was using the financial crisis as an excuse for escalating the campaign against "bourgeois specialist-wreckers" that had started with the Shakhty trial in 1928 and was an important instrument in the effort to discredit the "rightist Commu-

nists." In the mid-1930s this campaign—as evidenced by the coin affair—took a new turn. By attacking "wreckers" from among "bourgeois specialists," Stalin was shifting blame for the many failures in the
economy and the sharp drop in the standard of living caused by the policy of the great break (*veliky perelom*). He was also accusing rightist
leaders and a number of top Soviet administrators of having ties to and
even aiding and abetting the wreckers. Such accusations were an important part of the political game that Stalin was playing in the highest echelons of power.

To aid in the fabrication of a case alleging an extensive network of
counterrevolutionary wrecker organizations, during the summer of
1930 the OGPU began arresting high-level specialists from the central
agencies charged with running the economy. Those arrested were primarily well-known academics and experts who had played a prominent
role during the years of the New Economic Policy (NEP). Among them
were Nikolai Kondratiev, a former socialist revolutionary, a deputy to
the minister for food supply in the Provisional Government, who had
worked in Soviet agricultural agencies and headed the Finance Commissariat's Institute of Economic Trends (Koniunkturny institut); Pro-
fessors N. P. Makarov and A. V. Chaianov, who held positions in the
RSFSR Agriculture Commissariat; Professor L. N. Yurovsky, a member
of the collegium of the Finance Commissariat; Professor P. A. Sadyrin, a
former member of the Central Committee of the People's Freedom Party
who had joined the management of Gosbank; and V. G. Groman, an experienced statistician and economist who until 1921 had been a Menshevik and who worked in Gosplan and the USSR Central Statistical
Administration. Another prominent Menshevik, V. A. Bazarov, had followed a career path similar to Groman's and since 1921 had worked at
Gosplan. N. N. Sukhanov, who worked in economic agencies in the
1920s and in the Soviet trade offices in Berlin and Paris, was the author
of the famous *Zapiski o revoliutsii* (Notes about revolution).[34] On 10
October 1917, Sukhanov's apartment had been the site of the famous
meeting of the Bolshevik Central Committee (his wife was a Bolshevik)
where the decision was made to organize an armed revolt.

Through the efforts of the OGPU and with Stalin's attentive guidance,
materials were assembled demonstrating the existence of a network of
anti-Soviet organizations that were supposedly united under the "Peasant Labor Party," chaired by Nikolai Kondratiev, and the "Industrial

Party," led by Professor L. K. Ramzin. In addition to testimony about preparations to overthrow the Soviet government and ties to foreign anti-Soviet organizations and intelligence agencies, evidence of contacts with rightists and other members of the country's leadership and of the "wreckers'" desire to include rightist leaders in their government after the overthrow was beaten out of those arrested. Stalin intended to make this evidence available to a wide circle of party functionaries. At his request, on 10 August 1930 the Politburo adopted a decision to circulate the testimony of those arrested in the case of the "Peasant Labor Party" to all members of the Central Committee and the Central Control Commission, as well as to "managerial personnel in the economic agencies."[35] However, Molotov, who was handling Central Committee matters in Stalin's absence, decided not to circulate Makarov's testimony, which included allegations that, along with the finance commissar Grigorii Sokolnikov, Rykov, and others, the "wreckers" planned to install Kalinin in the "coalition government." On 11 August, Molotov wrote to Stalin, who was vacationing in the south, that Makarov was "intentionally smearing" Kalinin.[36] Stalin was adamant. In his reply to Molotov he insisted that all "testimony" be circulated. "There can be no doubt that Kalinin has sinned. [. . .] The Central Committee must definitely be informed about this in order to teach Kalinin never to get mixed up with such rascals again."[37] In another letter to Molotov, on 2 September, Stalin again asserted that the "wreckers" from the Groman-Kondratiev group "indisputably" helped Rykov, and Kalinin wound up being involved in the matter through his subordinates.[38] As a result of Stalin's insistence, on 6 September the Politburo adopted a decision to circulate additional testimony by Kondratiev, Groman, Sukhanov, and others.[39]

Once he had achieved his objective of having the "testimony" circulated, Stalin gave the already obedient Kalinin a scare for added effect and, in so doing, won the attention of other Politburo members. But the main targets of this operation were the rightists—primarily Rykov. Furthermore, the fact that the rightists were only indirectly implicated in sabotage probably did not seem sufficient to Stalin. The OGPU began to investigate another "lead" indicating direct involvement of the party opposition in the activities of the "underground parties" and their "terrorist plans." Several arrested instructors from the Military Academy gave testimony revealing a "military plot" supposedly headed by the commander of Leningrad Military District, Mikhail Tukhachevsky, who had ties to the party rightists. The OGPU asserted that the plotters were preparing to take over power and kill Stalin. On 10 September 1930, Stalin received all of these materials from Menzhinsky, who wrote, "It is dangerous to arrest the participants in this group one at a time. There seem to be two ways out: either we immediately arrest the most active participants, or we wait for your arrival, taking undercover measures so as not to be caught off guard. I feel I should point out that all insurrectional groups are maturing very quickly these days, and the latter option involves a certain risk."[40] Stalin was not frightened by the OGPU chief's warnings. Two weeks later, on 24 September, Stalin wrote to Ordzhonikidze:

> Take a look right away at the testimony by Kakurin and Troitsky [two arrested military instructors] and think about ways to liquidate this unpleasant business. This material, as you see, is top secret: only Molotov, I, and now you know about it. I don't know whether or not Klim knows about it. It would seem that Tukh[achev]sky was captured by anti-Soviet elements and was given quite a working over, also by rightist anti-Soviet elements. That's what the materials imply. Is it possible? Of course, if it can't be disproved, then it's possible. It appears that the rightists would go as far as military dictatorship if it will get rid of the TsK, of kolkhozes and sovkhozes, of a Bolshevik pace of industrialization. [. . .] The Kondratiev-Sukhanov-Bukharin Party—that's what we have here. What a business. . . . We can't put an end to this business the usual way (immediate arrest, etc.). We have to think things through thoroughly. It would be better to postpone the solution Menzhinsky suggests until the middle of October, when we will all be on hand. Talk to Molotov about all this when you're in Moscow.[41]

Stalin's letter shows that he knew the true value of this latest OGPU fabrication. Otherwise it is difficult to explain his good-natured willingness to "postpone the solution" for several more weeks, leaving the "conspirators" free, despite the dangers that Menzhinsky had signaled. Most likely, Stalin did not intend to arrest the army generals. As with Kalinin, this was purely a preventive measure as far as the military was concerned. Subsequent events confirm this. Upon returning from vacation, Stalin, together with Ordzhonikidze and Voroshilov, conducted simultaneous interrogations of Tukhachevsky, Kakurin, and Troitsky, apparently in mid-October. Tukhachevsky was pronounced innocent.[42]

Having abandoned the investigation of a military plot (undoubtedly on Stalin's orders), the OGPU continued fabricating cases concerning "terrorist organizations" and their connections with "rightist Communists." Correspondingly, moral responsibility for abetting "terrorism" and plotting Stalin's physical removal was placed on the shoulders of rightist leaders, primarily Bukharin. Upon returning to Moscow, Stalin stated as much to Bukharin over the telephone. Several months later, at a joint meeting of the Politburo and the Central Control Commission presidium on 4 November 1930, Stalin himself related how this had transpired: "On October 14 of this year, Com. Bukharin called me at my office, where I was talking with Coms. Kuibyshev and Molotov. Com. Bukharin demanded that I have a heart-to-heart talk with him about certain 'important,' in his opinion, issues. I replied that I had nothing to discuss with him heart to heart. I told him that it would be strange to have a heart-to-heart talk with him when he, Com. Bukharin, was cultivating terrorists among right deviationists through his unbridled personal agitation against Stalin. I alluded to the Smirnov-Orlov (right deviationists) terrorist group, which has direct ties to Uglanov, and therefore with Bukharin."[43] On 14 October, Bukharin had answered these charges in an emotional letter: "Koba. After our telephone conversation I immediately left work in a state of despair. Not because you had 'scared' me—you will not scare me and you will not intimidate me. But because those monstrous accusations that you threw at me are clear evidence of the existence of some sort of devilish, vile, and low *provocation,* that you believe, on which you are building your policy, and *that will lead to no good,* even if you were to destroy me physically as thoroughly as you are destroying me politically."[44] Bukharin demanded a face-to-face meeting and explanation from Stalin. Stalin stated that he was prepared only for official explanations in front of the Politburo.

On 20 October the conflict between Stalin and Bukharin was discussed in a closed session of the Politburo. As might have been expected, the Politburo supported Stalin, adopting a decision "To support Stalin's refusal to have a 'heart-to-heart' talk with Bukharin as correct. To propose that Com. Bukharin place all questions that interest him before the TsK."[45] Bukharin's assertive behavior, however—he accused Stalin of violating the truce they had reached, and, in the end, walked out of the session—cast a shadow over Stalin's victory. This is what Sergei Syrtsov told his supporters (information about the session has been preserved in investigative materials from the Syrtsov-Lominadze case). As A. Galperin, who was arrested in association with the case, wrote in his statement, "Com. Syrtsov told us that Bukharin's letter to Com. Stalin had been discussed in the Politburo on October 20 and that Bukharin had written in this letter that he recognizes his mistakes and asked, 'What else is wanted from me?' He then told us that Com. Stalin had refused to see Com. Bukharin for personal negotiations and that the PB [Politburo] had approved Com. Stalin's response to Com. Bukharin. In describing the significance that Stalin attributed to Com. Bukharin's letter, Com. Syrtsov said that in discussing this question Com. Stalin proposed drawing the curtain."[46] In a denunciation (the one that initiated the Syrtsov-Lominadze affair), B. G. Reznikov described this episode as follows: Syrtsov "described in great detail what happened and what had been said in the PB. He spoke in such great detail that he even felt the need to tell us things like 'Stalin ordered that the windows be closed, even though we were on the fifth floor.' He said that during Com. Stalin's second speech, Bukharin left, not waiting for it to finish. After that, Stalin ended his speech, saying, 'I wanted to give him a talking to, but since he's left, there's nothing to say.' [. . .] Syrtsov said that [Bukharin's] letter was written by hand, and Stalin read it without showing it to anyone."[47]

The Bukharin question was considered at the 20 October meeting in conjunction with a report by the OGPU administrators (Agranov, Menzhinsky, and Yagoda) on the testimony of the "wreckers." In this regard, the Politburo resolved:

a) That the OGPU report about the latest testimony by members of the *prompartiia* [Industrial Party] central committee concerning terrorist activity be taken into consideration and that it be proposed that further investigation be continued.

b) That it be proposed that the OGPU coordinate matters regarding necessary arrests with the TsK Secretary. Sabotage groups should be immediately arrested.

c) That Com. Stalin be immediately required to cease traveling around the city by foot.

d) That the necessity of moving the secret department of the TsK from Staraya Square to the Kremlin as soon as possible be recognized.

e) That Voroshilov be assigned to accelerate the further clearing of the Kremlin of a number of residents who are not entirely reliable.[48]

It is easy to see that the fabrication of cases against "terrorist organizations" in which the party opposition was supposedly involved was a sort of rehearsal for the political trials of 1935–1938, during which Stalin's political opponents were at first put in prison and later shot. In 1930 everything ended peacefully. In November, Bukharin published a statement in *Pravda* recognizing the correctness of the decisions of the 16th Party Congress and denouncing any factional work and attempts to conduct veiled struggles against the party leadership (in other words, Stalin). For now, Stalin neither wanted nor was able to take stronger measures. All of the provocations of this period were designed to achieve modest goals: to lay the groundwork for more decisive actions against the opposition and to intimidate those who were dissatisfied and wavering. Another step on this path was the removal of the unreliable Syrtsov from the Politburo.

THE SYRTSOV-LOMINADZE AFFAIR

Born in 1893, Sergei Ivanovich Syrtsov was younger than many Soviet leaders and had joined the party later, in 1913. But his entry into the party took place under propitious circumstances—his first moves within the party were guided by Molotov. Like Rykov, Syrtsov had abandoned his studies, having traded his place at Saint Petersburg Polytechnic Institute for a place as a political defendant and subsequent Siberian exile. During the Civil War he fought in the south, where he met several of Stalin's future comrades-in-arms (for example, Ordzhonikidze). In 1921 he joined the Central Committee apparatus as a department head. In 1926 he was sent as secretary to the Siberian territorial committee of the Communist Party. In early 1928 he was able to fulfill the dream of any party functionary—Stalin himself came to Siberia on a mission to organize emergency grain expropriations, which was successful, in part because of Syrtsov's efforts. Immediately after Stalin won decisive victory over Bukharin's group in 1929, he had the thirty-six-year-old Syrtsov appointed to the post of chairman of the RSFSR Council of People's Commissars, a post that had been held by Rykov, among his other duties. In June 1929, Syrtsov was made a candidate for membership in the Politburo.[49] But the young man did not justify the faith Stalin had placed in him, proving to be obstinate and excessively independent and siding with Rykov on a number of occasions.

Several documents indicate that Syrtsov was in rather close contact

Later on the morning of the denunciation, after Stalin informed Ordzhonikidze, chairman of the party's Central Control Commission, and Pavel Postyshev, secretary of the Central Committee (Kaganovich and Molotov were out of town), he ordered that Syrtsov be summoned. Syrtsov was not found until it was almost evening. Then he read the denunciation and announced that he would give official testimony only in front of the Central Control Commission. As soon as Syrtsov entered the Central Committee building, Reznikov also arrived, and he wrote a new statement. He alleged that Syrtsov had come to the Central Committee straight from a meeting that he had conducted with his supporters (including Reznikov). At the meeting, as Reznikov described it, the topic under discussion was talks with Lominadze on both groups' decision to prepare to replace Stalin using both legal and illegal means. Reznikov also alleged that Syrtsov had described to his followers in great detail the 20 October Politburo meeting where Stalin had raised the issue of Bukharin's letter. In the new denunciation, Reznikov quoted Syrtsov as saying:

> A significant portion of the party's most active members, of course, are unhappy with the regime and the party's policies, but this portion evidently feel that there is a unified Politburo that is following a firm line, that there exists a TsK, even if it isn't Lenin's TsK. These illusions should be dispelled. The Politburo is a fiction. In fact, everything is decided behind the Politburo's back by a small circle that meets in the Kremlin, in Tsetkin's former apartment; such Politburo members as Kuibyshev, Voroshilov, Kalinin, and Rudzutak are outside this circle, and inside the circle there are those who are not Politburo members, such as [Yakov] Yakovlev, [Pavel] Postyshev, etc. Then he said that Com. Voroshilov had been kicked out of his job; he had been replaced by Uborevich, an unprincipled man, devilishly proud, an obvious Thermidorian. They were thinking of putting Voroshilov in Rykov's place.[56]

Syrtsov also refused to say anything about Reznikov's second statement. Then other participants in the meeting were summoned—I. S. Nusinov, V. A. Kavraisky, Galperin. In front of Reznikov they denied his accusations and were therefore arrested and sent to the OGPU.

Through the joint efforts of the Central Control Commission and the OGPU, every one of the accused, including Syrtsov and Lominadze, confessed to anti-party factional activities. On 4 November 1930 there was a joint session of the Politburo and the Central Control Commission presidium to consider, based on a report by Ordzhonikidze, the matter "Concerning the factional work of Comrades Syrtsov, Lominadze, Shatskin, and others." After lengthy discussion, a decision was adopted to expel Syrtsov and Lominadze from the Central Committee and Lazar Shatskin from the Central Control Commission. A special Central Committee and Central Control Commission was set up to draft a resolution. Ordzhonikidze, Stalin, Stanislav Kosior, Kaganovich, Kuibyshev, Voroshilov, Rudzutak, Matvei Shkiriatov, Yaroslavsky, Kalinin, Molotov, and Sergei Kirov were all appointed members. The resolution prepared by the commission was approved only a month later, on 1 December, and published in newspapers on 2 December. It stated that Syrtsov and Lominadze had organized a "left-right" bloc whose platform coincided with the views of the right deviation. The decision to expel Syrtsov from the Central Committee and Shatskin from the Central Control Commission was approved.

In his presentation to the joint session of the Politburo and the Central Control Commission presidium on 4 November, Ordzhonikidze stated that Syrtsov believed the case against him was "manufactured." "He actually thinks, for example," Ordzhonikidze said, "that the TsK and TsKK knew what Nusinov, Kavraisky, Reznikov and he were up to and allowed him to follow that path. Even now he is convinced that Kavraisky, Nusinov, and Reznikov were either agents of the GPU or agents of the TsK and TsKK who had been assigned to look after him. All one can do is throw up one's hands and wonder how Syrtsov can make such absurd and criminal assertions. That is all you can do."[57] Ordzhonikidze's bewilderment was probably feigned. Syrtsov was undoubtedly right in many of his suspicions. As in similar cases, the Syrtsov-Lominadze affair involved the interweaving of certain events with deliberate provocations. The preparation of this case serves as a good example of Stalin's method of political warfare during the stage when he was consolidating one-man rule but still had to use subtle measures against his comrades-in-arms. Two circumstances are of particular relevance here. The first is Syrtsov's accusation regarding Stalin's limitation of the Politburo's rights. The second concerns the reasons why the leaders of the "anti-party group" were dealt with unusually leniently.

As already stated, Reznikov reported Syrtsov's allegations that Stalin's faction met separately and that a portion of the Politburo leadership was "cut off" in his 22 October denunciation. On the next day, 23 October, the issue arose again when Syrtsov was being interrogated by the Central Control Commission, headed by Ordzhonikidze. Ordzhonikidze, who was "having a discussion" with Syrtsov, tried to steer away from it. The corresponding stenographic record reads as follows:

SYRTSOV: It doesn't seem right to me to have a situation where a good number of Politburo decisions are made in advance by a certain group. I can completely understand why Rykov is excluded as a person who has committed rightist errors and has been following an incorrect political line. But as I understand it, Kuibyshev, Rudzutak, and Kalinin have not been taking part in this ruling group and are purely mechanical [pro forma] members of the Politburo, and this creates a situation whereby . . .

ORDZHONIKIDZE: Who makes up this group?

SYRTSOV: Those in the remainder, evidently, or a portion of the rest of them.

ORDZHONIKIDZE: Well, if you're the one talking, you should know.

SYRTSOV: This is how I am explaining it, that concerning a number of questions, individual Politburo members—if there were some other discussion, if there were some other approach—would not be tied down by preliminary discussion and would be putting questions somewhat differently.[58]

Syrtsov's testimony in this case has particular significance. As a candidate member of the Politburo, he knew a lot about the relationships between Politburo members and was aware of subtle nuances that were accessible only to those directly involved in events. The fact that Syrtsov was not fully informed in some key areas (for example, his belief that Voroshilov was being prepared for Rykov's post as chairman of the Council of People's Commissars, even though Stalin had already agreed with his closest associates on Molotov's candidacy) attests to the level of conspiracy within the Stalin "faction." It also confirms Syrtsov's observation about the existence of such a faction. Syrtsov most likely had good reason to talk about "factions" and "purely mechanical" members of the Politburo. Knowing the complex situation within the Politburo, he was probably hoping for some support from the "purely mechanical" members whose rights were being ignored by Stalin.

An accusation of factionalism was the most serious of all possible accusations that could have been leveled against Stalin. While the situation in the country was still under control, nobody was able to convince top party officials (primarily the members of the TsK) that the general line chosen was mistaken and ruinous. Collectivization and dekulakization had been taken too far, and the members of the Central Committee who had supported Stalin against the rightists bore direct responsibility for this. But certain accusations would upset even his most loyal followers. In a fight Stalin always tried to come out looking like a victim of the intrigues of his political opponents, so the implication that immediately after victory in the drawn-out fight against the opposition, he began to cut his loyal comrades-in-arms off from the leadership—preparing for yet another split—could be damaging. Stalin undoubtedly understood this. In his speech before a joint session of the Politburo and the Central Control Commission presidium on 4 November, he immediately stated that there had been no meetings in the former apartment of Klara Tsetkin (one of the leaders of the German Communist Party), that the only thing he did there was work on his speech for the 16th Party Congress ("far from ringing telephones") and speak with individual members of the Politburo. "While I was working in this apartment, at different times Molotov, Kalinin, Sergo, Rudzutak, and Mikoyan each came to see me once. Despite what Com. Syrtsov says, neither Kaganovich, nor Yakovlev, nor Postyshev were in this apartment and no meetings were held there and nor could have been held in that apartment. Did certain Politburo members occasionally meet? Yes, we met. Mostly we met in the TsK building. And what's wrong with that?"[59]

There is every reason to believe that Stalin was lying. The practice of holding "factional" meetings of the Politburo—at which the most important questions to be raised at the official meetings were discussed and decided in advance—had taken shape back in the 1920s. The group of seven (semyorka) that existed during the period of struggle against Trotsky was a "factional" Politburo, which included all the members except Trotsky. In 1926–1927, after Stalin broke with Zinoviev and Kamenev, he and his supporters in the Politburo also coordinated their stances on key issues, acting as a united front during official Politburo sessions. Stalin's letters to Molotov, for example, many of which were essentially addressed to the majority faction in the Politburo, serve as evidence of this. It is still unclear exactly how Stalin and his supporters in the Politburo coordinated their actions against the rightists in 1928–1929, but that such coordination took place regularly is attested to by the entire course of Stalin's fight against Bukharin, Rykov, and Tomsky. In 1930, Stalin used tried and true methods of political intrigue. He had reasons—Rykov was still in the Politburo. What was new in this case

was that Stalin had decided to distance not only his political opponent—Rykov—from decision-making but a number of his close associates as well. Maybe he felt that they were not sufficiently "stead-
fast," and he was worried that they might waver at the decisive moment,
or maybe he simply assumed that they were not capable of being useful
in such a delicate matter. I will point out that Syrtsov placed Kalinin
among the "purely mechanical" members of the Politburo, and at that
time Stalin was indeed purposefully discrediting Kalinin, accusing him
of ties with the "wreckers."

In any event, Stalin surely wanted to avoid any rumors of a factional
Politburo and to limit the dissemination of the other accusations that
Syrtsov was making. This appears to be one of the main reasons that
such an important matter was not even discussed in a Central Committee plenum. As early as the joint session of the Politburo and the Central
Control Commission presidium on 4 November, Stalin had stated that
the business concerning the Syrtsov-Lominadze bloc was not serious.[60]
And on 20 November 1930, on Stalin's suggestion, the Politburo
adopted a decision, in response to reports by a Western news agency,
not to publish any denials in the Soviet press and to have TASS indicate
through the foreign press that the report of a "military plot" and the arrest of Comrades Syrtsov, Lominadze, and others was nothing but "ma-
licious falsehood."[61]

The motives behind such decisions are understandable. It was not advantageous for Stalin to have the idea get out that he was facing opposition from those who had recently been his strong supporters. Such reports would have weakened Stalin's position and cast further doubt on
the durability of his regime. In the Syrtsov-Lominadze affair, we see
Stalin's efforts to find the optimal balance in suppressing dissent within
the party leadership. By exercising just the necessary degree of tough-
ness, Stalin avoided the brutality that later became commonplace and
thus underscored his confidence in the strength of his position and the
lack of seriousness of opposition members' intentions.[62] Based on what
we know, Stalin was also forced to deal with the positions of individual
Politburo members, or at least that of Ordzhonikidze. Ordzhonikidze
spoke openly about his friendships with Syrtsov and Lominadze in his 4
November speech. Publicly Ordzhonikidze demanded harsh punishment for the "factionalists," but privately to Stalin he probably expressed different feelings. Later, in 1936–1937, when the conflict be-

tween Stalin and Ordzhonikidze reached the breaking point, Stalin openly accused Ordzhonikidze of condoning Lominadze's anti-party activities.

RYKOV'S REPLACEMENT

The Syrtsov-Lominadze affair forced certain adjustments to plans for replacing Rykov as head of the Council of People's Commissars. Stalin first communicated his intention to remove Rykov in a letter to Molotov written in the south on 13 September 1930. The letter was confidential and was intended only for Molotov. Stalin wrote, "Our top Soviet hierarchy (Labor Defense Council, Council of Commissars, Conference of Deputies) suffers from a fatal disease. The Labor Defense Council has been transformed from an active, businesslike body into an idle parliament. The Council of Commissars is paralyzed by Rykov's insipid and basically anti-party speeches. The Conference of Deputies [. . .] has now tended to become the headquarters [. . . and] is now *opposing* itself to the Central Committee. Clearly this can't go on. Radical measures are needed. As to what kind—I'll tell you when I get to Moscow."[63] But soon he decided not to wait for a face-to-face meeting with Molotov in Moscow. In a letter to Molotov dated 22 September, Stalin made a more clear-cut proposal to "definitively resolve the question of the Soviet top leadership" by removing Rykov and Vasily Shmidt, Rykov's deputy, from the Council of People's Commissars and undertake a reorganization of the government. Stalin proposed reducing the number of members in the Labor and Defense Council, organizing an Implementation Commission within the Council of People's Commissars with the goal of monitoring the implementation of decisions by the center, and abolishing the council chairman's Conference of Deputies as a permanently functioning government body. He suggested handing over the duties of chairman to Molotov. Stalin now asked Molotov to discuss all of these ideas within the "small circle of close friends" and let him know about any objections.[64]

Politburo members met on 7 October to discuss Stalin's letter. As they agreed among themselves, each of them sent Stalin his own letter on the matter.[65] Voroshilov spelled out the overall discussion and its conclusions in a letter to Stalin dated 8 October. First of all, Voroshilov reported unanimous support for the idea of replacing Rykov: "The current situation cannot be tolerated any longer." However, opinion was divided over the new candidate. "I, Mikoyan, Molotov, Kaganovich, and to some extent Kuibyshev believe that the best solution would be to consolidate leadership. It would be good to put you in the SNK so you could really take over running the entire country as only you can." Voroshilov went on to justify this proposal. First, he flattered Stalin ("As never before, the SNK now needs someone who has a strategist's gift"). Second, in Voroshilov's opinion, having the "main office and general headquarters" on Staraya Square (where the party Central Commitee apparatus was located) was "cumbersome, inflexible, and [. . .] poorly organized." "Under such circumstances," Voroshilov wrote, Lenin "would be at the SNK and would be running the party and Comintern." Trying to anticipate Stalin's objections, Voroshilov wrote about possible obstacles to implementing such a decision. "They generally fall into three categories. 1. International questions. 2. Your personal attitude, and 3. Questions of direct party leadership." Voroshilov did not elaborate on the first two points, leaving unclear what he meant by "international questions" (probably Stalin's reduced involvement in Comintern matters). But being well grounded in matters of high-level Kremlin politics and knowing Stalin's moods and inclinations, Voroshilov outlined "questions of direct party leadership" in some detail—in other words, the threat of having Stalin's attention distracted from managing party affairs. Such a threat, Voroshilov acknowledged, was truly present. But he dismissed it using a purely demagogic technique, again citing the example of Lenin: "I think [. . .] there is no basis for presuming that the party and its organizations in 1930 are any less organized, durable (in every regard), etc., than they were ten years ago."[66]

Voroshilov's letter reflected his perspective on the change of SNK leadership as well as his understanding of the positions of individual Politburo members on the change. The letters of other Politburo members to Stalin painted a somewhat different picture than that presented by Voroshilov. Mikoyan was unequivocal in expressing his support of the idea of a "consolidated leadership" ("like we had when Ilyich was alive").[67] It is possible that Kuibyshev was equally unequivocal, but his letter has not yet been found. As far as Molotov and Kaganovich were concerned, both of whom Voroshilov had listed among his supporters, things were not so simple. In a letter to Stalin dated 9 October, Molotov pointed to the "tremendous pluses" of making Stalin chairman of the

Council of People's Commissars, especially at a time when the council's authority had diminished. But he also introduced arguments against such a decision. Stalin would not be able to manage the Comintern and the party the way he had been (in which case it was not out of the question that the post of Central Committee general secretary would be abolished). In the end, Molotov avoided clearly stating his position. "In any case, this question can and should only be discussed with you," he concluded. As for his own candidacy, Molotov, as might have been expected, took himself out of the running, citing his weakness as a worker and his lack of authority.[68]

Kaganovich's letter of 9 October, in which he, as usual, bent over backwards to please Stalin, demonstrated equal skill in navigating the issues. He essentially left it to Stalin to decide the matter as he saw fit, expressing support in advance for any outcome. "From the mouths of party members one often hears something to the effect that 'If only Stalin were appointed, that would be the real thing [. . .]. Of course it would be the real thing, and the party and the masses would see this as the real thing." However, Kaganovich immediately expressed his doubts: "First, would this decision restrict the scope of your work, in regard to the Comintern line in particular, and second, of life within the party? After all, especially in recent years the leading role of the party and the TsK has risen to unprecedented heights and this, Com. Stalin, speaking without exaggeration, is all thanks to you. The most important strategic maneuvers in the economy and in politics were determined, and will and should be determined, by you, wherever you might be. But will things get better if there is a change? I doubt it. The details of economic questions could even make it harder to see the entire field of battle." All of this, Kaganovich concluded, forces one to "decide in favor of Molotov's candidacy."[69]

More direct and less diplomatic, Ordzhonikidze expressed himself in a letter dated 9 October: "Of course Molotov should be put in Rykov's place."[70]

As Voroshilov's letter indicates, a number of Politburo members did not accept the proposal about forming an Implementation Commission, either. "First Kuibyshev, then I, and then Sergo expressed doubts about what purpose such a commission would serve," Voroshilov reported. Ordzhonikidze was particularly unhappy with the idea, expressing "concern that the creation of an IC would involve an element of weakening the role of the RKI [Workers' and Peasants' Inspectorate]"—of which he was head.

On the basis of these letters it is possible to re-create a fairly detailed picture of the meeting of the "small circle of close friends." Six men had gathered in Moscow on 7 October: Voroshilov, Molotov, Kuibyshev, Kaganovich, Mikoyan, and Ordzhonikidze. Other members of the Politburo based in Moscow—Kalinin and Rudzutak—were away on vacation (and in any event were not part of the group of "close friends"). Sergei Kirov and Stanislav Kosior, Leningrad and Ukraine party heads respectively, who were also members of the Politburo, only rarely came to Moscow. Rykov was still formally a member of the Politburo, but he was not invited to the meeting for obvious reasons.

Molotov probably opened the meeting, since Stalin's letters had been addressed to him. Because his task at this meeting of "equals" was to exhibit appropriate modesty and not express a particular interest in promotion to the new position, he talked mostly about his reluctance to accept such an elevated post. "He expressed doubts about how much authority he would hold for the likes of us and, in particular, for Rudzutak, but of course that's all nonsense. We will all support him, including, I believe, Rudzutak. If it turns out that we are wrong, then Rudzutak could be given another job," Ordzhonikidze wrote Stalin.[71] Rudzutak, as deputy chairman of the Council of People's Commissars, would be directly affected by the changes.

This aspect of the discussion deserves special attention. The comparisons drawn by Molotov between Rudzutak's "authority" and his own are evidence that a hierarchy still existed within the highest circle of leadership, a hierarchy not yet governed by closeness to Stalin (in that regard, Molotov stood much higher than Rudzutak), but by previous service. This hierarchy was an important component of the system of "collective leadership." At the same time, Ordzhonikidze's statement about the option of transferring Rudzutak to another job indicates that this hierarchy was more a thing of the past than a vital political factor.

In justifying his wholehearted support for Molotov's candidacy at the 7 October meeting, Ordzhonikidze cited his previous conversations with Stalin. In particular, he insisted that Stalin had always objected to the idea of his being made chairman of the Council of People's Commissars because of the "undesirability at present of a complete merger (including the appearance of such a merger before the entire world) [. . .]

of party and Soviet leadership."[72] Molotov's letter suggests that Ord-zhonikidze's information about previous conversations with Stalin was confirmed by Voroshilov. Voroshilov, however, did not consider the idea of Stalin's weakened control over the Comintern and the party as suffi-cient reason for rejecting the new appointment. Mikoyan felt the same way, and, so, apparently, did Kuibyshev. The discussion within the "small circle of close friends" apparently left a very distinct impression on the final two members, Kaganovich and Molotov. In letters sent to Stalin two days after the meeting, they expressed understanding of cer-tain negative consequences of Stalin's possible appointment that Stalin himself had not mentioned in his letters to Molotov. Kaganovich and Molotov may have had a change of heart after hearing what Ord-zhonikidze and Voroshilov had to say. This would explain the contra-diction between Voroshilov's assertion that Kaganovich and Molotov had supported the proposal to appoint Stalin as council head and the content of letters from these two men, in which they favored the solu-tion proposed by Stalin.

The discussion among the "small circle" sheds a good deal of light on Stalin's frame of mind and that of his closest comrades-in-arms, as well as on interactions within the party leadership during the early stages of the consolidation of Stalin's position as the unquestioned leader of the Politburo. Stalin's strength rested in his ability to concentrate on per-sonnel decisions and control of the party apparatus, but essentially without answering for the specific actions of the economic and political leadership. Only occasionally did Stalin intervene in the resolution of economic or social problems that were either, in his opinion, of funda-mental political significance or from which he would be able to derive specific political benefit. This extremely strategic advantage—being able to observe events from the side and act as arbiter—would be im-possible to maintain if Stalin were appointed chairman of the Council of People's Commissars.

It is easy to imagine that Stalin did not want to take on the enormous burden of running the government. This would have demanded a great deal of experience and skill at handling a torrent of daily problems, qualities that Stalin did not have. The job would have come with a grueling workload, which is something Stalin always avoided. It would also have limited Stalin's opportunities for political maneuvering and would have made him directly responsible not only for political solutions but for the day-to-day implementation of policies that even by 1929–1930 were a great strain on the society and the economy. All this tempered any desire he might have had to take on the post of chairman of the government and formally establish himself as Lenin's heir. Replacing Rykov dragged on for some time, however, which leaves room for speculation that Stalin was wavering, weighing the advantages and disadvantages before making up his mind to give the post of council chairman to Molotov. Ten years later he nonetheless took on the post, an indirect indication of his hidden desires.

The time needed to coordinate decisions about the new leader of the Council of People's Commissars and Stalin's own wavering may have been among the reasons it took so long to convene a party Central Committee plenum to enact the necessary resolution. The need to convene a Central Committee plenum was first put before the Politburo on 15 September 1930; however, an exact date was not immediately chosen. On 29 September the Politburo returned to this question and resolved to convene the plenum on 5 December.[73]

During the months leading up to the plenum, major personnel reorganizations implemented at the Supreme Economic Council, Gosplan, and the Finance Commissariat constituted lateral assaults on Rykov. The ideological ties between Rykov and the opposition were variously underscored during the 4 November joint session of the Politburo and the Central Control Commission presidium, where the case of Syrtsov and Lominadze was considered. A significant portion of Stalin's speech was devoted to these ties. Accusing Rykov of defending "wreckers" and "rotten Communists," Stalin stated, "The Chairman of the Sovnarkom exists in order, through daily practical work, to carry out the instructions of the party, instructions that he himself has a hand in developing. Is this being done or not? No, unfortunately, it is not being done. That is the problem, and that is the source of our dissatisfaction. And of course this cannot go on for long."[74] The same themes came up in Molotov's speech. He accused the rightists of "totally supporting, shielding, and inspiring the struggle of anti-Bolshevik elements against the party." Within the Politburo, Molotov stated, "Com. Rykov, without formally declaring war, has in fact been engaged in this very thing in recent weeks, while the TsK has been forced to work hard at fixing the crude mistakes of the economic, finance-credit, and other government bodies."[75]

Against this backdrop, on the very next day, 5 November, the Politburo approved the agenda for the upcoming plenum based on Stalin's speech. The plenum was scheduled to consider targets for 1931, a report by the Supply Commissariat on procurement of meat and vegetables, and a report from the Central Cooperative Society (Tsentrosoiuz) on consumer-goods cooperatives. On 20 November the Politburo again moved the start of the plenum, to 15 December. On 30 November the question of council elections was added to the agenda.[76]

While the plenum was being prepared, Rykov was essentially kept from power. On 29 November 1930, for example, a Politburo commission headed by Voroshilov considered questions having to do with developing Red Army forces in 1931 and a procurement plan for the Military and Naval Affairs Commissariat for 1931. Politburo members in attendance were Stalin, Ordzhonikidze, Kuibyshev, Molotov, and Rudzutak. Rykov, chairman of the Council of People's Commissars, was absent, although such questions came under his purview and should not have been dealt with, nor had in the past been dealt with, except when he was present.[77]

On 11 December 1930 the Politburo discussed drafts of resolutions on the main issues to be addressed by the plenum, but on the eve of the plenum's being convened, its start was again rescheduled, this time for 17 December.[78] The reason became clear the following day. On 15 December a member of the presidium of the Central Control Commission, Ivan Akulov, sent a special letter to the Politburo on the presidium's behalf proposing that a joint plenum of the Central Committee and Central Control Commission be convened instead of a Central Committee plenum. Such joint plenums of the Central Committee and Central Control Commission were usually convened to decide the most critical party and government matters. The last time such a joint plenum had taken place was in April 1929, when the final blow had been delivered to the rightists. This time, Akulov argued, a joint plenum was necessary to discuss "major economic questions." In actuality, the reason for a joint meeting was undoubtedly the upcoming replacement of Rykov. Akulov's proposal was accepted.[79]

The machinations surrounding the convening of the plenum were evidence that Stalin was trying to hide his true intentions regarding Rykov as long as possible. This effort continued even during the plenum itself, where the question of Rykov arose as if by chance.

The first two days of the plenum did not seem to foretell the emergence of any organizational issues. There was the usual discussion of agendas, and there were the traditional bureaucratic reports. Signs that an attack on Rykov had been prepared appeared on the third day. On the morning of 19 December, Rykov's remarks, made during discussions of Kuibyshev's report on economic targets for 1931, were repeatedly interrupted by comments from the floor reminding him of his past "sins" and demanding repentance. Rykov defended himself forcefully, asserting that it was pointless to recall "old arguments," although in closing he did assert his loyalty. "I am absolutely convinced that the general line of the Party is the only correct line, that our achievements point to this completely and categorically, that any double-dealing—as the vilest form of infighting is now called—any passivity, any neutrality, is now absolutely unacceptable for a member of the Party."[80] Nonetheless, plenum participants who spoke subsequently competed in condemning Rykov, accusing him of insincerity and calling his speech opportunistic.

At the evening session of 19 December, Kuibyshev made his closing remarks. Setting aside the subject of his talk—the economic plan for 1931—he denounced Rykov and essentially proposed removing him from the post of chairman of the Council of People's Commissars.

> I believe that tremendous cohesion will be needed between top Soviet and Party leaders in carrying out the exceptionally difficult plan that confronts us in 1931. There should not be the tiniest crack between the Council apparatus and the comrades and party leadership heading it. [. . .] The fact that Comrade Rykov has not taken a place among active champions of the general line, has not become a champion against the system of views the harm of which he himself has recognized, shows that such a crack exists as long as Comrade Rykov heads the Council apparatus. [. . .] What we wind up with is a TsK and its leadership, represented in the Politburo, and a TsK plenum—this is a leadership gripped by heartfelt enthusiasm for socialist construction that is leading the proletariat into ever newer and newer battles, that is bitterly fighting class enemies and every manifestation, even veiled manifestations, of hostile class ideology, and then there is the top of the Soviet government that is doing "what it can"! This cannot go on.[81]

Kosior, who was given the floor at the conclusion of the plenum, proposed relieving Rykov of his duties as chairman of the Council of People's Commissars and as a member of the Politburo, making Molotov the new chairman and making Ordzhonikidze a member of the Politburo. The plenum unanimously accepted this proposal.[82]

Stalin had no apparent role in Rykov's replacement. But throughout the operation, his guiding hand could be sensed—starting with the way things were handled leading up to the plenum and ending with the way the break between the party and the Soviet leadership was formulated. Stalin had expressed the formulation in his September letter to Molotov, and the December plenum repeatedly echoed it. Molotov, during his plenum appearance, publicly introduced Stalin's proposals for reorganizing the Council of People's Commissars (without naming their author, of course): the creation of an Implementation Commission and the introduction of changes to the makeup of the Labor and Defense Council. The action against the leadership of the Council of People's Commissars that had been painstakingly planned over a long period had finally taken place.

The year 1930 was the period when the Stalinization of the Politburo was completed. The year that saw the final and tragic victory of Stalin's Great Leap policy—brutally forced industrialization and mass collectivization also saw Stalin confirmed as the sole leader of the Politburo. The Stalinization of the Politburo was not an inevitable outcome of the defeat of the rightists in 1929, although Stalin's victory here was critical. Throughout 1930, Stalin persistently and purposefully worked to secure his leadership through political intrigue and the suppression of dissent. This was all the more necessary inasmuch as the policy of the Great Leap subjected the country to a growing crisis. Stalin's policies (and, correspondingly, the authority he gained through his policies) could not enjoy a victory grounded in positive outcomes and therefore had to be based primarily on force and terror.

Mass arrests, executions, and deportations affecting a wide swath of the country's population were accompanied by smear campaigns and personnel purges at the highest echelons of power. The main objects of Stalinist attacks were still the rightists, both Bukharin, who had been expelled from the Politburo, and Rykov, who had held on to his formal position within the Politburo and the Council of People's Commissars. As the situation in the country worsened, Stalin resorted to harsher and more radical ways of dealing with his opponents. During the first stage of the struggle against the rightists, Stalin had accused them of unscrupulous underground contacts with Zinovievites (with some justification), but in 1930 he made more sinister allegations that the opposition had been indirectly involved in "political terror" and "sabotage." Under Stalin's painstaking guidance, the OGPU fabricated numerous cases against "anti-Soviet organizations" whose plans, one way or another, relied on alliances with leaders of the "right deviation." Using this same template, on Stalin's orders (obviously to set an example before other members of top Soviet leadership), the OGPU undertook to discredit Mikhail Kalinin. The fabrication of the case against Syrtsov and Lominadze aided Stalin in consolidating his power. The December 1930 expulsion of Aleksei Rykov from the Politburo and his removal from the post of chairman of the Council of People's Commissars put the finishing touches on this campaign.

Despite the overall intensification of repressive policies, at this stage we do not yet see a double standard in their application. Stalin was not yet accusing oppositionists (as he would several years later) of direct involvement in terrorist organizations. They were merely shouldered with moral responsibility for encouraging "terror" and "sabotage." Although they were dismissed from their posts, participants in the Syrtsov-Lominadze "organization" remained free. To a significant degree, such a policy was determined by the situation at the highest echelons of power. The surviving traditions and practices of collective leadership and "intra-party democracy" provided for a degree of loyalty toward distinguished members of the party, even those who succumbed to "heresy." Stalin was forced at this point to contend with such traditions and with the fact that the Politburo was still a collective body of the highest authority. Stalin's public self-justification when faced with Syrtsov's allegations of a "factional Politburo" is indicative in this regard, as are the drawn-out and detailed preparations to replace Rykov, in which members of the Politburo were included.

As subsequent events demonstrated, the model of collective leadership with a single leader at its head, which had taken shape in 1929 and 1930, could not withstand Stalin's moves toward a dictatorship. Nonetheless, the mechanisms of such a model deserve close examination, which they will be given in the following chapter.

2 Power in Crisis
1931–1933

THE DEVASTATING CRISIS that became increasingly evident from 1931 proved the criminality of Stalin's Great Leap policy. Terrible famine, which hit its peak in the winter of 1932–1933, the collapse of agriculture, the failure of forced industrialization, and growing social tensions raised questions about the soundness of the regime and Stalin's own political viability. The response to the growing crisis offered by Stalin and his comrades-in-arms was intensified repression and terror to the point where state violence threatened the very foundations of the system. And while repression and coercion remained the cornerstones of Stalin's chosen course, occasionally, under the weight of circumstances, the country's leadership opted for certain concessions in the interest of preserving fundamental policies. Such wavering could be observed in 1931–1933.

THE FAILURE OF THE GREAT LEAP

The Great Leap policies of forced industrialization, collectivization, and liquidation of *kulachestvo* (kulaks as a class), which were pursued throughout 1929–1931, inflicted incalculable hardship. In 1930–1931, more than 380,000 peasant families—a total of 1.8 million people—were sent to special settlements in remote areas of the country.[1] Historians estimate that 200,000–250,000 families (approximately 1 million peasants) fled to the cities and to construction projects before repressive measures forced them elsewhere. Another 400,000–450,000 families (approximately 2 million peasants) were thrown off the land as members of a "third category" (that is, they were forced to move elsewhere within their own province). In most cases people in this category, having lost their possessions, also left for the cities and construction projects.[2] Collectivization and dekulakization significantly undermined the productive capacity of the countryside. In 1931 a number of regions were gripped by famine, which over the next two years reached devastating proportions.

Accelerated industrialization, extravagant capital investment in heavy industry, a disregard for the principles of economic management, and mass repressions of specialists, prompting the baiting and harassment of engineers and technically skilled workers, along with a breakdown of discipline in industry, all of which led to an industrial crisis.[3] This crisis was of particular concern to the country's leaders, so in late 1930 and early 1931 they allowed changes that permitted discussion of certain adjustments to economic policy. The new openness took shape gradually as a chain of separate, inconsistent and contradictory decisions, which R. W. Davies refers to as "minireforms."[4] These minireforms affected only industry; the strong-arm tactics used in the countryside remained unchallenged.

The minireforms comprised attempts to apply economic incentives and to deal with some of the most odious methods of wartime industrial management. The government officially condemned theories predicting a rapid dying-off of commodity-money relations and the introduction of direct "socialist" commodity exchange and proclaimed money and material incentives to be the foundations on which the new economy would be built. The most obvious and tangible manifestations of the new trends, however, were the condemnation of mass repressions of engineers and technically skilled workers and state support for the authority of industrial managers.

After a series of isolated decisions affecting specific cases in which the rights of industrial managers were infringed, as well as cases involving the rehabilitation of certain previously convicted specialist wreckers, in mid-1931 more far-reaching steps were taken. On 10 July the Politburo adopted two resolutions that significantly changed the situation for specialists and somewhat limited the rights of the OGPU. The first resolution, entitled "Questions concerning the OGPU," stipulated that the OGPU did not have the right to arrest Communists without the knowledge and approval of the party's Central Committee or to arrest specialists (engineering, technical, or military personnel, agronomists, doctors, and so forth) without authorization from the appropriate commissar (on either the national or the republic level). Furthermore, in cases of disagreement between a commissar and the OGPU, the matter was to be decided by the Central Committee. The resolution also stipulated that the OGPU could not hold "citizens arrested based on allegations of a political crime" for "more than two weeks without interrogation or [hold them] under investigation for more than three months, at which point the case must be resolved either through referral to a judge or by independent decision of OGPU collegia." Henceforth, all death sentences handed down by OGPU collegia were to be affirmed by the Central Committee.[5]

The second resolution, entitled "Concerning the Work of Technical Personnel in Enterprises and Improvements to Their Material Well-Being," contained a comprehensive program for the legal and political rehabilitation of specialists. The resolution consisted of two parts: a highly secret "special folder" part and a confidential part that was sent to all party members and government and industrial managers. Just two clauses were contained in the highly secret portion, but they were of fundamental significance: "Release arrested specialists starting with experts in ferrous metallurgy and then in coal using the list approved by Ordzhonikidze and Menzhinsky, and send them to work in factories; rescind the STO [Labor and Defense Council] resolution requiring the OGPU to hold specialists responsible for the overconsumption of fuel."[6] Sergo Ordzhonikidze and Viacheslav Menzhinsky were the heads of the Supreme Economic Council (VSNKh) and OGPU, respectively.

The portion of the resolution intended for wider circulation provided for an amnesty for specialists who had been sentenced to compulsory labor, and removed limitations on the positions that specialists could hold in enterprise management. The children of engineering and technically skilled workers were allowed the same rights as the children of industrial workers when they entered postsecondary education (previously they had been subject to discrimination). One clause in the resolution required that party organizations not be allowed to interfere in the operations of enterprise management. Finally, the 10 July resolution forbade the police, criminal investigators, and the procuracy from interfering in the productive life of enterprises and from conducting investigations into industrial matters without special permission from enterprise management or the government agencies that oversaw them. The practice of having official OGPU representatives within industrial enterprises was abolished.[7] In late November 1931, OGPU deputy chairman Ivan Akulov reported to Stalin that between May and November 1931, a total of 1,280 convicted specialists were released and subsequently assigned to particular enterprises, in cooperation with economic agencies.[8]

These concessions to the engineering and technical intelligentsia were never more than an insignificant departure from the general line, which by and large brooked no changes. The country was sinking deeper into a socioeconomic crisis that was particularly evident in the countryside. Burdened with crushing government taxes, peasants were fleeing collective farms to escape starvation. During the first half of 1932, the number of collectivized household farms was reduced by 1,370,800 in the Russian Federation and by 41,200 in Ukraine.[9] The countryside held significant social unrest. According to incomplete data from the OGPU for October 1931–March 1932, there were 616 riots recorded for the RSFSR, Ukraine, Belorussia, and Kazakhstan, representing 55,400 participants. In fact, rioting became more widespread from month to month.[10] Among the most prevalent types of disorders were resistance by hungry peasants to forcible grain removal and attacks on government storage facilities. Such events in Ukraine, not far from Poltava, were described to Council of People's Commissars chairman Molotov by one of the chiefs of the Central Control Commission of the Communist Party who had conducted an inspection in these districts. He wrote that on 3 May 1932 approximately three hundred women from the village of Ustinovtsy captured the chairman of the village soviet and, carrying a black flag, marched on the railway station at Gogolevo, where they started to break down the door to the warehouse. At first the warehouse supervisor was able to keep the crowd at bay using a fire extinguisher—the women dispersed, thinking it might contain gas. But the next day the peasants congregated again. Armed police and others authorized by the GPU were called on to suppress the disorder. The grain stored in the warehouse was shipped out the same day.

The next day, 5 May, a crowd of approximately the same size, made up of women from the village of Chasnikovka, overran a warehouse at the Sencha railway station and took thirty-seven sacks of wheat. On 6 May, emboldened by their initial success, the peasants returned to the station and removed 150 poods (nearly 2.5 tons) of corn from freight cars. The Communists who were trying to stop the crowd by shooting into the air were chased away. Toward evening, fifty armed policemen and Communists arrived at the station. The peasants were not frightened—approximately four hundred people had gathered at the station and were again attempting to open the freight cars. On 7 May mounted police and armed Communists chased away an even larger crowd of peasants.

On 5 May at the Sagaidak train station approximately eight hundred people barged past two policemen and village activists who were guarding the grain and opened the warehouse, taking close to 500 poods of grain, 400 poods of which they distributed on the spot, carrying away 100 poods. On 6 May approximately four hundred peasants from the villages of Liman and Fedunki attempted unsuccessfully to take grain.[11] Similar incidents took place across the entire country.

During the spring of 1932 a reduction in the grain ration triggered antigovernment riots in the cities, too. On 7–9 April, for example, large groups of residents of the Belorussian city of Borisov stormed grain warehouses and organized a march on the Red Army barracks by women and children. According to official estimates, which were probably low, four hundred to five hundred people took part in the unrest. Local authorities and police were sympathetic, and although the troops were loyal, "signs of commiscration could be seen among the Red Army soldiers and officers present."[12]

Much more serious occurrences followed several days later in the textile districts of Ivanovo Province.[13] Urban centers of this type held an intermediary position between the countryside, with its extreme suffering, and the large cities, which were meagerly, but more regularly, supplied. Delays in issuing food rations and low incomes due to breakdowns at technically backward and poorly supplied manufacturing facilities were part of daily life in the settlements surrounding textile mills. In early 1932 in Vichuga, for example, no flour was distributed for several months; children, who had been receiving only one hundred grams of bread per day, were now provided with only a sixty-gram ration.[14] The textile workers' political frame of mind was affected by events in the surrounding countryside, where many of the workers had relatives. Collectivization was bringing them to financial ruin. Into this volatile mix came the order to reduce rations.

On 5 April the Nogin Mill in Vichuga went on strike. By 9 April almost all the mills in the city were striking. At six o'clock the following afternoon, 10 April, OGPU leadership received a report from the deputy to the OGPU's authorized representative in Ivanovo Province. It stated that the situation at manufacturing facilities throughout Vichuga district was becoming critical. The report painted a picture of unrest. Approximately three thousand strikers had taken to the streets, forced their way into police headquarters, disarmed and beaten a policeman, and wounded the chief of police. Out of fifty policemen, seventeen remained in the ranks. The OGPU building had been surrounded by a crowd of up to one thousand people, and several chekists (secret police) had been beaten or injured by stones. The chekists had started to shoot back, wounding two demonstrators.[15] After the shots, the crowd dispersed. The OGPU representative for Ivanovo Province and the province party leaders set out for Vichuga, but talks with the strikers were not fruitful. Workers at mills in Teikovo also went on strike. The strikers demanded that the March food ration be left unchanged. A report was forwarded to Stalin, along with a note from OGPU deputy chairman Akulov saying that the Ivanovo Province authorities had been instructed not to use weapons and to mobilize all available agents, including agents from the city of Ivanovo, in order to "foment incohesion among the strikers." Stalin doodled all over a corner of the document with a pencil (a sign of anxiety or pensiveness?) and wrote the meaningless comment, "Why is the *obkom* [provincial party committee] silent?"[16]

Riots continued in Vichuga the following day. Overall, between 8 and 11 April (according to official reports) fifteen policemen were seriously wounded and forty policemen and between five and seven government representatives received minor injuries. On 12 April, Lazar Kaganovich arrived in Vichuga. A combination of repression and promises put an end to the strike in the mills there. Besides Vichuga, strikes and riots had taken hold elsewhere in the Ivanovo-Voznesensk area—in the Teikovo, Lezhnevo, and Puchezh districts. The Ivanovo leaders took energetic measures to keep the riots from spreading. On 14 April they adopted a decision to "eliminate anti-Soviet elements" in large cities. To prevent the Teikovo workers from marching on the provincial center of Ivanovo-Voznesensk they decided that the train would not stop in Teikovo.[17] Strike leaders were rounded up and arrested in the districts where there had been unrest. All of this prevented workers in other centers from being drawn into the strike movement, although the situation in the area remained very difficult.

While the unrest in Ivanovo Province was rather easily suppressed, these events brought a number of things to light that the regime found alarming. The strikes and demonstrations had taken place in the center of the country, not far from the capital, in one of the largest industrial regions, and had engulfed several districts at once. At any moment, workers from other enterprises who had a "sullen frame of mind" might have joined the strikers. Many peasants in Ivanovo Province supported the striking workers. So-called *volynki*—collective refusals by kolkhoz workers to do their jobs—spread across the countryside, and the collapse of kolkhozes accelerated.[18] Local Communists played an active role in the strikes and demonstrations (in a number of cases they were their organizers).[19] The local authorities demonstrated their helplessness.

Such disturbances could at any moment lead to unpredictable outcomes. It is not surprising that Moscow took the unrest in Ivanovo Province very seriously. The Central Committee wrote a letter to the party organization asserting that local Communists had missed the way "the detritus of the counterrevolutionary parties of SRs [Socialist Revolutionaries], Mensheviks, as well as counterrevolutionary Trotskyites and former members of the 'workers' opposition' who had been expelled from our Bolshevik ranks, had tried to build themselves a nest and organize disturbances against the party and Soviet authorities."[20] The Council of People's Commissars immediately decided to send additional food supplies to Ivanovo Province to diffuse tensions.

It may have been the events that took place in Ivanovo Province that compelled the government to take more decisive "liberal" measures. In May 1932 the Council of People's Commissars, the Central Executive Committee, and the Central Committee adopted measures that represented a policy shift. After significantly lowering plan targets for forcible state grain and meat collections, the government permitted peasants to sell grain (starting from 15 January 1933, after the completion of grain collections) and meat (so long as centralized collection stations continued to meet their targets). Furthermore, the independent farmers and collective farmers who came to sell their goods at market were now able to charge what the market would bear; previously, countless taxes and low price ceilings had hampered the sale of these products. The goal of such decisions was clear. The system of compulsory requisitioning and centralized supply had brought the country to the point of starvation. The Stalinist leadership recalled the NEP years and decided to resort to peasant self-interest to address the crisis.

During the spring and summer months of 1932, the policy that has occasionally been called NeoNEP seemed to be gaining momentum. One after another, resolutions were adopted asserting the impermissibility of liquidating collective farmers' private plots, requiring the return to private hands of livestock that had been requisitioned for communal farms, and mandating observance of "socialist legality." Meaningful modifications were even applied in the area of forced industrialization. In August 1932, for the first time in several years, a decision was adopted to significantly reduce capital investment, with the most drastic reductions affecting heavy industry.[21] These isolated measures came too late, however. A defective life preserver was being thrown to a drowning man. During the fall of 1932 the crisis took on enormous proportions. Starving peasants had only one concern: how to survive the winter and spring. Buffeted by years of arbitrary rule and with little faith in the authorities, the last thing on their minds was the fate of the harvest in the kolkhoz fields. To fulfill the impossibly optimistic plan for grain collections, the authorities requisitioned the last remaining resources of the countryside, including the supplies that families had set aside for their own use.

Stalinist policy was the main cause of the brutal famine. At its peak, from the end of 1932 into early 1933, it had its greatest impact on regions whose population comprised 70 million of the 160 million Soviet citizens.[22] The total number of famine victims cannot be precisely determined, in part because the regime did everything it could to mask the actual scale of the tragedy. Recent estimates of those who died from the immediate effects of the famine range from 5 million to 7 million.[23] Even the most conservative estimates are enormous. Furthermore, it is impossible to calculate, for example, how many people suffered devastating illnesses as a result of the famine, leaving them permanently disabled, even if they did not die until several years later. The secret reports compiled by the OGPU and the party (known as *informatsionnye svodki*), particularly during the first months of 1933, were replete with accounts of cannibalism. Masses of peasants and homeless children from the starving countryside flooded the cities. Epidemics gripped the country, and not only in rural areas but in the relatively well-off industrial centers. In November 1932, more than 160 cases of typhus per day were diagnosed in Leningrad.[24] In 1932–1933 more than 1.1 million cases of typhus and 500,000 cases of typhoid fever were registered in the country as a whole.[25]

Although the authorities tried to maintain high rates of industrial production, throwing the country's last resources into this effort, the deepening crisis eventually engulfed the industrial sector. Even official estimates show labor productivity remaining essentially stagnant in 1932. The cost of industrial production exceeded what the depleted country could bear. Impulsive purchases of equipment and materials in foreign markets led to an enormous foreign debt.[26] This debt had to be paid off not only through the reduction of imports, the massive requisitioning of hard currency and gold from the population, the sale of cultural treasures that filled the country's museums but also by exporting food that was desperately needed by the starving population.

Dozens more pages could be filled with similar facts and descriptions of the calamity that befell the Soviet Union. During a time of peace, more than ten years after bloody conflicts had drawn to a close, the Soviet Union found itself in a situation as devastating as war.

The only way the Stalinist leadership was able to hold on to power during this crisis was through brutal repression. The main methods of grain collection were house-to-house searches, mass arrests, shootings, and deportations, including the evictions of entire villages from the Kuban River valley. The OGPU "cleansed" industrial enterprises of "disruptors," "kulaks," and "wreckers." The 1933 introduction of internal passports was accompanied by a large-scale purging of cities. In April 1933, to supplement the multitude of camps, colonies, and special settlements, the Politburo enacted a decision to establish "labor settlements," where peasants accused of sabotaging grain collections would be joined by "urban elements who refuse to leave Moscow and Leningrad in connection with passportization," as well as "kulaks who had fled from villages and were expelled from industrial enterprises."[27] A total of 270,000 new special settlers were sent into exile in 1933. Despite high mortality, the camp population increased by approximately 200,000 over the course of the year.[28] Both the number of people condemned to forced labor and the number of years to which they were sentenced were enormous. According to data cited by the chairman of the RSFSR Supreme Court in a report to Stalin and Molotov in November 1935, more than 738,000 people during the first half of 1933 and more than 687,000 during the second half were convicted in the Russian Federation alone.[29]

As was usual in times of crisis, opposition to the general line intensified within the party itself. There is evidence to suggest that Communists increasingly viewed Stalin's policies as corrupt and blamed him for inciting an unjustified confrontation with the peasantry. Some members of the party attempted to unite and to conduct anti-Stalin propaganda within the party. Writings by members of the so-called Union of Marxist-Leninists, whose formation and writings were inspired by an old member of the party, Martemian Riutin, are among the best-known records of these attempts. In 1932, Riutin prepared a document entitled "Stalin and the Crisis of the Proletarian Dictatorship" and an appeal "To All Members of the VKP(b)." The appeal stated in part:

> Stalin and his clique have led the party and the proletarian dictatorship into an unprecedented dead end and they are experiencing a mortally dangerous crisis. Through deceit and defamation, as well as by duping party members, through unbelievable violence and terror [. . .] Stalin has over the past five years cut off and eliminated from the leadership all of the best, genuine Bolshevik cadres of the party and has established his personal dictatorship within the VKP(b) and the entire country. [. . .]
>
> An adventuristic pace of industrialization, entailing colossal reductions in the actual earnings of workers and personnel, backbreaking taxes, both obvious and concealed, inflation, price increases [. . .]; [and] adventuristic collectivization using unbelievable violence, terror [. . .] have led the entire country into the depths of crisis, to a monstrous impoverishment of the masses and famine both in the countryside and in the cities. [. . .]
>
> Not even the most daring and ingenious agent provocateur could have come up with a better way to destroy the proletarian dictatorship, to discredit Leninism, than the regime of Stalin and his clique did.[30]

Especially worrisome for the Stalinist center was the virtual sabotage of emergency grain collections by many local party workers. This circumstance was the main reason behind the announcement in November 1932 of yet another party purge. Many Communists were arrested for not fulfilling directives from the center regarding the removal of grain from starving villages. In total, approximately 450,000 people were expelled from the party in 1932 and 1933 (as of 1 January 1933 the party had 3.5 million members).[31]

REORGANIZATION OF THE POLITBURO

The new alignments that had developed within the Politburo after the decisive victory of the Stalinist faction, along with the growing crisis in the country, prompted unique minireforms in the party-state apparatus. Although these reforms did not affect the foundation on which the mechanisms of power rested, they reflected the intermediate state in which those in power found themselves in the period between the defeat of the opposition and the final consolidation of Stalin's dictatorship. Chief among them was a reorganization within the government apparatus, undertaken after Rykov's replacement, that made Stalin's idea about overcoming the "gulf between the party and the Council leadership"—stated in his letter of 22 September 1930—a reality. Molotov, the new chairman of the Council of People's Commissars, began by carrying out those measures that Stalin had enumerated in that letter. On 23 December, on Molotov's initiative, the Politburo approved a resolution that, clause by clause, substantially corresponded to Stalin's September proposals. The resolution provided for the abolition of the council chairman's Conference of Deputies and the creation of an Implementation Commission within the council. Most Politburo members were included in the Labor and Defense Council—Molotov, Rudzutak, Kuibyshev, Andreev, Stalin, Ordzhonikidze, Voroshilov, and Mikoyan, as well as the agriculture commissar, Yakov Yakovlev; the finance commissar, Grigory Grinko; and the chairman of the board of Gosbank, Moisei Kalmanovich. The tendency to merge party and state leadership was also seen in the decision to abolish the executive meetings of the Labor and Defense Council, which considered questions of the country's defenses and military construction, and replace them with a special commission, the Defense Commission, affiliated with the Council of People's Commissars and the Politburo. This commission comprised Molotov, Stalin, Voroshilov, Kuibyshev, and Ordzhonikidze.[32]

The emerging agreement to join the two branches of power was reinforced by Politburo decisions enacted on 30 December 1930. Based on
a report by Molotov, the Politburo approved a directive "to urgently re-
examine the SNK apparatus (the structure and personnel) and maximally simplify and reduce it in size, raising the necessary qualifications
for most party and special-scientific workers in the apparatus managing
the business of the SNK." It established, in addition to the Defense
Commission, a Currency Commission, both to come under the Council
of People's Commissars and the Politburo and to be chaired by Rudzutak.[33]

On a proposal by Stalin, the same day, 30 December, the Politburo
considered questions pertaining to its own operations. The resulting decision mandated that the Politburo meet six times per month. Three
meetings (on the 10th, 20th, and 30th of each month) would be closed
and would be dedicated to questions pertaining to the GPU, the Commissariats of Foreign Affairs and Defense, classified currency matters,
and certain internal party matters. Other less secret problems would be
dealt with at the regular Politburo meetings (on the 5th, 15th, and 25th
of each month). It was the responsibility of the Central Committee Secretariat to prepare the Politburo meeting agendas together with Council
of People's Commissars chairman Molotov.[34] The Politburo's new
schedule and the legalization of the practice of regular closed meetings
represented to a certain degree Stalin's response to the allegations aired
during the course of the Syrtsov case that he had usurped the rights of
the Politburo and had held limited, secret meetings.

The regular (open) meetings of the Politburo had many participants.
In addition to Politburo members and candidate members, a large
group of members and candidate members of the Central Committee
and members of the Central Control Commission presidium attended.
The closed meetings had more limited attendance—Politburo members
and candidate members, certain Central Committee members who held
high positions (for example, Central Commitee secretary Pavel Postyshev regularly attended the closed meetings), and the top members of
the Central Control Commission.

According to the protocols of Politburo meetings, on average the
group convened more than six times per month in 1931, apparently because of the large volume of work. There were therefore constant attempts to somehow limit the flow of issues coming before the Politburo.

On 30 April, on Stalin's recommendation, the Politburo decided, for example, that issues relating to requests from local party organizations around the country should be decided by the Central Committee Secretariat, together with Molotov, and "only in cases of exceptional importance" should such questions be brought before the Politburo.[35] The situation was complicated by the fact that the schedules of Politburo members involved in various government agencies simply did not permit them to attend all the meetings necessitated by their duties. To address this problem, on 25 November 1931, in response to a report by Kuibyshev and Kaganovich, the Politburo adopted a new meeting schedule for all the main bodies of the party and government. Starting on 1 December 1931, the Politburo was to convene at 2:00 PM on the 1st, 8th, 16th, and 23rd of each month; the Orgburo was to meet at 6:00 PM on the 5th and 17th of each month; the Secretariat was to meet at 6:00 PM on the 7th, 15th, 22nd, and 29th of each month; the Council of People's Commissars was to meet at 6:00 PM on the 3rd and 21st of each month; and the Labor and Defense Council was to meet at noon on the 9th, 15th, and 27th of each month.[36]

This resolution did not mention the closed Politburo sessions. But as the protocols show, closed sessions took place on the 1st and 16th of each month, and regular meetings were held on the 8th and 23rd. On 29 May 1932 the Politburo resolved "to draft Politburo agendas during closed sessions of the Politburo."[37]

As the protocols indicate, four Politburo meetings per month proved to be insufficient. The Politburo met much more often. The Politburo agendas grew in length. It was not uncommon for up to fifty items to be reviewed at a single meeting. On 1 September 1932, for example, the Politburo considered forty-one matters: six were postponed to the following meeting, one was removed from consideration, and on another matter, Politburo members were to be polled the following day. At the end of the meeting Stalin, apparently dissatisfied with its outcome, suggested limiting the number of issues brought before the Politburo. At his suggestion it was decided to "assign the TsK Secretariat the job of drafting Politburo meeting agendas so as to include no more than fifteen items."[38]

Such limitations led to an increase in the number of decisions made by polling Politburo members. This, in turn, made the job of the Central Committee's secret department, which was responsible for collecting

members' votes, more difficult. Unable to keep up with the flood of issues to be decided, they used every opportunity to organize a vote and,
in particular, polled members during Politburo meetings. Formally,
then, the procedure adopted by the Politburo on 1 September was not
being violated. The questions that did not fit within the established limit
were settled by poll, although in essence they were being decided (albeit
without discussion) at Politburo meetings. Nevertheless, this bit of arti-
fice provoked Stalin's displeasure. On 16 October 1932, at his request,
the Politburo resolved "to point out to the Secret Department of the TsK
the necessity of ceasing to conduct polling during Politburo meetings to
avoid distracting Politburo members from matters included on the
agenda."[39]

All of these structural and procedural reorganizations were evidence
of the burden that the party leadership, Stalin first and foremost, bore
by conducting regular meetings with numerous agenda items. It was
much easier to make decisions by polling members or holding informal
meetings of Politburo members. The country's worsening socioeconomic crisis and the proliferation of emergency methods of governing
became a convenient excuse for abandoning the way business had previously been conducted in the Politburo. Starting in late 1932, meeting
protocols indicate a sharp reduction in the number of Politburo meetings. This circumstance was formalized on 23 April 1933: the Politburo
approved a new meeting schedule—three per month, on the 5th, 15th,
and 25th.[40] Even this schedule was often not adhered to over the next
year and a half. On average, the Politburo convened twice per month.
Logs of visits to Stalin's office in 1931–1933 indirectly attest to the
increasing replacement of official Politburo sessions with informal
meetings between Stalin and his comrades-in-arms. They show a persistent tendency toward more frequent meetings between Politburo members in Stalin's office.[41]

In the early 1930s, the secret department of the Central Committee,
which handled the clerical and technical aspects of the Politburo's work,
was reorganized in conjunction with the simplification of the Politburo's operational procedures. The secret department was created by
resolution of the Orgburo of the Central Committee on 19 March 1926
to replace the Central Committee office, which had previously handled
technical services for the top bodies of the Central Committee and classified correspondence for the Central Committee apparatus. One of

Stalin's assistants, Ivan Tovstukha, headed the secret department. In July 1930 the Politburo released him from his Central Committee duties (at his own request, made because of ill health) and appointed him deputy director of the Lenin Institute. On 22 July, Aleksandr Poskrebyshev, who would head this department (which changed its name and structure over the years) almost until Stalin's death, was appointed director of the secret department.[42]

In the late 1920s and the early 1930s, the secret department performed a large number of functions. It hired and supervised the assistants to Central Committee secretaries (experts in various areas, aides) and their apparatuses. Four subdivisions provided clerical assistance: two provided clerical services for the Politburo and the Orgburo, a third handled the distribution of enciphered documents, and a fourth tracked the return of documents from top party offices, documents that had been sent out for implementation or information, as well as to a certain circle of party and government leaders. The secret department was also responsible for the secret Central Committee archive. The secret department chancellery handled support services: registration, communication, retyping of documents, and the creation of stenographic records of meetings of the highest bodies of the party leadership.[43] According to an organizational table of Central Committee departments approved on 28 January 1930, the secret department had a staff of 103. In combination, all the departments under the Central Committee had a total of 375 employees. The secret department was significantly larger than other departments, with the exception of the administrative department (Upravlenie delami), which had 123 employees. Other departments were assignment (51 employees), organizational-instruction (41 employees), culture and propaganda (36 employees), and agitation and mass campaigns (21 employees).[44]

On 13 November 1933, the Secretariat adopted a decision to reorganize the secret department. In essence, this reorganization left the secret department as the Politburo support apparatus. The secret department was essentially transformed into Stalin's personal chancellery. The resolution stated, "The Secret Department is directly subordinate to Com. Stalin and, in his absence, to Com. Kaganovich. The hiring and dismissal of Secret Department employees is to be carried out with the knowledge and consent of TsK Secretaries." Salaries for secret department employees were set at a level 30–40 percent above those for the equivalent categories of workers in other branches of government. The Central Committee administrative department was assigned the task of "satisfying all requests for apartments by employees of the TsK Secret Department within one month" and "put[ting] at the full disposal of the TsK Secret Department five dachas, to be maintained by the apparatus of the TsK Administrative Department."[45]

Between 1931 and 1934, the makeup of the Politburo did not undergo any significant changes. With the exception of Rykov, all Politburo members elected at the 16th Party Congress kept their positions and were again elected at the party's Central Committee plenum that took place after the 17th congress in early 1934. Those who joined and left the Politburo did so primarily for purely formal reasons. For example, in accordance with party regulations, the chairman of the Central Control Commission could not be a member of the Politburo, so in December 1930, Ordzhonikidze became a Politburo member upon leaving his post as Central Control Commission chairman, and Andrei Andreevich Andreev, who replaced Ordzhonikidze at the commission, left the Politburo. In February 1932, Rudzutak, who had been appointed to replace Andreev as commission chairman, left the Politburo, and Andreev, who was appointed transport commissar again, became a member.[46]

Cadre stability notwithstanding, a certain redistribution of functions and influence took place during the early 1930s, particularly among the Central Committee secretaries. Since the early 1920s, the assignment of responsibility among Central Committee secretaries had been established through special resolutions. Each secretary dealt with a particular area and with particular Central Committee departments (although each department also had its own director). On 26 January 1930 the Secretariat adopted yet another in a series of decisions concerning the assignment of responsibilities among the Central Committee secretaries. The resolution made Stalin responsible for the "preparation of issues to be dealt with at PB meetings and the overall management of the TsK Secretariat." Molotov, who was mentioned second in this resolution, was charged with "directing the Culture and Propaganda Department and the Lenin Institute." Kaganovich, who came third among the secretaries, was to direct the organizational-instruction department and the department that handled staffing for administrative and labor union positions. The last to be mentioned was Central Committee secretary

Aleksandr Smirnov, who was assigned to oversee the agitation and mass campaigns department, as well as the administrative department.[47]

The order in which the secretaries were mentioned in this resolution corresponded to the actual hierarchy within the party leadership. In 1930 (as in the 1920s), Molotov was essentially Stalin's deputy within the party, as well as his closest and most trusted comrade-in-arms, a fact reflected in the intensive correspondence between the two men.[48] Molotov managed all party business (including the workings of the Politburo) whenever Stalin was unavailable. This is formally reflected in the fact that it was Molotov who signed the protocols of all Politburo meetings when Stalin was vacationing in the south. In 1930, Kaganovich was essentially third secretary of the Central Committee (although officially no such position existed). He not only oversaw the most important Central Committee departments but managed the Central Committee apparatus when both Stalin and Molotov were away, and also signed the protocols of Politburo meetings at such times. After Molotov took over the Council of People's Commissars, Kaganovich assumed Molotov's duties within the Secretariat. During the early years of the 1930s, Kaganovich oversaw the functioning of the Politburo whenever Stalin was not in Moscow. In many cases he personally formulated Politburo decisions and managed the flow of items being considered, although he tried to get Stalin's approval of decisions on matters of consequence and often even on inconsequential matters.[49] During this period all documents sent to the Central Committee by department heads and regional party organizations were addressed to him. Stalin himself usually addressed all the directives he sent from the south as follows: "Moscow. TsK VKP(b) for Com. Kaganovich and other Politburo members."[50]

Kaganovich's political career was at its acme in the early 1930s. The scope of his responsibilities gradually expanded. On 17 August 1931 the Politburo adopted a decision to appoint Kaganovich to the Currency Commission while Stalin was in the south.[51] On 5 June 1932, on Stalin's suggestion, the Politburo named Kaganovich his deputy on the Defense Commission.[52] On 15 December 1932, the Politburo adopted a decision to organize an agriculture department within the Central Committee—a key department within the party apparatus given the famine. Kaganovich was appointed director.[53] On 18 August 1933, the Politburo adopted a decision to form a commission on rail transportation under the chairmanship of Molotov. Kaganovich, together with

Stalin, Voroshilov, Andreev, Ordzhonikidze, and G. I. Blagonravov, were named members of this commission. Just two days later, on August 20, Kaganovich was confirmed as deputy chairman, and on 15 February 1934 he was made chairman.[54]

Kaganovich's special role within the leadership of the Central Committee apparatus was established by a resolution of the Central Committee Secretariat concerning the hiring of personnel within the Central Committee apparatus. Approved on 17 January 1934, it stated: "a) It is hereby affirmed that the hiring and dismissal of all employees within the TsK apparatus, without exception, be carried out only with the approval of Com. Kaganovich or Com. Stalin. b) All department directors within the TsK VKP(b) are strictly required to adhere to this resolution." The story behind this resolution is significant. The initial draft of the resolution was written by Kaganovich and took the following form: "It is hereby affirmed that the hiring of all employees within the TsK apparatus, without exception, be carried out only with the approval of the TsK secretary." Stalin changed Kaganovich's text, placing Kaganovich's name before his own. The Central Committee Secretariat confirmed Stalin's version.[55]

Kaganovich's role as deputy within the party did not, of course, mean that the other members of the Politburo had lost their influence. In the early 1930s, each of them continued to occupy the position within the highest echelons of power that they had achieved during the previous decade. The actual participation of various Politburo members in decision making is indicated by the records of their visits to Stalin's office.[56] If we judge by this indicator, Molotov remained closest to Stalin despite his move from the Central Committee to the Council of People's Commissars. Kaganovich's second place in this list of intimates fully corresponds with the facts of Kaganovich's career, cited above. The remaining Politburo members who were administrators of major departments visited Stalin with approximately the same regularity. The members of the Politburo who directed regional party organizations—Sergei Kirov, Vlas Chubar, Stanislav Kosior, and Grigory Petrovsky—were all busy with local matters and came to Moscow only occasionally. Rudzutak, who was often ill and gradually withdrew from government, held little interest for Stalin.

The facade of stability in the political activity of Politburo members concealed a gradual and largely unnoticed curtailment of their rights and opportunities as power became concentrated in Stalin's hands. The numerous conflicts within the Politburo played a role in this process and are a source of eternal fascination for historians.

THE QUESTION OF FACTIONS: THE MINIREFORMS
AND THE RIUTIN AFFAIR

The political developments of the early 1930s can, at first glance, be fully explained by the existence of two opposing groups within the Politburo: those advocating a radical course and those advocating a moderate course. Kaganovich and Molotov (who were later joined by Nikolai Yezhov) are usually placed in the first group (the "radicals"), while Kirov, Ordzhonikidze, Kuibyshev, and occasionally other Politburo members are included in the second (the "moderates"). Until the mid-1930s, Stalin was a variable in this formula. Although his tendencies were radical, from time to time he was forced to contend with the presence of the moderate group and consequently fluctuated and maneuvered. The fluctuation of the political line between liberalization and terror can be interpreted as the result of the alternating predominance of the moderate and radical groups within the Politburo. It is obvious, however, that if such groups truly existed, there was bound to be a clash sooner or later, especially at times of a shift in policy. The only evidence supporting the existence of opposing factions within the Politburo, then, would be conflicts among top Soviet leaders that were at least partially grounded in overall policy considerations.

In this connection, the 1931 minireforms in the industrial sector have attracted significant scholarly attention. It is well known that one of the first official signals heralding these reforms was the First All-Union Conference of Workers of Socialist Industry that took place in Moscow in late January and early February 1931. It was attended and addressed by the country's leadership, including Stalin and Molotov, but the most significant moderate positions were expressed in the speech by Supreme Economic Council chairman Ordzhonikidze. Unlike Stalin, who limited himself to political appeals and demands for the unconditional fulfillment of the plan for 1931, as well as reminders of the dangers of sabotage, Ordzhonikidze displayed great flexibility and demonstrated detailed knowledge of the situation within industry. Two moments in Ordzhonikidze's speech stood out. First, he advocated giving greater authority to industrial managers and freeing them from the dictates of political personnel, stating that the majority of specialists had nothing to do with wreckers. Second, he called for strict adherence to *khozraschet* (the principle that enterprises should be self-financing), the establishment of contractual relations, and the financial responsibility of suppliers toward their customers.[57]

This circumstance, along with other signs of Ordzhonikidze's active commitment to a new course, gave historians reason to believe that the commissar of heavy industry was the initiator of the minireforms and even reason to view these very reforms as a result of Ordzhonikidze's victory in a clash with Stalin and Molotov, who adhered to the former line.[58] As is often the case, there was also an opposite, "skeptical" point of view, whose adherents presumed that a certain change in course in 1931 was the manifestation of a coordinated policy on the part of the party leadership, and questioned the existence of conflict between Stalin and Ordzhonikidze.[59] Archival documents tend to support the latter viewpoint. They also support the supposition that the relative retreat in 1931 was carried out largely on the initiative of Stalin, not Ordzhonikidze.

On 5 November 1930, at a meeting of the Politburo, Stalin proposed creating a special commission to work on "questions of commerce on a new basis." With Mikoyan as chairman, the commission included Stalin himself and representatives of various departments, and it was joined a little later by Molotov.[60] In 1931 and 1932, Stalin's intent in proposing the formation of this commission revealed itself in a series of resolutions calling for a strengthening of the position of commerce so that the rationing system could gradually be phased out. The practical consequences of these decisions were insignificant, inasmuch as the overall policy of forced industrialization and collectivization remained inviolable. However, it is important to note that it was specifically Stalin who supported measures permitting the political "rehabilitation" of commerce and commodity-money relations, which in 1930 had often been labeled vestiges of the past, bound to give way to the onrush of direct commodity exchange.

Soon after the Commerce Commission was created, something happened that could be viewed as one of the first real attempts to rein in the baiting and harassment of specialists. In late November, Ordzhonikidze received a report from Yezhov, director of the Central Committee assignment department, concerning attacks against Ya. Shmidt, head of construction for the Magnitogorsk Combine. Ordzhonikidze sent the following note to Stalin: "Soso, Yezhov says that in Magnitogorsk they are hounding Shmidt in the press. They—the Magnitogorsk party organization—evidently want to put the Central Committee in the way before they succeed. If we really want to save Shmidt, we should immediately suggest to [Ivan] Kabakov [secretary of the Ural Province party committee] that he influence Rumiantsev (secretary of the district committee) to make him stop the agitation against Shmidt. Yezhov is calling Rumiantsev to the TsK." Stalin wrote on Ordzhonikidze's note, "Agreed," and even placed this item before the 5 December 1930 meeting of the Politburo. In the decision that resulted (its text was written by Kaganovich and edited by Stalin), the Ural Province party was instructed to "ensure the immediate cessation of hounding and show their support for Com. Shmidt."[61]

Just a month later, Stalin himself was behind a decision to defend industrial managers in an analogous situation. On 4 January 1931, Gorbachev, director of the Petrovsky Metallurgical Factory in Dnepropetrovsk, wrote Stalin a letter in which he complained about constant hounding by the Dnepropetrovsk Province party organization and the party press. "Instead of letting factory management concentrate our energies on corrective measures and assisting us in this," Gorbachev wrote, "what is happening is constant harassment, the dragging of workers to meetings, and all of factory management's energies have to be turned to refuting the flood of accusations from party leadership, both verbal and in the press."[62] Stalin took an interest in this letter and wrote the following comment on it: "Com. Ordzhonikidze. I think Gorbachev's complaint has merit. What do you think should be done to correct the situation? Would it be enough to just put the party organization in its place?"[63] Not long afterward, on 20 January, a report by Ordzhonikidze raised the matter of Gorbachev's letter in the Politburo. Following Stalin's lead, the Politburo defended Gorbachev and "put the party organization in its place." At the same Politburo meeting Stalin initiated a decision to instruct party committees on the territorial and provincial level, as well as the central committees of republic Communist parties, not to "allow the removal of directors of factories that have all-union importance without the sanction of the USSR TsK and VSNKh."[64] This decision had fundamental significance. It marked the beginning of the gradual strengthening of the position of industrial managers and the weakening of political control over their operations.

As for Ordzhonikidze's speech at the industrial conference in January, the main positions he expressed did not go beyond the new approaches initiated by Stalin in the Politburo, which had undoubtedly been discussed within the circle of Stalin's comrades-in-arms. In that Ordzhonikidze's speech dealt with actual problems made it appear to be more radical than Stalin's speech. Documents show that Stalin's views were also evolving, however, as reflected in the spirit of his proposals concerning the Gorbachev matter. For example, when the speech he made at the industrial conference was being prepared for publication, he removed or softened a number of harsh statements concerning specialists. He deleted criticism aimed at Communist industrial managers who demanded help "from old, worn-out specialists," and crossed out a long passage about sabotage and added that only "some old" engineers and technicians "stray down the path of sabotage."[65]

This is not to deny that Ordzhonikidze was one of the most passionate advocates of the changes being introduced. Having confronted, in his role as chairman of the Supreme Economic Council, the devastating consequences of the policy of accelerated industrialization and the fight against wreckers, Ordzhonikidze sharply changed his previous position and advocated a more reasoned economic and political course and made every attempt to implement this course at the council. In doing so he was relying on the support of the Politburo and, first and foremost, Stalin. One anti-specialist controversy in the North Caucasus provides a window onto the mechanisms of this interaction between Ordzhonikidze and Stalin. On 20 May 1931, Ordzhonikidze sent Stalin, Molotov, and Kaganovich a copy of a telegram from N. G. Myshkov, chairman of the Stal (Steel) industrial complex. Myshkov reported that the local authorities had started legal proceedings against Venchel, foreman of the blast-furnace shop of the Sulinsky Metallurgical Factory and "one of the best blast-furnace operators, who works day and night in the shop," who had been nominated for a medal. The investigation, "which involves highly technical questions," Myshkov wrote with a hint of irony, was being conducted by a policeman, who found evidence that Venchel was a "wrecker." Myshkov asserted that this was not an isolated case and that in the North Caucasus the local police often called in shop foremen to interrogate them about technical problems, which demoralized technical personnel.[66] That very day, 20 May, Stalin personally brought this telegram to the Politburo, which resolved to halt the legal proceedings and provide Venchel with "normal working conditions in the shop" (this phrase of the resolution is written in Stalin's own hand) and also proposed that the "North Caucasus regional party committee bring a halt to the practice of police interrogation of specialists."[67]

That the Politburo was unified in its approach to the "rehabilitation" of specialists is evidenced by a new meeting of the officials of the Supreme Economic Council and the Supply Commissariat convened by the Central Committee on 22–23 June 1931. The meeting was distinguished from the January conference by a much greater degree of candidness and by the radical nature of its conclusions. (This must have been why the Politburo adopted a special resolution not to publish the stenographic record of the deliberations.[68] The only items published were several talks by government leaders that had been edited beyond recognition.) The attitude toward specialists and the relationships between industrial managers and the punitive organs received particular attention at the conference and were the subject of frank discussions. Molotov and Stalin were largely responsible for setting the critical tone of these discussions. "Even now there is always a GPU agent on duty, ready for any opportunity to bring one specialist or another to accountability," said Molotov. "It is clear that under such circumstances there will [always] be a case; under such circumstances it can happen that you wind up with some kind of work." Stalin proclaimed, "There's no need to allow policemen to be industrial technical experts. There's no need to allow a special OGPU office in a factory with a plaque, where they're sitting and waiting to be given work to do—and if there isn't any, they'll make some up."[69] (When the text of his speech was being prepared for publication, Stalin deleted this passage.) After fully justifying the past repression of specialists, Stalin announced a change of course due to the consolidation of socialist transformation and the specialists' change of heart—they were coming over to the side of Soviet power. Ordzhonikidze spoke on the first day of the conference. The main issues he addressed were also addressed by the other speakers, including the change in attitude toward specialists, an increased independence for enterprises, and the immediate allocation of enterprises' working capital.[70]

Speeches by Ordzhonikidze and other economic managers at the conference reflected the interests of those working in industry—primarily their desire for relative industrial independence and protection from the whims of the party and the punitive organs. In 1931–1932 the country's political leadership met these aspirations with a degree of sympathy. The Politburo adopted cardinal decisions on 10 July 1931 solidifying policy changes in regard to specialists and enterprise management. These decisions sprang from generally held views within the Politburo and were, first and foremost, Stalin's initiatives. As can be seen from the original protocols of Politburo meetings, its decision on issues relating to the OGPU dated 10 July 1931, a decision that limited its ability to arrest industrial specialists, was written by Stalin himself.[71]

In the spring of 1932, corrections were also made to policies affecting the countryside. A number of Politburo members made timid appeals for the introduction of certain changes in forcible grain collection at least as early as the start of 1932, when the threat of widespread famine was growing increasingly obvious. In January 1932, for example, Rudzutak wrote a note to Stalin proposing that the grain collection plan be fixed by the start of the fiscal year in order to "give the kolkhozes an opportunity to plan for the sale of a portion of their production in the market after they have fulfilled their government quotas."[72] This sensible proposal was adopted a year later, after many millions of lives had been lost to famine. But in 1932 it was ignored. Stalin had a similar reaction to an initiative by another member of the Politburo, Ukrainian Communist Party secretary Kosior, who, in a telegram to Stalin dated 15 March 1932, proposed "announcing, in the name of [Soviet] Union bodies, that future grain collections would be calculated so that the size of the harvest a kolkhoz and a kolkhoz worker achieve determines the allocation they receive for personal use."[73] Ukrainian leaders, suffering the impact of famine, were increasingly persistent in demanding food aid from the center.[74] In March and early May 1932, when the Politburo was considering the question of deporting kulaks who had been expelled from kolkhozes, Kalinin expressed his objection. On 4 May, Kalinin wrote on a tally sheet for votes on a resolution concerning the deportation of thirty-eight thousand peasant families, "I believe such an operation to be unjustified."[75]

To explain Kalinin's opposition, researchers point to the greater exposure the apparatuses of the All-Russian and All-Union Central Executive Committees that he headed had to the consequences of dekulakization, compared to the exposure of other high-level government bodies. Kalinin was the one who had to review the flood of complaints stemming from the punitive actions in the countryside.[76] To put it another way, Kalinin, like the Ukrainian leadership, was moved by the interests of the specific areas of government he was involved in and by his familiarity with information about the actual state of affairs in the country. In this sense, the actions of these men were comparable to actions by Ordzhonikidze during the period of the minireforms of 1931 (when he was serving as Supreme Economic Council chairman). And Stalin followed roughly the same script in 1932 as he had in 1931. Under the weight of crisis, ignoring periodic signals indicating the need for change, he began to initiate changes himself, essentially adopting the proposals of his comrades-in-arms. An example was his recommendation in May 1932 to enact resolutions permitting a certain reduction of plan targets for grain collections and loosening the rules in order to allow "kolkhoz commerce." Two weeks after Kalinin's protest of the deportation of thirty-eight thousand kulak households, the Politburo rescinded its own decision and brought the operation that had already been started to a halt.[77]

These facts suggest that the "moderate" initiatives of 1931 and early 1932 should not be viewed as evidence of factions inside the Politburo. Instead, the initiatives resulted from interactions between individual members of the top Soviet leadership who were standing up for the interests of their own institutional domains and Stalin, who, giving in to the pressures of circumstance, ultimately accepted or even went beyond their initiatives. Stalin always had the final word. It could not be said that Stalin made any of these decisions, "moderate" either in form or content, as a result of pressure or (even less so) categorical demands by the Politburo or a faction within it. It is known, however, that as the crisis grew, the political line hardened—notably so by the end of the summer of 1932. New documents fully support the idea that the force behind this hardening was Stalin. The question arises, Did this radicalization of Stalin's position lead to a sort of "schism" within the Politburo or enable the formation of a group of relatively moderate members who somehow opposed Stalin? Most political historians of the 1930s are to a certain degree inclined toward the opinion that such a moderate faction did exist, at least in 1932. Evidence supporting this version has come in the form of information provided by Boris Nikolaevsky concerning a discussion of the Riutin affair at a meeting of the Politburo.

It was at the end of 1932, when the situation in the country was reminiscent of the time of the Kronstadt Rebellion," Nikolaevsky wrote in his famous *Letter of an Old Bolshevik*. "It is true that there were no actual uprisings, but there were many who said that it would have been better if they had been contending with uprisings. A good half of the country was afflicted with a terrible famine. [. . .] Throughout broad swaths of the party, all the talk was about how Stalin's policies had led the country into a dead end, 'had put the party at odds with the peasant,' and that the only way out was to get rid of Stalin. A lot of influential members of the TsK were expressing these sentiments; they were saying that even in the Politburo there was an anti-Stalin majority all ready. [. . .] Not surprisingly, every conceivable platform and declaration was being passed around. Among them, Riutin's platform was attracting particular attention. [. . .] Of all the platforms, Riutin's was set apart by his harsh personal opposition to Stalin. [. . .]

"Many people were talking about this platform, so it is not surprising that it soon wound up on Stalin's desk. [. . .] Riutin, who at the time was being held in some sort of exile or detention (where his platform had been written), was brought to Moscow, and under interrogation he admitted his authorship. His fate was decided by the Politburo, since the GPU (on Stalin's instructions, of course) had expressed its support for the death sentence, and Riutin was an old and distinguished party activist, a group that Lenin's testament exempted from execution.

"It is said that the discussions were extremely tense. Stalin supported the GPU proposal. His most forceful argument was the growth of terrorist inclinations among young people, even in the Komsomol. GPU intelligence was filled with reports of such conversations among young workers and students throughout the country. They also detailed quite a few separate acts of terrorism committed by these groups against relatively low-level representatives of the party and the Soviet leadership. Despite the fact that they were Komsomol members, the party did not hesitate to apply the 'supreme penalty' to such acts, and Stalin argued that it would be incorrect and illogical to so severely punish those who had carried out such acts and spare the one whose political rhetoric served to justify such practices. [. . .]

"I no longer remember exactly how the votes were divided in the Politburo. The only thing I do remember is that Kirov was adamant against execution and that he managed to persuade the majority of

Politburo members. Stalin was rather cautious, to avoid letting the matter lead to sharp conflict. Riutin's life was then spared: he was sent for many years to one of strictest prisons."[78]

Even though Nikolaevsky's account has never been corroborated with hard or even circumstantial evidence, it is widely treated as credible within scholarly literature and textbooks on Soviet history. It is also widely believed that after being so strongly rebuffed in such an important matter, Stalin decided to gradually prepare mass repression against the party's old guard, and that the conflict between Stalin and Kirov over the Riutin affair was one of the reasons for Kirov's murder in December 1934. With time, Nikolaevsky's account of Politburo discussions of the Riutin case has taken on new details. For example, Boris Starkov has added to information outlined by Nikolaevsky: "It was S. M. Kirov, supported by G. K. Ordzhonikidze and V. V. Kuibyshev, who spoke forcefully and most decisively against the death penalty for Riutin. L. M. Kaganovich and V. M. Molotov abstained from voting."[79] Unfortunately, Starkov does not provide a source for this information.

Not a single archival document yet found supports Nikolaevsky's account or the accounts of those who have elaborated on his version of events, such as Starkov. Nor did a detailed study of the circumstances of the Riutin case, which took place at the time of his rehabilitation in 1988, unearth evidence of discord within the Politburo.[80] We now know that the collegium of the OGPU gave Riutin a ten-year prison term on 11 October 1932. It handed down the sentence after the case was discussed at a Central Committee plenum on 2 October and by the Central Control Commission presidium on 9 October. The presidium decreed that twenty-four people be expelled from the party as "members and accomplices of the Riutin-Ivanov-Galkin counterrevolutionary group [. . .] as traitors to the party and the working class who attempted to create, through underground measures [. . .] a bourgeois kulak organization to restore capitalism in the USSR and, in particular, the kulachestvo." The OGPU was assigned the task of taking legal and administrative measures against the organizers and participants of this "counterrevolutionary group," "subjecting them to the full force of revolutionary law."[81] This 9 October resolution was approved *through polling* of Politburo members on 10 October 1932. Stalin made only insignificant changes to the text of the presidium resolution, placing the notation "Agreed" on it. Below this notation, Molotov, Kaganovich, Mikoyan, Voroshilov, and Kuibyshev signed to show their agreement.[82] Kirov's signature was missing in this case, but that is not exceptional. Kirov was in Moscow very rarely and took little part in the workings of the Politburo. It can, of course, be supposed that Riutin's fate was sealed at a highly secret Politburo meeting, but there is no mention of such a discussion even in the special protocols of the Politburo (special folder), which contains decisions on much more important and secret questions. Finally, there were no meetings of the Politburo attended by the full membership between 25 September and 23 October, including in Stalin's Kremlin office.[83] If we presume something even less likely, that Riutin's fate was determined at a secret, unofficial meeting of Politburo members that was specially convened in some unknown location without the keeping of protocols, this raises at least two questions. First, why did such a generally routine question merit such secrecy, especially if Stalin did not anticipate opposition, as Nikolaevsky's document suggests? And second, how could Nikolaevsky's source have found out about such a top secret meeting, even if this source really was Bukharin?

Available documents force us to recognize Nikolaevsky's account of a clash between Stalin and Kirov over the fate of Riutin as mere legend, the likes of which are no rarity in Soviet history. Furthermore, what we currently know about the behavior of the Leningrad leadership in the early 1930s gives us no reason to believe that it was following a different, more moderate line from that pursued by the leadership of other regions of the country. As elsewhere, Leningrad dealt harshly with terrorism during the period of crisis. Certain statistics relating to repression in Leningrad Province in 1932, when the hypothetical clash between Kirov and Stalin specifically over the issue of terror is purported to have taken place, are available in recently published OGPU records. In 1932, according to these records, thirty-seven thousand people were arrested in Leningrad Province, representing approximately 9 percent of all OGPU arrests in the Soviet Union.[84] The population of Leningrad Province at this time constituted only 4.2 percent of the entire Soviet population.[85] Whatever questions there might be about these statistics, state terror in the area under Kirov's authority was certainly no less severe than in the Soviet Union overall. Given the arrests in the border territories of Leningrad Province, it was apparently even more severe.

Attributing this repression entirely to Kirov would be incorrect.

However, he did help incite the new wave of terror. On 16 April 1932, Kirov signed a resolution of the Leningrad Province party secretariat entitled "On Purging the City of Leningrad of Criminal Fringe [*deklassirovannykh*] Elements" (classified as a special-folder resolution). This resolution assigned the leadership of the province OGPU to work with Moscow in settling the question of the necessary "removal" of two thousand "criminal, fringe elements" for transport to Svirlag, an OGPU camp.[86] On 6 August 1932, *Pravda* published a speech by Kirov at a meeting of district party officials of Leningrad Province. Publishing this speech helped lay the ideological groundwork for the announcement of the famous and draconian Law of 7 August concerning the theft of socialist property, which Stalin proposed and formulated. "It is time to raise the accountability of people who deal with kolkhoz and cooperative property," said Kirov. "We have to candidly admit that our punitive policy is very liberal. We have to introduce a correction here. After all, if we try some embezzler, then we must understand that we are dealing with people who can adapt to any situation, they usually are very quickly released under an amnesty, and it's as if there never was any trial. We view cooperative kolkhoz property as belonging to society. It seems to me that in this regard, the time has come to raise kolkhoz and cooperative organizations to the level of government agencies, and if someone is caught stealing kolkhoz or cooperative property, he should be subjected to the harshest measure. And if the punishment is softened, then it should be to no fewer than ten years' incarceration."

Kirov's speech before the joint session of the Politburo and the Central Control Commission presidium, convened on 27 November 1932 to deal with the "counterrevolutionary group" of A. P. Smirnov, N. B. Eismont, and V. N. Tolmachev, also gives us an idea what his political manners were like at the time. This speech stood out for its aggressiveness and crudeness. Accusing Tomsky (Stalin was trying to label Tomsky and Rykov as supporters of the new "counterrevolutionary organization") of reluctance to defend the general line, Kirov exclaimed, "Your position is completely unique in this regard. If every party member should now punch an oppositionist in the snout, then you should be punching twice as hard and twice as strongly, assuming that you have really broken with your past."[87]

This speech does not conclusively disprove that Kirov was also conducting a separate, "moderate" program. Still, a significant body of documents now available to historians supports a skeptical view of Kirov's "oppositionism."

THE TRUE ORIGINS OF CONFLICT

A possible argument against relying on archival material to corroborate tales of clashes within the Politburo could be that documents of this sort would have been destroyed. In reality, however, the archives are literally overflowing with evidence of all kinds of conflicts within the Politburo in the 1930s. This allows us to better understand both the reasons for such conflicts and their nature, as well as how they influenced the mechanisms of power at the highest levels of Soviet government.

Historians studying one of the leading members of Stalin's Politburo, Ordzhonikidze, have noted the striking role of institutional interests in his approach to his governmental duties.[88] After being transferred to a new post, he substantially changed his positions in accordance with his new responsibilities. While he was chairman of the Central Control Commission, Ordzhonikidze had advocated superaccelerated industrialization and a struggle against wreckers in industry, but now that he was in charge of the Supreme Economic Council he advocated for a more balanced and moderate rate of industrial development, fought for the rights of specialists, and favored greater authority for industrial managers. Other members of the Politburo held views that were analogously influenced by the particular interests they were currently representing, with Molotov advocating for the Council of People's Commissars, Kuibyshev for Gosplan, Mikoyan for the Supply Commissariat, Voroshilov for the military, Andreev for the Transport Commissariat, and Kosior and Kirov for Ukraine and Leningrad Provinces, respectively. A multitude of documents can be found in the archives reflecting conflicts among the various branches of government, with the Politburo members who headed them taking active part. Bitter and lengthy arguments flared over the distribution of labor, equipment, and capital investment. These conflicts reached the peak of their fury when decisions were being drafted and finalized concerning quarterly, annual, and five-year plan allocations. During the early months of 1930, each member of the Politburo considered it his exclusive right to punish or reward his subordinates and was extremely upset by any attempts by outside regulators or inspectors to interfere in his domain. Politburo members had a hard time dealing with criticism of their agencies, taking such criticism as a personal insult and almost always responding with counterattacks.[89]

Such a politically motivated counterattack can be found in the 5 April 1931 Politburo decision concerning the newspaper *Ekonomicheskaia zhizn'*, which had taken the liberty of criticizing two government bodies headed by Politburo members—the Supply Commissariat and Gosplan. In response to demands by Mikoyan and Kuibyshev, the Politburo adopted a decision "to reprimand the editorial board of *Ekonomicheskaia zhizn'* for transforming correct and necessary criticism of the workings of the commissariats into libel against Soviet government agencies in articles concerning Narkomsnab [the Supply Commissariat] and Gosplan in the issue dated 24 March of this year." (In a move suggestive of retribution, the Politburo also decided to reduce the size of the newspaper.)[90] The administrators of Soviet government bodies successfully used this formula—turning criticism into libel against the Soviet authorities—both in the 1930s and in subsequent decades.

Gosplan's next conflict with the press—this time with *Pravda*—erupted in July 1931. On 8 July, *Pravda* printed an item accusing V. A. Levin, director of Gosplan's industrial division, of saying at a commission meeting convened to discuss a purging of Gosplan that "the plan for 1931 was drafted during the transition from the old Gosplan to the new. I had no part in this and am not responsible for that 'useless scrap of paper.'" (The transition that Levin referred to was the replacement of G. M. Krzhizhanovsky by Kuibyshev as Gosplan chairman in November 1930.) The item in *Pravda* characterized Levin as a "party freeloader": "It should be said that among individual Gosplan workers, there is talk about not fulfilling the plan and that Levin is by no means alone." The newspaper called on the commission and the Gosplan party cell to put the "opportunists" in their place.

At first the Gosplan leadership did not react to this attack by *Pravda*. A week later, however, a long poem appeared in *Pravda* by the Komsomol poet A. Bezymensky, a "response" in rhyme by a fictitious shock worker named Akulina Frolova to the "party freeloader" Levin. Bezymensky's literary "heroine" hurled unrestrained accusations at Levin, referring to his "meager brains" and his opportunism and promising to overfulfill every plan. It is likely that Gosplan chairman Kuibyshev found out that *Pravda* was preparing additional items about his agency.

He threw himself into battle. On 15 July, the day Bezymensky's poem was published, he brought the matter up in the Politburo. Kuibyshev's complaints were assigned to be handled by a commission made up of Stalin, Kaganovich, and Kuibyshev himself.[91] Exhibiting rare expeditiousness, the Politburo adopted a resolution the very next day, ordering that no further materials relating to problems at Gosplan be published. The editors of *Pravda* received a reprimand in the name of the Politburo: "Regardless of mistakes committed by Com. Levin and duly exposed by *Pravda,* it should be recognized that *Pravda* acted improperly in printing the item about Com. Levin (in which Com. Levin was incorrectly described as a 'party freeloader') and the poem by Com. Bezymensky without the knowledge of the TsK secretary."[92]

But having tasted victory, the leadership of Gosplan decided not to settle for what they had achieved. Levin apparently lodged a countercomplaint, stating that his testimony before the commission had been incorrectly recorded in the protocols. Levin's petition was reported to Stalin and on his suggestion was placed at the top of the agenda for the Politburo's 25 July 1931 meeting.[93] The Politburo charged the Orgburo with examining the petition and asked, "if it turned out that Com. Levin is correct, that the appropriate retraction should be printed in *Pravda.*" On 16 August, after Stalin had left for vacation, the Orgburo upheld Levin's complaint on Kaganovich's recommendation and instructed *Pravda* to print an explanation "rehabilitating Com. Levin."[94]

Such clashes left their mark. They clearly strengthened the positions of the government agencies and encouraged their lack of constraint. Stalin must have understood this, but for the time being he gave in to his comrades-in-arms.

One method that Politburo members used to put pressure on Stalin in fighting for the interests of their agencies (and, correspondingly, their own interests) was to submit their resignations. This method had become a party tradition. Lenin resorted to it on several occasions, as did Stalin in the 1920s. From this perspective, in the early 1930s the threat of resigning can be viewed as a holdover of the way things had been done within the party in the past, although by now these resignations were submitted and considered exclusively within the small circle of the top leaders.

On 26 June 1930, for example, Mikoyan wrote a letter to Stalin that read, in part,

I have already been working for four years in NKtorg [the Trade Com-
missariat]. All of the difficulties of socialist construction are most keenly
concentrated in NKtorg, since it is at the center of economic life. [. . .]
Furthermore, while blunders and errors in other areas of Soviet work
often go unnoticed by the party, in the area of NKtorg's work they are at
the center of politics.

Mikoyan complained most bitterly about the problems associated with
the foreign trade apparatus:

It's such a difficult, complex matter, which demands exceptional effort
and exceptional vigilance on the part of the NKtorg leadership. I have to
answer for everything done, for every little detail of NKtorg's operations. Meanwhile, I am so worn out and harassed—after all, I have gone
two years without a vacation—that I'm not in any shape to deal successfully with the management of NKtorg. Furthermore, a fresh person
(as I've been at this job for four years) would be better able to move
things forward. I therefore ask the Politburo:
• to release me from my job at NKtorg;
• to give me a two-month vacation;
• to assign me to a local job, a party or management job (some new construction project).[95]

Mikoyan's letter remained among his papers, with no sign that it was
ever given to Stalin. But even if Stalin never saw the petition, he was apparently aware of Mikoyan's frame of mind, although he decided not to
bring it out into the open. A month later, on 24 August, Stalin wrote to
Molotov, "We keep forgetting about a certain 'trivial matter,' that is, that
Trade is now one of the most important commissariats (and one of the
most complicated, if not the most complicated of all). And what do we
find? At the head of this commissariat is a person who is not coping with
a job that, in general, is difficult, if not impossible, for one person to handle. Either we must remove Mikoian, which shouldn't be assumed, or we
should prop him up with outstanding deputies, which, I think, won't
meet with any objection."[96] The issue was resolved in keeping both with
Stalin's proposal and Mikoyan's complaint. At first, Mikoyan was given
a deputy for foreign trade—A. P. Rozengolts—and later he was relieved
of responsibility for foreign trade. A Politburo resolution dated 15 November 1930 split the Trade Commissariat into two commissariats—a
Supply Commissariat (Narkomsnab) headed by Mikoyan, and a Commissariat of Foreign Trade headed by Rozengolts.[97]

The handling of Kuibyshev's letter of resignation, which he submitted to Kaganovich on 10 August 1931 (while Stalin was on vacation), involved concessions. Kuibyshev was unhappy with the circumstances under which the plan for 1932 and the Second Five-Year Plan were being drafted. Citing illness, he asked for a six-week vacation and in concluding wrote, "Since I clearly cannot manage the duties of head of Gosplan, I request that I be relieved of this job and provided with a job that I can handle (it would be better if it were in a province or territory)."[98] Stalin was very unhappy with Kuibyshev's complaints. "Comrade Kuibyshev's memo has created a bad impression; in fact, so does his behavior in general. He seems to be trying to avoid work," Stalin wrote to Kaganovich.[99] However, it appears that Kuibyshev's immediate boss, Molotov, was given the job of dealing with him. On 14 August, Molotov, who was away on vacation, sent Kuibyshev a letter on the matter. "Comrade Kaganovich sent Koba your letter to the Central Committee, and I read it. [. . .] There cannot be any question of your leaving Gosplan. I am sure that everyone would be decisively against it. [. . .] What you need is a break. I think this could happen soon, from the beginning of September. I therefore strongly advise you to drop the question of leaving Gosplan and not to ever raise it again. It is not the time for this—what's needed is to get down in earnest to the improvement of Gosplan. We must help you here, and I think that in the fall things will begin to get better, with success."[100] The question of resigning was off the table. As Molotov had promised, Kuibyshev was given a vacation and some support in the exhausting struggle with the various bodies of government that drafting the plans entailed.

In early September 1931, after calming Kuibyshev's concerns, Stalin was drawn into a heated conflict with Ordzhonikidze regarding the allocation of hard currency for imports needed by the Supreme Economic Council. Ordzhonikidze was being supported to a certain extent by several other members of the Politburo. Kaganovich, who was coordinating the work of the Politburo during this time, was forced to navigate the situation. Facing a standoff, Stalin and Molotov, who were vacationing in the south, were compelled to send an ultimatum, on 6 September, to the Politburo members who remained in Moscow. "We insist that both of your decisions on orders for steel and for railroad-car axles and wheels be revoked. If you disagree, we propose a special session of the Politburo to which both of us should be summoned."[101] After this ultimatum, the question was settled in Stalin's favor, although Ord-zhonikidze let Stalin know in private letters how upset he was.[102] To neutralize the impact of the conflict, Stalin had to send Ordzhonikidze several friendly letters, filled with gentle admonitions and explanations of exactly how Ordzhonikidze had been at fault.[103]

Several days later, on 12 September, Mikoyan submitted a new letter of resignation to Stalin. This time he was unhappy about the reprimands that his commissariat had been subjected to as a consequence of the dif-ficult food supply situation in Georgia.[104] Even though this conflict was resolved, on 15 October, the Politburo was forced to consider yet an-other letter of resignation from Mikoyan. This conflict appeared to be tied to a report that Mikoyan was drafting to be presented at the Central Committee plenum scheduled for the end of October. The Supply Com-missariat had been subjected to harsh criticism, and Mikoyan was at-tempting to deflect it by submitting a letter of resignation. The Politburo was firm. The resulting decision stated, "Com. Mikoyan's request to re-sign is denied, which obligates Com. Mikoyan to present a timely draft resolution on the Narkomsnab report to the plenum."[105]

In 1931 relations between Supreme Economic Council chairman Ord-zhonikidze and the Council of People's Commissars leadership (chair-man Molotov and his first deputy, Gosplan chairman Kuibyshev) were fraught with conflict. The temperamental Ordzhonikidze incurred Sta-lin's strong displeasure with his fierce defense of the interests of the Supreme Economic Council and of his rights as master of his own do-main.[106] In August 1931, Stalin wrote to Kaganovich (obviously in-tending that his words be conveyed to Ordzhonikidze): "Comrade Ord-zhonikidze is still misbehaving. [He] is apparently not aware that his conduct (which is aimed against Comrades Molotov and Kuibyshev) ob-jectively leads to the undermining of our leadership group, which histor-ically evolved in a struggle against all types of opportunism—and cre-ates the danger that the group may be destroyed. Is it really possible that he doesn't realize that he will find no support from us *whatsoever on this path*? What foolishness!"[107] In September–October 1931, in con-nection with a further intensification of the conflict between Ordzho-nikidze and Molotov, Stalin personally reprimanded Ordzhonikidze.

> I don't agree with you about Molotov. If he's giving you or VSNKh a hard time, raise the matter in the PB. You know perfectly well that the PB will not let Molotov or anyone else persecute you or the VSNKh. In

any event, you're just as much to blame as Molotov is. You called him a "scoundrel." That can't be allowed in a comradely environment. You ignore him, the SNK, the STO. You see the TsK, but don't notice the SNK, STO, Molotov. Why, what's your justification? Do you really think that Molotov should be excluded from this ruling circle that has taken shape in the struggle against the Trotsky-Zinoviev and Bukharin-Rykov deviations? [. . .] To isolate Molotov and *scatter* the ruling Bolshevik circle [. . .]—no, I won't go for that "business," however much that might upset you and however close our friendship might be. Of course Molotov has his faults, and I am aware of them. But who doesn't have faults? We're all rich in faults. We have to work and struggle together—there's plenty of work to go around. We have to respect one another and deal with one another.[108]

Not long after that he wrote again, "You still haven't learned to get away from the *personal* element in relationships between political leaders. This is bad [. . .] Molotov shouldn't be isolated and Sergo [Ordzhonikidze] shouldn't be isolated! We work together, come what may! The preservation of the unity and indivisibility of our ruling circle! Understood?"[109]

Despite such remonstrances, several months later another conflict erupted, now tied to plans to divide the Supreme Economic Council into several commissariats. Ordzhonikidze was against this decision.[110] Stalin and Molotov felt that the council had to be divided. Stalin proposed a draft resolution on the reorganization. Ordzhonikidze submitted his resignation and advanced various accusations against Molotov. As a result, on 23 December 1931, the Politburo adopted the following decision:

a) To adopt the draft resolution proposed by Com. Stalin on restructuring the work of the economic commissariats and submit it for final editing to a commission comprised of Coms. Stalin, Molotov, Ordzhonikidze, and Kaganovich. Com. Stalin is to convene the commission.
b) To refuse Com. Ordzhonikidze's letter of resignation.
c) To convene a special Politburo session to consider Com. Ordzhonikidze's memorandum concerning his relationship with Com. Molotov.[111]

On 25 December the Politburo adopted a finalized resolution on the operations of the economic agencies that legalized the division of the Supreme Economic Council into three separate commissariats: heavy industry, forestry, and light industry.[112] Evidence has yet to be found concerning a special Politburo meeting to consider the relationship between Ordzhonikidze and Molotov. Most likely the conflict was resolved behind closed doors.

The severity of this conflict forced Stalin to exercise caution. Several years later, on 3 June 1934, when the time came to further divide the huge Heavy Industry Commissariat, the Politburo enacted a decision to establish the position of deputy commissar of heavy industry fuel (coal, oil, shale, peat) and appointed M. L. Rukhimovich to hold it.[113] Molotov, who advocated further subdividing the People's Commissariat of Heavy Industry (NKTP), was away on vacation at the time (it is entirely possible that this question was intentionally raised when Molotov was out of town). Faced with a fait accompli, Molotov merely grumbled to Kuibyshev in a letter dated 5 June, "I am sorry that all they did was appoint Rukhimovich as NKTP deputy (fuel). I believe the time has come to settle the question of a *new people's commissariat* (fuel + power plants)."[114]

Acting as arbitrator in the numerous interagency arguments between his comrades-in-arms in the early 1930s, Stalin often preferred to find compromises. An example is the outcome of a conflict between Kuibyshev and Andreev, the transport commissar. On 14 November 1932, Kuibyshev approached the Politburo with a note concerning the arbitrary releasing of coal on orders of the deputy transport commissar, P. B. Bilik. Citing reports from the secretary of the Reserves Committee, E. A. Zibrak, and the OGPU deputy chairman, Genrikh Yagoda, Kuibyshev demanded that the Politburo punish those guilty of illegally using coal and, in particular, that a number of railroad employees be arrested and that Bilik be given a harsh reprimand.[115] The day before the question was to be considered by the Politburo, Andreev sent Stalin the following note: "Com. Stalin. My deputy Bilik is being reprimanded for nothing. He did not take a single ton of fuel from the reserves. I am attaching the explanation I required him to give me. He is quite a disciplined worker."[116] Given what followed, Stalin was apparently inclined to support the leadership of the Transport Commissariat. Stalin gave Andreev's note to Kuibyshev (it has been preserved in his Secretariat archives). Kuibyshev undertook some additional investigation. In response to Bilik's explanation, Zibrak prepared a new document showing that the releasing of supplies occurred in one case through a direct order from Bilik and in another with his knowledge.[117]

Despite the evidence of Bilik's guilt, the Politburo, which reviewed the matter on 25 November, adopted a compromise decision. Bilik was shown the "illegality of arranging for the release of coal from the Reserves Committee supply without the Committee's permission" and was issued a warning "that if such illegal actions should recur," he would be held "to the most stringent party and state accountability." As usual, it was those lower down who paid the price—the Politburo approved the arrest of a number of railway employees and charged the OGPU with "investigating and holding to account all the employees of the NKPS [the People's Commissariat of Transport] and roads guilty of the illegal releasing of supplies."[118]

The Politburo quite frequently had to sort out conflicts between the military and the economic commissariats concerning deferments of army service. This issue arose in August 1933. On 16 August the leadership of the Donetsk Province party organization sent a cipher addressed to Stalin in which it requested a deferment for ten thousand coal miners until 1 January 1934. This request was undoubtedly supported by Ordzhonikidze, whose purview included the mines, and it may even have been initiated by him. Understandably, Voroshilov, who was in charge of military matters, opposed this request. Upon receiving the encoded request for deferment from Kaganovich, who was handling it in Stalin's absence, Voroshilov added an annotation: "I am against it." Finding himself in the midst of yet another interagency conflict, Kaganovich arranged yet another compromise. On his recommendation, the Politburo granted a deferment for five thousand workers.[119]

The list of such compromise solutions to interagency conflict achieved with the help of the Politburo could go on. At the same time, Stalin took a more hard-line stance in quite a few cases and prevailed.[120] One of the more heated conflicts of this sort, one demonstrating the balance of power at the highest echelons toward the end of the period being examined in this chapter, broke out in August 1933. Molotov stood at its center. At the end of July 1933, several telegrams addressed to Molotov from throughout the country were delivered to the Council of People's Commissars concerning the shipment of new combines by the Communard factory in Zaporozhe that were missing a number of important parts.[121] On the basis of these telegrams, on 28 July the council adopted a resolution entitled "On the Criminal Dispatch of Incomplete Combine-Harvesters to MTS [Machine Tractor

Stations] and State Farms," which demanded that the Commissariat of Heavy Industry immediately halt shipments of faulty combines and equip previously shipped combines with the missing parts. It also authorized USSR procurator Ivan Akulov to arrest and bring to trial the factory managers guilty of shipping the incomplete combines.[122] The decision provoked protests. The secretary of the Dnepropetrovsk Province party committee, M. M. Khataevich, sent a special letter to several addresses: to the Council of People's Commissars, to the Central Committee of the Ukrainian Communist Party, to the People's Commissariat of Heavy Industry (Ordzhonikidze), to the Central Control Commission, and to the procurators of the Soviet Union and Ukraine. He argued that the Communard factory had performed well, that the shipment of incomplete combines was the result of an effort to prevent the theft of parts: certain combine parts were transported in separate boxes. "In general the factory has more successes than failures. In this light the regional committee would consider it expedient not [. . .] to undertake a criminal investigation against the management of the factory."[123] Molotov nonetheless took a firm stance. "We are well aware of the achievements of Communard, and so is the procurator. This will be borne in mind by the court. This trial is certainly not merely significant just for the factory itself, and to cancel it is entirely inexpedient," he replied.[124]

On 16 August 1933 proceedings began before a panel of criminal judges of the USSR Supreme Court in the case of shipments of incomplete combines, for which representatives of a number of industrial agencies and managers of the Communard factory were being tried. Deputy procurator Andrei Vyshinsky was in charge of the prosecution. His closing statement included the following: "The trial gives us grounds for raising general questions concerning the work of Soviet economic organizations. [. . .] I refer to the People's Commissariat of Agriculture. [. . .] I refer to the People's Commissariat of Heavy Industry. [. . .] I refer to the republican authorities."[125] Such a framing of the issue outraged the heads of the Heavy Industry and Agriculture Commissariats, Ordzhonikidze and Yakovlev. On 24 August, with Stalin out of town, they succeeded in having the Politburo adopt a decision condemning the formulation that Vyshinsky had used in his speech, "which provides a pretext for incorrect accusations against the People's Commissariat of Heavy Industry and the People's Commissariat of Agriculture." The resolution was drafted by Kaganovich and edited by Molotov. Kaganovich, Molotov, Kalinin, and Ordzhonikidze voted in favor.[126]

After learning of this decision from a letter sent to him by Kaganovich, on 29 August Stalin sent a cipher to Moscow addressed to Kaganovich, Molotov, and Ordzhonikidze and intended for all the other members of the Politburo as well. "I learned from Kaganovich's letter that you had found incorrect one point in Vyshinsky's speech, where he refers to the responsibility of the people's commissars for the dispatch and acceptance of incomplete output. I consider this decision incorrect and harmful. The dispatch and acceptance of incomplete output is the crudest of violations of Central Committee decisions, and people's commissars are also bound to be held responsible for a matter of this kind. It is lamentable that Kaganovich and Molotov were unable to stand up against the bureaucratic assault from the People's Commissariat of Heavy Industry."[127] Although Stalin's message was deciphered (and landed on Kaganovich's desk) around six in the afternoon of 29 August, the decision to rescind the resolution was not submitted to a vote until three days later, on 1 September. Kaganovich, Andreev, Kuibyshev, and Mikoyan signed the decision.[128] On 1 September, Ordzhonikidze left for vacation. Kaganovich apparently delayed addressing the issue to avoid putting Ordzhonikidze in an awkward position.

Stalin seems to have sensed the tension within the Politburo on this question. He felt compelled to further explain his position to the participants in this conflict. On 29 August, Stalin wrote to Kaganovich: "It is deplorable and dangerous that you (and Molotov) failed to curb Sergo's bureaucratic impulses with regard to incomplete combine-harvesters and sacrificed Vyshinsky to them. If you are going to train cadres this way, you will not have a single honest member left in the party. It's an outrage."[129] On 1 September he expressed similar sentiments to Molotov. "I consider Sergo's actions with respect to Vyshinsky the behavior of a hooligan. How can you let him have his way? By his act of protest, Sergo clearly wished to disrupt the campaign of the Council of Commissars and Central Committee to provide proper equipment. What's the matter? Did Kaganovich pull a fast one? So it seems. And he's not the only one."[130] He then wrote to Kaganovich yet again and accused him of winding up in the "camp of reactionary elements of the party." In a letter dated 7 September, Kaganovich both justified himself and acknowledged his mistakes, although he also tried to shift the blame onto Molotov.[131]

Molotov sent Stalin a response on 8 September in which he acknowledged his error but blamed everything on Ordzhonikidze and Kaganovich. "At the meeting in the Central Committee [Politburo meeting] Kaganovich, Kalinin, Ordzhonikidze, Yakovlev, and Vyshinsky were present, as well as myself. You know Kalinin's attitude toward these matters—he is always 'in favor of the industrial managers,' 'insulted' by the court and the Workers' and Peasants' Inspectorate, even more so in the present case. When Ordzhonikidze confronted him, Vyshinsky immediately stated that he had made a glaring error, and was generally obsequious. Personal attacks were made on me of a most repugnant kind by Ordzhonikidze, who said that I set this all up, behind the back of the Central Committee, that it was impossible to work with M. [Molotov] and so on. [. . .] In spite of this, and in spite of the fact that Kaganovich tacitly agreed with Ordzhonikidze, I did not give way."[132] Stalin returned to this subject in a letter to Molotov dated 12 September, expressing his extreme displeasure.[133]

The lengthy correspondence (lasting almost two weeks) devoted to this matter and Stalin's strong reaction are quite indicative of Stalin's primacy—it ended with acquiescence to Stalin's demands—but also of the continuing existence of the various branches of government and the members of the Politburo who represented their diverse interests as still a force to be reckoned with. Without asking Stalin's permission, his comrades-in-arms were still able to bring up rather important issues in the Politburo and achieve the resolutions they needed. Stalin himself was forced to resort to lengthy explanations and ultimatums. It is significant that during this period there arose a "tradition" in the Politburo of considering contentious issues in the absence of the particular member from whom a strong objection to the proposed solution was expected. Generally, as Andrea Graziosi has noted, in the early 1930s Stalin was an authoritative "older brother" to his closest associates ("best friend," as Kaganovich called him), and fights with him were still possible.[134] During the second half of the 1930s, such attitudes toward Stalin on the part of his comrades-in-arms—along with the various maneuvers and letters of resignation, as well as Stalin's own tendency toward compromise that went with such a relationship—were no longer evident. The "best friend" had been completely transformed into a typical dictator.

Furthermore, the conflicts we know of within the Politburo had more to do with institutional rivalries than with policy. In looking out for the interests of their own commissariats, Politburo members might still stray from the political line. For example, the energetic objections by Stalin's comrades-in-arms to repression within their governmental domains essentially supported a relatively "moderate" course and stood in opposition to the policy of totalitarian terror that prevailed in 1937–1938. Nonetheless, there is no evidence of groups within the Politburo that held differing views on key questions of political and socioeconomic development. Any given member of the Politburo might, depending on the circumstance, appear to be a "radical" or a "moderate." The facts and documents at our disposal (in particular, the correspondence between Politburo members) suggest that special—one could say friendly—relations existed between, on the one hand, Kaganovich and Ordzhonikidze and, on the other, between Molotov and Kuibyshev. (Kaganovich and Molotov are most often counted among the fervent radicals, whereas Ordzhonikidze and Kuibyshev are viewed as supporters of "moderation.") At the same time, relations between Ordzhonikidze and Kuibyshev were far from trouble-free. Their governmental affiliations often brought them into conflict.

These conflicts began back when Ordzhonikidze headed the Central Control Commission and regularly exposed errors and "sabotage" at the Supreme Economic Council, which was under Kuibyshev's purview. They continued beyond this period when, under Kuibyshev's leadership, Gosplan cut the material and financial resources allocated to the Supreme Economic Council (later its subdivision the People's Commissariat of Heavy Industry), now under Ordzhonikidze's control. Thus, the relationships between Politburo members were primarily determined by their administrative interests and their personal biases.

Even though the conflicts during the period of sharp political confrontation among the top party leadership were not grounded in fundamental policy disagreements, the pretensions of his comrades-in-arms were a significant problem for Stalin. First of all, tempered in battle but also emboldened by concessions made by Stalin in the 1920s, members of the Politburo and the government agencies they headed constituted an obstacle on Stalin's path to absolute dictatorship. Politburo members who headed major commissariats and other government bodies were, as political actors, essentially products of a merging of the highest party and state-economic leadership, which significantly increased their actual influence. The power of the Moscow-based leadership may have been further enhanced by the cultivation of "clients" from among the heads of local party organizations and middle-level government officials seeking patronage from the center. (This idea, which is suggested by a number of recent findings, requires further study.) Enjoying significant independence and authority in deciding everyday administrative matters, the agencies of the Soviet government in many cases dictated their own conditions, exacerbating the already devastating policy of the Great Leap. They were constantly demanding ever more burdensome capital investments and imports of foreign equipment and resisted any oversight of their use of the funds and resources allocated to them. The huge party-state apparatus spawned bureaucratism, stagnation, and inflexibility and the various components doggedly asserted their institutional rights.

Stalin could not fail to notice these extremely significant developments. His official speeches and informal letters were filled with invective against bureaucratism, the "heroes of *vedomstvennost'*" (competing departmental self-interest), and "bureaucrat bigwigs." Stalin's letters to his comrades-in-arms from 1931 though 1933 largely consisted of instructions concerning "subduing bureaucratism" and vedomstvennost', "Bolsheviks cannot take such a path, unless, of course, they want to turn our Bolshevik party into a conglomerate of departmental gangs."[135] "Tell Postyshev not to give in to pressure from the high-and-mighty bureaucrats who are seeking medals for their fellow bureaucrat pals."[136] "It is time to begin *holding accountable* the management of plants that are obligated to supply motor-vehicle and tractor enterprises with steel. If Ordzhonikidze starts to make trouble, we will have to brand him a rotten slave to routine who supports the worst traditions of the right deviationists at the PC [People's Commissariat] of Heavy Industry."[137] "I'm afraid that if we publish such a resolution, we'll hold back industrial progress by at least six months, since instead of doing what needs to be done, the respected 'Bolsheviks' will waste all their energy endlessly shuffling personnel from one job to another."[138] "How long are you going to put up with the abominations at the enterprises of the PC for Supply, especially the canning and bottling plants?

They have poisoned more than 100 people again! Why aren't you taking measures against the PC for Supply and Mikoyan? How long is the public going to be abused? Your [the Politburo's] patience is downright astonishing."[139] The examples are plentiful.

At the same time, Stalin's attitude toward vedomstvennost' could not be called principled. Stalin's displeasure was generally provoked by any decisions (regardless of whose interests they served) that were made without consulting him. For this reason, whenever Politburo members were advancing a particular matter, they tried to get Stalin's preliminary support, even when he was out of town on vacation. Stalin himself encouraged this practice. "The number of Politburo inquiries has no effect on my health. You can send as many inquiries as you like—I'll be happy to answer them," he wrote to Molotov in June 1932.[140] "We are still getting regular and frequent directives from the boss, which helps us not to miss anything, but also actually forces him to keep working, but there's nothing to be done about it," Kaganovich told Ordzhonikidze in a letter dated 2 August 1932.[141] Given such tight control over the decision-making process, not a single decision of any importance could get by Stalin unnoticed. Turning this tendency into a rule was an important element in Stalin's consolidation of power.

By a number of measures, the system of ultimate authority that took shape in the early 1930s could be characterized as a mixed system. It combined a variety of tendencies. The Politburo operated as a body of collective authority, following formally prescribed procedures. At the same time, it became increasingly common for it to adopt decisions by polling its members and holding small meetings in Stalin's office. Politburo members maintained a certain political and administrative influence, as evidenced by a whole series of letters of resignation and conflicts between Stalin and his comrades-in-arms. But Stalin, as a rule, managed to get his way, restraining initiative on all questions of fundamental importance. Although the grave socioeconomic crisis and the growing famine weakened Stalin to a certain degree, the threat hanging over the regime prompted Politburo members to rally around him.

Archival documents do not support the idea that subgroups within the Politburo with differing approaches to policy were competing for influence over Stalin. What archival materials do show are numerous conflicts at the highest echelons of power that arose out of the competing interests of the various agencies of government in which Politburo members were involved. This circumstance did promote the formation of certain informal alliances; however, these alliances did not fit the model of "moderates" versus "radicals." The immediate causes of conflict were the distribution of financial and other resources, criticism aimed at government agencies by oversight organizations or the press, personnel reorganizations, and other such matters. Politburo members charged with responsibility for a particular agency felt it was their inherent right to rule over their domains without outside interference.

The impact that these interagency conflicts had on the alignment of power within the Politburo was twofold. On the one hand, they provided opportunities for members of the Politburo to fight for the inviolability of their own spheres of influence and the remnants of collective leadership. On the other hand, the conflicts promoted disunity within the Politburo and allowed Stalin to play the role of arbitrator. By exploiting real problems caused by institutional self-interest, Stalin (the main culprit in the policy of the Great Leap and the resulting antagonisms between the agencies of government) was in a number of instances able to pose as an ardent foe of bureaucratic excesses. Harsh criticism of agencies and their leadership for "anti-government" actions was a convenient way for Stalin to control Politburo members, both in decision making and overall.

The numerous reprimands that Politburo members were subject to as a result of problems arising in their particular areas of responsibility not only kept the party-state apparatus in a state of anxiety but infected Stalin's entourage with a sort of inferiority complex. Stalin was constantly instilling his comrades-in-arms with the idea that his leadership was just as essential to victory as Lenin's leadership had been when power was first seized and consolidated. As can be seen from the evidence introduced in this chapter, Stalin preferred to elevate even secondary questions to the level of principle, taking every opportunity to demonstrate his superiority as a theoretician of Marxism-Leninism and as a sophisticated political strategist. The tone of Stalin's directives was nonetheless categorical. It is not surprising, therefore, that all important undertakings—whether of a reformist or a repressive nature—appear, based on the evidence, to have come from Stalin himself or from a unified Politburo. This does not mean that Stalin was the sole author of all initiatives. However, archival evidence has yet to be found that there was any active group within the Politburo exerting influence over Stalin or independently promoting a particular political line. The events of 1934, which have been repeatedly characterized by historians as the highpoint of "moderation" for the period of the prewar five-year plans, shed further light on this question.

3 A Facade of Liberalization
1934

THE BRIEF PERIOD between the surge in state terror in 1932–1933 and the new hardening of the general line that followed the murder of Sergei Kirov on 1 December 1934 had many of the features of a thaw, however limited it might have been by the systems that had taken shape over the previous few years. In the opinion of Mikhail Gefter, this brief period offered an opportunity—an opportunity that was missed—to choose, on the one hand, between further bloodletting and a continuation of the same course and, on the other, normalization of the "anti-Fascist democratization of the *Stalinist result.*"[1] Indeed, foreign policy considerations—the threat from Fascist Germany and the desire to conclude an anti-Fascist pact with France and its allies—largely determined the direction that Stalinist policy took now. On 19 December 1933 the Politburo adopted a highly classified (special folder) resolution concerning the possibility of the Soviet Union's joining the League of Nations and concluding regional mutual defense pacts with a number of Western countries (a list that would be sure to include France and Poland) in case of German aggression.[2] New foreign policy factors dictated the need for a softening of the general line. Undoubtedly there were also domestic reasons for putting an end to "lashing and prodding the country," as Stalin put it in January 1933. To some extent, the terrible crisis of 1932–1933 forced the Stalinist leadership to recognize the perniciousness of the Great Leap. This recognition, which came at the cost of millions of lives, prompted adjustments to economic and social policy and a reduction in repression. Some forces within the Politburo promoted this liberalization, and some hindered it.

THE VIRTUES OF MODERATION

The policy of repression, whatever the cost might have been, did stabilize the situation in the country. The autumn of 1933 saw a relatively good harvest, and some signs of improvement were also noted in industry.[3] The 17th Party Congress in early February 1934, which was meant to mark the end of the "great crisis," was labeled the Congress of Victors.

Many believed that the worst was behind them. Now that the Stalinist team had emerged victorious after a five-year struggle with society, established that collectivization and accelerated industrialization were here to stay, and destroyed even the most loosely organized party opposition, the time seemed to have come for certain concessions to appease the harried citizenry. And so it was. The relative stability at the end of 1933 was achieved not only through force. To a certain extent it was also the result of relatively moderate policies.

Even the Central Committee plenum of January 1933, which proclaimed the launching of new class struggles, featured promises by Stalin that during the Second Five-Year Plan the rate of industrial development would be significantly slowed. Unlike many other plenum slogans, this one was carried out. When in early 1933, economic agencies disregarded economic plans and started making their usual unauthorized capital expenditures, the country's leadership took measures to enforce budgetary discipline. After complaints from Gosplan, on 2 March 1933 the Politburo issued a firm decision: "In light of attempts by certain commissariats to set the volume of capital expenditures for 1933 higher than would correspond to the overall sum of eighteen billion rubles allocated for capital expenditures, as determined by the January Plenum of the TsK and TsKK, the Politburo points to the unconditional impermissibility of such attempts."[4] Reducing spending on capital construction to reasonable levels was a critical precondition for a return to economic health and the creation of conditions for efficient industrial production.

Tendencies toward moderation were not as evident in the countryside as they were in the industrial sectors. But with the approach of 1934, faint signs of a softening of the policy of collectivization and the struggle against kulachestvo could also be seen. Punitive actions by the political departments of machine tractor stations, numerous purges of personnel, and repressive campaigns to "strengthen kolkhozes" coexisted with a trend toward limiting forcible grain expropriation. In January 1933, attempts were made to stimulate peasant interest in more productive labor by introducing rules governing the amount of grain that had to be handed over to the state (the principle of *prodnalog,* or tax in kind), as well as by liberalizing rules regarding the cultivation of personal plots.

Repression was somewhat eased in the countryside as a result of instructions issued on 8 May 1933 by the Central Committee and the Council of People's Commissars to party and council personnel, OGPU bodies, and the courts and procuracy. The instructions prohibited the mass eviction of peasants (making allowances only for individual evictions of active "counterrevolutionaries" and limiting such evictions to twelve thousand households for the entire country), barred those not legally authorized to carry out arrests from doing so, and forbade using pre-trial detention as a preventive measure in cases of "inconsequential crimes." A limit was set on the maximum number of convicts that could be held in the prisons of the Commissariat of Justice, the OGPU, and the Main Police Administration (excluding camps and colonies)—400,000 instead of the 800,000 that were actually incarcerated toward the end of April 1933. Those condemned to serve fewer than three years were, according to the instructions, to have their sentences reduced to no more than one year of forced labor, with the remainder of their term conditional.[5] To facilitate the realization of this directive, special discharge commissions were created in every republic, territory, and province, with responsibility for the overall administration of the operation given to the RSFSR commissar of justice, Nikolai Krylenko. On 19 July 1933, Krylenko reported to Stalin and Molotov that as of 10 July 1933 prisons for all systems (the Justice Commissariat, the OGPU [not counting camps], and the Main Police Administration) contained 397,284 people. In other words, the objective set by the 8 May 1933 directive had been achieved.[6]

The first signs of moderation seen during the years of crisis had by

1934 grown into a new policy direction. To some extent, the 17th Party Congress marked its beginning. A relatively balanced economic policy was set for the Second Five-Year Plan, which was approved at the congress: in comparison with the First Five-Year Plan, it significantly reduced the rate at which industrial output would increase and officially recognized the need to make development of "group B" industries (those producing consumer goods) a priority. Certain new political trends also became evident at this congress. It is impossible to read the stenographic records without noticing that it was different from other meetings convened to thrash out five-year plans, primarily in the absence of incendiary rhetoric and the reduced emphasis on escalating the class struggle. However timid, veiled, and hinted at, there were also condemnations of the recent excesses in the countryside that had led to famine in many regions of the country. "It should be said forthrightly and clearly that during these breakthrough years repression was a crucial method of 'administration' for many party organizations in Ukraine," said, for example, second secretary of the Central Committee of the Ukrainian Communist Party (Bolshevik) Pavel Postyshev. "After all, the enemy used this method of 'administration' and used it widely in order to turn particular groups of kolkhoz workers and individual farmers against the building of kolkhozes, against the party and Soviet power."[7]

On the eve of the congress, decisions were urgently adopted to restore the party membership of several leaders of former opposition groups. On 12 December 1933 the Politburo issued a decision that arrangements be made for Grigory Zinoviev and Lev Kamenev to be readmitted into the party at one of the district party offices in Moscow, and a 20 December decree ordered that the leading theoretician of the Trotskyite opposition, Evgeny Preobrazhensky, be reinstated as well.[8] As subsequent events showed, these measures had a particular purpose—the oppositionists Kamenev, Zinoviev, Preobrazhensky, Lominadze, Tomsky, and Rykov were to be allowed to repent before the congress. Acknowledging their errors and generously peppering their speeches with insipid encomiums to Stalin, the former leaders of opposition movements and "deviations" made Stalin's victory and the consolidation of his sole leadership within the party eminently clear. But their very presence at the congress tribune symbolized a new policy of reconciliation within the party, characterized by Stalin as the "extraordinary ideopolitical and organizational drawing together of the ranks of our party."[9] The rehabilitation of many of Stalin's highly placed political opponents was seen within the party as the first step on the road toward the gradual rehabilitation of rank-and-file oppositionists and a suspension of repression and purges.

Moderation seems to have been the dominant mood of the 17th Party Congress, along with a desire to replace the policies of terror that had dominated the preceding years with a more balanced and predictable approach. "The main difficulties are already behind us" were the words with which Sergei Kirov closed his speech.[10] Undoubtedly, many other delegates felt the same way. Having survived exceptionally tense crises, famine, personnel shakeups, and uncertainty about what the coming day would bring, most party officials had turned into advocates of stability and a non-confrontational approach. The top leadership of the party had to take this into account.

What happened over the succeeding months seemed to confirm that expressions of support for moderate policies heard at the congress were more than empty declarations. After the 17th Party Congress the rehabilitation of opposition leaders continued. On 20 February, at the first meeting of the newly reconstituted Politburo, on Stalin's initiative Bukharin was named editor in chief of *Izvestia*.[11] This appointment appeared to be the first step toward returning Bukharin to the main political arena. On 13 March 1934 the Politburo confirmed a Party Control Commission decision to reinstate another leader of the right deviation to the party—former Central Committee secretary and first secretary of the Moscow party committee Nikolai Uglanov.[12] At approximately the same time, a request arrived in Moscow via the OGPU hot line that one of the most famous leaders of the Trotskyite opposition, Khristian Rakovsky, be allowed to return from exile in order to submit a statement of his "unconditional" break "with counterrevolutionary Trotskyism." This statement was circulated among Politburo members with the following note from Stalin: "To Comrades Molotov, Kaganovich, Voroshilov, Sergo [Ordzhonikidze], Kirov, Zhdanov. In my opinion Rakovsky can be permitted to come to Moscow." The Politburo issued the corresponding decision to summon Rakovsky on 18 March.[13] On 22 April, after *Pravda* published Rakovsky's statement, the Politburo resolved to put the matter of his reinstatement in the party before the Party Control Commission (which replaced the Central Control Commission).[14] During late April and early May, the Politburo also decided the question of employment for Zinoviev and Kamenev. The former became an editor of the journal *Bolshevik,* and the latter was named director of a literary institute.[15] On 22 July 1934 a resolution was adopted by the Politburo regarding the release from prison of Pyotr Petrovsky, son of Grigory Petrovsky. The younger Petrovsky had first been investigated in 1932 in association with the Union of Marxist-Leninists (the Riutin affair) and had later been condemned to a three-year prison term. Molotov wrote the text of the resolution (it features the following notation written in his hand: "In favor—Stalin, Molotov, Voroshilov, Chubar"). Rudzutak, Kalinin, and Mikoyan were later polled on the matter, a fact noted on the text of the resolution by the technical secretary.[16]

The expressions of repentance and "recognition of errors" that former oppositionists had to submit were extremely humiliating. Worse, those who had been "forgiven" were treated with contempt at every opportunity and with Stalin's evident encouragement. In 1934, Rakovsky, who was not reinstated in the party after all, was left hanging. Zinoviev was fired several months after his appointment to *Bolshevik,* on Stalin's initiative and amid an uproar. Nevertheless, the "forgiveness" shown leaders of former opposition movements was more than just a demonstration of Stalin's final victory (having oppositionists shot, as Stalin did two or three years later, for example, would have been sufficient for victory). It was also a gesture of reconciliation, the consolidation of the party around Lenin's sole heir, and a way to mark the end of the intraparty struggle.

The 17th Party Congress brought more substantial changes in the area of economic policy. Along with a reduction in the planned rate of growth for industrial output and capital investment, which signaled a turn away from the Great Leap strategy, the period of the Second Five-Year Plan was marked by numerous experiments and reforms in the industrial sectors aimed at expanding enterprises' economic self-sufficiency and revitalizing material incentives for labor. By this time talk of direct commodity exchange had been abandoned once and for all as "leftist" and was replaced by references to the role of money, financial accountability, and the need to strengthen the ruble. In November 1934 the Central Committee adopted a decision of fundamental importance—to eliminate ration cards for bread starting in 1935. In addition, the level of repression was significantly reduced in the countryside in 1934, especially in comparison with the level in 1932–1933. Concessions in areas such as the cultivation of household plots had tremendous importance in the lives of peasants.

In the final analysis, the foundation of this relatively moderate course was a recognition of the role of individual self-interest and the importance of material incentives in labor. The calls for asceticism and sacrifice coupled with the distrust of high incomes that had dominated the First Five-Year Plan were replaced with an ideology favoring a "cultured and prosperous life." Instead of the utopian promises of "garden cities" and abundant socialism made at the end of the 1920s, the Soviet people, especially the urban population, were now offered a future featuring attainable consumer comforts: a room, furniture, clothing, decent food, varied leisure activities. The attainment of this standard of living was actively used as a way to motivate labor.

The changes for the better that were gradually reaching certain subsets of the Soviet population were widely commented on in the West. "Red Russia Is Turning Pink" was the headline of an 18 November 1934 report by the *Baltimore Sun*'s Moscow correspondent. To support the notion of "pinkening," the author cited not only changes in the ways collective farms and industrial enterprises were run, the expanding practice of paying wages based on work performed, and the elimination of wage limits for party members but also the proliferating assortment of consumer goods available, including synthetic stockings (previously considered a sign of "ideological immaturity"), as well as the popularity of tennis, jazz, and the fox-trot, all of which had until recently been scorned as "bourgeois."

In Moscow this article, along with others like it, was noted and included in a secret abstract of foreign press translations that was circulated among the country's top leaders.[17] The selection of articles included for review suggests that the Soviet leaders took an interest in the West's reaction to the new moderate policies and that they had been counting on just such a primarily positive response. Filling store windows in major cities and expanding the leisure activities of the urban population was an effective way to create a positive image of the USSR in the West, since Western journalists were for the most part only able to visit such cities. It was important that signals of "normalcy" within the Stalinist USSR be sent out, for in 1934 the Soviet leadership was pursuing contacts with democratic countries (France and the United States in particular) in order to create alliances against Germany and Japan.

The easing of repression and the reorganization of the punitive apparatuses also served this dual purpose and was indeed noticed by the West. "I should mention another feature that is noticeable: the disappearance of terror," wrote, for example, Mark Khinoy, a correspondent for New York's influential Yiddish-language *Jewish Daily Forward,* after a five-week visit to the USSR. "The sense of mortal terror that used to be seen is no longer in evidence even toward the GPU and even less so toward the police. This absence of fear is seen primarily among the intelligentsia and former NEPmen and craftsmen. You also do not detect it among the broader mass of ordinary people. The exception is those Communists who have yet to be purged. But after purges, the Communists also become more open. One notices changes in attitudes toward the intelligentsia as a social class. They are courted, they are cajoled, they are bribed. They are needed."[18] There could be no talk of a dawning of democracy or the rule of law in 1934; nonetheless, in comparison with the preceding period, the level of repression had clearly been reduced.[19] For the first time in a long while, society was not in a fever over news of political trials of "wreckers" and "spies." The lull on the class-struggle front was associated to a certain extent with the continued effect of the 8 May 1933 Central Committee and Council of People's Commissars instructions easing eviction and detention (the official press was replete with references to it in 1934).

The reorganization of the punitive organs also played a part in stabilizing the political situation. In accordance with a Politburo resolution dated 10 July 1934 (and later issued as a Central Executive Committee decree), a new USSR People's Commissariat of Internal Affairs (NKVD) was established. The former odious political police apparatus—the OGPU—was formally abolished and became a subdivision of the NKVD, supposedly absorbed into the numerous routine administrative directorates: the worker and peasant police, the border and domestic guards, the civil registry office, and the administrative office. It was of fundamental importance that the newly created NKVD was deprived of authority to carry out a significant portion of the judicial functions that the OGPU had previously possessed. The judicial collegium of the OGPU was abolished, and the powers vested in the analogous body within the Commissariat of Internal Affairs—the special board—were somewhat curtailed. Whereas OGPU personnel had carried out arrests, conducted inquiries, and pronounced verdicts (assisted, for example, by a "troika" [a tribunal of three]), now cases investigated by one of the divisions of the NKVD were to be forwarded to the judiciary.[20] To implement this measure, the same day, 10 July, the Politburo adopted a decision to expand the network of judges, as well as the judicial support system, the procuracy, and the collegium of defenders.[21]

The creation of the NKVD was propagandized as a sign of democratization, a guarantee of a strengthened rule of law. "The government of the Union," *Izvestia* wrote under Bukharin's editorship on 11 July, "has decreed that a USSR Narkomvnudel [People's Commissariat of Internal Affairs] be organized, merging the OGPU into it and removing judicial affairs. This means that enemies within the country are for the most part destroyed and beaten; this means that the struggle that is not yet finished will continue, but to a large extent through other methods; this means that to a great extent the role of revolutionary legality is growing, the role of precise rules, established by law; this means that the role of judicial establishments, which try cases in accordance with set standards of legal procedure, is growing."

The thaw of 1934 has proved as great a source of questions among historians as it was a source of hope among those who lived through it. Most important, investigators have sought to establish who stood behind this shift in policy and what the balance of power was at the highest level of power, first and foremost within the Politburo.

THE POLITBURO OF THE 17TH PARTY CONGRESS

The thaw of 1934 did not involve significant changes at the highest echelons of power. The Politburo constituted after the 17th Party Congress differed little from the one elected after the 16th Party Congress in 1930. Among the members of the 16th Politburo, only Yan Rudzutak was demoted to candidate member, something that was evidently tied to his not being very active. Pavel Postyshev was the Politburo's new candidate member in 1934, as a reward for implementing Stalin's policies in Ukraine, where he had been sent in 1933 as second secretary of the Ukrainian Central Committee to "bolster the leadership."

Available documents suggest that there also were no significant changes in the assignment of responsibilities among Politburo members.

All indications are that after the 17th Party Congress, Lazar Kaganovich retained his position as Stalin's deputy within the party. Original protocols of Politburo meetings show that Kaganovich drafted many Politburo resolutions, that during Stalin's vacations he continued to manage the operation of the Politburo and the Central Committee apparatus, and that he chaired many Politburo commissions. In 1934, Kaganovich took on several new and important positions. While still holding the post of Central Committee second secretary, he was appointed chairman of the Party Control Commission, the new party administrative body created by decision of the 17th Party Congress to replace the Central Control Commission. On 15 February 1934, Kaganovich replaced Molotov as chairman of the joint Central Committee—Council of People's Commissars commission on rail transport, created in August 1933.[22] It was logical that Kaganovich then be appointed head of the Central Committee transportation department, an appointment made on 10 March 1934.[23] Kaganovich, who had been head of the agriculture department in the Central Committee apparatus, gave the post to the newly appointed Central Committee secretary Andrei Zhdanov. All of this testifies to Kaganovich's remaining one of the most active party leaders. It is telling that once a degree of stability had been achieved in the area of agriculture, he was assigned to tackle another complex and traditionally weak sector—transportation.

The distribution of responsibilities among Central Committee secretaries determined by the Politburo on 4 June 1934 shows that the party leadership hierarchy had not changed. Stalin was assigned to oversee the Central Committee's culture and propaganda departments, the Special Sector (the former secret department, which provided clerical services to the Politburo and to Stalin personally), and the Politburo.[24] Kaganovich managed the operations of the Orgburo, the Central Committee's industrial and transportation departments, the Komsomol, and the Party Control Commission. Zhdanov controlled the Central Committee Secretariat, the departments that managed agriculture, finance, trade, and planning, the "political-administrative department" (which oversaw the procuracy, the Commissariat of Justice, and other such sections), as well as the department that handled party personnel matters.[25] The large number of responsibilities carried by Kaganovich forced him to ask the Politburo to relieve him as head of the transportation department. On 9 July 1934, the Politburo granted his request, although it did leave Kaganovich in charge of "oversight and general management of this department."[26]

After the 17th Party Congress, Leningrad Province party secretary and Politburo member Sergei Kirov was also formally appointed Central Committee secretary. Since Kirov remained in Leningrad, he did not actually perform the duties of Central Committee secretary, because of a conflict that arose between Kirov and Stalin. The essence of this conflict is described in the memoirs of Mikhail Rosliakov, who headed the Leningrad Province finance authorities in 1934 (Rosliakov quotes Kirov, as well as the chairman of the Leningrad Soviet, I. F. Kodatsky). Rosliakov reported:

> The [17th party] congress was concluded on 10 February, and on the same day there was a TsK plenum to constitute the party's governing bodies. As was usual, before any organizational questions were brought before the Plenum, they were preliminarily discussed in the Politburo. So it was on this occasion. Everything was going smoothly, with general agreement. When the subject of candidates for TsK secretary came up, Stalin proposed electing S. M. Kirov as one of the secretaries and relieving him of his work in Leningrad. Sergei Mironovich [Kirov] was adamantly opposed to this, his main objection being that he should be allowed to work another couple of years in Leningrad and finish out the Second Five-Year Plan with his Leningrad comrades; there were also references to his lack of preparation for working in the center and the state of his health. Stalin insisted on his proposal, arguing for the necessity of strengthening the Central Committee's operations apparatus, promoting those younger, considering his own—Stalin's—age (he was then fifty-four). Kirov was energetically supported by Sergo, who mostly based his arguments on the problems of heavy industry faced by Leningrad. Kuibyshev also supported Kirov's reasoning.
>
> Stalin, seeing that his proposal was not meeting with the usual full support, became angry and left the meeting "in a huff." The comrades, who understood perfectly well that the question had to be resolved one way or another, proposed that Kirov go to Stalin and look for an agreeable solution with him. Most likely nobody knows just what was said between Kirov and Stalin, but Kirov stood his ground and a compromise solution was found: Kirov would be elected Central Committee secretary, but would keep his position of Leningrad Province secretary. And A. A. Zhdanov from Gorky would be brought in for TsK work.[27]

According to Rosliakov, the unexpected transfer of Zhdanov to Moscow created a number of organizational problems. In particular,

E. K. Pramnek, who was appointed first secretary of the Gorky Province party committee in Zhdanov's place, had to be made a Central Committee candidate member ex post facto (this status was expected of the head of such a large organization). As Alla Kirilina has shown, archival materials confirm Rosliakov's assertions: Pramnek was not listed among the Central Committee candidate members present at the first plenary session of the newly constituted Central Committee on 10 February 1934.[28] Other analogous irregularities indirectly support Rosliakov's assertions concerning the unexpectedness of Zhdanov's appointment. Zhdanov, who was not even a candidate member of the Politburo, took part in all Politburo meetings because of his position and was included in Politburo polling. Furthermore, in September 1934, in Stalin's and Kaganovich's absence, Zhdanov essentially ran the Politburo—it was he who signed Politburo protocols. Letters regarding various issues that were being considered by the Politburo came addressed to Zhdanov.[29] Such violations of party rules could have been avoided if Kirov had actually carried out the duties of secretary or if advance preparations had been made before Zhdanov's appointment.

All of these details support the assertion that a conflict over Kirov's transfer to Moscow did take place. There was nothing unusual, however, in this clash. Stalin's motives in insisting on Kirov's appointment are obvious. After Postyshev's transfer to Ukraine, the Central Committee needed a new, energetic secretary to take on work in important areas. It is also possible that Stalin wanted to counterbalance Kaganovich's influence (something he did in 1935–1936), and for the same reason he wanted a Politburo member to be made Central Committee secretary. Kirov's objections are just as easy to understand. A move to Moscow meant disrupting the familiar rhythm of his life that had taken shape over the course of eight years and becoming embroiled in Moscow's convoluted squabbles and problems. Perhaps, too, Kirov did not like being made directly subordinate to Kaganovich, who stood a step above him in the leadership hierarchy. Moves within the top leadership in the late 1920s and early 1930s had also often been associated with conflicts and stormy disputes. In 1926, Kirov himself was extremely reluctant to move to Leningrad from Baku, where he held the post of secretary of the Azerbaijan Communist Party. A great brouhaha had also attended Ordzhonikidze's 1926 move from the Caucasus to Moscow to chair the Central Control Commission.[30] In general, the conflict between Stalin and Kirov was a typical bureaucratic confrontation and did not reflect a policy disagreement. In all likelihood, Kirov was bargaining for more time to tie up matters in Leningrad, and Stalin agreed to postpone his move to Moscow. As the log of visits to Stalin's office shows, however, Kirov was forced to spend much more time in Moscow in 1934 than he had in the past.[31]

The compromise over Kirov's appointment fits perfectly within the tradition of resolving such disagreements within the Politburo during the early 1930s. In this sense, it confirms that the status quo was being more or less preserved within the Politburo even in 1934. Records of visits by Politburo members to Stalin's office also indirectly support this notion.[32] In 1934, as in the preceding three years, Molotov and Kaganovich visited Stalin more often than the other members and stayed longer. In third place in this list of visitors, previously Postyshev, was Zhdanov, who replaced Postyshev as Central Committee secretary.

Several years earlier a different version of events appeared in the Russian press, one that alleged a weakening of Stalin's power on the eve of Kirov's murder and of growing opposition toward Stalin on the part of a number of Politburo members. The following story of a major scandal that was purported to have taken place in the Politburo in September 1934 is told in support of this version.

> The Politburo adopted a decision to undertake a major modernization of the army. It was kept strictly secret. Suddenly, soon after this, information was received that foreign intelligence, German intelligence in particular, already knew about the decision that had been made and was making concerted efforts to get information about how this modernization was being carried out. Mikhail Tukhachevsky, who was in charge of the army's modernization, ordered that the source of the leak of information about our secret measures be found. It turned out to be from . . . Stalin himself, who in semi-official discussions with representatives of Czechoslovakia boasted that the reorganization of the Red Army being conducted under his leadership not only would put the Soviet armed forces on a level with European armed forces, but would put it ahead of them. He also wanted to attribute the achievements of modernization to himself. When he found out about this, Tukhachevsky went to Kuibyshev. The latter called Ordzhonikidze. Hearing what Stalin had done, Ordzhonikidze just said, "The ass." He shared Kuibyshev's opinion that the matter of Stalin's tactless behavior should be placed before a closed session of the Politburo. Valerian Vladimirovich

[Kuibyshev] took it upon himself to gather all the facts with which Stalin should be reproached.

Tukhachevsky's conversation with Kuibyshev and Ordzhonikidze took place in the middle of September 1934. At the end of that month, at a closed session of the Politburo, Stalin was forced not only to listen to many unpleasant things but suddenly to sense that his position was somewhat tenuous. If Molotov and Abel Yenukidze had not abstained from voting and if the placable Kalinin had not made a conciliatory speech, Stalin might even have been issued a reprimand.[33]

As is often the case, the source of this story is difficult to trace. The commentator, N. A. Zen'kovich, vaguely cites the writer Vladimir Karpov. It is possible that Karpov relied on a conversation with Vladimir Valerianovich Kuibyshev (son of the Politburo member), who himself published this story in the pages of *Moskovskie novosti*.[34] The persistence of such legends is inevitable, for they provide simple answers to complex historical questions. If incidents like the one described above actually took place, then all the well-known events that occurred in late 1934 and early 1935 arrange themselves into a logical chain: attacks on Stalin by members of the Politburo were followed by the removal of the attackers (Kirov in December 1934, Kuibyshev in January 1935, Ordzhonikidze in February 1937). Perhaps, Zen'kovich writes, the Politburo incident of September 1934 "accelerated the course of subsequent events. After that session, Stalin, probably, decided that he should not subject himself to such danger in the future."

Those who published this story, which spread with great ease, did not think to question it, even though one does not have to dig deep to find aspects that deserve scrutiny. By some strange means, Yenukidze, who would not have been allowed anywhere near a closed session of the Politburo, makes an appearance in it. It also takes quite a stretch of the imagination to come up with exactly what Stalin might have told the "representatives of Czechoslovakia" about the modernization of the Red Army. Perhaps he showed them designs or told them the locations of defense manufacturers? The absence of such details is telling. If we untangle the logic of this myth, what we are left with is that Stalin was accused of boasting about the growth of the Soviet army's fighting power at a time when boasts of this sort could be read in any Soviet newspaper. Finally, the authors of the legend were not well informed, for they did not know the vacation schedule of Politburo members. If they had, they would have placed this uproar in some other time, because for the entire month of September (as well as August and October) Stalin was vacationing in the south and admonishing his comrades in stern letters.[35]

The real balance of power at the highest levels of the Soviet party and state had reached a tipping point: not only did Stalin have to justify himself before members of the Politburo, but members of the Politburo had to justify themselves before Stalin. Kuibyshev was no exception. During the same September 1934, Kuibyshev was assigned to oversee preparations for the launch of the USSR-2 high-altitude balloon. Between one and six in the morning on 5 September he watched over the inflation of the balloon with hydrogen gas. This process ended calamitously in a fire and the destruction of the balloon. Realizing that responsibility for this failure would one way or another be placed on his shoulders, Kuibyshev took all the bureaucratic measures necessary. The same day, on Kuibyshev's orders Tukhachevsky, the deputy defense commissar, prepared an explanatory note for submission to Stalin. In it, Tukhachevsky reported that the commission that had urgently been convened to investigate the accident was advancing the theory that the fire had been started by electrical discharge from the unfurling of the silk balloon, that a number of circumstances surrounding the accident remained unexplained, and that the commission would continue its investigation until 7 September.[36] Kuibyshev felt that it was necessary to send his own commentary along with Tukhachevsky's note to Stalin. He explained that he, together with Zhdanov, had been on site and had been convinced of the technical readiness for flight and that he had kept watch over the filling of the balloon all night. In anticipation of possible accusations of hastiness, Kuibyshev wrote that the launch, owing to meteorological conditions, could either have been made on 5 September or delayed for a year. Kuibyshev's conclusion was characteristic. "In Com. Tukhachevsky's report, sent to you by me via mail, there is an attempt (not on Tukhachevsky's part) to attribute the fire to an electric spark generated by the unfurling of the silk envelope. I doubt this and presume that sabotage was involved. The matter is being rigorously investigated."[37]

Kuibyshev's self-justification and show of severity (intended to demonstrate that he had the necessary decisiveness and sense of responsibility for his assignment), along with his use of the formal second-person pronoun in addressing Stalin, attest to Kuibyshev's real political influence. Just a year earlier, in September 1933, Stalin had written to Molotov, "It's obvious that it would be rash to leave the center's work to Kaganovich alone (Kuibyshev may start drinking)."[38]

Overall, evidence has yet to be found indicating that Stalin's position was at all tenuous or that the alignment of power within the Politburo changed at all in 1934. During this period anything resembling even a mild reproof to Stalin was not possible in the Politburo. As before, Stalin determined the government's most important political and economic actions and had the final word in all matters. That the Politburo was also still part of the political equation is a separate issue. The balance of power in 1931–1933 and in 1934 could be characterized the same way, albeit with a few qualifications. In particular, we can observe that after the 17th Party Congress the procedures governing the functioning of the Politburo as a collective body were simplified. The first meeting of the 17th Politburo took place on 20 February 1934. As with earlier meetings, in addition to Politburo members and candidate members, a large number of Central Committee members and candidate members were present, as were members of the offices of the Party and Soviet Control Commissions. In the future, such meetings would be conducted with decreasing frequency. In 1934 only sixteen regular Politburo sessions were convened; only one meeting was held in September, one in November, and none at all in October. The vast majority of issues brought before the Politburo were decided either by polling the Politburo members or by having unofficial meetings between Politburo members and Stalin. As can be seen in the log of visits to Stalin's office, virtually all members of the Politburo visited him much more frequently in 1934 than they had during the preceding few years.[39]

The original protocols of meetings provide an additional means for reconstructing how the Politburo functioned in 1934. They show, for example, that a large number of Politburo resolutions were written in the hand of Aleksandr Poskrebyshev, head of the Special Sector of the Central Committee. The text of a resolution would be followed by his notations on the voting—for example, "Com. Stal[in,] Mol[otov,] Kag[anovich]—in favor (A[.] P[oskrebyshev])" or "Com. Stal[in,] Mol[otov,], Kagan[ovich,] Vor[oshilov]—in favor." Further down on the same page the secretary would note the results of polling of other Politburo members: "Com. Kuibyshev—in favor, Com. Kalinin—in favor."[40] Such procedures for processing resolutions suggest that they were essentially discussed and adopted by the group of Politburo members whose surnames Poskrebyshev noted (most often Stalin, Kaganovich, and Molotov). Either Poskrebyshev himself was present at these meetings of the "small leadership group" and wrote down the adopted decisions, or he was instructed to draft the decisions immediately after such sessions.

A significant portion of decisions included in the original Politburo protocols for 1934 are recorded in Poskrebyshev's hand or the hand of his deputy, Boris Dvinsky, with no notation of voting by Politburo members. It is entirely possible that in a number of cases the signatures of Politburo members are on the documents that initiated the decision (draft resolutions, letters, reports), which are stored among Politburo materials in the Presidential Archive of the Russian Federation. On the other hand, there are often clerical notations on the original resolutions stating that there were no initiating documents. This means that a significant portion of Politburo resolutions were adopted without voting by Politburo members. Poskrebyshev or Dvinsky recorded the decisions dictated to them by one of the country's leaders (most likely Stalin), and the decisions were processed as Politburo decisions. On the original protocols from September 1934 many resolutions feature the notation "no polling conducted." Only Kaganovich signed them (Stalin was away on vacation at the time), and when both he and Stalin were unavailable, Zhdanov did.[41]

All of this suggests that the procedures followed by the Politburo became increasingly simplified as it was transformed from a collective body into an appendage of a decision-making system that rested on Stalin's sole authority. The procedures were not unique to 1934, but this period did feature a strengthening of tendencies seen in the previous stage of the Politburo's development.

The stable makeup of the Politburo and the preservation of the former distribution of political roles and procedures in the Politburo suggest that the thaw of 1934 did not stem from new political leaders moving to the fore but was the consequence of a consolidation of the moderate line, signs of which had occasionally cropped up in preceding years. Correspondingly, it can be assumed that the means by which reforms were initiated also remained the same. Some specific examples show how this process worked in 1934.

ORDZHONIKIDZE AND MOLOTOV: CORRECTING THE SECOND FIVE-YEAR PLAN

The history of how the Second Five-Year Plan (1933–1937) came to be adopted richly illustrates how decisions were made at the highest levels of power.[42] For some time, researchers have discerned a political subtext to the circumstances surrounding the adoption of a new, more moderate pace of industrial growth. The subjects of particular focus are Viacheslav Molotov and Grigory "Sergo" Ordzhonikidze, whose pronouncements at the congress are used to support the idea that it was divided between two opposing factions—the radicals (Molotov) and the moderates (Ordzhonikidze).[43]

As historians have noted, starting in mid-1932 the country's leadership, prompted by the growing economic crisis, cut back on capital expenditures.[44] These reductions set the stage for an intensification of the traditional clashes between the industrial commissars (Ordzhonikidze, Mikoyan, and others), on the one hand, and the leadership of the Council of People's Commissars (Molotov) and Gosplan (Kuibyshev), who were in charge of distributing resources, on the other. These clashes generally followed the same pattern: the commissariats tried to achieve the maximum capital investment and Gosplan, with support from the Council of People's Commissars leadership, tried to cut capital investment and demanded increases in output using existing manufacturing resources. This basic scenario was played out again as the Second Five-Year Plan was being negotiated.

The Gosplan targets for the new five-year plan were repeatedly lowered over the course of 1932, since the actual state of the Soviet economy did not justify any hope that accelerated industrialization could be sustained. In December 1932, Kuibyshev's apparatus prepared a draft resolution for the Central Committee plenum being convened to review the results of the First Five-Year Plan and set targets for 1933 and the Second Five-Year Plan. The initial draft resolution stated, in part, "The Central Committee plenum feels it is necessary to estimate annual growth in industrial output during the coming five-year plan at 12–16 percent instead of the 20 percent annual average of the First Five-Year Plan."[45] This draft was reviewed by a commission consisting of Stalin, Molotov, and Kuibyshev that had been created by a Politburo decision dated 28 December 1932.[46] Stalin made a significant revision to the document. He added a new subsection, entitled "From the First Five-Year Plan to the Second," in which he provided an ideological argument for a reduced rate of growth. The first draft of this new subsection contained the following specific figures: "a) average annual growth of industrial output for the Second Five-Year Plan must be set not at 21–22 percent, as during the First Five-Year Plan, but somewhat lower—approximately 14 percent." During subsequent work on the text, Stalin changed the figure to "approximately 13–14 percent."[47] These figures appeared in the resolution approved by the Central Committee plenum in January 1933.

Based on the resolution, in May 1933 a Gosplan commission headed by first deputy chairman Valery Mezhlauk proposed reducing the annual growth rate for industrial output to 13 percent and limiting increases in iron production (a foundational planning figure in the Stalinist economy) to a level that would bring output to 15 million metric tons by 1937.[48] The head of Gosplan tried to secure Stalin's support. On 28 May 1933, Kuibyshev and Mezhlauk sent Stalin a letter arguing for a 15-million-ton target for iron and corresponding targets for steel and rolled metal. They contended that trying to smelt 18 million tons of iron—which the People's Commissariat of Heavy Industry was pushing for—would demand additional capital expenditures and would set annual growth in heavy industry at 16 percent rather than the 14 percent that had been approved by the plenum. "In light of the fact that smelting 15.2 million tons of iron and 11.6 million tons of rolled metal will satisfy the demands of other sectors at the target rate of growth and that this projection involves quite a strain from the perspective of new equipment, especially as concerns steel and rolled metal, Gosplan asks to be permitted to conduct further work on the Five-Year Plan on the basis of the limit indicated," wrote Kuibyshev and Mezhlauk in conclusion.[49]

No response to this letter has been found, but it appears that this initiative by the heads of Gosplan was not approved. In June and July 1933 discussions in Gosplan were based on an 18-million-ton quota for iron.[50] This figure was included in directives presented to the 17th Party Congress six months later.

Gosplan, nonetheless, continued to insist on reductions in capital investment. In June it proposed reducing investment for 1933–1937 to 97 billion rubles, as compared with the 135 billion rubles being demanded by the commissariats.[51] These were the lowest figures that had ever been discussed. They meant that the annual level of investment for the five-year plan would be only slightly higher than it was for 1933. The origin of these levels is unknown. Most likely Gosplan intentionally reduced them in anticipation of the inevitable bargaining with the commissariats over the next five-year plan. Indeed, during the discussions with the heads of government agencies that soon followed, the Gosplan leadership acknowledged that capital investment levels were insufficient and promised to raise them. Kuibyshev, for example, agreed to expand the capital investment plan for the Timber Industry and Transport Commissariats.[52]

By the time the commissions that had been assigned to reconcile any differences with government agencies had completed their work, the level of capital investment had been raised to 120 billion rubles. This new figure was discussed at a meeting chaired by Kuibyshev on 19 July 1933. In summing up the discussion, Kuibyshev's deputy, G. I. Smirnov, stated that sufficient material resources were not available to support the 120-billion-ruble program and that the amount had to be reduced to at least 110 billion.[53] On 26 July at another meeting, again chaired by Kuibyshev, the "final" compromise figure of 112.75 billion rubles was set.[54]

By autumn 1933, Gosplan had arrived at spending levels for 1934 and the Second Five-Year Plan based both on the overall directives that had come out of the January plenum and on the demands of the industrial commissariats for increases in capital investment. Compromise figures resulted in spending that exceeded the 13–14 percent growth in industrial output (and corresponding capital investment) announced by the January plenum. Even such a stalwart opponent of institutional overreaching as Molotov accepted the compromise figures. On 6 September 1933 he wrote to Stalin, "Work is now in progress on 1934 at Gosplan and in the commissariats. [. . .] Cap[ital] works are set at 22 billion r., growth of ind[ustrial] production at 17%. I think it would be better to set some more cautious targets. For cap[ital] works I think it's better to stay under 21 billion r. following the 18 bln. r. we have for the current year (without additions, which are inevitable in any year). For ind[ustrial] production, limit growth to 15%. [. . .] Reasons: in 1932 we had + 8.5%, this year we will have less than 10%. Despite the good harvest of 1933, I don't think it makes sense to use targets higher than those mentioned above. Better to agree on this and decide in the TsK now."[55] The 15 percent growth in industrial production that, in Molotov's opinion, corresponded to 21 billion rubles of capital investment went counter to the directives of the January plenum, but evidently Molotov understood that it would not be possible to overcome resistance from the commissariats, and so he just tried to fix these new limits by means of Politburo decisions.

Events played out according to a different scenario. On 15 November the Politburo adopted a decision to convene a party congress in January 1934. The second item on the agenda was the Second Five-Year Plan, which Molotov and Kuibyshev were to report on.[56] Discussion of their reports was scheduled to take place in the Politburo on 20 December. Over the course of the discussions, the five-year plan spending limits were significantly increased. The plan for capital investment went up to 133 billion rubles as compared to the 113 billion approved by Gosplan in July. Correspondingly, the annual growth target for industrial production was now 18 percent as compared to the 13–14 percent approved by the Central Committee plenum in January 1933 and the 15 percent proposed by Molotov for 1934.[57]

The new projections appear to have been prepared at the Politburo level, possibly by Kuibyshev himself, but without the participation of Gosplan personnel. On 20 December, the day that the Politburo discussed the new proposals, one of Gosplan's top administrators, G. B. Lauer, sent an angry message to Kuibyshev and Mezhlauk. "I feel I must direct your attention," Lauer wrote, "to the fact that the way work on finalizing the Second Five-Year Plan has been organized within Gosplan is absolutely unsatisfactory and does not support sound planning. We were ordered *in one day* to check the tables for the Five-Year Plan and turn in our corrections. Somebody received additional information [. . .] concerning changes made by you to the initial plan. These changes, however, are so serious that they indirectly affect all sectors, and we cannot just correct the tables, but projections for each sector (each branch) have to be reconciled all over again with the overall economy. As far as I understand, the rate of growth for industrial production has been significantly changed (18 instead of 14%), the relationship between A and B has changed, capital investment has been significantly increased for the final year (34 bil. r. instead of 26 bil. r.). Machine construction has gone up sharply. This means a different balance of building materials, a different balance for metals, different demands for fuel and electricity."[58]

The new limits, which exceeded what had been decided on in 1933, undoubtedly reflected a compromise between the managers of the industrial commissariats, on the one hand, and the Council of People's Commissars and Gosplan, on the other. The former had been given higher rates of capital investment, and in exchange the latter demanded faster growth in industrial output, since "the more you get, the more you should give." But neither side changed their feelings about the situation, and the conflict between them—which had been suppressed but not resolved—erupted again at the 17th Party Congress.

On 3 February 1934, Molotov and Kuibyshev presented a new version of the plan to the congress—an average industrial growth rate of 19 percent and investment over five years of 133.4 billion rubles. The next day, on 4 February, a situation arose during the morning session of the congress that had come up in the past when five-year plans were being considered (both at the 16th conference in April 1929 and at the 17th conference in February 1932). Delegates began demanding increases in construction programs for their own regions. That evening, Ordzhonikidze appeared before the congress. He criticized those who demanded that the plan be reexamined, stating, "If we now start down such a path, including everything that our provinces and republics demand in the Second Five-Year Plan, then we will wind up not with a Five-Year Plan but something else. [Interjection from the audience: "A Ten-Year Plan."] Yes, we would wind up with a Ten-Year Plan. We, comrades, want to have the sort of Five-Year Plan that—through a great expenditure of effort and resources—can be accomplished by our country." He then took the delegates by surprise, offering a "compromise plan," reducing the overall annual industrial growth rate from 18.9 to 16.5 percent. Furthermore (and this deserves particular attention), Ordzhonikidze emphasized that plans for capital investment for the five-year period remained the same. He also stated that all of these corrections had been agreed to by other members of the Politburo.[59] Soon after Ordzhonikidze's remarks, Mikoyan, commissar of the food industry, followed by Isidor Liubimov, commissar of light industry, took the podium with proposals for reducing rates of development in their sectors.

In summing up discussions of the Second Five-Year Plan, Molotov labeled the decision to adopt a reduced growth rate an expression of "Bolshevik caution, which demands taking serious account of all the circumstances we live under."[60] But he also implied that the industrial growth rate could and should increase, despite approval of the five-year figures. "In our annual plans for the Second Five-Year Plan we must ensure not just the fulfillment but the overfulfillment of the targets for the Second Five-Year Plan. This also goes for the current year of the Second Five-Year Plan. In supporting the proposal for 16.5 percent annual growth in industrial production for the Second Five-Year Plan, we must fully achieve—not falling short by a single percent, not by a tenth of a percent—the objective set by the party and the government for 1934, the second year of the Five-Year Plan. And this objective, as is well known, was set at 19 percent. This means that for 1934 we are already taking on a higher target in respect to the average growth rates of the Five-Year Plan."[61]

Documents have yet to be found explaining just how the "Ordzhonikidze correction" came about. But those facts that are available do not support a view of the decision to lower growth rates as the result of a struggle between two political groups or a political confrontation between Molotov and Ordzhonikidze. The evidence introduced above about how the Second Five-Year Plan came about suggests that what took place during the congress should probably be viewed as a continuation of the struggle between different branches of government over ratios between production and capital investment. The administrators of government agencies, who, in exchange for increased funding, had been forced on the eve of the congress to agree to industrial growth rates that were disadvantageous to them, were able to exploit some as-yet-unknown circumstances during the congress itself to have this decision reconsidered. In essence, the industrial managers achieved a victory over Gosplan and the Council of People's Commissars at the congress. They preserved high rates of capital investment but were given the right to produce much less. In this context, Molotov's speech was an attempt to at least argue for the position of Gosplan and the council. Forced to agree to the concessions granted industrial managers (based on the political notion of "Bolshevik caution"), he warned them that if the situation developed favorably (even in 1934), they would have to pay for the capital investments with a much better growth rate than the 16.5 percent that they had managed to negotiate during the congress.

It is hard to say which was more detrimental to movement toward a more moderate economic policy—attempts to increase rates of industrial production with high rates of capital investment, favored by the Council of People's Commissars and Gosplan (and Molotov personally), or the successful endeavor of the industrial agencies (Ordzhonikidze in particular) to reduce rates of production while maintaining huge capital expenditures. In any event, it is difficult to label these competing institutional positions as either moderate or radical, or to assign them any particular political coloration.

STALIN AND KIROV

In any discussion of the forces behind a move toward more moderate policies, the name of Sergei Kirov is usually among the first to be mentioned. The mysterious circumstances of Kirov's murder and the abrupt hardening of the political line that followed led some to conclude that Kirov would have been able to advance and sustain a moderate political program and that he could have unified the forces opposed to Stalin.[62] Historians skeptical of this view feel that Kirov was a loyal follower of Stalin and remained so to the end, that within the party his political stature never came close to Stalin's, and that his views on policy were fully harmonious with Stalin's. Francesco Benvenuti, for example, after studying all of Kirov's published speeches and the official Soviet press, reached the conclusion that the only moderate course Kirov was in favor of was the one already in evidence in 1934. In fact, all of the Soviet leaders supported the "new" policies.[63] Some time later, J. Arch Getty also concluded that Kirov was not a moderate who opposed Stalin's hard line.[64]

What evidence is currently available to assist historians in resolving these questions? Sources that sustain the notion that Kirov had his own, relatively independent political platform include the memoirs of Nikita Khrushchev, the testimony of certain members of the commission created after the 20th Party Congress to study the circumstances of Kirov's death, and the memoirs of several participants in the 17th Party Congress. All of this evidence has been reproduced in the historical literature and widely disseminated.[65] Once we navigate past the numerous contradictions between these accounts, we arrive at the following scenario. At the 17th Party Congress a number of high-ranking party officials (the various names mentioned include Kosior, Robert Eikhe, Boris She-boldaev, Ordzhonikidze, and Petrovsky) discussed the possibility of re-placing Stalin with Kirov as party general secretary. Kirov rejected the proposal, but Stalin learned of the plans (some write that Kirov himself told Stalin and in so doing sealed his own fate). During Central Com-mittee elections at the congress, many delegates voted against Stalin (fig-ures cited range from 270 to 300 out of 1,225). After learning of this, Stalin ordered that the ballots on which his name had been crossed out be removed and that it be announced in the congress that only three votes had been cast against him. While historians who develop the idea of Kirov as an "oppositionist" are inclined to trust this evidence, histo-rians who deny that Kirov acted as an independent political force and who deny that Stalin was involved in his murder denounce such eyewit-ness testimony as sheer invention.[66] Overall, however, it should be rec-ognized that theories concerning a double conspiracy (delegates to the congress against Stalin and Stalin against Kirov) appear less convincing in light of recently uncovered archival materials.[67]

The entire course of Kirov's career within the party tends to counter rather than support the idea that he might have taken an independent political position. Kirov, like the other members of the Politburo in the 1930s, was Stalin's man. It was on Stalin's insistence that Kirov took over leadership of the country's second most important party organiza-tion, ensuring that he would enter the highest echelons of power. In ad-dition to the good personal relations that existed between Kirov and Stalin, Kirov's being politically compromised may well have been a fac-tor in Stalin's attitude toward him. Party members knew that before the revolution Kirov not only failed to join the Bolsheviks but held non-Bol-shevik, liberal political positions; as a journalist, he left evidence of his "crimes" in the form of newspaper articles. During the spring of 1917, for example, he showed himself to be an ardent champion of the Provi-sional Government and encouraged support for it.[68]

Armed with these facts, in late 1929 a group of Leningrad func-tionaries (including the leadership of the Leningrad Soviet and the provincial Party Control Commission) demanded of Moscow that Kirov be removed from his post for pre-revolutionary collaboration with the "leftist-bourgeois" press. The matter was considered at a closed joint session of the Politburo and the Central Control Commission presidium. Largely thanks to Stalin's support, Kirov emerged from this confrontation a victor. His opponents were fired from their posts in Leningrad. Nevertheless, in the decision of the joint session (which was given a special-folder classification), Kirov's pre-revolutionary activities were characterized as an "error."[69] This amounted to a mine that was underfoot for the rest of Kirov's political career. Whether or not it would ever go off depended on Stalin.

Within the party everyone was well aware of Kirov's dependence on Stalin. Several years after the joint session that ruled in Kirov's favor, Kirov was, in the famous "Riutin platform," lumped with former opponents of the Bolsheviks who, because of their complete lack of political principles, served Stalin especially loyally. "Our opportunists were also able to adapt themselves to the Stalin regime and camouflage themselves [. . .] Grinko [the finance commissar] and N. N. Popov [one of the editors of *Pravda*] are both former Mensheviks who were so well known in Ukraine; Mezhlauk—the dep. chairman of VSNKh—is a former Kadet [Constitutional Democrat] and was later a Menshevik; Serebrovsky—dep. to the heavy industry commissar, is a former loyal servant of capitalists; Kirov, a member of the Politburo, is a former Kadet and editor of the Kadet newspaper in Vladikavkaz. All of these, you could say, are the pillars of the Stalinist regime. They are all the ultimate opportunists. These people adapt themselves to any regime, to any political system."[70] A few dozen pages later, the authors of the platform continued their invective against Kirov. Pointing to the impunity of Stalin's "loyal bureaucrats and servants," they wrote, "Everyone knows how the attempt by Leningraders to expose Kirov as a former Kadet and editor of the Kadet newspaper in Vladikavkaz turned out. They got a punch in the mouth and were told to shut up. Stalin [. . .] definitely protects his own scoundrels."[71]

These accusations against Kirov and other "opportunists" had more than a grain of truth. Stalin really did prefer to rely on people who had black marks in their political biographies—examples are the former Menshevik Andrei Vyshinsky and Lavrenty Beria, who was accused of collaborating with Musavat (Azerbaijan Muslim party) intelligence in the early 1920s. And from time to time Stalin did indeed remind his comrades-in-arms of their sins, especially during intense political struggles.

It is difficult to say what effect his past "opportunism" had on Kirov, but documentary evidence suggests that he conducted himself less like a full member of the Politburo and more like an influential administrator of one of the country's major party organizations. Kirov's initiatives were limited to those that served the needs of Leningrad (requests for new capital investment and resources, attempts to transfer Leningrad personnel to Moscow, petitions concerning the opening of new stores). Kirov's appearances in Moscow for Politburo meetings were extremely rare. He also rarely participated in votes on Politburo decisions conducted through polling (primarily, it appears, because of the logistical difficulties of doing so from Leningrad). Overall, the documents that have so far become available make it impossible to paint Kirov as the leader of an anti-Stalin wing of the party or as a reformer, or even as a player of any significance in the development and implementation of high-level policy. Khrushchev, one of those largely responsible for the aura of mystery surrounding Kirov, wrote in his memoirs, "In general, Kirov was not a very talkative person. I, personally, did not have direct interaction with him, but later I asked Mikoyan about Kirov. [. . .] Mikoyan knew him well. He told me, 'Well, what can I say? During meetings not once did he speak out about some issue. He sat there, and that was it. I don't even know what that means.'"[72]

Available information about the development and implementation of reforms also tends to support the view of Francesco Benvenuti that the country's leadership during the thaw of 1934 acted as a united front. As during the preceding period, the main initiator of any changes was Stalin.

An example is the elimination of ration cards for bread, which resulted from a decision by the November 1934 Central Committee plenum. This event, rightly considered one of the most important signs of liberalization, was the first step in phasing out the ration system and subsequently reorienting economic policy from being primarily based on repressive administrative measures to being more open and allowing the economy to be regulated by a mix of administrative and quasi-market forces. Some adherents of the idea of Kirov as a reformer attribute the November decision on ration cards to him. The source of this supposition can be found in a well-known book by Aleksandr Orlov. According to Orlov, during the spring and summer of 1934 Kirov began coming into conflict with Stalin and other members of the Politburo.

One of these conflicts is purported to have occurred in connection with supplying food to Leningrad. Without permission from Moscow, Kirov allegedly used reserve supplies from the Leningrad military command. Voroshilov expressed his displeasure at this during a Politburo meeting. In response, Kirov stated that these actions had been necessitated by extreme need and that the food supplies would be returned to the warehouses as soon as new deliveries arrived. Sensing that he had Stalin's support, Voroshilov asserted that Kirov was seeking "cheap popularity among the workers." Enraged, Kirov answered that the workers had to be fed. Mikoyan countered that Leningrad workers ate better than the rest of the country. "And why exactly should Leningrad workers eat any better than all the others?" Stalin broke in. Kirov again lost his temper and cried out, "I think the time is long overdue for us to abolish the ration system and start feeding our workers as they should be fed!"[73]

No documents have been found to support Orlov's account. However, conflicts between the Moscow and the Leningrad leadership (as well as the leadership of other regions) concerning the distribution of resources and the use of government reserves were frequent and began long before 1934. The friction markedly intensified during the famine of 1932–1933. The Politburo protocols for this period are replete with decisions related to petitions from throughout the country, including from Leningrad, about increasing centralized supply allocations and reducing procurement quotas. There were also many such conflicts in 1934. On 5 January 1934 the Politburo was polled on a decision concerning grain consumption in Leningrad that exceeded the approved allocation by five thousand metric tons in the third and fourth quarters of 1933. In accordance with a proposal by Mikhail Chernov, the agriculture commissar, the Politburo wrote off this debt, but it demanded that the Leningrad provincial committee and the provincial executive committee not allow excess consumption in the future.[74] The same day, Stalin demanded that the Politburo prohibit the opening of a department store in Leningrad for the sale of high-quality manufactured products. This request by Kirov (he had sent a special telephone message to Moscow) was supported both by Mikoyan, commissar of supply, and Molotov, chairman of the Council of People's Commissars. Stalin, nevertheless, dictated a negative decision. "I am against it. It should be opened only when we have a guarantee that there are enough goods for no less than six months." Stalin's demand was adopted by the Politburo.[75]

The Council of People's Commissars archives contain records of yet another conflict between Leningrad and the central authorities over the unauthorized use of food supplies by the Leningrad leadership. The matter concerned several hundred tons of meat and canned goods (valued at 653,000 rubles at government prices) that Leningrad had received from the USSR Supply Commissariat and sold at higher prices (for 1,143,000 rubles), using the difference to develop local pork sovkhozes. What must have happened was actually nothing out of the ordinary. Leningrad had probably asked for money from the Supply Commissariat for the development of local pork-producing sovkhozes, but Moscow had not provided the money, since getting additional capital funds was a complex and lengthy process. Instead, the Supply Commissariat had provided additional food supplies for sale. Such a transaction was simpler and faster than the allocation of financial resources. It was illegal but not at all unusual. Local administrators and enterprise directors regularly circumvented existing rules and laws to get the funds, raw materials, and supplies they needed. In the 1930s so-called barter transactions were widely used; enterprises might exchange their output independent of the established centralized reserves. Despite strict instructions from the government, such violations became commonplace, since the economy simply would not have been able to function without them. From time to time, certain violators were brought to justice. And the time came for the Leningrad leaders to have their turn as victims of the campaign to "establish order."

On 3 March 1934, Molotov sent I. F. Kodatsky, the chairman of the Leningrad Soviet and one of Kirov's closest associates, a telegram demanding that the Lensoviet presidium's resolution authorizing a special account for funds generated by the resale of food supplies be rescinded and that the guilty be punished.[76] The next day Kodatsky sent a telegram saying that the decision had been rescinded and asking Molotov for permission to report on the matter not in writing but in a face-to-face meeting in Moscow on 7 March. This request, which raised suspicion that Kodatsky did not want to punish his subordinates, left Molotov indignant. He sent a new telegram to Kodatsky, which was written in his own hand and read, "Any personal thoughts you offer would be insufficient. To avoid delay and eliminate confusion in the matter of the illegal establishment of a food reserve by the Lensoviet, I propose that a written explanation and report on punitive measures against the guilty be sent immediately."[77] Kodatsky ignored Molotov's order (we can presume that he consulted with Kirov before taking such a daring step). A month and a half passed before a furious Molotov sent a new telegram, on 20 April. "I feel it is absolutely intolerable for you to ignore the demand of the Sovnarkom dated 5 March to submit a written explanation of the establishment of an illegal Lensoviet food reserve. I am placing this matter before the Sovnarkom for 21 April. Your presence before the Sovnarkom is mandatory."[78]

On 21 April the matter was brought before a meeting of the Council of People's Commissars with Kodatsky in attendance. Despite the outrageous nature of the violation and the blatant insubordination of the Leningrad authorities to the government, the council issued a lenient decision. The Leningrad Soviet presidium was advised to punish the workers involved in creating the reserve. Kodatsky was shown his error in ignoring instructions from the council to submit a written explanation and punish the guilty. The deputy supply commissar, M. Belenky, who had allowed the soviet to create the reserve, was rebuked. The council also asked the Soviet Control Commission to look into whether there were any excess food supplies (above those provided for by the government plan) and, if so, what they were being used for in Leningrad and other cities—which seems to indicate that what the Leningrad leadership did was fairly common.[79] A week later, on 28 April, the Leningrad Soviet presidium adopted an exceptionally mild decision: to reprimand those responsible for establishing the reserve.[80]

Friction between local officials in Leningrad and central government officials in Moscow was rather typical, at least in the first half of the 1930s. Local governments were constantly demanding that the center give them new capital to invest and additional food and industrial appropriations—more resources of all sorts. At the same time, they had a lenient attitude toward violations and tried to protect their people when they were caught breaking the rules. Kirov and his subordinates behaved just like other local authorities. Conflict between local governments and the center over centralized distribution had nothing to do with the policy views of those involved. Moscow was not acting as a principled adherent of the rationing system and local governments were not demanding abolition of the system. Furthermore, those facts we now have at our disposal suggest that abolition of the rationing system was carried out on the initiative of the central authorities, primarily on Stalin's initiative.

In the early 1930s the top party leadership proclaimed the rationing system to be a necessary temporary measure. The slogans acclaiming a rapid transition to socialist commodity exchange and the abolition of commerce were condemned as "leftist." "Rationing is not a socialist ideal. [. . .] It would be good to get rid of it as soon as possible, as soon as we have sufficient goods," Mikoyan stated before a Central Committee plenum in October 1931, when he was supply commissar.[81] At the 17th Party Congress, Stalin placed special emphasis on problems of commerce, reiterating his condemnation of "leftist garbage": "Soviet commerce is a stage we have passed through" and "we have to work on direct commodity exchange."[82] On 22 October 1934, while vacationing in the south, Stalin wrote Kaganovich, "We must have in the state's hands 1.4 billion to 1.5 billion poods [22.9 million to 24.6 million tons] of grain in order to get rid of the *rationing system* for bread at the end of this year, a system that until recently was necessary and useful but has now shackled the national economy. We must get rid of the rationing system for bread (perhaps for *groats and macaroni* as well) and the related "bartering" of industrial crops and some animal-husbandry products (wool, leather, etc.). [. . .] This reform, which I consider an *extremely serious* reform, should be prepared right away, so that it can begin to be implemented in full in January 1935."[83] It was after this mandate by Stalin that preparations were launched to abolish ration cards. Available evidence indicates furthermore that this reform was determined less by political will than by the economic situation—in particular, serious fiscal difficulties.[84]

When abolishing the ration system was being discussed at the November 1934 plenum, Stalin again emphasized the importance of commerce and money as levers of economic policy. After listening to plenum speakers who were primarily concerned with the technical and logistical aspects of the matter, Stalin made the following comments (this speech was not published). "I have taken the floor in order to explain certain questions as I understand them because the speakers evidently do not quite represent, have not quite understood, why this reform is being introduced and its significance. Why are we abolishing the rationing system? First and foremost, it is because we want to strengthen the cash economy. [. . .] The cash economy is one of the few bourgeois economic apparatuses that we, socialists, must make full use of. [. . .] It is very flexible; we need it. [. . .] To expand commercial exchange, to expand Soviet commerce, to strengthen the cash economy—these are the main reasons we are undertaking this reform. [. . .] Money will start to circulate; money will come into fashion, which hasn't been the case for some time; the cash economy will strengthen. The value of the ruble will become more stable, undoubtedly, and strengthening the ruble means strengthening all of our planning and financial accountability [*khozraschet*]."[85]

Records of the November 1934 plenum do not support the assertion by Boris Nikolaevsky that this plenum was the "height of Kirov's success" and that "Kirov was the main speaker and hero of the day."[86] If there were any "heroes of the day" at this plenum, Stalin, Molotov, and Kaganovich would better fit the bill. They gave speeches on the most pressing questions and were particularly active. Kirov did not go beyond ideas that Stalin had presented. On 1 December 1934, the day of his death, Kirov was supposed to have given a speech at a meeting of the party's most active members summarizing the November plenum. The notes that Kirov prepared for the speech, which are preserved among his papers, indicate that Kirov was preparing merely to reiterate the most important points made by Stalin. "Industry is not a bad thing. Agriculture. Bring them together through commercial exchange. Direct commodity exchange—it's too early. Commercial exchange is not used, but at the same time [. . .] without commercial exchange [. . .]. Strengthening financial accountability [. . .]. The role of money [. . .]. New impetus forward."[87]

Available evidence points to Stalin's also playing the leading role in the reorganization of the OGPU and the relaxation of repressive measures, a question that should be addressed separately.

THE POLITBURO VERSUS THE NKVD

Stalin introduced a proposal to create the NKVD at the first meeting of the newly constituted Politburo, on 20 February 1934. Its creation had not been included on the agenda. Stalin introduced the idea personally at the meeting. The decision that was adopted resolved, in part, "to recognize the necessity of organizing a Union Commissariat of Internal Affairs [and] incorporating into it a reorganized OGPU."[88] Two weeks later the Politburo polled members on a decision to prepare a draft statute on the NKVD and an NKVD special board. A commission chaired by Kaganovich was to be created for that purpose. Records indicate that the commission was also proposed on Stalin's initiative. The original Politburo decision is a text written in pencil on a Central Committee form by the head of the Special Sector, Aleksandr Poskrebyshev. Immediately below the text of the decision, Poskrebyshev made the notation "Coms. Stal[in,] Kag[anovich,] Mol[otov]—in favor (A[.] P[oskrebyshev])." Further down it was noted that Voroshilov, Andreev, Kuibyshev, Mikoyan, Kalinin, and Ordzhonikidze were in favor of the decision (they were probably polled by telephone).[89] The manner in which the information was recorded suggests that the decision concerning the NKVD statute and the special board was adopted during a meeting between Stalin, Molotov, and Kaganovich. Undoubtedly Kaganovich, who was named chairman of the newly created commission, received thorough instructions on the main points to be included in the NKVD statute.

We can only guess what was said at such meetings regarding the reorganization of the secret police and changes to the policies that governed their operations, but there is sufficient consistency in the various assertions made by Politburo members and other highly placed officials within a variety of contexts to provide an idea of the general form such discussions must have taken. For example, on 9 July 1934 Voroshilov sent Stalin a draft Politburo decision to free A. Verkhovsky, a high-ranking military expert who had been arrested as a "military conspirator." In an accompanying letter, Voroshilov commented on Verkhovsky's petition to be released: "Although we presume that while he was in the ranks of the Red Army, A. Verkhovsky was not an active counterrevolutionary, he was never, however, our friend and is unlikely to become such. This is clear. Nevertheless, keeping in mind that *the situation has now changed significantly,* I feel that he can be released without particular risk and used for specialized scientific research." The Politburo approved Voroshilov's proposal.[90]

Kaganovich also spoke about the new circumstances as a factor in changing punitive policy. At a conference of Moscow Province's prosecutorial personnel on 21 September 1934, he explained that at this new stage, now that the kulaks have been defeated, it was essential "to bring our measures, repressions, the struggle with enemies, into legal frameworks [. . .] to educate our population in the framework of socialist awareness of the law, which is critically important. [. . .] The consolidation of our order—both the kolkhoz system and the entire Soviet order—it demands the education of our entire people of 160 million in the spirit of legal awareness. [. . .] It is necessary to train the population in order to make judgments in accordance with the law."[91] More specific guidance was offered in a speech by Genrikh Yagoda at a conference of operatives of the central NKVD apparatus.[92] He stated that the organization of the NKVD and the incorporation of the OGPU into it represented an organizational consolidation in accordance with the policy of "strengthening of socialist legality," which was outlined in instructions dated 8 May 1933. Like Kaganovich, he spoke of the need for "increased socialist awareness of the law among the toiling masses." Warning that the fight against enemies must not flag, Yagoda explained to his subordinates that under the new circumstances the main task of the NKVD was to uncover a relatively small number of underground "espionage and sabotage organizations." For this reason, instead of mass arrests, chekists should conduct "subtle, painstaking, and probing investigative work." Yagoda reminded his audience that with the liquidation of the OGPU judicial collegium, the option no longer existed to deal with cases outside the judicial system, and therefore investigations had to be conducted more carefully, with observance of procedural rules and without falsification. We can guess at what Yagoda was saying based on the testimony given in 1937 by G. A. Molchanov, former head of the secret political department of the NKVD, when he was under arrest. In 1934, according to Molchanov, "Yagoda repeatedly pointed out to me the necessity of following a more liberal course in our punitive policy. For instance, I remember a conversation that we had during the summer of 1934 at the Dynamo waterworks. During this conversation Yagoda came right out and said to me that it was perhaps time to stop shooting people."[93]

The concomitant ideas about strengthening "socialist legality" and the role of the courts, on the one hand, and raising awareness of the law among the masses and establishing new methods of operation for the NKVD, on the other, all of which could be heard in speeches by the Soviet leaders and read in the press, reflected official explanations of the new course. Besides foreign policy concerns (that is, the desire to create a favorable image of the country abroad), there were serious internal, systemic reasons to proclaim these changes. As historians of Soviet law have already noted, the periodic shifts in the balance between justice and terror and in the more or less active use of legal controls was essential for the survival of the regime.[94] The expansion of mass repression had undermined the system itself and had affected both the economy and social stability. Extensive evidence indicates that the party leadership in 1934 had indeed decided to somewhat reduce the level of repression, to reject the extremes of state terror, and to strengthen the role of legal mechanisms. The scale of this change of policy should not be exaggerated. At its core, the regime remained repressive and brutal.[95]

The practical effect of the new course was seen in a series of Politburo decisions related to the activities of the OGPU-NKVD. On 3 April 1934, USSR procurator Ivan Akulov sent Stalin a petition from A. I. Seliavkin, a former director of the Antiaircraft Defense Administration of the Heavy Industry Commissariat and a three-time recipient of the Order of the Red Banner who had been given a ten-year sentence by the OGPU collegium for allegedly selling secret military documents. Seliavkin wrote from a prison camp that under threat of being shot he had copied down false testimony dictated to him by the investigators.[96] An inquiry showed that the chekists had indeed falsified the indictment. This case was selected as representative. On 5 June 1934 the Politburo adopted two resolutions related to it. The first resolution overturned the verdicts brought against Seliavkin and the others convicted in the case. The second resolution advised the "entire top OGPU leadership" to take note of the "serious deficiencies in how investigators conducted OGPU investigations," and the procuracy was admonished not to ignore complaints submitted by the accused in the Seliavkin case.[97]

The shakeup that surrounded the Seliavkin case and the active involvement of the leadership of the procuracy in initiating it reflected a correction of Stalin's policy toward the NKVD. Further evidence for this is seen in how the Politburo dealt with the question of courts at NKVD camps. On 9 August 1934, Yagoda, the internal affairs commissar, after working with the leadership of the USSR Procuracy and the RSFSR Commissariat of Justice on the question, sent telegrams to local offices concerning the creation of territorial or provincial courts to try cases arising out of crimes committed in the camps.[98] The main points of the telegram contradicted the Politburo resolutions of 10 July on the reorganization of the judicial system. The NKVD proposals on procedures for approving death sentences were particularly provocative. While the rules for judicial procedure approved by the Politburo in July provided an opportunity to appeal a death sentence and a complicated system for confirming such sentences (including a Politburo commission on legal matters), Yagoda's telegram prohibited such appeals and required that death sentences be approved only by provincial (or territorial) procurators and judges.

On 4 September, USSR deputy procurator Andrei Vyshinsky submitted a request to Central Committee secretary Zhdanov to consider whether the 9 August circular should be reversed. He was supported by top officials at the RSFSR Justice Commissariat.[99] When the matter had still not been resolved after some time, Vyshinsky showed his persistence by contacting the Central Committee again, this time addressing his request to Kaganovich.[100] Kaganovich assigned Zhdanov to deal with the matter. On 7 October, Yagoda sent his objections to Vyshinsky's request to the Central Committee. He argued that most camps were very remote and in some cases were not easily able to contact the regional centers, much less Moscow, and that the red tape involved in trying the cases would have "the most deleterious effect on the maintenance of the necessary strict discipline in the camps."[101]

Despite Yagoda's objections, on 17 October the Politburo overturned the 9 August circular and assigned Yagoda, Nikolai Krylenko (RSFSR justice commissar), and Vyshinsky to prepare a new proposal on the matter.[102] The Politburo resolution that was confirmed on 9 November on the establishment of territorial (or provincial) courts at the corrective labor camps was in a certain sense a compromise. The Politburo agreed with Yagoda's proposal to create courts at the camps and established simplified procedures for trials there (they could be conducted quickly and without the participation of the plaintiff and the accused), but it upheld the overall procedure for confirming death sentences.[103]

The conflict over the camp courts, on its own, might have been attributed little significance if other actions by the country's top leadership had not accompanied it. In September 1934, Stalin ordered the formation of a Politburo commission to investigate chekist activities. This move was prompted by complaints submitted to the Central Committee concerning old cases of "sabotage" within the Agriculture and Sovkhoz Commissariats and in connection with a network of "spies and wreckers" supposedly working for Japan. These cases had been fabricated by the OGPU in early 1933. Approximately one hundred agriculture specialists had been arrested as part of an agricultural sabotage case involving, among others, F. M. Konar and A. M. Markevich, deputy agriculture commissars, and M. M. Volf, deputy sovkhoz commissar. During the trial, fourteen of the accused recanted the confessions they had made under interrogation. This did not affect the verdict. Forty people were sentenced to be shot, and the others were given prison sentences of varying lengths.[104] In March 1933 twenty-one out of the twenty-three accused of spying for Japan were sentenced by the OGPU collegium to be shot.[105]

Some time later, A. M. Markevich sent a petition from the camp where he was being held to Stalin, Molotov, and USSR procurator Akulov. He complained about the "incorrect methods for conducting OGPU investigations." "Yagoda harshly cut me short, [saying,] 'Don't forget that you're being interrogated. You're not deputy commissar here. Do you think that we'll be asking your forgiveness in a month and that we'll say we made a mistake? Since the TsK agreed to your arrest, it means that we gave them exhaustive and convincing evidence of your guilt.' The investigators in my case were interested only in confessions of guilt and brushed aside all the objective evidence of my innocence." At the same time, A. G. Revis, one of the two suspects in the Japan case who had not been shot, sent a petition to M. I. Ulyanova, head of the complaint office of the Soviet Control Commission. He also told of illegal investigative methods and stated that his testimony was shaped by pressure from the investigators and by the persuasion of a provocateur who had been placed in his cell.

Akulov sent Stalin Markevich's petition and Ulyanova sent him Revis's on the same day, 1 September.[106] Ten days later Stalin sent the following directive to Kuibyshev and Zhdanov:

> I bring the attached documents to your attention, especially Revis's note. It is possible that the content of both documents reflects reality. I advise:
> a) Assign a commission consisting of Kaganovich, Kuibyshev, and Akulov to verify the contents of the documents.
> b) Get to the bottom of the deficiencies of the "investigative techniques" used by the former OGPU.

c) Free the innocent victims, if there turn out to be any.

d) Purge the OGPU of perpetrators of the specific "investigative techniques," and punish them, "whoever they might be."
I think this is a serious matter and should be dealt with thoroughly.[107]

Four days later, on 15 September, the Politburo adopted a special-folder resolution on the "case of A. R. and A. M." As Stalin had suggested, a commission made up of Kaganovich, Kuibyshev, and Akulov (and chaired by Kuibyshev, who was the current chairman of the Soviet Control Commission) was assigned to look into the Revis and Markevich petitions and "present to the TsK all resulting conclusions and proposals."[108] On 4 October, Zhdanov, whose duties as Central Committee secretary included overseeing the Central Committee political-administrative office, was added to the commission.[109]

The commission did a thorough job. In addition to the Revis and Markevich cases, other instances of a similar nature were identified (in particular, the evidence from the Seliavkin case, which the Politburo had dealt with several months previously, was again brought up).[110] Other materials appear to have come from the procuracy. For example, the archive of the Kuibyshev Secretariat holds a copy of a report from the Saratov territorial procuracy dated 31 August 1934 that was forwarded to Kuibyshev and Zhdanov by Vyshinsky. In the report, the Saratov procurator wrote about illegal investigative methods used by the Lysogorsky district branch of the NKVD. An inquiry, the procurator reported, showed that, in order to extract the testimony they wanted, members of the NKVD had confined prisoners to cold cells and then kept them several days on a brick oven; deprived them of bread for six or seven days; threatened that they would be shot; forced suspects to stretch out their arms and bend them behind their heads and then gagged them during interrogations so they could not breathe; and kept large numbers of prisoners in the same cell, among other measures. Three of the Lysogorsky chekists found guilty had been arrested.[111]

Within the context of the Kuibyshev commission, a letter sent to the Politburo on 25 October 1934 by Akulov takes on significance. He reported that an inspection conducted by the procuracy had uncovered violations of the law by top officials of the Azerbaijani NKVD. In their desire to generate fanfare and demonstrate their achievements to Moscow, the Azerbaijani chekists fabricated a case of large-scale theft within cooperatives, using their agents as provocateurs and extracting testimony through "beatings and other illegal means." Akulov informed the party leadership that he had already ordered the arrest of several NKVD-Azerbaijan employees and asked that a commission be sent to Baku headed by a representative of the Central Committee or Party Control Commission to conduct an inspection of branches of the security and police forces, as well as the republic's procuracy. Stalin wrote on the report, "In favor of Akulov's prop[osal]." On 15 November the Politburo drafted a resolution on sending a special commission to Azerbaijan "to conduct a thorough inquiry into the operations and personnel of agencies of the NKVD, the police, and the procuracy of Azerbaijan."[112]

With such reports and the results of inspections before it, the Kuibyshev commission prepared a draft decision that called for "eradication of illegal investigative methods, the punishment of the guilty, and a review of the Revis and Markevich cases."[113] But before this resolution could be finalized, Kirov was murdered. On 7 January 1935, Markevich, who appears to have been transferred to a Moscow prison but whose case had not yet been reviewed, again wrote to Stalin with a request to be released. "If the members of Comrade Kuibyshev's commission still have some doubts about my guilt, I ask that they call me for questioning again." Stalin wrote his decision on this petition: "Send him back to the camp."[114] In 1938, Markevich was shot.

The Politburo decisions condemning OGPU-NKVD methods and demanding that "socialist legality" be observed were not empty declarations. First of all, let me note that these decisions were given the special-folder classification, which meant that they circulated only within the Politburo and among top NKVD officials. Obviously they were not intended for propaganda purposes. Second, arrest statistics attest to an actual decline in the activities of the secret police. In cases brought by the OGPU-NKVD, 205,000 people were arrested in 1934, compared to 505,000 in 1933. Arrests for "counterrevolutionary crimes" were sharply down—from 283,000 in 1933 to 90,000 in 1934.[115] For the moment we do not have monthly data and therefore cannot separate out December 1934, when there was a new surge of repression after Kirov's murder.

These figures indicating the level of repression in 1934 can be called low only in comparison with figures for the mass terror of the preceding period and the Great Terror of 1937–1938. The continuing arrests, party purges, and other repressive measures attest to the fundamentally unchanged nature of the regime. Minor reforms were instituted within the context of this repression. Even during the autumn of 1934, when the campaign to rein in the NKVD appears to have reached its peak, a tendency to encourage harsh measures was still evident. On 2 September 1934, for example, the Politburo ordered that the military collegium of the Supreme Court be sent to Novosibirsk to sentence to death a group of workers from the Stalin Metallurgical Factory who had been charged with spying for Japan.[116] On 19 September the Politburo violated the procedure for sanctioning death sentences that they themselves had established, which required that the sentences be upheld by the Central Committee political commission.[117] According to a telegram from Molotov, who was in Western Siberia, the Politburo had empowered the party secretary of the Western Siberian provincial committee, Eikhe, to independently confirm death sentences in Western Siberia in September and October.[118] On 2 November his period of authority was extended to 15 November.[119] On 7 November the "moderate" Kuibyshev, who was on an official visit to Central Asia, sent a telegram to Moscow addressed to Stalin and Molotov. He wrote, "A conspiracy among Bai elements is playing a major role in holding up cotton procurement. The TsK of Uzbekistan has been very slow in implementing broad measures in this struggle, and the arraignment of the perpetrators of the organized Baikulak resistance is being published until November 7. I request that for the duration of my stay in Uzbekistan a commission consisting of Kuibyshev, Ikramov [secretary of the Central Committee of the Communist Party of Uzbekistan], and Khodzhaev [chairman of the republic Council of People's Commissars] be given the rights of a TsK Political Commission—for example, the right to confirm death [shooting] sentences."[120] On 9 November the Politburo granted this request. On 26 November the same right was given to commissions in other Central Asian republics (Turkmenia, Tajikistan, and Kirgizia). Again, the commissions were composed of Kuibyshev and top leaders of the republic in question.[121] Similar examples could be given. In 1934 the foundation of Stalin's system of state terror was still solidly in place. No more than minor adjustments had taken place, with a slight decrease in the level of terror.

The evidence, then, suggests that Soviet policy in 1934 represented a pragmatic reaction to both domestic socioeconomic realities and international threats. The Great Leap of the First Five-Year Plan had led to a severe crisis. The collapse of the economy, famine, and the terror that affected a significant portion of the country's population raised doubts about the very survival of the regime and undermined its economic and social foundations. A moderate course was the only way to stabilize the situation. A reorienting of economic, social, and punitive policy, as well as fundamental changes in ideological norms, reflected the country's predominant moods and interests. Once again the regime managed to maneuver its way out of a crisis by exploiting a widespread desire for stability, moderation, and a "prosperous life." All of the relatively successful policies of the Second Five-Year Plan were rooted in these desires. Foreign policy considerations were also part of the Soviet government's calculations. The growing threats of German fascism from the west and Japan from the east forced Stalin to seek allies among the Western democracies and to convincingly demonstrate to the international community the fundamental difference between fascism and communism by showcasing the "democratic achievements" of Soviet power.

The historical record shows that Stalin played the initiating role in the transformations of 1934. It was he who formulated both specific proposals and the ideological and propagandistic bases for changes to the general line. Archival sources do not back up widely held beliefs about the reformist role of Kirov and his supporters within the Politburo. Instead, these sources suggest that Kirov was primarily focused on the concerns of Leningrad Province, whose interests he represented, just as other regional party secretaries represented the local interests of their constituencies. The part that Kirov played in the high-level policy decisions being made in Moscow was minimal. His position within the party, undermined by an unsavory political past, made him into a loyal follower of Stalin. Historians have yet to offer a single solid piece of evidence to sustain or develop the hypothesis that Kirov was seen as an alternative to Stalin. Analogous conclusions can also be drawn in regard to other suppositions about a struggle within the Politburo between moderates and radicals. As newly uncovered documents show, the famous episode involving a backroom polemic between Molotov and Ordzhonikidze at the 17th Party Congress can be viewed as part of the longstanding institutional tug-of-war over plans for capital investment and production targets.

The move toward moderation in 1934 shows us a version of the system that took shape in 1929, but one relatively free of the excesses of state terror and adventuristic economic policy. This model could be called "soft" Stalinism. Repressive in essence, it nonetheless set certain limits on state violence and consequently facilitated greater social stability. This model also allowed the government to better tap into the potential for improving production and stimulating labor productivity. Indeed, these moderate policies proved so important for the system that many aspects of them were continued beyond 1934, when Stalin unleashed the next campaign of repression. This coexistence of repressive and moderate tendencies in Stalinist policy and the reorganization at the highest levels of power that came with it will be examined in the following chapter.

4   Terror and Conciliation
1935–1936

WHETHER OR NOT Stalin was involved in Kirov's murder, he took full advantage of the opportunities it presented to further his own objectives. Principally, he used it as an excuse to eliminate his former political opponents, the leaders and members of the opposition movements active in the 1920s and early 1930s. Between 1935 and 1938 a large number of oppositionists were destroyed. In almost every case, the accusations of terror leveled against them included allegations of involvement in plans to kill Kirov. Besides serving as a vehicle for settling old accounts, his murder became the starting point for a large-scale fabrication of cases against "terrorist organizations," the deportation of "suspicious" population groups, and a new wave of purges within the party. Although the shot fired in Smolny Institute occasioned horrible reprisals, it was not used to justify a level of repression that matched what came later. Two and a half years would pass before mass terror reached its peak. In 1935–1936 two political tendencies were in evidence: attempts to continue the moderate line and placate the citizenry and a concurrent consolidation of hard-line policies. Because each of these trends is clearly delineated and was actively manifested, the period between Kirov's murder and the Great Terror of 1937–1938 is of significant interest in terms of fluctuations in the general line, the logic governing decisions made by the top leadership, and the balance of power within the Politburo, or rather between the Politburo and Stalin.

THE AFTERMATH OF KIROV'S MURDER

The surge in state terror during the months immediately following Kirov's murder seemed to irretrievably sweep away all the moderate initiatives of the preceding period. Within hours of learning of Kirov's death in Leningrad, Stalin wrote out the text of a Central Executive Committee decree that would be called the Law of 1 December. This emergency measure was put into effect essentially on the basis of Stalin's unilateral decision (the Politburo formally approved it on 3 December).[1] The law ordered that the investigation of cases involving terrorist acts be completed within ten days, that those accused be informed of the charges against them only one day before the cases were heard, that trials be conducted without the participation of the accused, that no appeal or petition for reprieve be allowed, and that those convicted be shot immediately after their death sentences were announced. This law signified a radical break with the practices of jurisprudence introduced in association with the reorganization of the OGPU, the courts, and the procuracy in 1934. The practices embodied in the Law of 1 December were optimal for conducting a far-reaching campaign of terror, and for this reason they were often applied in 1937–1938.

Over objections from the NKVD, Stalin ordered that the "Zinoviev trail" be pursued, and accused former political opponents—Lev Kamenev, Grigory Zinoviev, and their supporters—of Kirov's murder. As subsequent events showed, this had far-reaching consequences. One by one, all the former members of the opposition were accused of terrorism. By 16 December 1934, Kamenev and Zinoviev had been arrested. On 28–29 December in Leningrad a session of the military collegium of the USSR Supreme Court sentenced fourteen people accused of being directly involved in arranging Kirov's murder to be shot. The decision asserted that they were all, including the actual murderer, Leonid Nikolaev, "active participants in a Zinovievite anti-Soviet group in Leningrad" and that finally, after several years, having lost all hope of support from the masses, they had organized an "underground terrorist counterrevolutionary group" headed by the so-called Leningrad Center. On 16 January 1935 the NKVD special board reviewed the criminal case

against this fictional center—the "Leningrad Counterrevolutionary Zinovievite Group." The seventy-seven defendants involved in the case
were all sentenced to varying terms of incarceration or exile.[2] The same
day, 16 January, nineteen people tried in the case of the so-called Moscow Center, purportedly headed by Zinoviev and Kamenev, were given
prison sentences ranging from five to ten years.[3] All of these cases were
crudely fabricated. There was no evidence to suggest that the former oppositionists were in any way tied to Kirov's murderer. Stalin dealt with
his old political rivals by accusing them of crimes that they had not committed.

Immediately after the convictions of Zinoviev and Kamenev, a secret
Central Committee letter went to party offices throughout the country
enumerating "lessons from the events associated with the villainous
murder of Com. Kirov." Stalin himself took part in drafting this letter. It
contained categorical assertions that a Leningrad group of Zinovievites
who called themselves the Leningrad Center had planned the terrorist
act against Kirov. Their ideological inspiration came from the Moscow
Center of Zinovievites headed by Kamenev and Zinoviev, the letter said.
It also alleged that both of these centers were "essentially a form of
White [anti-Bolshevik] organization in disguise, making it entirely appropriate for their members to be dealt with as if they were Whites."[4]
This was a new and, to a certain extent, decisive step along the path to-
ward the complete destruction of the former oppositionists.

Having dealt this powerful blow against the Zinovievites, Stalin reminded the letter's recipients that the party had seen other "anti-party
groups" in its history—Trotskyites, "democratic centralists," "the worker
opposition," "right deviationists," and "rightist-leftist freaks." This history constituted a "tip" as to where more "enemies" and "saboteurs"
could be found. Local authorities were being encouraged to suspect all
Communists who had ever expressed any concerns over the Stalinist
leadership or who had shown the slightest signs of dissent. Readers of the
letter understood that these were not empty words, but instructions
meant to be translated into action. Large groups of former oppositionists
from the capitals and major cities were sent to Siberia or to the north or,
at best, to remote provincial centers.[5] A number of opposition leaders
were tried. In Moscow in March–April 1935 the NKVD special board
convicted leaders of the "workers opposition," A. G. Shliapnikov, S. P.
Medvedev, and others, based on fabricated evidence.[6]

Settling accounts with oppositionists was a main element of the new policy of repression. Another was ridding major cities and border areas of "anti-Soviet elements." One of the most famous of these efforts was the purging of "people of the past" (members of the pre-revolutionary elite—the nobility, government officials, military officers, and industrialists) from Leningrad. During February and March of 1935, when this operation was under way, 11,702 people were sentenced to confinement in camps or sent into exile.[7] In late 1934 and early 1935 the Politburo also sanctioned mass arrests and deportations of kulaks and "unreliable elements" in Azerbaijan and the border regions of Ukraine, Leningrad Province, and Karelia.[8]

The campaign of repression against former oppositionists continued under the guise of an "inspection of party documents." In May 1935 a letter from the Central Committee on disarray in the recording, issuing, and filing of party documents went to local party headquarters. The letter demanded that the party put its house in order and ensure that no alien elements be allowed to penetrate it. Officially, the instructions were to verify the existence and genuineness of party membership cards and party registration cards. The inspections that took place from May to December 1935 actually constituted a purge involving arrests.

This inspection, over the course of which approximately 250,000 people were expelled from the party, was conducted jointly by the party and the NKVD. The nature of their collaboration can be seen in reports by the heads of republic and provincial offices of the NKVD that arrived in Moscow addressed to Nikolai Yezhov, who was in charge of the purge. As the heads of the NKVD of Belorussia reported: "In accordance with directives of the USSR NKVD, special instructions were given to local offices of the NKVD concerning the reexamination of records regarding party members involved in various cases. [. . .] It was proposed that all of these materials be given to the corresponding party organizations and that in all cases where obvious enemies and suspected enemies are uncovered, they should be immediately arrested and investigations should be conducted to determine exactly by what means and channels these people had entered the party and how they exploited their party membership to further their counterrevolutionary and espionage objectives."[9] Over the course of the inspection, which lasted several months, the Ukrainian NKVD handed over to the party dossiers on 17,368 people, the Ivanovo Province NKVD handed over dossiers on 3,580 people, and the Zapadnaya Province NKVD handed over dossiers on 3,233 Communists.[10] For its part, the party provided information to the NKVD about those expelled from the party over the course of the inspection. The chekists then initiated surveillance of those expelled, many of whom were arrested. As Yezhov reported at the Central Committee plenum in late December 1935, preliminary figures as of 1 December 1935 showed that 15,218 "enemies" had been arrested and more than one hundred "enemy organizations and groups" had been uncovered in association with the party expulsions.[11]

The campaigns of repression conducted in 1935 were in many ways similar to the actions that took place two years later and served as a prologue to the massive operations of 1937–1938. The difference here was that what took place in 1935–1936 was not immediately followed by large-scale operations. During this period the Stalinist leadership also took steps that could be seen as a continuation of the moderate policies of 1934.

On 31 January 1935, at the height of the post-Kirov repressions, the Politburo, following a proposal by Stalin, enacted a fundamental decision involving essential changes to the USSR constitution, in particular to its electoral system. The primary issue at hand was the extension of voting rights to those many groups in the population who had previously lost this right as "alien elements." Several days later this extension was reported in newspapers. At the same time, measures were taken that to a certain extent limited the mass repression and rehabilitated hundreds of thousands of people who had been tried during preceding years.

An important step of a similar nature was the decree issued by the Council of People's Commissars and the Central Committee entitled "On Procedures for Conducting Arrests," enacted on 17 June 1935. More radical than the famous instructions issued 8 May 1933, the decree stated that "arrests in all NKVD cases without exception must henceforth be made only with the consent of the appropriate procuracy," and it established a complex procedure for obtaining authorization for arrests of high-level personnel, specialists, and party members from the heads of the appropriate commissariats, government agencies, and party committees.[12] The new procedures made the job of the NKVD somewhat more difficult. Not surprisingly, in 1937–1938 this decree was essentially rescinded.

On 26 July 1935 the Politburo adopted a decision entitled "On Expunging the Criminal Records of Kolkhoz Workers." This was aimed at peasants who had been given sentences of less than five years or some milder form of punishment and who had already served out their sentences. Those who had been conscientious kolkhoz workers could receive full pardons and have their records expunged. The commission formed to conduct this campaign was ordered to complete its work by 1 November 1935.[13] While the decree did not apply to those who had been convicted of counterrevolutionary crimes, those given sentences of five years or more, or recidivists, or some others, it affected hundreds of thousands of peasants. Expunging these records had little effect on their lives, which were oppressed by material hardships and lack of legal rights, but it did have a certain symbolic weight.

By 5 December 1935, according to a report submitted to the Politburo by USSR procurator Andrei Vyshinsky, the records of 125,192 kolkhoz workers had been expunged throughout the Soviet Union, and in Chelyabinsk Province alone 40,000 cases were still pending. On Vyshinsky's recommendation the Politburo extended the deadline for completion of the expunctions to 1 March 1936.[14] On 25 April 1936, in a periodic report addressed to Stalin, Kalinin, and Molotov, Vyshinsky summarized the campaign. He reported that between 29 July 1935 and 1 March 1936 the conviction records of 556,790 kolkhoz workers from throughout the country had been expunged (an additional 212,199 kolkhoz workers had had their records expunged in Ukraine in 1934 by decision of the government of that republic). Despite the large numbers, Vyshinsky proposed conducting additional inspections in those regions of the country where a high percentage of expunctions had been rejected. The Politburo supported this proposal.[15]

The lengthy campaign to expunge the conviction records of kolkhoz workers coincided with something that was of much greater significance for peasants—an amnesty for those convicted on the basis of the notorious Law of 7 August 1932 concerning the theft of public property. Since this law was exceptionally harsh, several months after it was published, the government was forced to make changes to the way it was implemented. A Politburo resolution dated 1 February 1933 and a corresponding published decree of the Central Executive Committee presidium dated 27 March 1933 prohibited prosecutions based on the Law of 7 August "of persons guilty of petty, sporadic theft of public property, or of workers stealing out of need, out of a lack of awareness, or under other mitigating circumstances." On 11 December 1935, Vyshinsky wrote to the Central Committee, the Council of People's Commissars, and the Central Executive Committee asserting that these requirements were not being followed. He proposed adopting a new decision, one ordering a review of convictions based on the Law of 7 August. Members of the Politburo considered this matter on 15 January 1936. Stalin agreed with Vyshinsky and wrote on his note, "In favor (the resolution should not be published)."[16] A decree issued by the Central Executive Committee and Council of People's Commissars that was signed on 16 January ordered a review of convictions based on the Law of 7 August to verify their compliance with the 27 March 1933 decree of the Central Executive Committee presidium. The commissions assigned to carry out this review could propose reducing sentences as well as releasing prisoners ahead of schedule. Six months later, on 20 July 1936, Vyshinsky reported to Stalin, Molotov, and Kalinin that the review of cases mandated by the 16 January decree had been completed. More than 115,000 cases had been reviewed. In more than 91,000 of them the application of the Law of 7 August had been found to be incorrect. As a result of sentence reductions, 37,425 people (32 percent of those whose cases had been reviewed) were released from incarceration.[17]

Approximately the same number of convicts gained their freedom as a result of a Politburo resolution dated 10 August 1935. This resolution provided for the release and expunction of the records of officials convicted in 1932–1934 of "grain collection sabotage" and of various financial machinations perpetrated under conditions of high inflation and shortages of rubles (paying workers in "local" currencies, making loans to workers, issuing bonds, and so on). As Vyshinsky reported to the government and the Central Committee on 10 December 1935, preliminary figures showed that 54,000 people had been released based on this decision, and more than 24,000 had been proposed for release.[18]

Although these campaigns were modest in scale, they did demonstrate the regime's desire to make peace with segments of the population who were "socially close"—for example those who, despite occupying positions within society that would tend to ally them with the authorities, nevertheless had been engulfed by the terror. They were a minority among those who had been repressed. "Socially alien" elements—who had lost their civil rights and been transformed into second-class citizens, or *lishentsy* (outcasts)—posed a much greater problem for the authorities.[19] Members of this population category were rather numerous. As of 1 January 1936, *spetspereselentsy* alone (special settlers, primarily peasants) numbered more than a million.[20] In addition to exiled kulaks, Cossacks and members of the pre-revolutionary "ruling classes" were among the segments of the population that suffered discrimination. The Stalinist leadership faced additional problems posed by millions of children of outcasts who were coming of age, burdened by the stigma of their family backgrounds. There was the danger that this group would generate ever-expanding "socially alien" populations.

The government, aware of the need for changes in this area, maneuvered and made promises, although it was in no hurry to carry them out. This tendency could be seen particularly clearly in the case of the kulaks. In 1935–1936 the five-year term of exile legally mandated for hundreds of thousands of peasants who had been targeted for repression during the first phase of collectivization (1930–1931) was coming to an end. The question of what would happen to them now was pressing. Past experience in restoring rights to kulaks had shown that most of them preferred to leave their place of exile. For this reason, at the suggestion of the NKVD leadership, the broad-based restoration of rights to exiled peasants that was undertaken in 1935 prohibited them from leaving their place of exile. This meant that the vast majority of former kulaks had their civil rights restored only on paper.[21]

The government attempted to compensate for this obvious violation of its own laws through a variety of propaganda campaigns. A bit of political theater acted out by Stalin in early December 1935 at a meeting of combine operators gave the signal for a new and sensational demonstration of "conciliation" with "socially alien elements." When a Bashkir collective farmer, A. Tilba, proclaimed from the meeting dais, "Although I am the son of a kulak, I will fight honorably for the cause of the workers and peasants and for the building of socialism," Stalin responded, "A son is not responsible for his father," a phrase that went on to become famous.[22] Subsequent events showed that Stalin's aphorism, which was widely used in propaganda, had been calculated. It represented the willingness of the country's leadership to institute a limited relaxation of restrictions affecting young people in hopes of drawing them away from the older generation of opponents to the regime.

A decree that was issued by the Central Executive Committee and the

Council of People's Commissars and approved by the Politburo on 29 December 1935 outlined new rules governing admission to institutions of higher learning and vocational training. The new law had a significant impact on the children of outcasts. In the past, "children of non-workers and those deprived of their right to vote" were prohibited from entering institutions of higher learning and technical schools. This new law repealed that prohibition.[23]

The new law on admittance to higher education complicated the issue of releasing the children of kulaks and other populations from exile. Although a blanket prohibition against leaving exile remained in force, the government made certain exceptions, especially in the case of young people. On 27 January 1936 a group of young people who had been exiled to Ufa along with their families sent a telegram addressed to Stalin, Molotov, and Yagoda. It read, "We, the undersigned young men and women, aged eighteen to twenty-five, exiled from Leningrad for the social pasts of our parents or relatives and living under extremely difficult conditions, appeal to you to release us from a punishment we did nothing to deserve—administrative exile—and to restore all of our civil rights and permit us to live anywhere within the territory of the [Soviet] Union. We cannot answer for the social pasts of our relatives. Because of our ages, we have nothing in common with the past, we were born into revolution, we have been raised and nurtured by the Soviet authorities, we are honest Soviet students, workers, and employees. We ardently desire to join the ranks of Soviet youth and be included in the building of socialism." Molotov forwarded the telegram to Vyshinsky the same day, with the notation, "I ask you on my own behalf and on behalf of Com. Stalin to attentively and quickly get to the bottom of this matter—a response should be sent, and it seems that we should meet them halfway."[24] Vyshinsky promptly replied to Molotov that he had ordered that the files of the Ufa petitioners be sent to him.

Vyshinsky also raised the possibility of adopting a resolution allowing freedom of movement for all young people sent into administrative exile with their parents.[25] This idea did not generate support. A decision was made to address only the particular case of young people exiled from Leningrad. On 28 February 1936 the Politburo approved a decree by the Council of People's Commissars and the Central Committee to release from exile all young people who had been expelled from Leningrad with their parents in 1935, so long as they themselves had untarnished records.[26] On 14 March, Vyshinsky reported to Stalin and Molotov that approximately six thousand cases were subject to review as a result of the 28 February resolution.[27] After local authorities made petitions, the Politburo approved another decision of similarly limited scope on 22 June in regard to young people exiled to a special settlement in the town of Igarka in Krasnoyarsk Territory.[28]

The government took other measures in parallel with campaigns to appease kulak youth, specifically in relation to Cossacks. Newspapers published a Central Executive Committee decree (adopted by the Politburo one day earlier) concerning the Cossacks of the North Caucasus and the Azov-Black Sea territories on 21 April 1936. "In view of the devotion that Cossacks have shown to Soviet authority," the government lifted restrictions on Cossack service in the Red Army. In another move, the Politburo issued an order to the people's commissar of defense concerning the creation of Cossack cavalry units.

With the healthy economic growth the country enjoyed in 1935–1936 the government could allow conciliatory policies. In fact, the healthy economy was both a cause and a result of certain moderate economic policies. Despite heightened repression after Kirov's murder, 1935 saw the most significant concessions to the peasantry since the beginning of collectivization. Documents drafted during the Second Congress of Outstanding Kolkhoz Workers in February and later enacted into law by the government guaranteed the right to maintain and expand private plots. Kolkhoz workers' production on private plots grew at an exceptional pace during the Second Five-Year Plan, enabling an increase in agricultural output and an improvement in the country's food situation. In 1937 the share of private plots in the overall gross output of the kolkhoz sector was 52 percent for potatoes and vegetables, 57 for fruits, 71 percent for milk, and 71 percent for meat.[29] Similar liberalization could be seen in 1935–1936 in the industrial sectors. The rights of economic managers were also further expanded. The economy's efficiency was enhanced by policies that provided material incentives for labor. It was also in 1935–1936 that slogans touting a "prosperous life" took on new significance for the urban population with the abolition of the rationing system and extra pay for high productivity.

The evidence points to a Stalinist leadership in 1935–1936 that was betting on combining repression with moderate policies. Although the level of terror was high, it did not reach the peaks attained during the dekulakization of the early 1930s or the Great Terror of 1937–1938. The relaxation of pressure on "socially alien" sectors of the population and the efforts to reconcile with children of outcasts and kulaks raised hopes of a peaceful trend toward social stability and the elimination of certain contradictions inherent in the more severe repressions of previous years.

The documents we have at our disposal show that Stalin remained the force behind both the repressive and the moderate measures taken in 1935–1936. Presumably, the motives for his political actions during this period were determined by several interrelated factors. The most important was the critical need to strengthen and develop the positive economic trends that emerged in late 1933 and 1934. After the bitter experiences of past crises, Stalin understood the economic costs that come with any campaign of repression.

Foreign policy considerations played a part in the desire to develop economically. The growing threats from Germany and Japan brought the Soviet Union closer to the Western democracies. The 7th Comintern Congress in July–August 1935, after reconsidering issues on which it had not been able to reach consensus in the past, came out in favor of establishing an anti-Fascist people's front. Hoping for a leftward turn in the countries of western Europe and an expansion of the ranks of supporters of the Soviet Union, Stalin recognized the need to form a favorable image of a thriving and democratic "birthplace of socialism." In a note accompanying a draft Politburo decision on changes to the constitution and the creation of a constitutional commission (adopted by the Politburo on 31 January 1935), Stalin wrote: "In my opinion, the matter of the constitution of the Union of SSR is a lot more complicated than might be apparent at first glance. First of all, the system of elections should be changed, not only in the sense of eliminating its many steps. It should also be changed in the sense of replacing open voting with *closed* (secret) voting. We can and must take this matter to a conclusion, not stopping halfway. The situation and alignment of forces in our country at the moment is such that we can win politically only by doing this. What's more, the necessity of such a reform is dictated by the interests of the international revolutionary movement, since such a reform will definitely be a mighty tool against international fascism."[30]

The balance of power at the highest echelons could also have effected Stalin's twisting political course. The members of the Politburo had lost a great deal of their clout. But their acquiescence to Stalin's dominance still did not resemble a retreat or a full capitulation—at least in some cases.

THE REMNANTS OF COLLECTIVE LEADERSHIP

To those positing the existence of factions within the Politburo, the shifts in policy in 1935–1936 might be explained by a struggle between moderates and radicals, with Stalin playing a more or less neutral role. Solid archival evidence has yet to be found to support the idea of such a struggle. Like many other persistent theories about the Stalin period, it remains unproved, despite active efforts by scholars.

On 1 February 1935 a Central Committee plenum confirmed Anastas Ivanovich Mikoyan and Vlas Yakovlevich Chubar as new members of the Politburo. Andrei Aleksandrovich Zhdanov and Robert Indrikhovich Eikhe were named candidate members. If we assess these changes to the makeup of the Politburo guided by theories of factions among Stalin's cohorts, we will conclude that after Kirov's murder it was the moderates who were in the ascendant. Chubar, who was criticized by Stalin for being "spineless" during the famine in Ukraine, was a cautious politician. He was arrested in 1938 for having ties with Rykov and "rightist" inclinations. Some historians also count Zhdanov among the moderates.[31]

In reality, the Politburo reshuffling did not have any particular political significance and was predetermined by the formal procedures for filling vacancies. Mikoyan and Chubar were taking the seats vacated by the recently deceased full members Kirov and Kuibyshev simply because, as senior candidate Politburo members (both had been elected candidate members in 1926), it was their turn to do so. Furthermore, they held important posts (Mikoyan was food industry commissar, while Chubar was deputy chairman of the Council of People's Commissars). Eikhe was formally nominated for the vacated candidate membership as secretary of the large Western Siberian party organization. Since he would be located thousands of kilometers from Moscow, he would not actually be able to participate in the workings of the Politburo. Zhdanov, on the other hand, was already deeply involved in the Politburo. As Central Committee secretary since 1934, he had essentially been functioning as a Politburo member and had frequently signed

Politburo decisions. A decisive factor in Zhdanov's election to the Politburo was his inheriting Kirov's post as head of the Leningrad party organization.

Of much greater significance for the actual assignment of roles at the highest echelons of power was the 27 February 1935 Politburo decision on new appointments within the Central Committee leadership. This decision removed Politburo member Andrei Andreev from his position as transport commissar and made him a Central Committee secretary. Lazar Kaganovich, who retained his position as Central Committee secretary but was relieved of his duties as chairman of the Party Control Commission of the Central Committee and secretary of the Moscow Province party committee, was appointed to replace Andreev at the Transport Commissariat. Nikolai Yezhov, who had also recently been made a Central Committee secretary, was appointed to fill Kaganovich's Party Control Commission spot. Another part of Kaganovich's patrimony—the post of secretary of the Moscow Province party committee—went to another up-and-coming party official, Nikita Khrushchev.[32] As we can judge by the original protocols of Politburo meetings, this important resolution may have been passed at a meeting of a group of Politburo members. Poskrebyshev signed the original resolution (a sign that Stalin probably dictated it), after which Stalin signed it. Under Stalin's signature Kaganovich, Ordzhonikidze, Molotov, Voroshilov, and Mikoyan signed their names with the same red pencil. Kalinin, as the clerical record indicates, was polled separately (evidently by telephone).[33]

The true meaning behind this step, initiated by Stalin, became clearer on 10 March 1935, when the Politburo passed a resolution entitled "On the Distribution of Responsibilities among TsK Secretaries." Newly appointed Central Committee secretary Andreev was put to work at the Orgburo and essentially became the head of that body—it was he who had the duty of chairing Orgburo meetings. However, the resolution included a notable stipulation: the drafting of Orgburo agendas was assigned to two Central Committee secretaries—Andreev and Yezhov. Andreev was further assigned management of the Central Committee's industrial department, previously headed by Yezhov, as well as oversight of its transportation and administrative departments. Yezhov, freed by this resolution from oversight of the industrial department, was given authority over the most important Central Committee department—the department overseeing party personnel matters (ORPO, "department of leading party organs"). Stalin was assigned responsibility for the workings of the rest of the Central Committee departments, "especially the department of culture and propaganda." Kaganovich, who remained a Central Committee secretary, was given (in addition to his new post as transport commissar) the task of overseeing the work of the Moscow Province and City party organizations. The post of transport commissar would be his primary responsibility, however, as the resolution emphasized in various ways. His responsibilities in Moscow should not come "at the expense of work at the NKPS [People's Commissariat of Transport]." The final item in the 10 March resolution read as follows: "To permit Com. Kaganovich to appeal to obkoms and kraikoms [provincial and territorial party committees] for help and support in his capacity as a TsK secretary on matters of rail transport whenever the circumstances might so dictate."[34]

The personnel reassignments of early 1935 could be described as a diffusion of influence among Stalin's closest comrades-in-arms. Kaganovich, who had been Stalin's first deputy within the party for several years, with a broad range of functions, was now deprived of many of his previous responsibilities. Officially, Andreev had taken his place, having been appointed Central Committee secretary in charge of the Orgburo, but Andreev's influence over the Orgburo was limited by Yezhov's having equal authority in drafting the Orgburo agenda, as well as by Kaganovich's remaining both a Central Committee secretary and a member of the Orgburo. Thus, the reassignments within the leadership of Central Committee departments essentially equalized the roles of Andreev and Yezhov. Andreev was given authority over the less-important industrial department. Yezhov was managing the key department within the party structure, which gave him authority over personnel issues. Zhdanov also assumed many of the responsibilities of a Central Committee secretary (unlike Kirov, who had not been very engaged in the affairs of Moscow when he served as Leningrad party chief). On 20 April 1935 the Politburo even adopted a special resolution, "Requiring Com. Zhdanov, in order to facilitate the work of the TsK Secretariat, to spend one out of three ten-day periods per month in Moscow to work with the TsK Secretariat."[35]

In 1935, as a result of all these reorganizations, two Central Committee secretaries (Andreev and Yezhov) were added to the three (Stalin,

Kaganovich, and Zhdanov) who had collaborated in managing the Central Committee apparatus at the beginning of 1934. The two new secretaries took over a significant share of the responsibilities. This had at least two important consequences. First, the powerful post of Central Committee second secretary—Stalin's deputy within the party—was essentially eliminated. This post had been held in past years by Molotov and Kaganovich. Now the responsibilities of the second secretary were distributed among several secretaries. Second, Stalin strengthened the positions of several of those who had been recently promoted—Yezhov, Zhdanov, and Khrushchev. All in all, these measures weakened Stalin's former comrades-in-arms—and the mechanisms of collective leadership within the Politburo.

Yezhov's entry into the highest echelons of power would have particular significance. Even though he lacked any official standing within the Politburo, Yezhov actively participated in its operations. Stalin entrusted him with his most important assignments related to NKVD operations, the organization of political purges, and the settling of personnel matters. After successfully carrying out Stalin's order to organize trials of the Zinovievites accused of Kirov's murder, Yezhov essentially became the party functionary responsible for overseeing the NKVD. On 31 March 1935, for example, the Politburo asked him to review the Statutes Governing the NKVD and the Main Administration of State Security of the NKVD.[36] After maintaining oversight of NKVD operations for a year and a half, Yezhov was finally appointed head of this commissariat. His work at the Party Control Commission overlapped. One of his first acts after being appointed to the Party Control Commission was to design and implement the campaign "to bring order to the recording, issuance, and filing of party membership cards." The secret Central Committee letter on this matter, which Yezhov drafted, was approved by the Politburo on 13 May 1935.[37] From this point on, for almost a year and a half, Yezhov was engaged in orchestrating party purges.

One of the most important tasks assigned to Yezhov in early 1935 was preparation of the so-called Kremlin case, which began with the arrests between January and April 1935 of a group of employees in government offices located in the Kremlin (cleaning personnel, librarians, staff members of the Central Executive Committee presidium and the Kremlin commandant, and others). They were accused of plotting terrorist acts against government leaders, primarily Stalin. Since those arrested included relatives of Lev Kamenev, he was lumped with those accused of inciting the conspiracy.[38] If the Kremlin case had been limited to these falsifications, it could have been seen as a logical extension of the repression against former oppositionists launched after Kirov's murder. But the case also targeted Central Executive Committee secretary Abel Yenukidze, who was accused of supporting the terrorists. He was fired and then expelled from the party. The accusation reached directly into the circle of Stalin's closest comrades-in-arms.

The fifty-eight-year-old Yenukidze was an old party member. He had begun his revolutionary path in Transcaucasia and had long had friendly relations with Stalin and other members of the Politburo (including Ordzhonikidze). His job involved taking care of the material and practical needs of the highest level of Soviet officialdom, which made him an intimate in many Kremlin households. Although Yenukidze was not a member of the Politburo, he was an important element of the Stalinist system of collective leadership that had arisen toward the end of the 1920s and that Stalin had gradually but purposefully destroyed over the period that followed. The attack against Yenukidze, launched on Stalin's initiative, was the first blow felt by the inner circle. The case reflected the relationship between Stalin and his comrades-in-arms as the period of collective leadership drew to a conclusion. It was one of a series of blows that destroyed what remained of the Politburo's influence.

There is strong documentary evidence that Stalin took a particular interest in the Kremlin case. He regularly received and read the transcripts of interrogations, making notes on them and issuing instructions to the NKVD.[39] As more and more damning "evidence" was gathered against Yenukidze, ever harsher measures were taken. On 3 March 1935 the Politburo adopted a decision to remove Yenukidze from the post of Central Executive Committee secretary and appoint him to the chairmanship of the Central Executive Committee of the Transcaucasian Federation.[40] This was a form of punishment, but a mild one. Two weeks later, on 21 March, the Politburo approved a new, harsher decision for distribution to members of the Central Committee and the Soviet and Party Control Commissions: "A Report to the TsK VKP(b) on the USSR TsIK [Central Executive Committee] Apparatus and Com. Yenukidze." This report accused Yenukidze of losing his "political vigilance." The document stated that the question of Yenukidze's membership in the Central Committee would be discussed at the next Central Committee plenum.[41] Yenukidze immediately wrote a letter to the Politburo stating his full support of the decision to remove him from the post of Central Executive Committee secretary. At the same time, on 22 March, he appealed to Voroshilov and Ordzhonikidze (and through them to all members of the Politburo) to reverse the decision to appoint him to the Transcaucasian post. After "those accusations, which were justly directed against me, I cannot show up to work there. [. . .] It is not false shame and pride that is speaking; I simply cannot psychologically and *physically* force myself to go there as TsIK Chair. [. . .] I implore you for the sake of our old friendship and as comrades to help me by granting my request."[42] His friends did come to his aid. On 25 March he wrote a petition stating that he could not go to Transcaucasia owing to his state of health and asked for a two-month vacation. The Politburo approved this request.[43]

Knowing that he had the support of friends in the Politburo, Yenukidze seems to have become emboldened. In May, while on vacation, he sent a letter to Yezhov in which he asked about work in Moscow or as a Central Executive Committee representative in the resort towns of Sochi and Mineralnye Vody. The letter seems to indicate that an unofficial offer of work in the resort towns had already been made. Apparently friends in Moscow had orchestrated the more or less favorable treatment of Yenukidze. On 13 May, Yezhov forwarded a letter from Yenukidze to Stalin with a note stating, "Since the petition indicates that his vacation will end in a few days, I ask permission to summon him for questioning on a number of matters." Stalin did not respond to Yezhov's request, but he proposed appointing Yenukidze as Central Executive Committee representative to the "Mineralnye Vody group." A decision to do so was adopted by the Politburo on 13 May 1935.[44]

An incident that took place at the Central Committee plenum on 6 June 1935 supports the idea that Stalin had agreed to this decision only reluctantly and that Yenukidze himself was counting heavily on help from his friends in the Politburo. The plenum had been convened to address the question of the Central Executive Committee apparatus and Yenukidze. Yezhov, who spoke on behalf of the leadership, proposed a mild decision—expulsion from the Central Committee. Yenukidze gave a dignified speech, expressing moderate repentance and even arguing against some of the accusations. His overconfidence made a renewed attack against him at the plenum's conclusion easier (although Stalin had probably planned one all along). A number of speakers, particularly Yagoda, argued for Yenukidze's arrest. But Stalin decided against such a move for now. A compromise was reached, according to which Yenukidze was expelled from the party.[45]

Stalin's attitude toward Yenukidze notwithstanding, his old friends, including at least one Politburo member—Ordzhonikidze—maintained relations with him. Stalin saw this as an act of defiance. On 7 September, Stalin sent Kaganovich, Yezhov, and Molotov a cipher from Sochi in which he asserted that appointing Yenukidze a Central Executive Committee representative had been a mistake, since that position gave him too many rights. "It turns out that people are talking about Yenukidze's expulsion from the party being in essence a maneuver to distract attention, [saying] that he had been sent to Kislovodsk for a vacation, and not as a punishment, that he would be reinstated [in the party] in the fall, since he has friends in Moscow. And Yenukidze himself, it turns out, is happy with his situation; he's playing politics, surrounding himself with the disgruntled and skillfully making himself out to be the victim of out-of-control passions within the party. The situation is made even more ambiguous by the fact that Yenukidze went to visit Sergo [Ordzhonikidze] and discussed 'business.'" In the end, Stalin demanded that Yenukidze be removed from his post and sent to a lesser position in Rostov or Kharkov.[46] The next day, 8 September, in a letter to Kaganovich, Stalin again accused Ordzhonikidze of continuing "to be friends with" Yenukidze.[47]

As Stalin had demanded, on 11 September the Politburo appointed Yenukidze to the secondary post of head of the Kharkov office administering motor vehicle transportation.[48] But on 22 September, Stalin was forced to again telegraph Kaganovich: "They say that Yenukidze has not yet received his orders to leave for Kharkov and is still sitting in Kislovodsk." The next day Kaganovich reported that Yenukidze was not carrying out the orders concerning his new appointment, but "now a categorical order has been issued, and no later than 25 September he will leave Kislovodsk for Kharkov."[49]

Despite Stalin's displeasure and Yenukidze's imprudent behavior, in June 1936, the Central Committee plenum adopted a decision to reinstate him in the party.[50] This decision was probably also the result of a compromise that Stalin entered into reluctantly. Just six months later Stalin launched a decisive offensive, and Yenukidze was arrested. This occurred on 11 February 1937, a week before Ordzhonikidze killed himself. In October, Yenukidze was shot.[51]

The change in Yenukidze's fortunes largely reflected the changes in Stalin's relations with those around him. Even though the political situation had changed after Kirov's death, Stalin could still rest assured that his loyal comrades-in-arms did not want to lose what remained of collective leadership and, in particular, its most important element—the right to influence personnel decisions and assure the security of "their people." Repression of the *nomenklatura* and the entourages surrounding Politburo members was restrained. In that respect, 1935 and 1936 can be viewed as a period of exceptional equilibrium. Stalin was still not able to unilaterally sanction arrests of certain categories of nomenklatura members. However, even Politburo members were no longer able to defend against NKVD actions, which were fully controlled by Stalin. This was a transitional period, marked by the coexistence of the remnants of collective leadership and by signs that a dictatorship was being solidified.

Stalin's former comrades-in-arms continued to carry out many important functions. As the Politburo protocols indicate, Kaganovich, for example, continued his active role as one of the party's leaders, although most of the matters that he now placed before the Politburo had to do with problems of rail transportation. As in past years, when Stalin was on vacation in August and September of 1935 and 1936, Kaganovich oversaw the workings of the Politburo, handling the flow of issues addressed and signing Politburo decisions and meeting protocols. During these vacation breaks, documents sent to the Central Committee were addressed to Kaganovich. Many Politburo decisions made during Stalin's vacation in 1935 were the result of consultation between Kaganovich and Molotov.[52]

Politburo protocols for 1935–1936 nonetheless show that Kaganovich tried to gain Stalin's approval for even minor matters and refrained from advancing his own initiatives. In September 1935, for example, when the Council of People's Commissars was considering a decree to give contractual agreements the force of law, Kaganovich wrote on an accompanying note from Molotov: "This matter affects large numbers of kolkhoz workers. We should ask Com. Stalin for his opinion." The document was sent to Stalin (it retains Stalin's response: "In favor"), and only then was it approved by the Politburo.[53] Kaganovich placed similar notations—"In favor (vote with Com. Stalin)"; "In favor, with a query to Com. Stalin"; "In favor (vote by telegraph with Com. Stalin)"—on such draft Politburo decisions in September 1935 to award the actor Vasily Kachalov the Order of the Red Banner of Labor, permit L. I. Lavrentiev, secretary of the Far Eastern Territory party committee to be given a vacation and permission to come to Moscow, and grant a vacation and treatment abroad to Yezhov.[54]

Kaganovich's letters to his Politburo colleagues also changed tone in 1935–1936. However ecstatic and optimistic Kaganovich's past letters may have been in their assessment of Stalin and his deeds, now they turned into fawning and ridiculous panegyrics: "Things are going fine here. To give a brief description, I can briefly repeat what Mikoyan and I told Com. Kalinin when he went to Sochi. Before he left he asked us what to tell the Boss. We told him: Tell him that 'the country and party are so charged up that things are getting done without the shooter having to do anything—the army is shooting.' What's happening with grain collections this year, for instance—it's an absolutely stunning victory on our part—the victory of Stalinism"; "The main news is the appointment of Yezhov. The right time came for this splendid, wise decision of our parent and met with a wonderful response in the party and the country"; "Overall, it is very difficult without the boss, and when you left, it became even harder. But unfortunately we have to burden the boss with a great quantity of matters and interrupt his rest, while at the same time words cannot express how valuable his health and vigor are to us, those who love him, and to the entire country"; "Here, brother, we have the great dialectic in politics, the sort [of dialectics] that our great friend and parent has mastered to perfection."[55]

Documents from 1935 to 1936 do not contain evidence of open démarches by Politburo members of the sort that were characteristic of the early 1930s (letters of resignation, refusals to present reports, ultimatums about institutional interests). At least on the surface, the Politburo of this period appears more "disciplined."

Stalin, as his position became stronger, had less and less need to interact with his comrades-in-arms. The log of visitors to Stalin's office shows a marked decrease in the number of meetings between Stalin and

members of the Politburo.[56] In 1935–1936 regularly scheduled Politburo sessions became a thing of the past—on average, the Politburo met
less than once per month. Most decisions were made through polling.
The way original Politburo protocols were put together shows that various sorts of meetings between individual Politburo members became
common practice and replaced official sessions. On 4 September 1935,
for example, Kaganovich wrote to Ordzhonikidze that "today we discussed the plan for the 4th qu[arter] and added 100 million rub. to your
annual expenditures, [then] the overall matter was sent to Sochi [where
Stalin was vacationing] for approval."[57] This clearly relevant discussion is not to be found in the protocols of any Politburo meeting. After
Stalin signed off on the plan, approval for it was processed as a decision
made by polling the Politburo members on 7 September. The polling did
not actually take place—the original resolution was signed by Molotov,
alone.[58] This scenario was fairly typical.

In 1935–1936, Stalin continued to be actively involved in the decisions that the Politburo issued. His notes and signatures are preserved
on many of the resolutions that were enacted. Even when he was away
on vacation, he monitored the Politburo's activities, managing the
progress of all important resolutions. From time to time, individual
members of the Politburo would travel to Sochi to discuss specific issues. Politburo decisions were frequently approved on the basis of
telegrams from Stalin. Such a telegram, signed by Stalin and Zhdanov
(who was also vacationing in the south), came to Kaganovich, Molotov, and other Politburo members in Moscow on 25 September 1936. It
read: "We consider it absolutely imperative and urgent that Comrade
Yezhov be appointed people's commissar of internal affairs. Yagoda has
clearly turned out not to be up to his task in the matter of exposing the
Trotskyite-Zinovievite bloc. The OGPU was four years late in this matter. All the party functionaries and most of the regional representatives
of the NKVD say this." The telegram also included a proposal to remove Rykov as communications commissar and replace him with
Yagoda; to change the leadership of the Timber Industry Commissariat;
and to leave Yezhov as chairman of the Party Control Commission and
Central Committee secretary as well as make him the new internal
affairs commissar.[59] The very next day, 26 September, Kaganovich
drafted the Politburo resolution on the changes in status of Yagoda,
Yezhov, and Rykov.[60]

The way these Politburo decisions were executed is worth noting. First, the resolution about Rykov and Yagoda was issued, followed by the one about Yagoda and Yezhov. The originals of both resolutions were handwritten by Poskrebyshev's deputy Boris Dvinsky on the heavy paper usually used to record Politburo decisions taken at regular sessions. Kaganovich made minor changes to each of the resolutions (for example, he replaced the word "remove" with the word "relieve" to describe Rykov's being fired from his post as communications commissar). Each resolution was certified with Kaganovich's signature. Each also has a secretarial notation: "Com. Petrovsky—in favor; Com. Rudzutak—in favor; Com. Postyshev—in favor."[61] Considering that Molotov and Voroshilov were in Moscow (Ordzhonikidze was on vacation, and Mikoyan was on official business in the United States), the question arises, Why are their signatures missing from these decisions? Does their omission signify disagreement with Stalin's proposal?

This question should be raised if only because historians have long speculated about a clash between Stalin and Molotov over heightened repression in 1936. The basis for this speculation was the failure to name Molotov one of the Soviet leaders against whom terrorist acts had been plotted when a list was publicized during the first "great" Moscow trial, of the so-called United Trotskyite-Zinovievite Center. In a secret letter to the Central Committee dated 29 July regarding "terrorist activities of the Trotskyite-Zinovievite counterrevolutionary bloc" and later during the August trial, it was revealed that the United Trotskyite-Zinovievite Center had conspired to kill Stalin, Voroshilov, Kaganovich, Kirov, Ordzhonikidze, Zhdanov, Kosior, and Postyshev.[62] The omission of one of Stalin's closest comrades-in-arms, the chairman of the Council of People's Commissars, attracted the attention of those following developments in the Soviet Union from abroad. It was seen as evidence of Molotov's possible fall from grace. Admittedly, several months later, during the second trial, in January 1937, Molotov (along with Stalin, Kaganovich, Voroshilov, Ordzhonikidze, Zhdanov, Kosior, Eikhe, Postyshev, Yezhov, and Beria) was named as a target of attempts being planned "by a parallel anti-Soviet Trotskyite center."[63] The addition of his name this time only heightened speculation. There were rumors that Molotov had given in and been forgiven by Stalin. The conflict between them, therefore, must indeed have existed.

By early 1937 the journal *Sotsialistichesky vestnik* (Socialist herald) was also alluding to a hypothetical clash between Stalin and Molotov. In the famous "Letter of an Old Bolshevik" published there it was alleged that preparations for the August trial had been conducted without informing all members of the Politburo. Some, including Molotov and Kalinin, had "gone on vacation, knowing nothing of the surprise that was being prepared for them."[64] Molotov comes out looking like an opponent of the campaign of terror against former oppositionists. Alexander Orlov backs up this version in his book on the subject. He asserts that Stalin himself crossed Molotov's name off a list provided by arrested oppositionists during interrogations about terrorist plots. Orlov further alleges that Yagoda ordered that Molotov, who was vacationing in the south, be placed under constant surveillance (supposedly to prevent a possible suicide). There were rumors, according to Orlov, that Molotov had fallen into disfavor after trying to dissuade Stalin from "arranging a shameful mockery of justice against old Bolsheviks."[65]

Evidence has yet to be found to support Orlov's version of events. Indeed, it is doubtful that Stalin would have used exclusion from a list of terrorist targets as a means of putting pressure on his comrades-in-arms. Each of the lists included Ordzhonikidze, with whom Stalin truly was in conflict over the heightened repression, and Postyshev, who was removed from his party post in Ukraine in January 1937. Kalinin, who posed no threat to Stalin, was not listed. This line of argument could be continued. But the most important evidence that there was no conflict between Stalin and Molotov over hardening the line is probably Molotov's own testimony. In the accounts recorded by Feliks Chuev in the 1970s and 1980s, Molotov reflected many times on the years of the terror and attempted to justify himself, but not once did he refer to the potentially convenient notion that he had been in conflict with Stalin. He did, however, speak openly of his conflict with Stalin over the arrest of his wife and of the disfavor he fell into during the final months of Stalin's rule. He recounted how over the course of the Great Terror his closest associates had been arrested and asked to give evidence against him.[66] As for his attitude toward heightened repression, Molotov stated unequivocally, "No, I never considered Beria to be the one most responsible [for repression], but always considered Stalin to be the one most responsible, and we, who approved of it, who were active, and I was always active, stood behind the taking of action. I was never sorry and will never be sorry that we took drastic measures"; "I do not deny that I supported this line."[67]

The only thing for which hard documentary evidence can be found that somewhat hindered Stalin's turn toward terror was the determined attempt by Grigory "Sergo" Ordzhonikidze to protect his commissariat from repressive measures and save friends and relatives from arrest.

STALIN AND ORDZHONIKIDZE

Ordzhonikidze, one of the most famous party leaders of the 1930s, headed the Commissariat of Heavy Industry—the largest Soviet commissariat, a ministry unique among ministries, each of whose main committees (glavk, short for glavny komitet) ran a major branch of the economy. The activities of the commissariat were constantly at the center of national attention. Its industrial complexes symbolized the country's burgeoning power. The enterprises under the purview of this commissariat were supplied with the most advanced equipment, much of which was purchased abroad. A lion's share of the country's hard currency resources were expended on this equipment.

During his years at the helm of this complex economic entity, Ordzhonikidze, an energetic and talented administrator, underwent a certain evolution. A vast divide separated the Ordzhonikidze of the late 1920s and the Ordzhonikidze of the mid-1930s. When he headed the Central Control Commission of the Workers' and Peasants' Inspectorate—essentially a penal agency—he was held in little account and could lash out at those who displeased him with impunity. When he headed the commissariat, he carried tremendous responsibilities on his shoulders for the successful functioning of this critical government agency. One important lesson he learned during the intervening years appears to have been that without a degree of workforce stability, economic success is impossible. Ordzhonikidze was extremely touchy when it came to even the slightest attempts to injure "his" commissariat and "his" people. This was a source of repeated conflict with other Soviet leaders, including Stalin.[68] Although generally he was a consistent and faithful supporter of Stalin, in many situations Ordzhonikidze's temper got the better of him.

A source of Stalin's extreme displeasure was Ordzhonikidze's friend-

ship with Vissarion Lominadze. At the February–March plenum of
1937, after Ordzhonikidze's death, Stalin recalled the Lominadze affair
and sharply criticized Ordzhonikidze for being conciliatory and liberal.
Stalin talked about Ordzhonikidze's open correspondence with Lominadze in the late 1920s, when he was well acquainted with Lominadze's
"anti-party inclinations" but hid them from the Central Committee. As
Stalin put it, Ordzhonikidze took the accusations leveled against Lominadze in 1930 very hard "because on a personal level he trusted the
man, and that personal trust had been betrayed." Stalin asserted that after learning of Lominadze's part in the "right-left bloc," Ordzhonikidze
even demanded that Lominadze be shot.[69]

Stalin was probably lying in this case, taking advantage of Ordzhonikidze's death. Not a single document related to the Lominadze
affair confirms that Ordzhonikidze spoke out in favor of shooting Lominadze. Ordzhonikidze even continued to help him. Thanks to Ordzhonikidze, Lominadze was able to shore up his position rather quickly;
he was awarded the Order of Lenin and was given (as a result of Ordzhonikidze's personal appeal to the Politburo) the prestigious post of
secretary of the Magnitogorsk municipal party committee.[70]

For the time being, Stalin did not interfere in Lominadze's fate. After
Kirov's murder, however, when measures began to be taken against former oppositionists, Stalin remembered Lominadze. The NKVD fabricated a case against him. Not waiting to be arrested, Lominadze killed
himself in January 1935. His deputy read his suicide note to Moscow
over the telephone: "I request that this message be passed on to Comrade Ordzhonikidze. I decided long ago to choose this ending in the
event that no one believed me. [. . .] I was ready to prove that this libel
was absurd and completely lacking in truth, to justify myself and attempt to persuade others—but even then I wasn't sure they would believe me. . . . An ordeal awaits that I am in no condition to endure. [. . .]
While I have made mistakes, I have devoted my entire adult life to the
Communist cause, to the affairs of our party. I only regret that I didn't
live to see a decisive fight in the international arena. It isn't far off. I die
fully believing in the victory of our cause. Convey to Sergo Ordzhonikidze the contents of this letter. Please help my family."[71]

Ordzhonikidze fulfilled this request. As long as he was alive, Lominadze's widow received a pension for her husband, and by Council of
People's Commissars decree, Lominadze's son, named Sergo after Ord-

zhonikidze, was granted a sizable monetary benefit.[72] Such a grant was unheard of—generous state support to the family of someone labeled an enemy of the people! This may well have precipitated heated discussion between Stalin and Ordzhonikidze. In any event, immediately after Ordzhonikidze's death, Lominadze's wife was deprived of her pension, and not much later she was arrested.

Lominadze was among the former Caucasian bosses whom Ordzhonikidze considered his people and to whom he provided ongoing patronage. In the early 1930s, Stalin removed Ordzhonikidze's cronies from positions of leadership in Transcaucasia (this action, which occasioned a number of clashes, also did nothing to improve relations between Stalin and Ordzhonikidze).[73] Ordzhonikidze continued to patronize his disgraced Caucasian cronies. In September 1937, after Ordzhonikidze was already dead, one member of his inner circle, former first secretary of the Transcaucasian territorial committee Mamia Orakhelashvili, who had been arrested by the NKVD, signed the following testimony.

> First of all, being very closely associated with Sergo Ordzhonikidze, I was a witness to his patronage and his conciliatory attitude toward people with anti-party and counterrevolutionary inclinations. This applies primarily to Beso Lominadze. In my presence, in Sergo Ordzhonikidze's apartment, Beso Lominadze, after a number of counterrevolutionary slurs aimed at the party leadership, made an exceptionally insulting and hooliganistic slur against Stalin. To my surprise, in response to this counterrevolutionary audacity by Lominadze, Ordzhonikidze, smiling, turned to me and said, "Have a look at him!"—and continued to conduct conversation with Lominadze in a calm tone. [. . .] In general, I have to say, the parlor in Sergo Ordzhonikidze's apartment, and, on days off, his dacha (first in Volynskoe and later in Sosnovka), was a frequent meeting place for members of our counterrevolutionary organization, who, while waiting for Sergo Ordzhonikidze to arrive, conducted the most candid counterrevolutionary discussions, which continued right on after Ordzhonikidze himself showed up.[74]

Even considering the methods the NKVD used to obtain testimony, it can be presumed with a degree of certainty that the protocol signed by Orakhelashvili is not sheer invention. Disgraced Soviet leaders tended to have little affection for Stalin. Countless examples illustrate Ordzhonikidze's acerbic and blunt style. If the NKVD passed on to Stalin denunciations concerning the inclinations of his comrades-in-arms, those reports have not yet been found (the archives most likely to contain them have not yet been opened to scholars); still, it is extremely likely that someone reported to Stalin on the meetings and conversations among the Transcaucasians who met at Ordzhonikidze's. In any event, extensive evidence suggests that Stalin strongly disliked the members of Ordzhonikidze's circle. As a result, they were among the first victims of mass repression.

With the public trial in Moscow of the United Trotskyite-Zinovievite Center in August, the situation for Ordzhonikidze's Transcaucasian clients and those who worked at his Commissariat of Heavy Industry took a sharp turn for the worse. The purge that followed the trial primarily affected those who worked for the commissariats managing the country's economy. Many former oppositionists worked at these commissariats, since it was considered safer to assign former oppositionists practical tasks within industry than allow them to engage in more ideologically sensitive work. A large number of Ordzhonikidze's commissariat employees fell victim to this purge. Attacks against industrial managers were of such scope that Stalin agreed to issue a directive to the secretaries of provincial, territorial, and republic party committees, which was sent out on 31 August 1936, prohibiting the removal of managers without approval from Moscow, especially those enterprise directors who had been appointed by decision of the Central Committee. All compromising evidence related to this category of manager was ordered sent to Moscow for review.[75] The story behind this directive is not yet known. On 29 August 1936, Kaganovich and Yezhov sent a draft of it in a telegram to Stalin in Sochi for approval, writing: "In accordance with your instructions we have drafted the following text for the directive."[76] Since the directive primarily affected Ordzhonikidze's domain, he presumably also had a hand in its appearance.

A piece of evidence supporting this presumption is that on 29 August—the same day this directive was sent to Stalin for approval—a resolution was sent to the Politburo that directly affected the Commissariat of Heavy Industry. It overturned a decision by the local authorities to expel the director of the Magnezit Factory in the city of Satka, Chelyabinsk Province, from the party. Undoubtedly initiated by Ordzhonikidze, the resolution was included in the Politburo protocol for 31 August and was published in newspapers the next day.[77]

Paralleling the decision concerning the director of the Satka factory, was a 31 August resolution passed by the Politburo concerning the Dnepropetrovsk provincial committee of the Ukrainian party, one article of which dealt with the fate of the director of the Krivoi Rog Metallurgical Plant, Ya. I. Vesnik. This well-known industrial manager, whose name was familiar to readers of Soviet newspapers, had been accused of abetting counterrevolutionary Trotskyites and expelled from the party. The Politburo intervened on Vesnik's behalf and returned his party membership card.[78] On 5 September, *Pravda* published information about a plenum of the Dnepropetrovsk provincial committee at which the Politburo resolution of 31 August was discussed. After issuing the necessary statements about redoubling the fight against enemies, the plenum "emphatically warned" against allowing further excesses "taking the form of indiscriminate inclusion of party members among Trotskyites and their abettors without sufficient basis for doing so."

Several days later, on 7 September 1936, Ordzhonikidze wrote to Stalin from vacation in the south emphasizing his particular desire to defend economic managers and explicitly expressing his disagreement with the campaign against former oppositionists.

> While the trial of the traitorous rabble [Kamenev, Zinoviev, and other former oppositionists] was under way, I wanted to write to you, but somehow it never worked out. I listened to part of the trial in the TsK, in Com. Kaganovich's office. I listened to the closing words of almost everyone. It is impossible to imagine that anyone could have a more odious downfall than the one they exhibited. Shooting them wasn't enough; if it had been possible, they should have been shot at least ten times. [. . .] They caused tremendous harm to the party; now, knowing what they're made of, you don't know who's telling the truth and who's lying, who's a friend and who's a double-dealer. This is the poison they injected into our party. Today, we are paying a heavy toll for this. Nerves in the party now are taking quite a thrashing: people don't know whether or not they can trust this or that former Trotskyite, Zinovievite. There are quite a few of them in the party. Some people think that we should toss them all out of the party, but that is not wise and should not be done; instead we should take a good look, figure out what's what— our people don't always have enough patience and skill. They messed things up with a lot of directors; almost all of them were saved, but they remained "tarnished." [. . .] I'm very worried about the army. [. . .] A skillful enemy could deal us an irreparable blow here: they'll start to spread rumors about people and instill distrust in the army. Here, we need to be very careful.[79]

Ordzhonikidze's "summer offensive" appears to have been the result of compromise at the upper reaches of the party. Stalin, who was fueling the engine of repression, had encountered resistance. Ordzhonikidze was not the only one to defend his people; the heads of other government agencies did so as well.[80] Stalin made concessions and sanctioned the Politburo's decision to defend economic managers. But soon this short-lived compromise fell apart. Its demise was signaled by the arrest of Ordzhonikidze's first deputy, Yury Piatakov, during the earliest hours of 12 September 1936. This further exacerbated the situation at the Commissariat of Heavy Industry and worsened Ordzhonikidze's situation, for it placed him in the position of having worked side by side with the "enemy."

To what degree Ordzhonikidze actually believed that Piatakov was guilty is hard to say. On 7 September, in the letter to Stalin, Ordzhonikidze cautiously hinted that it would be possible to manage without arresting Piatakov, then on a business trip in the Urals. His wife had been arrested and had given evidence against him, which he refers in his first sentence. "Piatakov's wife really buried him. Whatever we decide to do, we can't leave him as deputy [chairman], that is completely impossible, it would be harmful at this point. He has to be immediately removed. If we're not going to arrest him, let's send him somewhere, or leave him right there in the Urals."[81] But when Stalin decided to do away with Piatakov, Ordzhonikidze did not resist and even expressed his support. The telegram that Ordzhonikidze sent from Piatigorsk on 11 September 1936 to vote on Piatakov's fate was loyal. "Am in full agreement with the Politburo's [proposed] decree to expel [Piatakov] from the TsK VKP(b) and on incompatibility with his retaining his membership in the VKP(b) in the future. I vote 'Yes.'"[82]

Ordzhonikidze's "full agreement" with Piatakov's expulsion from the party (which essentially meant arrest) did not, however, save Ordzhonikidze from further tribulation. Stalin, it seems, had decided to break Ordzhonikidze once and for all before the decisive events that lay ahead. This is the only explanation for the arrest soon afterward of Ordzhonikidze's older brother Pavel (Papulia). Ordzhonikidze's character and the special importance he placed on family and friends made this a very hard blow, as evidence from a variety of sources indicates. For example, in testimony on the case of Beria in 1953, the secretary of the Communist Party of Azerbaijan, M. Bagirov, said, "Several months before his death, Sergo Ordzhonikidze visited Kislovodsk for the last time. This time he called on the telephone and asked that I come to see him. I fulfilled Ordzhonikidze's request and came to Kislovodsk. [. . .] Ordzhonikidze asked me in great detail about Beria and spoke out rather harshly about him. In particular, Ordzhonikidze stated that he could not believe that his brother Papulia, who had been arrested at that time by Beria, was guilty."[83]

In addition to Papulia Ordzhonikidze, others close to Sergo were arrested by Stalin's order. In early October 1936, Stalin sent the following directive to Yezhov: "Concerning Vardanian—he is currently the secretary of the Taganrog city committee. He is undoubtedly a secret Trotskyite, or at least he is a patron and protector of Trotskyites. He should be arrested. L. Gogoberidze—secretary of one of the factory party committees in the Azov-Black Sea territory—should also be arrested. If Lominadze was a secret enemy of the party, then Gogoberidze is also a secret enemy of the party, since he was as close as could be with Lominadze. He should be arrested."[84]

The October arrests within Ordzhonikidze's close circle were particularly cynical because they were conducted on Ordzhonikidze's fiftieth birthday, the occasion of boisterous (arranged) celebrations across the country. Hints as to Ordzhonikidze's state of mind can be found in the memoirs of Ordzhonikidze's wife, Zinaida. "On 27 October," she writes, "in Piatigorsk there was a ceremonial meeting to mark Sergo's fiftieth birthday. He refused to attend and I went by myself."[85] At the very end of October, Ordzhonikidze left for Moscow. Soon after his arrival in the capital he had a heart attack.

Ordzhonikidze's depression and illness apparently did not force him to completely lay down his arms. At the February–March plenum Stalin, who launched a full-scale attack against the deceased Ordzhonikidze, exclaimed, "How upset he allowed himself to get defending all those, as is now evident, scoundrels, like Vardanian, Gogoberidze, from everyone. [. . .] How upset he got himself and how upset he got us."[86] Stalin's words can be interpreted to mean that the October arrests of Vardanian and Gogoberidze triggered some sort of clash between Stalin and Ordzhonikidze.

But Ordzhonikidze was no match for his opponent. The chekist attacks that Stalin directed against the Commissariat of Heavy Industry became more and more brutal. In late November 1936 the so-called Kemerovo trial of "wreckers" in the mines of Kuzbass was being widely publicized in the press. The second public Moscow trial in the case of the so-called Parallel Anti-Soviet Trotskyite Center, held from 23 to 30 January 1937, gave new impetus to repressive measures aimed at economic managers. Basically, the commissariat was on trial. Out of seventeen defendants, ten were managers from the Commissariat of Heavy Industry who had served under Piatakov.

Ordzhonikidze was increasingly vulnerable. In addition to worrying about protecting his employees, he now had to worry about saving his own political reputation. In early December 1936, apparently in response to a demand by Stalin, Ordzhonikidze gave Stalin letters that Lominadze had written in 1929 that contained criticism of Stalin's policies. Immediately afterward, on 4 December, Stalin sent these letters to members of the Politburo. In the cover note, Stalin criticized Ordzhonikidze for committing a crude political mistake. "It can be seen from these letters that Lominadze, even back in 1929, was engaged in a struggle against the TsK and its decisions, and furthermore he was counting on the fact that Com. Ordzhonikidze would not tell the Central Committee of the party about Lominadze's anti-party inclinations and ideas. It is completely obvious that if the TsK had had Lominadze's letters in their hands in time, it would never have agreed to send Lominadze to Transcaucasia to serve as first secretary of the Zakkraikom [Transcaucasian territorial committee]."[87] In the context of his arguments with Ordzhonikidze over the new waves of repression, this démarche by Stalin served an obvious goal. Ordzhonikidze was being warned that his patronage of "enemies," which had a long history, would not be tolerated any longer.

Politically compromised, Ordzhonikidze could only hope that Stalin would change his stance. He tried to convince Stalin that continuing the repressions would bring irreparable harm. To avoid irritating Stalin, Ordzhonikidze cast events in the following light: the NKVD had already exposed the vast majority of enemies; the main task now was to work conscientiously toward repairing the consequences of the sabotage. This was a view that Ordzhonikidze constantly brought up in his final speeches.

His desire to thwart a new wave of repression can be seen in the documents he prepared for the upcoming Central Committee plenum, scheduled to open in late February 1937. The Politburo had assigned him the task of reporting to the plenum on the sabotage of heavy industry and the measures being taken to rectify its consequences. The text of the speech itself has yet to be found, but a draft resolution that he sent to Stalin gives us an idea of what he was planning to say. He wrote in a calm tone and discussed the sabotage in a dry and unsensational manner. His primary focus was on the technical measures that had to be taken to improve industrial productivity. The speech opened with an overview of the successes that had been achieved "thanks to our cadres of engineers, technical experts, and economic managers who had been cultivated by the party from among the sons of the working class and the peasantry."[88]

At the time this resolution was being drafted, accusations of sabotage made against workers in heavy industry were based solely on information extracted during interrogations of arrested managers who came from the central apparatus of the Heavy Industry Commissariat—Piatakov, S. A. Rataichak, and the directors of several enterprises. In one case, L. M. Mariasin, the construction manager, had been arrested along with others working on the construction site of a train manufacturing facility in Nizhny Tagil. Those overseeing the construction of the Kemerovo Chemical Plant were put on trial in January 1937 in the case of the "Parallel Trotskyite Center." There were similar cases. Ordzhonikidze proposed having the Commissariat of Heavy Industry conduct an independent review of the cases. He also included an article in the draft resolution in which he called for the commissariat to be assigned to report to the Central Committee within ten days on the status of construction of the Kemerovo Chemical Plant, the Nizhny Tagil Train Factory, and the Sredne-Uralsky Copper Smelting Plant with specific recommendations for "liquidating the consequences of sabotage."

As later became evident, in proposing this arrangement in the draft resolution, Ordzhonikidze was pursuing a specific goal. With the aim of amassing additional ammunition to use in his talks with Stalin, Ordzhonikidze was inventing an appealing pretext for setting up an independent commissariat review. Ordzhonikidze had even sent separate commissions out to review the construction projects without waiting for the plenum's decision. Officially, the task of the proposed commissariat commission was to come up with measures to remediate the "consequences of sabotage." In actuality, Ordzhonikidze gave his people quite different instructions.

Fortuitous timing has given us a piece of evidence that helps clarify what Ordzhonikidze was trying to achieve during the days leading up to the February–March plenum. A 21 February 1937 article written by Professor N. Gelperin would not have seen the light of day had it not been published at just the right time. The article, which was published in the commissariat newspaper *Za industrializatsiiu* under the heading "The Commissar's Directives," contained a rather candid assessment, written under the immediate influence of events, that managed to slip through a small crack in censorship during the brief period of confusion between Ordzhonikidze's death and the February–March plenum. After Molotov's report to the plenum criticizing Ordzhonikidze's commission, Gelperin's article could not have been printed (and Gelperin himself would not have dreamed of writing it).

As Gelperin described events in his article, Ordzhonikidze had summoned him on 5 February and asked that he go to Kemerovo to the chemical plant construction site. Ordzhonikidze sent him off with the words: "Keep in mind [. . .] that you are going to a place that was one of the rather active centers of sabotage. All of the honest workers there—and they make up the vast majority—are really upset by this story. You are also probably still feeling the effects of the recent trial [of Piatakov and other "Trotskyites"]. But remember that cowardly or insufficiently conscientious people might want to blame everything on sabotage to, so to speak, cover up their own mistakes in the sabotage trial. It would be fundamentally wrong to allow this. We would not be getting a full picture of what happened, and, consequently, we would not know what needs to be done to fix things or how it should be done. Approach it like a technician; try to distinguish intentional sabotage from inadvertent mistakes—this is the main task."

In other words, Ordzhonikidze was not asking his people to confirm the evidence fabricated by the NKVD but to give their own economic and technical assessments. Since in the official view all economic problems and shortcomings were the clear-cut result of sabotage, such an assignment was inherently seditious. Nevertheless, Gelperin acted in accordance with Ordzhonikidze's wishes. Upon returning from Kemerovo, the commission presented a comprehensive report in which the words "sabotage" and "wrecker" were nowhere to be found. The report of another commission—headed by Ordzhonikidze's deputy O. P. Osipov-Shmidt and assigned to investigate the coke by-product industry in Donbass—was compiled in the same spirit. Both of these commissions managed to return to Moscow before Ordzhonikidze died. He met with Gelperin and Osipov-Shmidt and was given a thorough account of their findings.

Things turned out differently with a third commission, which included the head of the commissariat's Main Construction Administration, S. Z. Ginzburg, and another of Ordzhonikidze's deputies, I. P. Pavlunovsky. This commission went to the train factory. Ginzburg, the only participant in these events to live to see post-Communist Russia, later gave the following account.

> In early February 1937 Sergo told me what had happened at Nizhny Tagil Uralvagonstroi. [. . .] He proposed that Pavlunovsky and I [. . .] immediately travel there in a commissariat train car and take a detailed look at just what the arrested construction saboteurs did. [. . .] In mid-February Sergo called from Moscow and asked what state the construction site was in, what kinds of criminals had been found. I answered that the factory had been well built, without shoddiness, although certain budget items had been somewhat overspent. At present, the construction has ground to a halt, the workers don't know what to do with themselves. [. . .] To Sergo's question, Had I been to other construction sites? I answered that I had and that in comparison with other construction sites, in N. Tagil things are better in many ways. Sergo asked again: Is it really so? I told him that I always tell it the way it is. In that case, said Sergo, find Pavlunovsky and immediately return to Moscow. In the train dictate to the stenographer a brief report addressed to me about the state of affairs at the Uralvagonzavod and come to see me as soon as you get back.[89]

After receiving these reports, Ordzhonikidze again wrote to Stalin, but this only prompted another fit of irritation. Stalin was also very displeased with the draft resolution that Ordzhonikidze was proposing for the plenum. A copy of the draft proposal with margins covered by Stalin's comments and criticisms has survived. The markings seem to indicate that what annoyed Stalin most of all were the passages in the document that revealed Ordzhonikidze's desire to soften the assertions of sabotage and to give the document a more objective tone. Words in Stalin's hand are scrawled across the first page of the document: "1) Which sectors are affected by sabotage and how were they affected (specific facts). 2) Reasons they got away with it (an apolitical, business-oriented selection of cadres, insufficient political education of cadres)."[90]

The decision passed during the February–March plenum after Ordzhonikidze's death took a harder line than the initial draft prepared by the Commissariat of Heavy Industry.

The arguments and conflict between Ordzhonikidze and Stalin, the months of tension, peaked in the days before the opening of the Central Committee plenum. On 15 and 16 February, in addition to fulfilling his duties at the commissariat, Ordzhonikidze worked on plenum materials, hurrying to complete the resolution on sabotage in industry that the Politburo had assigned him to draft, and working on his speech— "throwing together the main points on pieces of paper and on a pad," as Ordzhonikidze's widow, recalled two years later.[91]

We are able to ascertain in great detail how Ordzhonikidze spent 17 February from the summary prepared by his secretary and from the testimony and memoirs of witnesses.[92] Ordzhonikidze left home that morning and went to the commissariat, arriving at ten minutes after noon, although, as his deputy A. P. Zeveniagin testified, he usually arrived earlier, at ten.[93] Any number of reasons could account for Ordzhonikidze's late arrival, but it does indirectly support an assertion made in one of Ordzhonikidze's biographies, evidently based on the words of his widow, that on the morning of the 17th, Ordzhonikidze had a face-to-face talk with Stalin that lasted several hours.[94]

We will never know what was said during this conversation, but certain available pieces of evidence let us guess at the nature of Stalin and Ordzhonikidze's final confrontation. Since Stalin was energetically preparing for the Central Committee plenum and since a session of the Politburo was scheduled to convene at three to discuss plenum documents, it is reasonable to assume that plenum issues were raised. Perhaps Ordzhonikidze spoke of the arrests at the commissariat and of Bukharin's fate, which would be decided at the plenum. He may also have brought up his brother, Papulia Ordzhonikidze. There were other possibilities as well. The next day, 18 February, Ordzhonikidze was scheduled to meet with the director of the Makeevsk Metallurgical Factory, G. V. Gvakharia, who enjoyed Ordzhonikidze's patronage. Gvakharia had recently been accused of ties with Trotskyites, and he had probably come to Moscow to seek Ordzhonikidze's protection.[95] Ordzhonikidze may well have spoken of Gvakharia's fate with Stalin. (Gvakharia was arrested some time after Ordzhonikidze's death.) Almost certainly the conversation touched on the results of Ginzburg's inspection. Ginzburg had returned to Moscow early on 18 February and soon afterward Poskrebyshev informed him by telephone that "I. V. Stalin has asked that he be sent the report about the state of affairs at Uralvagonstroi, which Sergo talked to him about."[96] The other commissariat commissions may also have been discussed.

But whatever Stalin and Ordzhonikidze did discuss on 17 February, their conversation apparently ended on a calm note. Stalin is unlikely to have brought matters to a head right before a Politburo meeting; he probably left Ordzhonikidze with some cause for hope. Indeed, Ordzhonikidze's workday seems to have followed its usual course, without his exhibiting signs of particular anxiety or alarm. After spending a little more than two hours at the commissariat, at two thirty he left to see Molotov in the Kremlin. The Politburo meeting got under way there at three. The meeting was well attended. In addition to all the Politburo members, a large contingent of Central Committee members and candidate members were there, as were the heads of the Party and Soviet Control Commissions. Only one item was on the agenda—the decisions drafted to go with the various speeches to be delivered at the plenum. After discussion, the draft resolutions on Zhdanov's speech about the upcoming elections, Stalin's speech about the shortcomings of party work, and Yezhov's speech about the "lessons of sabotage, wrecking, and spying" were approved more or less unchanged. The draft resolutions on the speeches by Ordzhonikidze and Kaganovich about sabotage in the economic commissariats were passed, too, but with the stipulation that their final versions reflect corrections and additions approved by the Politburo.[97]

Of course, Stalin proposed corrections and additions. The original Politburo protocols for 17 February include a draft resolution on Ordzhonikidze's speech with changes in Stalin's hand. As before, Stalin crossed out a number of phrases about the achievements of workers in industry and transport. Having given up on getting the necessary formulations out of Ordzhonikidze, this time Stalin made extensive insertions. In the section outlining the obstacles to exposing enemies, Stalin included a reference to "bureaucratic corruption of the principle of *edinonachalie* [greater authority for managers of enterprises]." He also stated that "based on edinonachalie, many economic managers consider themselves absolutely unconstrained by the public opinion of the masses and rank-and-file economic workers," thereby depriving themselves "of the support of the forward ranks in exposing and liquidating shortcomings and deficiencies used by enemies for their wrecking work." Another lengthy insertion that Stalin entered was of a programmatic nature. "Finally, the TsK VKP(b) plenum cannot overlook the objectionable phenomenon that the very uncovering and exposure of Trotskyite wreckers, after the wrecking work of Trotskyites became evident, was achieved despite the passivity of a number of agencies of industry and transport. It was usually the NKVD and individual party members—volunteers—who exposed the Trotskyites. The industrial agencies themselves, and, to a certain degree, the transport agencies as well, exhibited neither active effort nor—to an even lesser extent—initiative. Furthermore, certain industrial agencies were even a drag on this case."[98] This was Stalin's response to Ordzhonikidze and all those who tried to limit the purge of cadres. The ensuing harsh criticism of Ordzhonikidze's agency during the plenum was delivered under the banner of these ideas, put forward by Stalin.

One and a half hours after the opening of the Politburo session, at four thirty, Ordzhonikidze and Kaganovich went to Poskrebyshev's office and stayed there for two and a half hours. The amount of time they spent there suggests that they must have been working on the draft resolutions, incorporating remarks expressed during the Politburo meeting. At seven Ordzhonikidze and Kaganovich left Poskrebyshev's office and walked around the Kremlin grounds. Near Ordzhonikidze's apartment the two men said good-bye and went to their respective homes. Ordzhonikidze entered his apartment at seven fifteen. He probably had dinner. ("He ate irregularly: sometimes at six or seven in the evening, and sometimes at two in the morning," Ordzhonikidze's wife recalled of the final months of his life.)[99] At nine thirty that evening he again set out for the commissariat.

It was a short trip from the Kremlin to the commissariat on Nogin Square. By ten o'clock Ordzhonikidze was meeting in his office with Professor Gelperin, who had returned that day from his inspection in Kemerovo. The haste with which this meeting was arranged tells us that Ordzhonikidze was eager to review the commission findings. As Gelperin recalls, Ordzhonikidze listened to what he had to say, asked questions about the construction and the state of equipment, and asked that a written report be prepared. Ordzhonikidze scheduled another meeting with Gelperin for ten o'clock on the morning of 19 February.[100] Since the head of the Main Administration for the Nitrogen Industry, E. Brodov, was scheduled to report to Ordzhonikidze at the same time, there must have been a chemical industry meeting at the commissariat that morning.[101]

The very timing of these meetings is significant. Ordzhonikidze was planning to work as usual. The other matters that occupied him at the commissariat during the evening of 17 February did not seem to foretell anything unusual either. As always, he signed a lot of papers and listened to a few reports. The final three orders issued by Ordzhonikidze are dated 17 February. Close to midnight Ordzhonikidze met with O. P. Osipov-Shmidt, his deputy in charge of the chemical industry.[102] Osipov-Shmidt had headed the commission to visit the coke by-product industry in Donbass, and this was most likely the topic of their conversation. Twenty minutes after midnight Ordzhonikidze left work and went home.

Up to this point, everything that happened indicates that Ordzhonikidze was working just as he usually did. Undoubtedly, however, something of significance occurred after Ordzhonikidze returned home. Unfortunately, very little information is available about the final hours of Ordzhonikidze's life. Most likely, he had another heated conversation with Stalin, a conversation culminating in Ordzhonikidze's tragic suicide.

Although many details of these events will remain a mystery, it is possible to assert a critical fact: Ordzhonikidze died because he was attempting to counter mounting repression, in particular the destruction of industrial cadres. This conclusion raises another question: How far was Ordzhonikidze prepared to go in his fight with Stalin? Robert Tucker expresses the following opinion: "By virtue of his very old intimacy with Stalin, their common Georgian origins, his tendency to become infuriated to the point of ignoring dictates of prudence, and his loyalty to the party's cause, Ordzhonikidze was the one prominent leader left who was capable of openly resisting Stalin at the upcoming plenum and possibly becoming the core figure in a last-ditch concerted opposition to the general secretary's rampage of terror. Stalin had, at all cost, to forestall that."[103]

This view is widely held. Taking it to its logical conclusion, some historians have suggested that Stalin ordered Ordzhonikidze's death. For now, all available evidence indicates that Ordzhonikidze was trying to

change Stalin's mind but that he had no intention of bringing their conflict out into the open. (A characteristic detail is the fact that over the
forty-seven days of 1937 that Ordzhonikidze was alive, he met with
Stalin in his office twenty-two times, for a total of almost seventy-two
hours spent with Stalin in that setting alone.)[104] Everything we know
about Ordzhonikidze's political biography, his behavior over the final
months of 1936 and the first months of 1937, and his extremely poor
state of health appears to support the supposition that he killed himself. This was a suicide of protest, the final, desperate argument Ordzhonikidze made in his unsuccessful attempt to convince Stalin to put an
end to the repression of his people.[105]

Ordzhonikidze's inconsistent attempts to stop Stalin were the exception to the rule, however. Other members of the Politburo even if they
sensed a growing threat, actively supported Stalin in his efforts. Starting
with the former oppositionists, the terror engulfed a widening swath of
party-state officialdom before it came crashing down on society at large.

5 Stalin and the Great Terror
1937–1938

AN EXTENSIVE BODY of scholarship is devoted to the history of the Great Terror, the mass repression that engulfed all segments of Soviet society in 1937 and 1938. One question central to this scholarship and to the subject of this book has been debated for many years: To what extent was the terror centrally orchestrated, determined by orders from the top, and to what extent did more elemental, spontaneous factors affect the course of events? A number of historians believe that elemental forces played a greater role than is generally recognized. Though not denying the role of the center in directing the repression, they argue that the Great Terror was the result of contradictions inherent in the party-state, the uncontrolled actions of regional bosses who, in their desire to deflect attacks away from themselves, directed the terror against countless scapegoats, or the active support that broad sectors of the population gave to the repression.[1]

Increased archival access has permitted a clearer picture of the Great Terror. As documents show, over the course of 1936, on Stalin's initiative, a policy aimed at the "wholesale liquidation" of former oppositionists was conducted, reaching its culmination in the Moscow trials of August 1936 and January 1937. During the first half of 1937 army officers were also purged, and attacks were undertaken against the middle-level nomenklatura. Throughout the rest of 1937 and continuing into

1938, the attacks became large-scale purges of managerial cadres. Despite their breadth and cruelty, within the context of the Stalin era, these measures were somewhat limited in nature. Had the purges stopped with the destruction of former oppositionists, party-state functionaries, and the military, we would probably not be justified in calling this repression the Great Terror.

The Great Terror began when repressive measures engulfed the broadest strata of the country's population. This, as we now know from archival investigation, occurred between August 1937 and November 1938, when a series of mass operations against "anti-Soviet elements" and "counterrevolutionary national contingents" took place, including mass deportations. There is now a basis for believing (and the literature increasingly reflects this belief) that the Great Terror was a series of purposeful and carefully planned centralized operations. The repressive measures differed from others organized by the Stalin regime in terms not only of scale (arrests and deportations of peasants in the early 1930s also encompassed a significant portion of the population) but also in exceptional cruelty, especially in the enormous numbers of people shot.[2]

Considering the fundamental importance of the Great Terror, it is inevitable that every interpretation, in the end, shapes both our understanding of the mechanisms by which key political decisions were made and implemented within the Stalinist system and our overall characterization of the system. It is therefore essential that the tragic events of 1937–1938 be reevaluated with a focus on their political aspects.

THE MOTIVES BEHIND MASS OPERATIONS

A great number of conjectures and assertions have been produced to explain the mass repressions of the late 1930s and the motives of Stalin and his comrades-in-arms in unleashing the Great Terror.

Official Stalinist propaganda gave a single, unequivocal explanation: the targets of these purges were enemies. Honest citizens had nothing to fear. The only way innocents could be swept up by the terror was if they fell victim to enemies who had infiltrated the NKVD (in which case Stalin would see that the victims were expeditiously rehabilitated). Even today, there are those who adhere to such views.

Justly rejecting any apologies for the terror, some anti-Stalinists succumb to the opposite extreme. Not wishing to explain anything, they view any analysis of the reasons for the terror as attempts to justify it. Insofar as information about the terror does have to be somehow interpreted, everything is boiled down to Stalin's mental deficiencies, to the brutal nature of the leader and his comrades, and to generalizations about the totalitarian nature of the regime.

While the psychological tendencies of Soviet leaders certainly may have played a role in shaping many of the events of 1930–1950, the leaders' actions were not necessarily devoid of a certain criminal logic. Reconstructing the calculations made by the organizers of the terror is an essential step in studying the principles governing the political system that took shape during the late 1930s because the large-scale repression of 1937–1938 is the clearest expression of what sets the Stalinist political regime apart from other regimes in Soviet history.

The factors shaping the Great Terror can be conditionally divided into two categories. First, there are the overall reasons behind the use of terror and milder forms of violence by the Soviet state over the entire span of its existence, especially from the late 1920s to the early 1950s. Here, a wide range of ideas support the theory of a "permanent purge," according to which constant repression was essential to the viability of the Soviet regime, as it would be to any similar regime. Historians note that repression, the "subsystem of terror," served many functions. Among the most important were ensuring that society was kept in a state of submissiveness, suppressing dissent and opposition, and solidifying the sole authority of the leader. The campaigns against saboteurs and "degenerate" officials were also an effective method for manipulating social consciousness and shaping the myth of a just leader. Repression was also undoubtedly an essential condition for the functioning of the Soviet economy, which was based on compulsory labor, supplemented at various stages by the large-scale exploitation of convicts. The list of such observations could be continued. Every repressive act, including the large-scale operations of 1937–1938, to a certain degree served these overall functions.

Even once we have understood the reasons for the terror as an underlying element of the Stalinist system, we must still explore its application during particular periods of Soviet history. At different stages, state terror was used to varying extents and in varying forms not only as a way to bolster the regime but as a means of solving problems specific to a particular period.

We can analyze the specific reasons for acts of state terror both in terms of the acts themselves and on the basis of political slogans used in laying the groundwork for particular campaigns. The theoretical basis for the mass repression of the late 1930s was enunciated most clearly during the notorious plenum of February–March 1937. The stenographic record of the plenum, in combination with other documents, suggests that the mass arrests and executions of 1936–1938 pursued two primary interrelated goals: the large-scale purge of leading cadres in light of a growing military threat and the destruction of a potential "fifth column" in society.

During the first months after the trial of former oppositionists that took place in Moscow in August 1936, the main thrust of the purge was directed against the administrative cadres of the party and the state economic apparatus. A clamorous anti-bureaucratic propaganda campaign, launched during the February–March plenum, accompanied these shake-ups. In a plenum speech, Stalin announced the objective of pouring "fresh forces awaiting deployment" into the administrative ranks. Indeed, over the course of the two years that followed, the old cadres were largely destroyed and replaced with a new generation of officials.

On the eve of the February–March plenum, the Central Committee department in charge of party personnel (ORPO), headed by Georgy Malenkov, compiled names of nomenklatura workers from various agencies who had been involved in opposition movements or in other parties or who had in any way "wavered." The compilation was divided into two lists. The first included administrators who had been removed from their posts, expelled from the party, and arrested. The second enumerated the political "sins" of workers who still held their jobs.[3] Most of those included in the second list were soon arrested, and the majority were shot.

Stalin wanted to get rid of the old guard for several reasons. He was particularly suspicious of those who had been involved in opposition movements, as many who held party-state posts at the middle- and lower-management level had been. Stalin was undoubtedly aware that he was not an indisputable authority even for those veteran Bolsheviks who had never taken part in opposition movements and who had followed him loyally. Whatever these people might say in their speeches, however fervently they might pledge their loyalty, Stalin knew that long-time party members remembered the numerous policy failures of the

1930s and that Lenin's testament had at one point come close to dooming Stalin's political career. At one time the party leadership had every reason to see Stalin as merely one among many equals. Even though such a time seemed increasingly distant, Stalin was suspicious of his comrades-in-arms who could recall the heyday of party democracy. To make matters worse, the influence of the "party generals," though reduced to a minimum, had not fully disappeared.

Through long years of collaboration, the old cadres had grown close and established strong mutual ties. Stalin periodically reshuffled the party bosses, moved around provincial party committee secretaries, replaced secretaries and Central Committee department heads. But to completely sever the ties, to break up groups that had grown up around leaders at various levels based on the principle of personal loyalty, was impossible. Moving from one place to another, party bosses often brought their people with them. Groups had formed within the party-state apparatus whose members had a dual allegiance: to the top leader (Stalin) and to their own patrons within the Politburo or other government entities. Although we have yet to hear of a single instance where such a group posed the slightest opposition to Stalin's sole authority, the existence of such informal structures was a source of apprehension for Stalin.

Stalin expressed these apprehensions with particular candor in his concluding remarks at the February–March plenum. "People are sometimes selected based not on a political or business principle but on personal acquaintance, personal allegiance, friendships—generally criteria of a narrow-minded nature." He singled out for particular criticism the secretaries of the Central Committee of the Communist Party of Kazakhstan, Levon Mirzoyan, and the Yaroslavl Province party committee, A. R. Vainov. The former, according to Stalin, brought thirty to forty of his people to Kazakhstan from Azerbaijan and Ural Province, where he had worked previously, and placed them in positions of authority. The ones who had been brought to Yaroslavl from Donbass had also brought a group of his subordinates. Stalin was frank in explaining what he did not like about such a practice. "What does it mean to drag a whole group of cronies with you? It means that you have acquired a certain independence from local organizations and, if you want, a certain independence from the TsK. He has his group, I have my group, they have a personal allegiance to me."[4]

In speaking out against groups based on personal allegiance to a patron, Stalin was not just talking about secretaries of local party organizations. He appears to have seen a similar threat in all structures, however loosely organized, and leveled particular criticism for pursuing institutional self-interest (vedomstvennost') and placing the interests of a given group above those of the state against the People's Commissariat of Heavy Industry and its head, Ordzhonikidze. The concern that Stalin expressed over the question of sabotage in the army and the NKVD, which was the subject of special discussions at the plenum, may have masked his anxiety over such dual loyalties within these organs of government. One institution where personal allegiances clearly played an oversized role was the Politburo itself. The damage it suffered as the result of purges had a character all its own.

Stalin did not have a very high opinion of the managerial abilities of the older administrators. In his plenum speech, as if warding off charges that he was destroying highly skilled cadres, Stalin asserted, "Today's saboteurs do not have any technical advantages over our people. To the contrary, our people are technically better trained." The advantage of the saboteurs, Stalin insisted, was only their "possession of a party membership card."[5] This appears to have been Stalin's opinion about old Bolsheviks as an "estate." The old cadres, in Stalin's opinion, had lost their revolutionary zeal and were drawn to a tranquil, "petit bourgeois" life. A significant portion of Stalin's speech at the plenum was devoted to denouncing a "mood of nonchalance and self-satisfaction," an "atmosphere of grand ceremonies and mutual salutations," that "undermines people's sense of direction and tends to make them rest on their laurels."[6]

The older cadres were also accused of widespread abuse of power. As the new wave of terror got under way, the anti-bureaucratic propaganda campaign in the press intensified. Many administrators were accused of breaking the law, being degenerate, having a heartless attitude toward people, suppressing criticism, encouraging sycophants, and creating local cults. All of these themes were developed during the February–March plenum. Boris Sheboldaev, secretary of the Azov-Black Sea party territorial committee, and Pavel Postyshev, secretary of the Kiev Province committee, were the butts of criticism at the plenum, especially for encouraging toadies and creating their own cults. But to varying degrees, analogous accusations were leveled against the heads of almost all major organizations. One of Stalin's closest aides, Lev Mekhlis, editor of *Pravda,* devoted almost his entire speech to criticism of the secretaries of provincial committees. Citing numerous examples from local newspapers, he excoriated a flourishing "toadyism and *vozhdizm* [leaderism]." In Gorky Territory, according to Mekhlis, a newspaper was named *For the Implementation of Comrade Pramnek's Instructions,* and the territorial committee halted its publication only after sharp criticism in the pages of *Pravda.* In another case, the newspaper *The Chelyabinsk Worker* had published a report that concluded with the words "Long live the head of Cheliabinsk Bolsheviks, Com. Ryndin!"[7]

As a rule, those so criticized were eventually labeled enemies of the people. They were assigned full responsibility for lawlessness, violence, economic failures, and the unprecedented hardships endured by the populace in the past.

Stalin seems to have felt that the best way to strengthen the regime was to promote a new generation of leaders. They were better educated, energetic, and free of any inflated sense of their own worth due to "revolutionary service," nor were they responsible for the crimes and violence during collectivization and industrialization. Their life experiences and rapid advancement were the best guarantees of their loyalty to Stalin. It was from his hands that they received positions of authority; it was with him that hope for further advancement rested. In fact, a turnover of cadres in the late 1930s became not only possible but essential. Sheila Fitzpatrick, who has studied this question in detail, has shown that the mass advancement and training of new "proletarian cadres" in the late 1920s and early 1930s created a "potential problem: the *vydvizhentsy,* better qualified than the old cadres, were on the average only about ten years younger. In the natural course of things, they would probably have had to wait a very long time for top jobs."[8] Stalin's remarks at the plenum suggest that he was aware of this problem. "We have tens of thousands of free people, talented people. We just have to recognize them and promote them in time so they don't languish too long in one place and start to rot."[9]

Of course, the promotion of new officials did not require the murder of old ones. But like any dictator, Stalin preferred to destroy his aggrieved former comrades, suspecting that at a critical moment they might unite and remind their leader how unfairly he had treated them. Under Stalin, disgraced officials did not simply go into retirement, and this forced anyone fortunate enough to survive to work with redoubled effort to prove how indispensable and devoted he or she was.

While much of the Soviet nomenklatura was destroyed during this period, the vast majority of victims of the Great Terror—the mass operations conducted between August 1937 and November 1938—were ordinary citizens. Some of their contemporaries, in attempting to understand the brutal logic of the terror, advanced the theory that Stalin's main goal was the destruction of opponents of the regime that could potentially constitute a fifth column in case of war. This notion was expressed in letters to Stalin both by Nikolai Bukharin (writing from prison) in December 1937 and Mikhail Sholokhov in February 1938.[10] Analogous theories were proposed by Western observers. The U.S. ambassador to Moscow Joseph Davies wrote about repression as a method for destroying a potential fifth column.[11] Isaac Deutscher expresses a similar viewpoint in his biography of Stalin.[12]

Documents that have become available in recent years support these theories. In and of themselves, we should note, the numerous assertions by Stalin and his comrades-in-arms of a military threat are not proof that the Kremlin actually believed that one existed. In many cases, especially in the 1920s, the flames of war hysteria were fanned purely as a propaganda tool to distract the people from failures in the domestic policy arena. But in the mid-1930s things were different. Suffice it to point out that in 1936–1937 there was a significant (even explosive) growth in the military budget, both in absolute terms and as a percentage of total expenditures.[13] The international situation in 1936 and 1937, when the mass purges were under way, had all the hallmarks of a prewar period. An important indicator from the perspective of the Soviet leadership, besides the increasingly aggressive posture of German Fascists, was the war in Spain. Events in Spain convinced Stalin, who was already highly mistrustful of the Western democracies, that England and France were not able to effectively resist Germany. These events also served as reminders of the destructive potential of foreign intervention in a civil war, as well as of the fifth-column factor, which had emerged as a concept within the Spanish context. There is documentary evidence that Stalin, who devoted a lot of time to Spain, was convinced that one of the main reasons the republicans had been defeated was the presence of traitors in their camp, and he demanded that traitors be dealt with decisively.[14] Interestingly, at the same time that Stalin was demanding the liquidation of spies in Spain, preparations were being made in Moscow to launch the case against a "counterrevolutionary organization" in the Red Army.

In July 1937, when decisions were being made about large-scale operations against "anti-Soviet elements," Japan invaded China, heightening tensions in the Far East. Soon afterward, on 21 August, two important events coincided: the Soviet Union and China signed a non-aggression treaty aimed against Japan, and the Council of People's Commissars and the Central Committee issued a decree "On the Exile of the Korean Population from Border Regions of the Far Eastern Territory." The decree gave the goal of the deportations of Soviet Koreans as "stopping the infiltration of Japanese espionage into the DVK [Far Eastern Territory]."[15]

Stalin viewed the deteriorating international situation in 1936–1937 with extreme concern. Over the course of Russian history in general and the history of Bolshevism in particular, war was not just a threat from without; it was a time of social cataclysm and political upheaval. After the Bolsheviks emerged from the Civil War as victors, no force within the country had been capable of overthrowing the regime. Soviet leaders themselves had achieved power as a result of war and always believed that they might succumb to a combined effort by a foreign enemy and domestic anti-Bolshevik forces.

One of Stalin's closest comrades-in-arms, Viacheslav Molotov, spoke frankly about this several decades later.

> Nineteen thirty-seven was necessary. If you consider that after the revolution we were slashing left and right, and we were victorious, but enemies of different sorts remained, and in the face of impending danger of fascist aggression they might unite. We owe the fact that we did not have a fifth column during the war to '37. After all, even among Bolsheviks there were the sorts who were fine and loyal when everything was going well, when the country and party were not threatened with danger. But if something started, they would falter and switch sides. I think a lot of the military who were repressed in '37 shouldn't have been rehabilitated. [. . .] These people probably weren't spies, but they had ties to reconnaissance, and, most important, you couldn't count on them at a time of crisis.[16]

Another of Stalin's close comrades, Lazar Kaganovich, made similar statements in the early 1960s. Here is how he explained the reasons for the repressions: "This was a struggle against a 'fifth column' that came to power in Germany under Hitlerite fascism and was preparing war against the land of Soviets."[17]

There is good reason to believe that Molotov and Kaganovich were repeating ideas that had been circulating among the Soviet leaders in 1937 and 1938. Stalin's preoccupation with the threat of a potential fifth column is confirmed, for example, by notes he made on the draft of Molotov's speech to the February–March 1937 plenum. Stalin underlined the point in the speech where it was asserted that Trotsky had directed his supporters in the Soviet Union to "save their strength for a more important moment—for the beginning of the war—and at that moment strike decisively at the most sensitive areas of our economy."[18] In the margins of this document, opposite assertions that "we [the party] were left by those who were not up to the fight against the bourgeoisie, who intended to cast their lot with the bourgeoisie, and not with the working class," Stalin wrote: "This is good. It would be worse if they had left during wartime."[19] Stalin's speeches during the plenum contained this notion of the particular danger of saboteurs and spies at a time of war: "To win a battle in wartime several corps of soldiers are needed. And to subvert this victory on the front, all that is needed are a few spies somewhere in army headquarters or even division headquarters able to steal battle plans and give them to the enemy. To build a major railroad bridge, thousands of people are needed. But to blow it up, all you need are a few people. Dozens or even hundreds of such examples could be given."[20]

Along the same line, Stalin took active part in writing an article entitled "On Certain Cunning Techniques of Foreign Intelligence in Recruiting" that was published in *Pravda* on 4 May 1937. This lengthy feature, which spread across the bottom halves of three newspaper pages, was an important element in laying the ideological groundwork for the Great Terror. It was reprinted in several editions, used widely in propaganda and discussed in political meetings across the country. Since the First World War, the article asserted, German intelligence had maintained a vast file of citizens of Russia, France, and Great Britain who were seen as "a reserve that could be called on for espionage work." As evidenced by the initial version of the article, preserved in the archives, Stalin not only changed the headline of this feature, which started out with the prosaic title "On Certain Methods and Techniques

Used by Foreign Intelligence," but also added a page of new text about the subversion of a Soviet worker in Japan.[21]

The conviction held by Stalin and his comrades-in-arms that a potential fifth column existed in the Soviet Union was based on genuine data. The brutal confrontation that took place during the Civil War, repression during the period of the New Economic Policy, collectivization and dekulakization, the struggle against saboteurs, and party purges had affected many millions of people. The injured parties were, by definition, under suspicion. Along with their families, they constituted a significant proportion of the country's population.[22] The OGPU and later the NKVD had kept track of these "suspicious" elements. From articles by historians who have access to NKVD archives we learn that in 1939 (after the conclusion of the Great Terror) there were eighteen such categories, including, among others former nobility; tsarist officials; merchants; police; officers of the tsarist and White armies; former members of various parties hostile to the Bolsheviks (Socialist Revolutionaries, Mensheviks, and others); members expelled from the party for "anti-Soviet activities"; kulaks; and those convicted of counterrevolutionary crimes and members of their families. A number of categories contained those viewed as potential targets for recruitment by foreign intelligence: members of German, Polish, Japanese, Korean, and other ethnic groups; repatriated Soviets; those with foreign citizenship or contact with foreigners; and the clergy and members of religious organizations.[23] Documents governing the operations of 1937–1938 suggest that approximately the same categories of suspects had been used in preceding years as well. Criminals, too, were registered with the police.[24]

The OGPU-NKVD files were an important instrument of terror and were periodically used to act against population groups in a particular region. In July 1937, however, a decision was made to liquidate or isolate those groups that were being monitored by the secret police through these files. This decision does not appear to have been made abruptly. The same logic of "complete liquidation" had governed measures taken against former oppositionists, and since early 1937 the idea of a vast network of enemies—not only among former oppositionists but in the population at large—had taken hold at the highest echelons of power.

The leadership was worried about the number of people who had been expelled from the party over the course of numerous purges. We can see this, for example, in a memorandum dated 15 February 1937, where Malenkov draws Stalin's attention to this fact. "It should be noted in particular that there are currently more than 1,500,000 former members and candidate members of the party who have been expelled or lost their membership over the course of events at various times dating back to 1922. Many enterprises have large numbers of former Communists; in fact, they sometimes outnumber the members of party organizations working in these enterprises." The memorandum gave the following examples: at the Kolomensky Locomotive Factory there were 2,000 former party members and 1,408 Communists; at the Krasnoe Sormovo Factory this ratio was 2,200 to 550; and at the Moscow Ball Bearing Factory it was 1,084 to 452.[25] Stalin took note. During his concluding remarks at the February–March plenum he cited a number of figures from Malenkov's memorandum, stating, "All of these outrages that you have let by, this is all grist for the mill of our enemies. [. . .] All of this creates a situation that allows enemies' reserves to be augmented."[26]

The victims of dekulakization posed another thorny problem in the mid-1930s. As Sheila Fitzpatrick, who has studied this question in depth, has shown, the former kulaks tried to return to their native lands and lay claim to their confiscated property. In a number of cases they were able not only to regain a portion of their property but to reestablish their former influence over the rural population, to whom they now did not look so bad in comparison to the Soviet bosses who had replaced them as the dominant force in village life. The result was a new tangle of conflicting forces: the state versus the kulaks who had had their rights restored; the kulaks versus the new rural bosses, many of whom had distinguished themselves by "liquidating kulaks"; the kulaks versus the kolkhoz workers who were now farming their former property. Fitzpatrick concludes that the shadow of the kulak "hung over the countryside throughout the 1930s."[27]

By 1937 a decision was made to use terror to cut through this tangle. At the February–March plenum, all talk of repression was aimed at the kulaks. The secretary of the Western Siberian party territorial committee, Robert Eikhe, who in previous years had come forward with initiatives for a "peaceful" solution to the problem, asserted at the plenum that among a large number of kulaks who had been resettled in his territory there was still "a sizable group of inveterate enemies who would stop at nothing in their efforts to continue fighting."[28] The secretary of the Sverdlovsk Province committee, Ivan Kabakov, complained that the combination of intense industrial construction during the First Five-Year Plan and massive dekulakization had "opened up giant gaps through which flowed" "alien elements" into urban enterprises.[29] The secretary of the Turkmenian party organization, Yakov Popok, also brought up the dangers posed by kulaks returning from imprisonment or exile: "A large number of kulaks passed through Solovki and other camps and now are coming back as 'honest' toilers, are demanding an allotment of lands, and are laying all kinds of claims, going to the kolkhoz and demanding to be taken into kolkhozes."[30] As subsequent events showed, former kulaks were one of the main targets of the actions of 1937–1938.

During plenum discussions about preparations for elections based on the system outlined in the new constitution, much was said about the threat to Soviet authority supposedly posed by the country's millions of religious believers, especially those active in religious organizations and the Orthodox Church. The head of the Union of Militant Atheists, Yemelian Yaroslavsky, for instance, stated that the approximately thirty-nine thousand registered religious organizations (and approximately one million religious "activists") counted in the Soviet Union constituted an "organization for promoting anti-Soviet voting across the country." In addition to official religious organizations, Yaroslavsky acknowledged the existence of a large number of underground sects. The number of believers in the country was very large, as evidenced by the census of 1937. Yaroslavsky did not provide specific census figures (citing their unavailability), but as an example he gave the figure for two districts of Saratov Province: in the Cherkassky district 78.9 percent of the population was religious and in the Balandinsky district, 52.2 percent. "There are districts where it is even worse, with an even greater number of believers," Yaroslavsky lamented.[31] A large number of kolkhoz chairmen, according to Yaroslavsky, also served as church elders.[32]

As if trying to outdo one another, party functionaries speaking at the plenum pointed to one new target after another. Lavrenty Beria, secretary of the Central Committee of the Georgian Communist Party, reported that during the past year alone approximately fifteen hundred "former members of anti-Soviet parties—Mensheviks, Dashnaks, and Musavatists"—had returned from exile. "With a few exceptions, most of those returning are still enemies of the Soviet authorities; most are people who organize counterrevolutionary sabotage, espionage, diversionary operations. [. . .] We know that they have to be treated as enemies."[33] The secretary of the Eastern Siberia territorial committee, M. O. Razumov, asserted that "Buryat bourgeois nationalists" were joining forces with Trotskyites to spy for Japan.[34] The Moscow party secretary, Nikita Khrushchev, complained that vast numbers of people "who have something to hide" were creeping into the capital from all over the country in a desire to blend into the large city: "Not only people we have already made note of are creeping in, but so are people whom we haven't gotten to yet. [. . .] Those who have been expelled from the party are also making their way here."[35]

As documents show, the Soviet leadership continued to discuss the threat of a potential fifth column after the February–March plenum. On 20 May 1937, Malenkov sent Stalin a note in which he proposed abolishing the relatively simple procedure for registering religious associations (*dvadtsatki*). Malenkov asserted that because of existing laws, "we ourselves have created a wide-reaching legal organization that is hostile to Soviet authority." Throughout the entire Soviet Union, he said, more than 600,000 people belonged to dvadtsatki, and "in recent times the hostile activities of clerics have greatly intensified."[36] Stalin felt that it was necessary to circulate this note for review by members of the Politburo. Nikolai Yezhov also received it. On 2 June, Yezhov sent Stalin a response in which he heartily supported Malenkov. "From experience in the fight with religious counterrevolution in past years and at present, we are aware of numerous instances where the anti-Soviet forward ranks of the church use legally existing 'church dvadtsatki' as ready-made organizational forms and as cover in the interest of anti-Soviet operations."[37]

By attempting to play to Stalin's mood and by digging up more and more ominous signs of subversion, the Soviet leaders raised tensions and lay the groundwork for a "final solution" to the problem of "enemies." The idea that massive operations against a potential fifth column were essential took decisive hold of the top Soviet leadership in July 1937.

DIRECTIVES AND THEIR IMPLEMENTATION

In recent years most of the important documents concerning the large-scale operations carried out in 1937–1938 have become available, and historians now have an opportunity to investigate in detail the mechanisms involved in their implementation. While the country's political leadership was engaged in the discussions about the need to destroy "enemies," small-scale actions, serving as precursors to the large-scale operations, were conducted during the spring and summer of 1937. In March 1937 the NKVD published an order mandating that a special registry be created for all foreigners who had been given Soviet citizenship since 1 January 1936.[38] On 29 March 1937 the Politburo adopted a decision to remove any senior officer from the Red Army who had been expelled from the party for political reasons. For the time being, they were sent to work in economic commissariats.[39] On 23 May 1937 the Politburo approved a decision to exile two categories of "enemies" from Moscow, Leningrad, and Kiev: former oppositionists who had been expelled from the party and family members of former oppositionists who had been sentenced to death or to incarceration for a term of more than five years.[40] These measures were made more stringent by instructions approved by the NKVD on 15 June 1937. The list of cities from which exiles would be sent was extended to include Sochi, Taganrog, and Rostov-on-Don.[41]

These and other relatively limited actions laid the groundwork for the truly massive repressive measures that unfolded starting in August 1937.[42] The 2 July 1937 Politburo resolution entitled "On Anti-Soviet Elements," which ordered that directives be sent to local officials by telegram, can be seen as the starting point for the Great Terror, which was actually a series of large-scale operations. This telegram required local authorities to register criminal offenders (the meaning of this phrase was not elaborated) and kulaks who had fled their places of exile and determine how many of them should be arrested and how many should be shot. There were also instructions to organize local tribunals, "troikas" made up of regional bosses. These troikas would determine who would be imprisoned and who would be shot.[43]

On 30 July 1937, after some back-and-forth with the Politburo, the commissar for internal affairs issued Order no. 00447, entitled "On an Operation to Repress Former Kulaks, Criminals, and Other Anti-Soviet

Elements."[44] The order mandated that the operation begin between 5 and 15 August 1937 (depending on the region) and be completed within four months. First and foremost, it identified "contingents subject to repression." The order essentially targeted anyone who had shown the slightest resistance to Soviet authority or who had been a victim of state terror during its earlier stages: kulaks who had left their place of exile, even if they had completed their full term of punishment; former party members who had opposed the Bolsheviks (Socialist Revolutionaries, Georgian Mensheviks, Musavatists, Dashnaks, and others); former members of the White Guard; surviving tsarist officials; "terrorists" and "spies" involved in cases fabricated by the OGPU-NKVD in past years; political prisoners still in the camps—the list goes on. In addition to people in these political categories, ordinary criminal offenders were also mentioned as targets of the purge.

All those targeted in the order were divided into two categories. Those in the first were subject to immediate arrest and execution; those in the second were to be sent to a camp or prison for a term of eight to ten years. Each province, territory, and republic was given quotas for each of the two categories. A total of 268,950 people were to be arrested, and 72,950 of them were to be shot (this figure included 10,000 already in the camps). It is important to note that the order included a mechanism for escalating the terror, since local officials were able to ask Moscow to increase their quotas for arrests and executions. The special troikas that would hand down the sentences would be guided by the limits approved by Moscow. As a rule, the troikas comprised the local NKVD chief, the secretary of the regional party organization, and the procurator of the given republic, province, or territory. They were given extraordinary powers: they handed down sentences (including death sentences) and gave orders related to the implementation of the sentences with no oversight.

On 9 August 1937 the Politburo adopted another NKVD order, "On Liquidating Polish Sabotage-Espionage Groups."[45] This order specified procedures for dealing with "counterrevolutionary national contingents." In 1937–1938 operations were carried out against Poles, Germans, Romanians, Latvians, Estonians, Finns, Greeks, Afghans, Iranians, Chinese, Bulgarians, and Macedonians. A special operation was carried out against the so-called Harbintsy (former employees of the Chinese-Eastern Railroad who returned to the Soviet Union from China after the railroad was sold in 1935). The Stalinist leadership saw all of these populations as fertile ground for espionage and collaborationism and placed no limits on the numbers of arrests or executions that could be carried out in operations against them. However, the center did exercise a form of loose control over the operations through a procedure for approving the summary reports of sentences handed down, the so-called albums that were sent to Moscow to be signed by the heads of the regional NKVD administrations and the regional procurators.[46]

Archival materials give us the following picture. After receiving the quota for the arrest and execution of kulaks and "anti-Soviet elements" from Moscow, NKVD chiefs (on either the provincial or the territorial level) convened a board composed of municipal and district NKVD bureau heads to map out exactly what needed to be done. Initially, the files of "anti-Soviet elements" were used to compile lists of those to be arrested and shot. After the arrests, investigations were conducted. Their primary objective was seen as identifying the arrestees' "counterrevolutionary associations" and any "counterrevolutionary organizations" to which they belonged.[47] "Evidence" was obtained in various ways, but most often torture was used. New arrests were then made on the basis of "testimony" obtained under torture. Those arrested during this second wave provided new names, also under torture. Using this method for acquiring new names, the dragnet thrown out could, in theory, expand indefinitely to encompass the vast majority of the country's population.

In parallel with the large-scale operations that were at the core of the Great Terror, the purges of border regions that had begun at earlier periods continued into 1937–1938. The most significant was the September–October 1937 deportation of more than 170,000 Koreans from the Far East into Kazakhstan and Uzbekistan.[48]

As the targets that had been initially approved by the Politburo were achieved, local NKVD bureaus, as provided for by Order no. 00447, began to ask Moscow to authorize higher quotas for arrests and executions, and as a rule, these requests were approved.[49] As a result, by the beginning of 1938 more than 500,000 people had been convicted based on Order no. 00447.[50] The figure far exceeded the initial target set by the order (269,000). Furthermore, the four-month timetable indicated in the order had already come to an end.

Given this background, the political signals emanating from Moscow at the very beginning of 1938 take on special significance. On 9 January the Politburo labeled as incorrect the firing of relatives of "individuals arrested for counterrevolutionary crimes purely on the basis of their blood relations" and assigned USSR procurator Vyshinsky to issue appropriate instructions to the procuracy.[51] On 19 January newspapers published a Central Committee plenum decision entitled "On Decisions by Party Organizations Concerning Expulsions of Communists from the Party, and the Formal-Bureaucratic Attitude toward Appeals by Those Excluded from the VKP(b), and Measures for Fixing These Shortcomings," which mandated a more attentive attitude to the fate of party members. The leadership of the USSR Procuracy and the Commissariat of Justice took several steps as a result of these decisions.[52]

The true meaning of these political maneuvers is still not entirely clear. It is entirely possible that in early 1938 Stalin really was preparing to put an end to the purges and that the January plenum was supposed to send a signal to that effect. One thing that supports this theory is that when the purges finally ended in early 1939, their conclusion was proclaimed at the 18th Party Congress under the banner of fighting for an attentive attitude toward the fate of Communists. In any event, the decision adopted during the January 1938 plenum was never more than political theater. Despite the enormous scope of the terror during the second half of 1937 and initial statements about concluding operations against "anti-Soviet elements" in 1937, it was ultimately decided to continue the purges into 1938. In late January and early February 1938 the Politburo sanctioned a continuation both of the operations mandated by Order no. 00447 and of those targeting ethnic and national groups.[53]

The reasons behind these decisions are still unclear, but there is first-hand evidence that the idea of continuing the mass operations into 1938 had Stalin's support. Stalin was actively engaged in managing repressive measures in 1937. Documents show that he personally authorized increasing quotas for arrests and executions in many regions. Nor did he go away for vacation in 1937, something he had done in all recent years, usually leaving in July or August and staying away until October. On 17 January 1938, when the decision had to be made whether or not to put a halt to large-scale operations, Stalin sent Commissar of Internal Affairs Yezhov the following directive.

The SR [Socialist Revolutionary] line (both left and right) has not been fully uncovered. [. . .] It is important to keep in mind that there are

still many SRs in our army and outside the army. Can the NKVD account for the SRs (the "former") in the army? I would like to see a report
promptly. Can the NKVD account for "former" SRs outside the army
(in civil institutions)? I also would like a report in two–three weeks.
[. . .]
    What has been done to expose and arrest all Iranians in Baku and
Azerbaijan?
    For your information, at one time the SRs were very strong in Sara-
tov, Tambov, and the Ukraine, in the army (officers), in Tashkent and
Central Asia in general, and at the Baku electrical power stations, where
they became entrenched and sabotaged the oil industry. We must act
more swiftly and intelligently.[54]

Directives of this sort from Stalin (perhaps in the future other such
documents will be uncovered) were undoubtedly connected to Politburo decisions in support of continuing operations in 1938. In terms of
scope, operations against "national counterrevolutionary contingents"
took first place among operations in 1938.

In total, secret internal NKVD statistics indicate that in 1937–1938,
branches of the NKVD (excluding the police) arrested 1,575,259 people
(87.1 percent for political crimes). Of these, 1,344,923 were convicted
in 1937–1938, with 681,692 sentenced to be shot (353,074 in 1937 and
328,618 in 1938).[55] While these figures demand further study and re-
finement, overall they reflect the scale of the Great Terror. At the center
of the Great Terror were operations against "anti-Soviet elements"
(based on Order no. 00447) and operations against nationalities. Evidence for this can be seen in the following statistics. According to figures
from 1 November 1938, the number of people convicted during operations targeted at "anti-Soviet elements" was 767,000 (of these almost
387,000 were sentenced to be shot), and the number swept up in operations targeting nationalities was 328,000 (of whom 237,000 were shot).
In fact, these figures are low, since operations continued until mid-No-
vember.[56] These two operations thus accounted for more than 80 percent of those convicted and more than 90 percent of those shot.

The conclusion of large-scale operations was just as centrally orchestrated as their beginning had been. On 15 November 1938 the Politburo
approved a directive banning trial by troikas, and on 17 November a
Politburo decision prohibited all "mass arrest and banishment opera-

tions."[57] On 24 November, Yezhov was relieved of his post as commissar of internal affairs.[58]

Even a brief enumeration of the main actions making up what we call the Great Terror suggests that the center tightly controlled the large-scale repressive measures in 1937–1938. Instructions on the conduct of various operations and significant trials were issued by the Politburo, which also approved all of the main NKVD orders. The actions of the troikas were governed by quotas adopted in Moscow. Most sentences of high-level arrestees were officially handed down by the military collegium of the USSR Supreme Court; in actuality, they were decided by a small group of the highest-level Soviet leaders (Stalin, Molotov, Voroshilov, Kaganovich, Zhdanov, and, in some cases, Mikoyan and Kosior). The 383 lists containing the sentences (mostly death sentences, but in a few cases prison sentences) of more than forty thousand Soviet nomenklatura personnel were first publicly mentioned by Nikita Khrushchev during the 20th Party Congress.[59] The lists have since been made available on the Internet.[60]

Finally, regular trips by members of the Politburo throughout the country encouraged the Great Terror. The objective of the trips was to conduct purges of republic and provincial party organizations. We know of such trips by Kaganovich (to Chelyabinsk, Yaroslavl, and Ivanovo Provinces, as well as to Donbass), by Zhdanov (to Bashkiria, Tataria, and Orenburg Province), and by Mikoyan (to Armenia). In 1937–1938, Andreev acted essentially as a roving commissar dealing with repressive measures.[61]

Just because the center controlled the operations that made up the Great Terror (and other similar operations) does not mean, however, that "elemental factors" and local initiative did not play a role in shaping them. The elemental factors were officially labeled "excesses" or "violations of socialist legality." Among the aspects of the 1937–1938 operations that were attributed to "excesses" were the "inordinately large" number of deaths during interrogations; arrests and executions that surpassed the quotas established by Moscow (although local overages were generally approved retroactively by Moscow); and failures to terminate a given operation on schedule. However, such elemental factors and initiatives by local authorities were the inevitable results of incentives inherent in orders from Moscow coupled with a tendency to put unflinching people in charge of NKVD operations and to eliminate NKVD operatives who were not sufficiently ruthless.

Once we recognize the special role played by the center in carrying out the terror we are confronted with new questions. Who specifically among the top party leaders initiated the change in political course, and to what degree are we justified in assuming that there was at this stage a radical group within the Politburo putting pressure on Stalin? The first name to come up when such questions are raised is inevitably that of Nikolai Yezhov, who was directly in charge of the government's main instrument of terror—the Commissariat of Internal Affairs, the USSR NKVD.

STALIN AND YEZHOV

Yezhov was one of the figures most actively behind the Great Terror. In the historical memory of the Russian people, his name is inextricably linked with the mass repressions, called the *yezhovshchina*. Because historians often place Yezhov within the radical group supposed to have existed within Stalin's inner circle and blamed for the hardening of the political line and the turn toward terror, they have therefore looked to Yezhov himself when seeking some explanation for the unbelievable cruelty of the mass repressions. The physical shortcomings of the "bloodthirsty dwarf"—who was only one and a half meters (five feet) tall, with a malformed face and figure—are frequently mentioned and are apparent even in his meticulously retouched official photographs. Many historians have speculated that his physical unattractiveness was the source of an inferiority complex, emotional impairment, and a cruel nature. Even before Yezhov wound up at the helm of repression campaigns, many saw signs of cruelty in him. Robert Conquest cites the impression he made on one old Communist: "He was reminded of one of those slum children whose favorite occupation was to tie paraffin-soaked paper to a cat's tail and set fire to it."[62]

Such characterizations notwithstanding, up to a certain point Yezhov did not stand out among the Stalinist leaders. His political biography and administrative resume were typical of those of his colleagues.

Nikolai Ivanovich Yezhov was born into a working-class family in Saint Petersburg in 1895. Like many of his contemporaries, he had little education (in the questionnaire filled out after his arrest in 1939 he

wrote "incomplete elementary" on the line for educational background) and began to work early, at age fourteen. He apprenticed with
a tailor and then worked in the Putilov Factory. During the First World
War, when he was drafted into the army, he served on the northern front
and worked as a metalworker in ordnance shops. In May 1917 he
joined the Bolshevik party, and then he served as a commissar in one of
the combat support units in Vitebsk. During the Civil War he was appointed commissar for a number of Red Army units. He wound up
working in Kazan for the Tatar Province committee of the Russian
Communist Party (Bolshevik). In August 1921 he was called to work in
Moscow, where, as the historian Bulat Sultanbekov speculates, Yezhov
was probably able to gain the support of several Central Committee
members (for example, Lazar Kaganovich or Mendel Khataevich),
whom he had met earlier in Belorussia.[63] In early 1922, Yezhov was appointed secretary of the Mari Province party committee, and a year later
he was named secretary of the Semipalatinsk party committee. In 1925
he was appointed head of the organization department of the Kazakh
territorial party committee.

Many of those who encountered Yezhov during these years gained a
favorable impression of him. The Soviet writer Yury Dombrovsky (who
experienced his share of arrests, prison camps, and exiles) has left the
following recollections. "Three out of four of my investigations took
place in Alma-Ata, Kazakhstan, and Yezhov served for some time as
secretary of one of the Kazakhstan provincial committees (Semipalatinsk). Many of my contemporaries, especially party members, met him
through work or on a personal basis. Not a single one of them spoke ill
of him. This was a sympathetic, humane, mild-mannered, and tactful
person. [. . .] He would always try to settle any unpleasant personal
matter quietly, without creating a stir. I repeat: This was the general feeling. Was everyone really lying? After all, we were talking after the fall of
the 'bloody dwarf.' That's what a lot of people called him, the 'bloody
dwarf.' And it's true—in history there probably hasn't been anyone
bloodier than he."[64]

Anna Larina, Bukharin's widow, heard similar things about him. "In
particular, I clearly remember an exiled teacher, the Kazakh Azhgireev,
whom I chanced to meet in Siberian exile. He had gotten to know
Yezhov well when the latter was working in Kazakhstan, and expressed
utter bafflement at his terrible career. [. . .] He would often sit with me

and start talking about Yezhov: 'What happened to him, Anna Mik-
hailovna? They say by now he's not a man but a beast! I wrote him twice
to tell him I was innocent—no answer. And there was a time when he responded to any request at all; he was always ready to help in any way he
could.'"[65]

Yezhov was given a job in the party Central Committee apparatus in
Moscow in 1927. He served as deputy commissar for agriculture in
1929–1930, the period of forced collectivization and mass dekulakization, in which Yezhov had a hand. Later, he was returned to the Central
Committee, where he first held the important post of head of the department handling staffing for administrative and labor union positions and then of the industrial department. Yezhov's immediate su-
perior within the Central Committee was Lazar Kaganovich, whose
introduction of Yezhov led to a special Politburo decision on 25 November 1930 allowing Yezhov to be present at Politburo meetings and
to receive "all materials circulated to TsK members and TsK candidate
members."[66]

According to several of Yezhov's contemporaries, during this initial
period of his Central Committee career he did not distinguish himself as
particularly bloodthirsty.[67] The American historian Robert Thurston,
who studied repression in Soviet industrial enterprises in the 1930s, has
suggested that Yezhov's experience working in heavy industry in Saint
Petersburg, when conflict between workers and factory owners was in-
tensifying, may have played a role in the many cases the NKVD developed against enterprise managers.[68] However, Yezhov's actions as head
of the department in charge of Central Committee personnel does not
support speculation that he had strong "anti-specialist" inclinations. Indeed, documents show that on several occasions Yezhov took the initiative in defending economic managers. In November 1932, for example,
Yezhov's Central Committee personnel department introduced the
question of the high turnover in the coal industry. Investigations conducted by Yezhov's subordinates had revealed that the failure to meet
coalmining targets was directly tied to the high turnover rate among
mine managers. On average, mine managers and chief engineers served
just six months in one place, and mine superintendents served three to
three and a half months. For operations to run smoothly, senior personnel needed to spend several years at the same facility. Yezhov drafted a
memorandum on this matter, which served as the basis for discussion at

a session of the Central Committee's Orgburo on 19 January 1933.[69] The resulting decision established a new procedure for appointing and replacing the top management of coalmining enterprises. Now, trust administrators could be appointed or replaced only with approval from the Central Committee, with changes at the deputy level requiring an order from the commissar of heavy industry and changes at the superintendent level, an order from the trust administrator. The objective was to have management remain in one place no fewer than three to four years.[70]

In April 1933, Yezhov sent a report to Central Committee secretary Kaganovich about the dismissal of directors of four metallurgical plants in the Urals by local authorities who did not obtain authorization from the commissariat and the Central Committee. On 7 June the Orgburo issued a resolution in which it reversed the decisions to dismiss the directors and punished the guilty authorities.[71]

During the 17th Party Congress, Yezhov was made a member of the Central Committee. After the congress he became a member of the Orgburo, deputy chairman of the Party Control Commission, and head of the Central Committee's industrial department.

The turning point for Yezhov came after the death of Kirov. Stalin chose Yezhov as his main assistant in carrying out a political purge. His first assignment along these lines was an investigation into Kirov's murder. Despite a lack of evidence, Stalin ordered him to develop a case implicating Zinoviev, Kamenev, and their supporters. Top NKVD officials were skeptical about this approach and attempted to undermine Stalin's instructions. This is where Yezhov came in. Stalin effectively made Yezhov his representative within the NKVD. Delving into every detail, Yezhov coaxed the investigation down the necessary path. This upset the chekists, who were not used to such interference. But Stalin was adamant. During the February–March 1937 plenum, Yezhov gave the following account:

> Com. Stalin began, as I recall it now, by calling me and Kosarev, and he said, "Look for murderers among the Zinovievites." I must say, the chekists didn't believe this, and just in case they covered themselves by following up other leads here and there, foreign leads—maybe something would turn up. [. . .] At first our relations with the chekists, the relationship between the chekists and our oversight, took a while to smooth out. They didn't really want to show us [the results of] their in-

vestigations. [. . .] Com. Stalin had to get involved. Comrade Stalin called Yagoda and said, "Look here, we'll knock your teeth in." [. . .] Institutional considerations were at play here: this was the first time that suddenly the TsK was asserting some kind of control over the cheka. People found that hard to swallow.[72]

Yezhov fulfilled the mission Stalin had assigned him. The investigation into the case culminated in two trials of former oppositionists, including Zinoviev and Kamenev, who were held politically accountable for the act of terrorism. After being appointed Central Committee secretary and Party Control Commission chairman, Yezhov continued to oversee the NKVD. Working closely with the secret police, he orchestrated the party purge conducted in the guise of an inspection and reissuing of party membership documents.

Stalin showed Yezhov great favor during this period. On 23 August 1935, for instance, Stalin forwarded to Yezhov proposals by Lenin's widow, Nadezhda Krupskaya, on adult education, the publication of her article in *Pravda*, and organizing a Lenin museum. He appended the following note: "Com. Krupskaya is right on *all* three points. I am sending you this letter because when you commit to do something, it usually gets done, and there is hope that you will carry out my request—summon Krupskaya, have a talk with her, and so on. Greetings! How is your health? J. Stalin."[73] Stalin was satisfied with Yezhov's handling of these requests. "It is good that you took the matter firmly in hand and moved it forward," he wrote to Yezhov on 10 September. After making comments on plans for the Lenin museum, Stalin added, "Now the *most* important thing. You must go on vacation as soon as possible—to a resort in the USSR or abroad, as you wish, or as the doctors instruct. Go on vacation as soon as possible if you don't want me to raise a fuss."[74] Such letters attest to the high regard in which Stalin held this rising star. Upon returning from vacation with restored vigor, Yezhov was thrown into preparations for the trials of leaders of the former opposition movements.

Here again, as in early 1935, Stalin used Yezhov to advance his agenda within the NKVD over NKVD resistance. After making mass arrests among former supporters of Trotsky, the NKVD leadership wanted to try them and shoot them. Stalin, however, demanded that a case be fabricated demonstrating the existence of a United Trotskyite-Zinovievite Center being directed from overseas by Trotsky to wage a war of terror against the party leadership. For various reasons, NKVD leaders had reservations about this. Then Yezhov took the cases in hand. In carrying out Stalin's instructions, he became party to a scheme against Yagoda, the NKVD commissar, and his supporters, acting in concert with Yagoda's deputy, Yakov Agranov. Several months later, Agranov related details during a meeting at the NKVD headquarters: "Yezhov summoned me to come see him at his dacha. I have to say that this meeting had a conspiratorial tone. Yezhov conveyed Stalin's feelings about mistakes made in the investigation into the case of the Trotskyite Center and ordered that measures be taken to uncover the Trotskyite Center and expose the terrorist band that had obviously not been uncovered yet, along with the personal role played by Trotsky in this affair. Yezhov put the question like this: either he himself would convene an operational meeting or else I could get involved in this case. Yezhov's instructions were specific and put us on the correct path toward breaking the case."[75]

The result of Yezhov's efforts was the first Great Moscow trial of Kamenev, Zinoviev, and other former oppositionists in August 1936. They were all shot.

Enthusiastically taking part in the falsification of cases against a Unified Troskyite-Zinovievite Center, Yezhov became increasingly involved in the activities of the secret police. At this point it is hard to say whether Stalin was preparing Yezhov to take Yagoda's place or planning to exploit the antagonism between the two men. But in late August, during the final stage of the Kamenev-Zinoviev trial, something happened that increased the probability that Yagoda would be replaced.

On 22 August 1936, after Kamenev and Zinoviev testified in court about their ties to the rightists—Bukharin, Rykov, and Tomsky—and it was officially announced that this testimony was being investigated by the procuracy, Mikhail Tomsky committed suicide. In a suicide note addressed to Stalin, Tomsky renounced the testimony that had been given at the trial. "I am turning to you not only as the head of the party but as an old comrade in common struggles, and here is my last request—don't believe Zinoviev's brazen slander. I was never in any kind of blocs with him, I never took part in any kind of plots against the party."[76] The letter concluded with a surprising postscript: "If you want to know who it was that pushed me onto the path of right opposition in May 1928, ask my wife personally. Only then will she name them."[77]

After arriving at Tomsky's dacha, where the suicide had occurred,

Georgy Molchanov, head of the NKVD secret political department, had been given Tomsky's suicide note. Tomsky's widow had refused to give Molchanov the names of those referred to in the postscript, so Tomsky's note was sent to Stalin, who was in the south. At the same time, Kaganovich and Ordzhonikidze, who had been left in charge in Moscow, sent Yezhov to meet with Tomsky's widow. Yezhov was able to learn that Tomsky had been referring to Yagoda, who had supposedly "been actively engaged with the troika of top rightists, regularly providing them with materials about the situation in the Central Committee and in various ways supporting their activities." Upon returning to the Central Committee, Yezhov conveyed this news to Kaganovich and Ordzhonikidze, who were awaiting his return. At first they decided that Yezhov should go to see Stalin in the south and personally report to him on the latest developments. A little later, possibly after consultation with Stalin, Kaganovich instructed Yezhov not to make a trip, but to compile a written report.

The several rough drafts of this document that have been preserved among Yezhov's papers attest to the care he took in writing the report.[78] On 9 September 1936 the final version of the letter was sent to Stalin. After informing Stalin of the circumstances of Tomsky's suicide and the contents of his suicide note, Yezhov devoted a significant portion of the letter to efforts to uncover new organizations of Trotskyites and to criticisms of the NKVD for poor performance in this area. He reported on the lack of success in searches for a "military line" of Trotskyites, even though "undoubtedly [. . .] Trotskyites in the army still have some cadres that have yet to be exposed." He bemoaned as well the failure to uncover Trotskyite connections inside the NKVD, despite indications that chekists had ignored evidence of terrorist activity by Trotskyites, Zinovievites, and their bloc that had emerged in 1933–1934. "I would very much like to tell you about certain shortcomings in the work of the cheka that cannot be tolerated much longer. Without your involvement in this matter, nothing will get done," Yezhov concluded.[79]

All this creates the impression that Yezhov was calling for a change of leadership at the NKVD. Most likely, however, he simply was in tune with Stalin's mood and was playing up to it.[80] The idea that the NKVD had been slow in exposing conspiracies (an idea that most likely originated with Stalin rather than Yezhov) appeared a month later in a telegram from Stalin demanding that Yagoda be removed.

That Yezhov was not the author of the main scenarios according to which the terror played out is seen in portions of the drafts of the letter where he spelled out the accusations that would, in his view, ultimately be leveled against the Trotskyites and rightists (Bukharin and Rykov). "Personally," Yezhov wrote, "I doubt that the rightists formed a direct organizational bloc with the Trotskyites and Zinovievites. The Trotskyites and Zinovievites are politically so discredited that the rightists must have been afraid of forming such a bloc with them." He asserted that the rightists had their organization, that they believed in terror, and that they knew about the activities of the Trotskyite-Zinovievite bloc, but that they were biding their time, wanting to exploit the Trotskyite terror to their own ends. "The very least punishment" for the rightists, Yezhov felt, would be expulsion from the Central Committee and reassignment to jobs in remote areas. "Here we need your firm instructions," he wrote to Stalin. As far as Piatakov, Karl Radek, and Sokolnikov were concerned, Yezhov had no doubt that they were heading a "counterrevolutionary gang," he wrote, but he understood that it probably did not make sense to "undertake a new trial." "The arrest and punishment of Radek and Piatakov without a trial will undoubtedly get into the foreign press. Nonetheless, it has to be done." Yezhov reported that he had carried out Stalin's request for a review of the lists of everyone arrested in association with recent cases and the cases tied to Kirov's murder to see if any new sentences should be handed down. "A rather formidable number will have to be shot. Personally, I think that we have to do this and finish with this scum once and for all." "It is understood that no trials need to be arranged. Everything can be handled in a simplified manner based on the Law of 1 December and even without convening a formal trial."[81]

So Yezhov's writings show him to be a worthy disciple of Stalin's. He obviously did not yet know of Stalin's intention to organize new trials and a large-scale purge. For now, everything being done was for the purpose of dealing with former oppositionists—and without trials, as for Kamenev and Zinoviev. What Yezhov did do was bring this plan, devised by Stalin, to life during the summer and early fall of 1936. It is possible that Stalin himself did not know what he would do over the coming months. In any event, we can see that Yezhov was not the author of the scenario as it would play out, nor its inspiration.

While carrying out Stalin's will and acting in complete secrecy, Yezhov was able to maintain a reputation as a relatively moderate figure. From time to time he would help the heads of various agencies defend their own people from repression. On Stalin's instructions, Yezhov was already moving ahead full steam to prepare the case alleging rightist "terrorist activity." Not knowing this, Nikolai Bukharin, according to his widow, Anna Larina, liked Yezhov "very much." "He understood that Yezhov had become a creature of the Central Committee apparatus and that he ingratiated himself with Stalin, but he [Bukharin] also knew that he was not the only one. He considered him to be an honest man and sincerely dedicated to the party. [. . .] It seemed to Bukharin back then, paradoxical as it may seem, that Yezhov, while not a highly cultured man, had a kind heart and a clear conscience. [. . .] Bukharin was sincerely glad when Yagoda was replaced with Yezhov: 'He won't turn to falsification.'"[82] We also have evidence from V. F. Nekrasov that Ordzhonikidze's widow, Zinaida Gavrilovna, who had been friendly with Yezhov's wife, harbored no ill will toward Yezhov, who certainly bore some responsibility for her husband's death. She did not, according to Nekrasov, consider Yezhov to be a "horrid scoundrel." "He was a toy," she said. "They played with him as they wished."[83]

Yezhov was a major presence at the Central Committee plenum in February–March 1937. He delivered two reports: one on the Bukharin-Rykov case and another on sabotage within the NKVD. By dealing with high-priority government issues, Yezhov became part of the country's top leadership, even though he was not an actual member of the Politburo. On Stalin's suggestion, he was made a member of the permanent Politburo commission charged with formulating and resolving questions of a secret nature. During the mass terror, the old members of the Politburo depended on the NKVD and its head to a certain extent, checking with Yezhov on a number of matters, especially personnel issues. On 2 September 1937, for example, in asking the Politburo to approve a number of personnel changes in the Defense Commissariat, Voroshilov framed his request in the following way: "Yesterday Com. Yezhov met with Com. Gribov. Afterward I spoke with Com. Yezhov by telephone and he told me that he had no materials or cases unfavorable to Gribov. I believe Com. Gribov can be appointed com[mander] of SKVO [North Caucasus Military District] troops and Com. Timoshenko can be transferred to the KhVO [Kharkov Military District] as troop commander."[84]

To what extent does all this demonstrate that Yezhov had become an independent political figure? Extensive documentary evidence shows that what Yezhov did was carefully controlled and directed by Stalin. Stalin read the most important documents issued by Yezhov's commissariat, oversaw investigations, and determined the scripts that show trials would follow. Stalin spent a significant portion of his time in 1937–1938 reading the volumes of interrogation transcripts that Yezhov sent to him.[85] Stalin also gave Yezhov instructions urging particular arrests. Historians have noted that during investigations into the case of Tukhachevsky and other military leaders implicated in a "military conspiracy," for example, Stalin saw Yezhov almost every day.[86] Overall, as indicated by the log of visitors to Stalin's office, Yezhov visited Stalin 288 times in 1937–1938 and spent slightly fewer than 855 hours with him. This was something of a record—the only person to spend more time in Stalin's office was Molotov.[87]

Although the majority of directives concerning the terror took the form of Politburo decisions, available documents show that their true author, again, was Stalin. To varying degrees, all members of the Politburo—but most prominently Molotov, Kaganovich, Andreev, and Voroshilov—were involved in orchestrating the mass repression. They were all following Stalin, however, who determined its course and scale. Stalin signed all the Central Committee directives on arrests and trials sent to points across the country.[88] In many cases, Stalin sent out telegrams in his own name with instructions to take harsher measures than a report might have indicated. An example is Stalin's reaction to a telegram from S. M. Sobolev, secretary of the Krasnoyarsk territorial party committee, who reported on 27 August 1937 that there had been a devastating fire at the Kansk Mill and that arson by enemies of the people was suspected. Even though Sobolev promised to send additional details of the investigation to Moscow, Stalin immediately telegraphed, "Arson of the mill must have been carried out by enemies. Use any means to uncover the arsonists. Try the guilty expeditiously. Death sentence. Publish an account of the execution in the local press."[89]

Yezhov was, without doubt, a gifted and motivated disciple of Stalin. He deftly organized several public trials that, despite a few glitches, concluded with full confessions of guilt by the accused, who were active members of the Bolshevik party. Yezhov was personally involved in interrogations and ordered the use of torture. Under his leadership, the NKVD instigated many repressive actions. Wishing to please Stalin and prove his indispensability, Yezhov encouraged his subordinates to "overfulfill plans" for mass arrests and executions set by the Politburo. Stalin must have urged Yezhov on to ever harsher measures. Historians have widely commented on the unprecedented propaganda campaign surrounding the NKVD and Yezhov personally in 1937–1938. Yezhov was given every imaginable award and title, held numerous key party-state posts at once (Central Committee secretary, Party Control Commission chairman, commissar of internal affairs, and, starting in October 1937, candidate Politburo member). Cities, factories, and collective farms were named after him.

Overall, Yezhov should not be cast as the orchestrator of the Great Terror or considered an independent political force determining the scope and shape of repressive measures. He was a diligent executer of Stalin's will who acted on precise instructions from above. There is not a shred of evidence that Yezhov strayed from under Stalin's control. Then, when Stalin felt that it was expedient, Yezhov was relieved of his duties.

A change in the general line would come with a halt to the mass repression and the removal of Yezhov, and Stalin began preparing for the change far in advance, one step at a time, hiding his true intentions. On 8 April 1938 the Politburo approved the appointment of Yezhov to the additional post of water transport commissar.[90] This looked like a way to honor Yezhov in accordance with Bolshevik tradition: Felix Dzerzhinsky, while serving as the Soviet Union's first secret police chief, was placed in charge of rail transport in order to bring this critical sector under control. In truth, Yezhov's new appointment was a prelude to another reshuffling of NKVD cadres. Over the following weeks, the Politburo approved the transfer of a large number of high-level NKVD personnel to the Water Transport Commissariat.[91] Major reassignments of cadres continued for several months.

The erstwhile "chekist heroes" sensed that trouble was brewing, and some of them attempted to avoid arrest. News that Genrikh Liushkov, head of the Far Eastern NKVD administration, had fled abroad made a stunning impression. In 1937 and early 1938 he had overseen the arrests, executions, and deportations of ethnic Koreans from the border regions of Central Asia. In late May 1938 the Politburo adopted a decision to relieve Liushkov of his duties in the Far East and call him back to the central NKVD apparatus. Liushkov had enough experience to realize what this "promotion" meant. During the night of 12–13 June, with classified documents in hand, he left the office on an "inspection" and crossed the border into Manchukuo (Manchuria). He provided valuable intelligence to the Japanese, and in August 1945, when he had outlived his usefulness, the retreating Japanese shot him.

Liushkov's defection was a major blow to Yezhov, who would have to take responsibility for it. He realized then just how tenuous his position was. In late November 1938, after he had already been replaced as NKVD commissar, in a confessional letter written to Stalin he remarked, "A critical moment was Liushkov's defection. I literally went mad. I called Frinovsky and proposed that we go together to report to you. I didn't have the strength to do it alone. I said to Frinovsky then, 'Now we'll face serious consequences.' [. . .] I understood that you were bound to develop doubts about the work of the NKVD. And you did. I sensed that the entire time."[92]

Soon enough, Yezhov had further cause for concern. In August, Lavrenty Beria, Central Committee secretary of the Georgian Communist Party, was appointed as Yezhov's first deputy at the NKVD. On the surface, it appeared that Yezhov was still in favor and in power, but he now had a deputy serving under him that he would never have chosen of his own free will. "I also worried about the appointment of Com. Beria," Yezhov admitted in the same letter to Stalin. "I saw in this a lack of trust in me, but I thought that this would all pass. I sincerely believed and believe that he is an outstanding worker, and I presumed that he might take over the post of commissar. I thought that his appointment set the stage for my being relieved."[93]

The ease with which his closest aides were replaced and arrested showed just how powerless the commissar of internal affairs was in and of himself. In desperation, he attempted to undertake certain countermeasures. As he admitted to Stalin, he was encouraged in this by his other NKVD deputy, Mikhail Frinovsky, who did not get along with Beria. Frinovsky tried to convince Yezhov that it would be impossible to work with Beria and that Beria would give biased information to Stalin about the state of the commissariat. Frinovsky advised "keeping a firm hold on the reins. Not to sulk, but to stay firmly in charge of the apparat so it wouldn't split between Com. Beria and me [Yezhov]. Not to let

Com. Beria's people into the apparat." As a matter of routine, NKVD cadres began to gather materials compromising Beria, but on Frinovsky's advice, Yezhov gave them to Stalin.[94]

Obviously, Yezhov no longer had any control over the situation taking shape. While making fitful attempts to keep his head above water, he undoubtedly understood that the purge of NKVD cadres sooner or later would reach the top. Unable to cope with the emotional stress this created, Yezhov reportedly began to drink without restraint.

Beginning in October, Stalin's maneuvers that centered on the NKVD took on new life. On 8 October the Politburo appointed a commission to draft a Central Committee, Council of People's Commissars, and NKVD resolution outlining new policies on arrests, procuratorial oversight, and the conduct of investigations. For the time being, Yezhov was appointed chairman of the commission, which included Beria; USSR procurator Andrei Vyshinsky; chairman of the USSR Supreme Court Nikolai Rychkov; and Georgy Malenkov, who dealt with judicial matters for the Central Committee. The commission was given ten days to draft the document. In fact, the initial resolution creating the commission, which was written in Kaganovich's hand, did not stipulate a timetable. Stalin added the ten-day limit to the final version.[95] Nevertheless, the Politburo did not adopt a resolution entitled "On Arrests, Procuratorial Oversight, and the Conduct of Investigations" until 17 November, more than a month after the commission had been created. It is doubtful that the resolution took this long to draft. The protocols of Politburo meetings seem to indicate that Stalin needed this month to purge additional cadres from the NKVD apparatus. Between 8 October and 17 November the Politburo approved the appointment of a new head of the NKVD secretariat, placed a group of instructors from the party personnel department in top positions within the NKVD personnel department, and appointed new heads for the foreign and operational departments of the NKVD's Main Administration of State Security, as well as a new head for the Leningrad Province administration, among others. All of these new appointments were Beria's people.[96] Before landing the decisive blow, Stalin, as usual, was ensuring that nothing unexpected would happen—that is the impression created.

Apparently Stalin had reason to be wary of desperate moves by doomed NKVD bosses. Following in Liushkov's footsteps, Alexander Uspensky, commissar of internal affairs for Ukraine, went into hiding on 14 November 1938. As Nikita Khrushchev recalled, Stalin believed that Yezhov, who had listened in on a telephone call about Uspensky's fate that Stalin and Khrushchev (then Ukrainian party secretary) were having, had warned Uspensky of his impending arrest.[97] Experience and well-developed conspiratorial channels permitted Uspensky to hide in various cities around the country for five months. Not until 16 April and only after great effort did the secret police manage to find Uspensky—a success that resulted in a large number of medals for NKVD agents.

A resolution dated 17 November signaled the imminent demise of the old NKVD leadership. Even though it recognized the NKVD's success under the leadership of the party in rooting out "enemies of the people and espionage-sabotage by foreign intelligence agents" and the need to continue the task of purging the Soviet Union of "spies, saboteurs, terrorists, and wreckers," Yezhov's agency was harshly criticized. In the end, the NKVD and the procuracy were forbidden to conduct any mass operations involving arrests and resettlement, and arrests were heretofore to be carried out only with a court order and with the approval of the procurator. The judicial troikas were abolished, and the cases under their jurisdiction were either transferred to the courts or sent for review by the special board of the USSR NKVD. Chekists were reminded of the necessity of observing the code of criminal procedure in conducting investigations.[98]

Many such resolutions were no more than declarations, passed one day and forgotten the next. But the accusations against the NKVD and the allegations that saboteurs were present in the agency left no doubt that Stalin had decided to lay all the blame for the mass terror on the secret police. That is what happened, and one of the first victims of this new shift in policy was Yezhov. Just two days after the resolution about arrests and investigations was adopted, on 19 November 1938, the Politburo reviewed allegations by the head of the NKVD bureau in Ivanovo Province, V. P. Zhuravlev. There is reason to believe that his denunciation was arranged at the top. Zhuravlev stated that at one point he had reported to Yezhov about suspicious behavior among a number of high-ranking NKVD agents, but the commissar had not given the report appropriate attention, even though the allegations turned out to be well founded. The process of reviewing Zhuravlev's statements to the Politburo turned into a public rebuke of Yezhov. He was accused of clogging investigative departments with foreign spies but also, most important, with inattention to the department charged with protecting Central Committee members and the Politburo, allowing it to be infiltrated by conspirators.

On 23 November, Yezhov was called to a meeting with Stalin, Molotov, and Voroshilov in Stalin's office that lasted from nine in the evening to one the following morning.[99] They discussed, among other things, a letter of resignation from Yezhov. In this letter, which was addressed to Stalin and dated the same day, Yezhov took full responsibility for operational failures in his commissariat and for the infiltration of enemies into chekist ranks and asked to be relieved of his duties as head of the agency. Clearly seeing the direction events were taking, Yezhov furthermore attempted to remind Stalin about his faithful service and energetically pledged his limitless devotion to the leader. He closed his letter with the following words: "Despite all the major shortcomings and failures in my work, I must say that, with the daily guidance of the TsK, the NKVD really trounced the enemy. I give my word as a Bolshevik and my pledge before the TsK VKP(b) and before Com. Stalin to keep all these lessons in mind in my future work, to bear in mind all my errors, to reform myself, and, in any area where the TsK sees fit to use me, to justify the trust of the TsK."[100]

On 24 November the Politburo granted Yezhov's request. The decision was formulated charitably: the reasons that Yezhov had stated in his letter to Stalin were cited as the context for his departure, as were supposed health problems that did not permit him to simultaneously administer two major commissariats: internal affairs and water transport. While Yezhov would no longer head the NKVD, the Politburo allowed him to continue to serve as Central Committee secretary, chairman of the Party Control Commission, and water transport commissar.[101] Nevertheless, both the members of the Politburo and the many ordinary Soviet citizens reading the report of Yezhov's replacement in newspapers certainly understood that his fate was sealed. "The comrades with whom I had been friendly and who had seemed to like me—suddenly everyone has turned from me as if I have the plague. They didn't even want to talk," Yezhov lamented in a letter to Stalin.[102]

During the 18th Party Congress Yezhov was not even elected to the Central Committee. The well-known Soviet military commander Admiral Nikolai Kuznetsov, who took part in the plenum of current Central

Committee members that decided who would be included in the newly constituted body the day before actual voting, left the following recollections: "First they eliminated those TsK members who they felt had not coped with their duties or who had somehow tarnished themselves and therefore were not worthy of being included in the new membership. [. . .] I remember how Stalin spoke against Yezhov and, pointing to his poor performance, emphasized his drunkenness rather than any abuse of authority or unwarranted arrests. Then Yezhov spoke and, acknowledging his mistakes, asked to be appointed to less independent work, which he would be able to handle."[103]

Soon after the congress, on 10 April 1939, Yezhov was arrested. Almost a year later, in February 1940, he was shot, charged with heading a "counterrevolutionary organization" within the NKVD. None of this was accompanied by the usual fanfare. The low-profile manner in which Yezhov was removed is consistent with evidence that Stalin was worried about drawing attention to the activities of the NKVD or the Great Terror. Yezhov was just one of the many scapegoats who, having carried out the will of the leader, paid with their lives so that Stalin could remain above suspicion.

Newly available archival documents have contributed greatly to our understanding of the mass repression of the late 1930s known as the Great Terror. Starting with campaigns to eliminate former oppositionists who had survived thus far, the repression grew into a sweeping purge of party-state cadres. The next stage of the terror comprised the large-scale operations against "anti-Soviet elements" and "counterrevolutionary national contingents," conducted from June 1937 through November 1938, which affected a significant portion of the Soviet population. The purge of cadres and the large-scale operations were based on a common logic. They were motivated by Stalin's desire to eliminate a potential fifth column, solidify the state apparatus and Stalin's personal power, and forcefully unite society in the face of a growing threat of war. One of the important results of this wave of terror was the almost total destruction, with a single blow, of an entire generation of managers. The large-scale advancement of young cadres created a societal basis for the conclusive consolidation of Stalin's dictatorship.

There is extensive evidence that the terror was centralized in nature and was initiated and orchestrated from Moscow. The statutes circulated at its inception supplied the mechanism by which repression was undertaken and was escalated. Despite the enormous sweep and momentum of the huge undertaking, it began and ended almost simultaneously throughout the entire country with orders from Moscow. There is every reason to believe that the author and driving force behind the policy of terror was Stalin. The preparation and execution of measures aimed at destroying former oppositionists and conducting party-state purges and large-scale operations, as well as the formulation of the ideological grounds for doing so, were the focus of Stalin's unflagging attention in 1937 and 1938. To varying degrees, each and every member of the Politburo shared responsibility for the immense crimes of this period. Nikolai Yezhov, the commissar of internal affairs, played the most direct role in carrying out Stalin's plans and directives. But despite Yezhov's exceptional diligence in prosecuting the terror, there is no evidence whatsoever to indicate that he ever acted independently in conducting repressive measures or had any particular influence on Stalin in shaping policy. Yezhov's position, which was enhanced as the terror grew, nevertheless was always fully dependent on Stalin. Once Stalin made the decision to halt large-scale operations, he used Yezhov as a scapegoat for "violations of socialist legality" and destroyed him.

6   On the Eve of War
The New Structure
of Stalin's Government

AFTER SEVERAL YEARS of relative stability, there was significant turnover in the membership of the Politburo in 1937–1938, during the period of mass terror. Proportionally the Politburo was not as severely affected as other party-state structures, but the political influence of individual members, even the remainder of Stalin's old guard, was reduced to a minimum by mass arrests and executions (especially within the nomenklatura). The Politburo's total dependence on Stalin was a key indicator that Stalin's personal dictatorship was firmly in place.

With the new political realities came changes to the fundamental institutions of power. This rearrangement, undertaken during the final weeks before the war with Germany, was never completed. Still, it established precedents that would greatly influence the model of power that took shape after the war.

REPRESSION WITHIN THE POLITBURO

Whether Ordzhonikidze committed suicide or was murdered, he was the first Politburo member to become a victim of heightened repression. The second was Yan Rudzutak. Rudzutak was one of the oldest party leaders. He first became a candidate Politburo member back in 1923, reaching full membership in 1926. Having demonstrated the requisite loyalty to Stalin, he held the important post of chairman of the party's Central Control Commission from 1931 to 1934. Since party rules forbade the chairman of the commission from holding other elected positions, Rudzutak was temporarily removed from the Politburo. After the 17th Party Congress he again became a candidate member. Then, in May 1937, Rudzutak was expelled from the Central Committee and arrested. He was shot in 1938, charged with espionage and plotting terrorist attacks against the country's leadership. During the Central Committee plenum of October 1937, Yezhov was elected to take his vacated candidate seat on the Politburo.

The next change in the makeup of the Politburo took place in January 1938. Pavel Postyshev was removed as a candidate member and Nikita Khrushchev was put in his place. Unlike other Politburo members who were removed during the terror, Postyshev was destroyed gradually. His disgrace serves as an interesting illustration of the sorts of political intrigues and practices that held sway in Stalin's Politburo during the years of terror.

Pavel Petrovich Postyshev was one of the most prominent figures within the party. He had become involved in the Social Democratic movement back in 1901 and worked as a professional revolutionary. During the Civil War he commanded partisan detachments in the Far East. Beginning in 1930 he held the post of Central Committee secretary and was part of a circle of influential party functionaries who enjoyed Stalin's trust. In 1933, during the height of a famine in Ukraine, Stalin appointed Postyshev second secretary of the Ukrainian Central Committee and first secretary of the Kharkov Province committee. After the capital of Ukraine was moved from Kharkov to Kiev, Postyshev became first secretary of the Kiev Province committee. Stalin was pleased with Postyshev's performance and in 1934 rewarded him with a candidate membership in the Politburo.

The first signs of trouble for Postyshev came in the fall of 1936, when large numbers of his people were arrested. On 13 January 1937 the Central Committee of the Communist Party adopted a special resolution on the Kiev Province committee and the Ukrainian Central Committee in which it was alleged that the leadership of the republic's party organization had been infiltrated with enemies. Postyshev was issued a reprimand and removed from the post of Kiev Province secretary.[1]

In organizing the attack against Postyshev, Stalin did not stop at fabricating cases against "saboteurs" in the Ukrainian party leadership, but he also incorporated actual sins of the Kiev leadership (sins that were not uncommon among leaders of many regions) into the allegations: clannishness, abuse of power, and the creation of local cults. While officially Postyshev held the title of second secretary of the Ukrainian Central Committee, he was in fact the most powerful man in Ukraine. His personal qualities—he was ruthless, assertive, and domineering—as well as the support he had long enjoyed in Moscow and the fact that he was Stalin's personal emissary to the republic had helped him achieve this status. Postyshev had used his position to populate the Ukrainian party organization with people who were personally devoted to him. They, in turn, went to great lengths to promote a cult of Postyshev within the republic. Up to a certain point in time, Stalin had encouraged a worshipful attitude toward his "loyal comrades-in-arms," seeing this as enhancing his own status as the supreme object of deification.

As was not unusual during these years, Postyshev's wife, Tatiana Postolovskaia, used her husband's position to further her own political standing, even attempting to take active part in personnel decisions in the republic's party organization. She held the post of secretary of the party committee for the Ukrainian Association of Marxist-Leninist Scientific Institutes (UAMLIN) and became embroiled in the countless conflicts and squabbles that erupted among the "soldiers of the ideological front."

Stalin fully exploited all of this. Accusations of personal aggrandizement and abuses were showered on Postyshev during the plenum of the Central Committee in February–March 1937. In his remarks at the plenum, the new secretary of the Kiev Province committee, S. A. Kudriavtsev, said, "The fuss around Com. Postyshev became so clamorous that people started talking out loud about Postyshev's closest, truest, finest, most devoted comrades-in-arms, and those who had not quite attained this status just called themselves Postyshevites."[2] Postolovskaia was also criticized, and her denunciation by Stalin's helpers was yet another blow against Postyshev. The main accusation leveled against Postolovskaia had to do with her treatment of a woman by the name of P. T. Nikolaenko, who, thanks to Stalin, came to enjoy a brief moment of fame. A party member, Nikolaenko had so taken to heart Stalin's teachings about intensification of the class struggle that she was afflicted with relentless visions of enemies and spies. After joining the party in her youth, she had worked in women's organizations and furthered her studies. In 1935 she was hired to work in the Kiev museum complex. At one point she approached the director of the complex with her suspicion that one of her coworkers was stealing from the museum exhibits. When the director did not act on her accusations, she went higher up and informed on him as well. To get rid of Nikolaenko, her employers arranged for her to attend graduate school, but soon she was back to her old habits, identifying and exposing "enemies." The party organization of the Ukrainian Association of Marxist-Leninist Scientific Institutes, with the involvement of Postolovskaia, managed to have Nikolaenko expelled from graduate school. Nikolaenko went on to teach in the political departments of the Yugo-Zapadnaia Railroad, where she told anyone who would listen that enemies had taken over UAMLIN and that Postolovskaia "sits like a tsarina, surrounded by enemies." Postolovskaia learned about this from her supporters and did the only thing she could think of—she had the party city committee expel Nikolaenko from the party. To please Postolovskaia, this was done rather hastily and a few corners were cut: the documents were fixed to make it look as if the expulsion decision made in January 1936 had been recorded in September 1935. Nikolaenko appealed directly to Stalin. In April the Party Control Commission adopted a decision to restore Nikolaenko's party membership. In Kiev, however, the local party committee was in no hurry to reissue a party membership card and reinstate her in her job.[3]

A key determinant of Nikolaenko's fate came after a Central Committee resolution dated 13 January 1937. On arriving in Kiev to talk about the resolution, Lazar Kaganovich was told about this "heroine of denunciation," and after returning to Moscow, he reported about her to Stalin, who took a genuine interest in Nikolaenko. He devoted an entire paragraph of one of his speeches during the February–March plenum to her. Furthermore, he included this paragraph in the official, widely distributed text of the speech.

> Nikolaenko is a rank-and-file member of the party. She is an ordinary "little person." For an entire year she sent out signals about problems in the Kiev party organization and exposed clannishness, a petit bourgeois approach to workers [. . .] the preponderance of Trotskyite saboteurs. She was waved away like a troublesome fly. Finally, to get rid of her, they went ahead and expelled her from the party. [. . .] But the intervention

of the Central Committee of the party helped untangle this tangled knot. And what emerged after the matter was investigated? It emerged that Nikolaenko was right, and the Kiev organization was wrong. [. . .] After all, what is Nikolaenko? Of course, she's not a member of the TsK, she isn't a commissar, she's not a secretary of the Kiev Province organization, she isn't even a secretary of any cells—she is a simple rank-and-file member of the party. As you see, simple people sometimes turn out to be much closer to the truth than certain elevated institutions.[4]

It is not difficult to guess why Stalin decided to promote this cult of the "little person." Just as, in another era, he had called on the Soviet people to follow the example of Stakhanovites, those heroes of labor, now, given the new political tasks at hand, Stalin highlighted new opportunities for heroism in the "denunciation of enemies." By defending the "little person" Nikolaenko from the wife of the omnipotent Postyshev, Stalin also reinforced the image of the just leader taking a stand against degenerate bureaucrats. And while Nikolaenko was bathing in glory, Postyshev was kicked out of Ukraine and sent into honorable exile as secretary of the Kuibyshev Province party committee.[5]

Many historians believe that Postyshev suffered because he attempted to oppose Stalin's policies of repression. One source of this notion is Khrushchev's "secret speech" to the 20th Party Congress.

During the February–March TsK plenum (1937) the speeches of a number of TsK members essentially expressed doubts concerning the correctness of the emerging policy of mass repression under the guise of a struggle against "double-dealers." These doubts were most strikingly expressed in the speech by Com. Postyshev. He said: "As I saw it, we went through such tough years of struggle: rotten party members broke and went over to the enemies, the healthy fought for the cause of the party. These were the years of industrialization, collectivization. I couldn't imagine that, having gone through this tough period, Karpov and those like him would wind up in the enemy camp. (Karpov was a TsK Ukraine party worker whom Postyshev knew well. [Khrushchev's interjection.]) But there was testimony that Karpov had allegedly been turned by the Trotskyites back in 1934. I personally think that in 1934 for a healthy member of the party who had traveled a long road of bitter struggle against the enemy for the sake of the party, for the sake of socialism, to wind up in the enemy camp is unlikely. I don't believe it . . . I can't imagine how it's possible to get through the difficult years with the party and then, in 1934, go over to the Trotskyites. That's strange."[6]

Later in the speech Khrushchev returned to the subject of Postyshev.

> Attempts to speak out against unfounded suspicions and accusations
> led to a situation where those who protested were subjected to repres-
> sion. In this regard, the story of Com. Postyshev is typical. During a dis-
> cussion, when Stalin showed dissatisfaction with Postyshev and asked
> him the question, "Who are you?" Postyshev firmly stated with his
> usual exaggeration of the letter "o," "I'm a Bolshevik, Comrade Stalin,
> a Bolshevik!" And this statement was at first seen as a sign of disrespect
> toward Stalin, and later as a harmful act, and ultimately led to the de-
> struction of Postyshev, who was proclaimed an "enemy of the people"
> without the slightest justification.[7]

It is impossible to establish the veracity of this last story about the
conversation between Stalin and Postyshev. Khrushchev gives neither
the time nor the setting for the exchange. But we can easily compare the
citation of Postyshev's speech at the February–March plenum with the
stenographic record. If we do so, it immediately becomes evident that
the fragment used by Khrushchev (this portion of Khrushchev's speech
was prepared by Central Committee secretary Pyotr Pospelov) takes
Postyshev's words out of context, with small changes that completely al-
ter the meaning. In fact, Postyshev said the following (the quotation is
taken from the unedited stenographic record of the plenum—in other
words, the words are exactly as they were pronounced from the plenum
tribune).

> Here's how I see it: we went through such tough years, after all, there
> were such twists where people either broke or they kept their footing, or
> they went over to the enemies—the period of industrialization, the pe-
> riod of collectivization, it was, after all, a cruel struggle between the
> party and enemies during that period. I couldn't imagine that it was pos-
> sible to live through all these periods and then go over to the enemy
> camp. And now it turns out that he, since 1934, had fallen into the ene-
> mies' clutches and become an enemy. Of course, here it is possible to be-
> lieve all that, or you can not believe it. I personally think that it is aw-
> fully hard after all those years, in 1934, for a person who managed to
> keep a sure footing throughout the path of bitter struggle to go over to
> the enemies. It's very hard to believe. [Molotov: It's hard to believe that
> he only became an enemy in 1934? He probably was one even earlier.]
> Of course earlier. I can't imagine how it's possible to get through the dif-
> ficult years with the party and then, in 1934, go over to the Trotskyites.
> It's strange. He must have had some worm the whole time. When that

worm appeared—in 1926, or in 1924, in 1930—that's hard to say, but it's obvious that there was some worm that did some work in order for him to have gone over to the enemy camp. [. . .] That's not how Com. Stalin puts the question, that we have to be vigilant only toward those people who at one point sinned against the party. You can be more vigilant with those people, but the enemy can purposefully keep himself clean. From the testimony by the rightists we see how they kept themselves and their cadres so they wouldn't stick out.[8]

The rest of Postyshev's speech took a similar tone. This is not surprising. When Postyshev came to the February–March plenum he was no longer the secretary of the largest republican party organization, but a mere provincial committee secretary, one who had recently been publicly censured for political blindness and being soft on the enemy. Undoubtedly, Postyshev did not support the new course. Unlike most of the other party bosses attending the plenum, he had firsthand experience of just what a policy of expanded repression would mean. Nevertheless, neither Postyshev nor any other members of the Central Committee (Khrushchev mentioned no other names) expressed even the slightest doubts during the plenum.

Postyshev's speech to the February–March plenum was received calmly. He was not bombarded with the hostile interjections that usually punctuated speeches by disgraced functionaries. The reception, however, was deceptive. In mid-1937 the Politburo suddenly began planning to denounce Postyshev. Someone named Gubelman submitted the denunciation, probably by arrangement at a high level. Gubelman alleged that in 1910 Postyshev had submitted a degrading petition addressed to the commander of the Moscow Military District pleading for a reduction of his sentence. The Politburo summoned Postyshev for an explanation. He repented, blaming his youth and lack of awareness. For the time being, he was merely issued a reprimand for concealing this fact from the Central Committee.[9] Several weeks later, Stalin sent Central Committee secretary Andrei Andreev to Kuibyshev Province. A visit by Andreev foretold no good. Wherever this emissary of Stalin appeared (and he traveled extensively in 1937), repression took on new vigor. We can only imagine what Postyshev was going through as he awaited Andreev's arrival. But once again the storm clouds blew over. Andreev merely convened a meeting of the provincial committee bureau, at which he expressed to Postyshev the party leadership's dissatisfaction with the struggle against enemies in Kuibyshev Province and ordered that the situation be promptly remedied. To get things rolling, several provincial officials were arrested.

After receiving such a stern admonition, Postyshev tried to prove himself a capable eradicator of the "enemy underground." In doing so, he gave Moscow a pretext for further attacks. On 8 January 1938, Georgy Malenkov, head of the party personnel department, sent Stalin a memorandum reporting that the Kuibyshev Province committee had disbanded thirty district committees whose heads had been labeled enemies of the people. "I consider such actions by the Kuibyshev Province committee of the VKP(b) to be politically harmful and bound to have blatantly provocative consequences," Malenkov wrote. In the draft Politburo resolution that Malenkov presented on this matter he proposed that a reprimand be issued to the provincial committee bureau and Postyshev. Stalin added a new paragraph to Malenkov's draft calling for Postyshev's dismissal as first secretary of the Kuibyshev Province committee, with the matter of his subsequent fate to be decided by the Central Committee of VKP(b).[10] With this addition, the resolution entitled "On the Politically Mistaken Decisions of the Kuibyshev Provincial Committee of the VKP(b)" was adopted by the Politburo on 9 January 1938.[11]

Several days later the Politburo decision served as the basis for a free-for-all against Postyshev during the January Central Committee plenum. Officially, the Postyshev question was not on the plenum agenda. Regardless, almost an entire day was devoted to a performance in the best traditions of the Stalinist school of political intrigue. As the plenum got under way, there was nothing to give Postyshev particular cause for concern. The criticism leveled against him, which came primarily in Malenkov's speech, did not go beyond what had already been expressed in the recent Politburo decision about the Kuibyshev Province committee. Nobody questioned Postyshev's legitimacy as a candidate member of the Politburo, and Postyshev therefore came to the tribune prepared to give a speech appropriate to his status as such. Briefly recognizing his mistakes, Postyshev began to address the agenda items. Suddenly he was subjected to a barrage of accusatory remarks and questions, the tone of which was set by Yezhov, Molotov, Malenkov, and others sitting at the tribune. This was a tried-and-true method for dealing with those out of favor during party congresses and plenums. A firestorm of indig-

nant objections, accusations, and degrading remarks prevented oppositionists and those who had fallen from grace from speaking.

From then on, everyone who spoke from the tribune began and ended
their speeches with condemnations of Postyshev. The speech by Nikolai
Ignatov, second secretary of the Kuibyshev Province committee, was
particularly vehement. He sharply attacked his boss, accusing him of
numerous sins.[12]

The speech by Lazar Kaganovich was decisive. As a member of the
Politburo, Kaganovich, obviously acting on Stalin's behalf, was demonstrating the party leadership's impartiality toward Postyshev, but his
remarks were unequivocally condemnatory. "Com. Postyshev, in my
opinion, is bankrupt as a major political leader," Kaganovich asserted.
"The Central Committee of the party had intended to nominate Com.
Postyshev to serve as chairman of the Soviet Control Commission. [. . .]
Now, after such a speech, I think that it is unlikely that the Central Committee will be able to entrust him with such a post. [. . .] If Com. Postyshev has no hidden causes and diseases shaping his attitude toward the
Central Committee of the party, if he is able to sincerely and honestly re-
make himself, to rein in his ambition and work as a Bolshevik in any
job, then he can preserve himself as a party worker. And if he doesn't
have the guts to do this, then however well he may have served in the
past, whatever his background might be [. . .] the party must condemn
such gross errors."[13]

After listening to these accusations, Postyshev at first attempted to
protest and explain himself, but he finally gave in and began to repent,
clutching at the straw that Kaganovich seemed to be offering him. "I can
only say one thing, comrades, and that is that I recognize the speech that
I gave earlier to be fully and totally incorrect and incompatible with the
party spirit. I do not myself understand how I could have made that
speech. I ask the TsK plenum to forgive me. Not only have I never associated with enemies but I always fought against them. I have always
fought on the side of the party against enemies of the people with all my
Bolshevik soul, and I shall fight the enemies of the people with all my
Bolshevik soul."[14]

Now Postyshev appeared before the members of the Central Committee and a wide circle of the initiated (the stenographic record of the
plenum was, as usual, distributed to party offices throughout the country) not as an unrepentant victim, capable of inspiring sympathy, but as

a remorseful sinner who had gotten what was coming to him. (Stalin constantly used this technique of forcing an absolute public repentance.) And, as usual, after the repentance came the blow. Speaking at the very end of the meeting on 14 January, Stalin suddenly announced that it would be necessary to remove Postyshev from among the candidate members of the Politburo. He proposed Khrushchev for the vacated seat.[15]

Postyshev's fate was sealed. A few weeks after the January plenum the Politburo decided to turn the matter of Postyshev over to the Party Control Commission. At the commission, accusations of provocative assaults against cadres were joined by others: it turned out that the people Postyshev had hired were spies and that "at the very least" he knew about the existence of a "counterrevolutionary organization" and had been informed that some of his closest aides were involved in it. On 17 February the Politburo approved a decision by the Party Control Commission to expel Postyshev from the party.[16] Soon afterward he was shot.

The circumstances of Postyshev's downfall do not seem to indicate that he was a serious opponent of Stalin. Undertones of dissatisfaction in Postyshev's speeches during both the February–March 1937 and the January 1938 plenums most likely represent attempts to defend his position within the party leadership and a sense of injury at being unjustly persecuted. Postyshev's fate differed from the fates of other repressed members of the Politburo in only one way: Stalin toyed with few of them for so long. As time went on, people were disposed of with increasing haste, and no trouble was taken to create an appearance of "impartiality." Bolsheviks of the Lenin generation proved absolutely helpless before Stalin. He easily quashed their few feeble attempts at self-defense by using fear and their own lack of solidarity, as well as the power of the NKVD.

The next Politburo victim of the terror was candidate member Robert Indrikhovich Eikhe. Up to this point, Eikhe's career was unmarred. A member of the party since 1905, for many years he headed a Siberian party organization and enjoyed Stalin's complete confidence. Even in 1930, when many highly placed officials in Siberia demanded that Eikhe be replaced, accusing him of incompetence, Stalin came to his vigorous defense. Eikhe's opponents were harshly punished and removed from their posts.[17] The special favor Stalin showed Eikhe was also reflected in his 1935 election as a candidate member of the Politburo. In October 1937, Eikhe advanced further: he was brought to Moscow to fill the important post of agriculture commissar. Then in April 1938, Eikhe was arrested, although he was not officially removed from the Politburo. Nikita Khrushchev told the story of what happened to him in his famous speech to the 20th Party Congress. Using torture, the NKVD coerced a confession of sabotage and involvement in a counterrevolutionary organization. Eikhe wrote two petitions to Stalin begging him to get to the bottom of the case and telling him about the torture used by the NKVD. It was of no use. In February 1940, Eikhe was shot.[18]

The removal of Postyshev from his post and his arrest signaled the vulnerability of two other members of the Politburo from Ukraine: Stanislav Vikentievich Kosior and Vlas Yakovlevich Chubar. After heading the Ukrainian party organization for almost ten years (from 1928 to 1938), Kosior was brought to Moscow in January 1938 to serve as deputy chairman of the Council of People's Commissars and as chairman of the Soviet Control Commission (the position for which Postyshev had supposedly been considered). But by May 1938, Kosior, too, had been arrested, and few months later he was shot. Nor was he officially removed from the Politburo. Testimony that the NKVD beat out of Kosior and other highly placed arrestees became the official basis for charges against Chubar. This was not difficult to achieve, because for many years, until Chubar was transferred to Moscow, he had headed the Ukrainian Council of People's Commissars and worked closely with both Kosior and Postyshev. He was linked to many "conspirators" through professional relationships established after his 1934 appointments as deputy chairman of the Council of People's Commissars and of the Labor and Defense Council (he was first deputy starting in January 1938). On 16 June 1938, using evidence fabricated by the NKVD, Stalin shepherded a decision through the Politburo expressing political distrust of Chubar: "The Politburo of the TsK does not feel it is possible to leave him as a member of the Politburo of the TsK and deputy chairman of the SNK of the Union of SSRs and feels it is possible only to assign him work in the provinces on a trial basis."[19] The next day, 17 June, Chubar was appointed head of construction for the Solikamsk Paper Combine.[20] He was arrested almost immediately after arriving in Solikamsk, and a few months later he was shot.

As we can see from the fates of Stalin's liquidated comrades-in-arms, the procedure for fabricating charges during the terror could lead to the destruction of any member of the Politburo. Nonetheless, repression in the Politburo was selective, and in comparison with many other party-state structures, it could even be characterized as limited. The members and candidate members of the Politburo who were destroyed (Kosior, Chubar, Eikhe, Postyshev, Rudzutak), and Ordzhonikidze, who ended his own life, as well as Grigory Petrovsky, chairman of the All-Ukraine Central Executive Committee and candidate member of the Politburo, who survived but was banished from the nomenklatura—these together made up less than half (seven out of fifteen) of the members of the Polit-buro who had been elected after the 17th Party Congress and survived until 1937. All of the repressed members of the Politburo had been second-tier members of the leadership. The core members of the Politburo, Stalin's most "distinguished" and well-known comrades-in-arms, kept their positions, at least officially.[21] Knowing the reasons for repressing some and sparing others permits a better understanding of the place held by each Politburo member within Stalin's decisively consolidated dictatorship.

STALIN'S OLD AND NEW COMRADES-IN-ARMS

Although historians will never be able to penetrate the gloomy depths of Stalin's psyche to fully understand the calculations and inclinations that wound up determining the fates of those with whom he had shared the leadership up to the Great Terror, certain patterns do appear. Stalin seems to have sanctioned the destruction of members of the Politburo who were the most "guilty," "useless," and "exposed" from his point of view. Exactly how these three interrelated qualities led some to be accused and not others is a puzzle worthy of scholarly attention.

As far as Stalin was concerned, the worst sin any functionary, to say nothing of Politburo members, could commit was to have indiscriminate contacts with former oppositionists and other "suspicious elements." This is what, for the most part, led to Postyshev's downfall. He was surrounded by "enemies" in Kiev and even tried at first to protect them. It mattered little that his impulse to protect his people had nothing to do with political convictions but was the desire of a patron to protect his clients and thereby prevent any erosion of his own position. In the case of Rudzutak, Stalin was extremely suspicious of his political loyalties and connections. As for Kosior and Chubar, their reputations had been seriously undermined during the famine of 1932–1933. Attempts by both men to maneuver and to some small degree serve the interests of Ukraine prompted fits of irritation in Stalin. In 1932 he even planned to remove Kosior and Chubar from the republic, but he thought better of it. Instead, in 1933 he sent Postyshev there as his commissar.[22] Chubar, as the memoirs of Molotov and Kaganovich make clear, was also vulnerable as someone known to maintain good relations with rightists (in particular, Rykov) and prone to "rightism."[23]

In Stalin's attitude toward his subordinates, suspicions of insufficient political loyalty often went hand in hand with a low opinion of professional competence and accusations of shirking hard work. The stigma of "uselessness" in and of itself, even in the absence of political accusations, could, however, be sufficient basis for destruction. The Soviet system, inherently unwieldy and inefficient, constantly demanded extraordinary efforts from the heads of its administrative apparatuses. Stalin, therefore, strove to surround himself with workaholics with organizational skills. By the same token, Stalin got rid of those who were not performing because of poor health or who simply failed to exhibit sufficient energy and competence.

In addition to being tainted by real or imagined political "rightism," Chubar, for instance, was not physically robust, and the Politburo had been compelled to adopt several special decisions allowing him to undergo lengthy treatments abroad. Eikhe also suffered from serious health problems, which had become acute not long before his arrest.[24] Rudzutak had ceased carrying a full workload several years before his arrest. He was often ill and, based on doctors' recommendations, was repeatedly granted long vacations. On 11 June 1936, the Politburo adopted a decision to send Rudzutak, with an attendant, to Paris for treatment, to be followed by a three-month vacation. A huge sum was allocated for this—four thousand U.S. dollars.[25] The idea that Rudzutak was "useless" proved so enduring that decades later Molotov was still talking about this side of him.

> Up to a certain point he was not a bad comrade. [. . .] He had conducted himself pretty well in the [tsarist] prison camp, and that, so to speak, helped him maintain his authority. But by the end of his life—I already formed this opinion when he was my deputy—he had become self-indulgent. He no longer was engaged in real struggle like a revolutionary.

And in those days this was very important. He liked to relax. He never stood out as being particularly active and involved in work. [. . .] He was off to the side, to the side. With his people, who also liked to relax. And he didn't contribute anything new, that could help the party. They understood, he had been through forced labor, he wants to take it easy, they didn't give him a hard time—go ahead and rest. He became such a philistine—he would sit, have a bite with friends, hang around with his crowd—he wasn't a bad companion. For the time being that was all right, but [. . .] It's hard to say what got him into trouble, but I think it was that he hung around with a certain type of people, there were some non-party leftovers, God only knows what kind. The chekists, evidently, saw all this and reported on it.[26]

Molotov's description jibes with several official views from the late 1930s. During the height of the terror, for example, on 3 February 1938, the Politburo approved a joint resolution of the Central Committee and the Council of People's Commissars limiting the size dacha a government official could have "in light of the fact that [. . .] a number of arrested conspirators (Rudzutak, Rozengolts, Antipov, Mezhlauk, Karakhan, Yagoda, and others) had built themselves grandiose dacha-palaces with fifteen–twenty rooms or more, where they lived in luxury and spent the people's money, thereby showing their commonplace utter decay and degeneracy."[27]

Using such formulas as "guilt" and "uselessness" to explain the targeting of Politburo members for repression does not always work. Given the broad sweep of arrests within the Soviet nomenklatura, all members of the Politburo had inevitably had contact with "enemies" and therefore could be seen as guilty. As for "uselessness," Mikhail Kalinin managed to hold on to his position even after he was nearly blind and had essentially been relieved of his duties. This suggests that given the same degree of "guilt" and "uselessness," some Politburo members were less "exposed" than others. Leaving aside any emotional attachments Stalin might have had, it can be asserted that "exposure" had a purely institutional and political basis.

Stalin's comrades-in-arms, at least the most distinguished among them, were bearers and symbols of revolutionary legitimacy, embodying the connection between Stalin's dictatorship and the Lenin period. They were also bearers of collective responsibility for the policy of the Great Leap. These men had been too close to Stalin for too long for accusations against them not to tarnish the reputation of the leader himself.

Furthermore, by carrying out the most important functions in the party-state apparatus, the top Soviet leaders held real levers of administrative, if not political, influence and were important elements of the system of government. Stalin had to take this into account. In relation to the Politburo he was much more circumspect than he was in regard to other power structures. It was the Politburo members of the second echelon, who were subject to repression. But they were destroyed under a shroud of secrecy: not one of them was convicted in an open trial, and in some cases there was not even a formal expulsion from the Politburo at a Central Committee plenum.

Did this mean that the surviving Politburo members were capable of limiting Stalin's power in any meaningful way? Years of archival research have not uncovered any evidence to confirm the exotic view that Stalin's power weakened as the Great Terror came to an end.[28] To the contrary, all available documents have bolstered the traditional view that the terror marked the consolidation of Stalin's dictatorial power and put an end to previous traditions of collective leadership.

While preserving the core of the old Politburo, Stalin did everything necessary to keep his comrades-in-arms in a state of submission, to fill them with fear and deprive them of the slightest trace of independence. He achieved this primarily through actions against their relatives and close associates. The range of potential targets from the circles of his Politburo colleagues was limitless. The flood of denunciations and slanders obtained during NKVD interrogations produced the most diverse names, and Yezhov regularly reported them to Stalin. It was up to Stalin whether a given "suspect" would be pursued or not.

To prevent such arrests from generating undesirable conflict, Stalin instilled in his fellow Politburo members an ideology of "duty before personal attachments" and sternly rejected any attempts on their part to interfere in NKVD matters. Stalin's reaction to negotiations between Yezhov and Kosior regarding the fate of Kosior's brother is indicative. Kosior's brother Vladimir, a supporter of Trotsky, was living in exile with his wife in Minusinsk. In early 1936, Vladimir's wife was sent to prison, accused of involvement in a "counterrevolutionary organization." Vladimir sent his Politburo-member brother an irate letter in which he demanded Stanislav's intervention and the release of his wife. He threatened to kill himself otherwise. Stanislav Kosior wavered. On 3 May 1936 he approached Yezhov with a request: "I am sending you a letter from my brother Vladimir, a Trotskyite. Obviously he isn't lying; in any event it's clear that he's become desperate. In my view this matter should be straightened out. If he writes to me it means he's reached the breaking point. Get involved in this case, please, and decide what to do."

After receiving this carefully worded letter, which did not ask any outright favors, Yezhov decided not to ignore this request by a Politburo member and sent for Vladimir Kosior's file. At the same time, however, he consulted with Stalin, as he always did. Stalin reacted to Yezhov's inquiry with a gruff refusal. "It's completely obvious that Vl. Kosior is a specimen alien to the working class, an enemy to Soviet power and a blackmailer. The yardstick by which he measures everything—the party, the working class, the authorities, legality—is the fate of his wife, and only that. It's obvious that Vl. Kosior is a real bourgeois, a philistine, and his wife is really 'on the hook,' otherwise he wouldn't be trying to blackmail his brother with suicide. It is shocking that St. Kosior felt he could interfere in this case of blackmail."[29]

Stalin may have resorted to such shameless demagoguery about "the party, the working class, the authorities, legality" in his conversations with Ordzhonikidze as well. Stalin's refusal to release Sergo Ordzhonikidze's older brother, Papulia, was an important signal for members of the Politburo. As subsequent events showed, they came to terms with the futility of approaching Stalin over the fates of family members.

After Ordzhonikidze, one of the first to take such a blow in 1937 was Lazar Kaganovich. First, there were mass arrests among his closest associates and deputies at his Transport Commissariat. Then, as Kaganovich recalled in the 1980s, Stalin interrogated him about his friendship with one of the main military "conspirators," Iona Yakir. That was how Kaganovich learned that some of the arrested officers had alleged his, Kaganovich's, involvement in their "counterrevolutionary organizations."[30] More followed. Before the war, Kaganovich's older brother, Mikhail, killed himself after being removed as commissar of the aviation industry and accused of "counterrevolutionary activities."

Stalin's relationship with Molotov posed a particular problem. Viacheslav Mikhailovich Molotov was his closest comrade-in-arms. For almost two decades they had collaborated in solving the most important and secret problems. Molotov was perceived in the country as number one in Stalin's circle, as his unofficial heir. Even after the significance of the Politburo as a political force reached its nadir, Molotov remained Stalin's main advisor. "Closest of all to Stalin, in the sense of decisions taken on various questions, was Molotov"—that is how Khrushchev expressed his understanding of the situation in the prewar Politburo.[31] There is extensive evidence to support this view. It was with Molotov that Stalin worked on the most important problems before the war, primarily those of international politics.

While Molotov was wholly devoted to Stalin, he at times permitted himself to be stubborn and intractable, in contrast to the obsequiousness of the other Politburo members. "He impressed me as someone independent, who thought for himself, with his own views on matters; he spoke his mind and told Stalin what he thought. It was obvious that Stalin didn't like this, but Molotov stood his ground. In this, I would say, he was an exception. We understood why Molotov was so independent. He was Stalin's oldest friend," wrote Khrushchev.[32] Georgy Zhukov formed an analogous impression of the relationship between Stalin and Molotov. "While taking part many times in discussions on a number of matters in Stalin's office in the presence of his inner circle," Zhukov told the writer Konstantin Simonov many years later, "I had an opportunity to see the arguments and contention, to see the stubbornness exhibited on several issues, especially by Molotov; at times it even reached the point where Stalin raised his voice and even lost his temper, but Molotov, smiling, got up from the table without changing his view."[33]

Undoubtedly chafing at such familiarity, Stalin did everything he could to put Molotov in his place. Molotov's secretaries and aides were destroyed one after another (the Politburo removed two of his aides in August 1937: A. M. Mogilny, head of his secretariat, on 17 August, and M. R. Khluser, Molotov's assistant, on 28 August).[34] Molotov's wife, Polina Semyonovna Zhemchuzhina, commissar of the fishing industry, was attacked in 1939. On 10 August , the Politburo adopted a secret (special folder) resolution which stated that Zhemchuzhina "had exhibited imprudence and indiscriminateness in regard to her associations, as a result of which, many hostile espionage elements made their way into Com. Zhemchuzhina's circle, who unwittingly facilitated their spying." The Politburo ordered that a "careful check of all materials concerning Zhemchuzhina" be conducted, and determined that she would be relieved of her duties as commissar gradually.[35]

Storm clouds gathered over Zhemchuzhina. During subsequent weeks the NKVD obtained testimony alleging her involvement in "sabotage and espionage work." Now it was up to Stalin whether this testimony should be taken seriously. For whatever reasons, Stalin decided to stop short of arrest at this point. On 24 October the Politburo was convened to consider the Zhemchuzhina question; all members and candidate members were present, with the exception of Khrushchev. Zhemchuzhina was partially exonerated, probably on Stalin's initiative (in any event, the corresponding Politburo resolution was written in his hand). In this decision—now not a special-folder decision and therefore subject to wider dissemination—the accusations against Zhemchuzhina were labeled "slanderous." Nevertheless, the resolution repeated the allegations of "imprudence and indiscriminateness" that had been contained in the 10 August resolution. This was enough to justify a decision to remove Zhemchuzhina from her post as fishing industry commissar.[36] In February 1941, during the 18th party conference, Zhemchuzhina was deprived of her candidate membership in the Central Committee. Later, after the war, Zhemchuzhina was finally arrested, and she spent several years in exile.[37]

There is also documentary evidence that in the late 1930s, Stalin increased pressure on Molotov, rebuking him on numerous occasions over particular Council of People's Commissars decisions. On 28 January 1937, for instance, Molotov submitted a request to the Politburo to approve additional capital funds for the NKVD. Stalin responded with a harsh note: "To Com. Molotov. Why wasn't it possible to take care of this matter when the itemized lists of construction projects were being reviewed? Did that slip by you? This should be discussed in the PB."[38] The council's proposal was adopted the next day, which implies that the proposal itself was not the source of Stalin's irritation.

On 17 October 1937, Molotov approached the Politburo with a request to approve additional funds for two chemical industry enterprises. Stalin wrote the following note on the request: "To Com. Chubar. Who wrote this memorandum? Who checked the figures? It is hard to vote in favor of Com. Molotov's proposal."[39] Stalin made similar comments to Chubar over Molotov's head, even though Molotov was apparently in Moscow at the time, according to Politburo protocols, thus violating the existing line of authority and snubbing Molotov. Chubar, deputy chairman of the Council of People's Commissars and finance commissar, was subordinate to Molotov, and Molotov's signature on the letter to the Politburo indicated that the matter had been agreed on at the level of the Council of People's Commissars. Stalin repeated this maneuver several days later. On 20 October 1937, Molotov wrote to the Politburo with a request to approve the allocation of forty million rubles from the council's reserve fund to replenish the working capital for trade within the system of the Commissariat of Domestic Trade. Stalin again wrote a comment on the letter: "And what does Com. Chubar think of this?"[40] In the end, both decisions were adopted. This meant that Stalin had no objections to the resolutions but was probably just making a political point. Numerous examples of such potshots at Molotov by Stalin regarding decisions by the Council of People's Commissars can be found.[41]

Molotov was placed in a humiliating position at the 18th Party Congress. On 14 March 1939 he presented the traditional update by the chairman of the Council of People's Commissars on the five-year plan for the development of the Soviet economy. The report did not contain any content out of the ordinary, and his main assertions had been approved in advance by the Politburo. Nevertheless, the following day, 15 March, the Politburo, undoubtedly on Stalin's initiative (the original resolution shows Stalin's corrections), adopted a resolution entitled "On Molotov's Report on the Third Five-Year Plan at the 18th VKP(b) Congress." It found fault with Molotov's report. The members agreed "1) To recognize as incorrect that Com. Molotov in his speech . . . did not take time to summarize the discussion and analysis of the main corrections and additions to his theses. 2) To propose to Com. Molotov that this point be corrected."[42] In response to this Politburo decision, on 17 March Molotov reviewed the main points of the pre-congress "discussions" in his concluding remarks and recognized (without referring to the 15 March resolution) that he was correcting an "omission" in his report.[43]

Asking that a report include an account of pre-congress discussions was not unusual. What was unusual was that this request was made using a Politburo resolution that officially enumerated Molotov's errors. In analogous situations back in the 1920s and the early 1930s the procedure was strikingly different. On 7 November 1926, for example, Stalin had written to Molotov about publishing the speeches they made at the 15th party conference: "I have only now realized the whole awkwardness of not having shown anyone my speech. [. . .] I already feel awkward after the disputes of a couple of days ago. And now you want to kill me with your modesty, once again insisting on a review of the [your] speech. No, I had better refrain. Better print it in the form that you consider necessary."[44] Surviving letters show that, at least until 1936, Stalin heartily approved of the quality of Molotov's public speeches. "Today I read the section on international affairs. It came out well," he wrote in January 1933 about an upcoming speech by Molotov to a session of the Central Executive Committee.[45] "Reviewed. Not bad. See comments in the text," is how Stalin assessed the preliminary text of a speech Molotov would give about the Soviet constitution in February 1936.[46] When Stalin wanted to make critical remarks to Molotov, he did so privately. "The section on 'forced' labor is incomplete and unsatisfactory. See the comments and corrections in the text," Stalin wrote Molotov about a draft speech the latter was preparing to present to the Congress of Soviets in March 1931.[47]

Another old comrade-in-arms of Stalin who found himself discredited before the war was Kliment Yefremovich Voroshilov. After conducting a large-scale purge of the army under Stalin's orders, Voroshilov, who even in the best of times had not exhibited great talents as head of the military, was completely demoralized. "The longer things went on, the more he lost face. Everyone knew that if something came up for Voroshilov to deal with, he would be long weeks getting ready before any kind of answer would come," recalled Admiral Nikolai Kuznetsov.[48] On top of everything else, responsibility for defeats during the Soviet-Finnish War was placed on his shoulders. In May 1940, Semyon Timoshenko replaced him as defense commissar. While he was turning over the Defense Commissariat to its new commissar, a commission that included Zhdanov, Malenkov, and Voznesensky made an inspection. The official statement summarizing the results of the inspection contained harsh criticism of the state of affairs in the Military Administration.[49] Although Voroshilov's departure was carried out in an orderly fashion and on the surface appeared to be a promotion—he had just been appointed deputy chairman of the Council of People's Commissars and chairman of the council's Defense Committee—within the inner circle it could be felt that Stalin had cooled toward his longtime friend. As Khrushchev recalled, "Stalin [. . .] in discussions criticized the military administration, the defense commissariat, and especially Voroshilov. Sometimes he focused everything on the person of Voro-shilov. . . . I remember that one time Stalin, when we were at his dacha near town, in a fit of anger sharply criticized Voroshilov. He became very agitated, got up, and launched into Voroshilov. Voroshilov also got angry, turned red in the face, got up, and in response to Stalin's criticism hurled the accusation at him. 'That's your fault, you destroyed the military cadres.' Stalin also responded. Then Voroshilov grabbed a plate . . . and smashed it against the table. This is the only time I saw something like that with my own eyes."[50]

Stalin's bias during the late 1930s encompassed other old members of the Politburo who were as yet untouched by repression. All of them lost someone from among their relatives, close friends, or associates (the best-known case is of Kalinin's wife, who was sent to a labor camp). All of them lived with the fear that a political accusation could emerge at any moment. Speaking at an extended session of the defense commissar's military council on 2 June 1937, Stalin reminded his audience, for example, that Central Committee secretary Andrei Andreev had been "a very active Trotskyite in 1921"—a reference to the position Andreev had taken when the role of labor unions was being debated during the 10th Party Congress, where Andreev had supported Trotsky's position—although now he was "good at fighting with Trotskyites."[51] And Mikoyan recounted, twenty years later, soon after Ordzhonikidze's death, another of Stalin's threatening remarks: "The business of how the twenty-six Baku commissars were shot and only one of them—Mikoyan—survived is dark and tangled. And you, Anastas, don't make us untangle this business."[52]

Overall, available evidence supports the view that the old Politburo members were totally dependent on Stalin. This dependency, as Moshe Lewin has aptly pointed out, was characterized by slavishness: "Stalin could remove, arrest, and execute any of them, persecute their families, forbid them to attend meetings of the bodies of which they were members, or simply rage against them uncontrollably."[53] While such formulations strike some historians as exaggerated, those of us who have seen the available documents have every reason to insist on their accuracy.[54] Leaving aside many other considerations, let me again underscore the chief one: Stalin really could (and often did) suddenly deprive any Politburo member he chose not only of his job but of his life.

An important step in establishing the new system of power was the appointment of young leaders who had received their positions and authority directly from Stalin. In March 1939, during the plenum of the Central Committee that had been elected at the 18th Party Congress, Andrei Zhdanov and Nikita Khrushchev were made full members of the Politburo, joining the ranks of Andreev, Kaganovich, Kalinin, Mikoyan, Molotov, Voroshilov, and Stalin. Lavrenty Beria and Nikolai Shvernik were made candidate members. More fresh faces were brought in two years later. In February 1941, three up-and-coming party figures were all made candidate members: Georgy Malenkov, Aleksandr Shcherbakov, and Nikolai Voznesensky.

These Politburo appointments reflected a change of standing within the hierarchy of power. During the terror there was a further expansion of the areas for which Zhdanov—who represented the middle generation of Politburo appointees—was responsible. On 16 April 1937 the Politburo adopted a decision mandating that Zhdanov work alternate months in Moscow and Leningrad, beginning in May 1937.[55] (This followed the 20 April 1935 Politburo decision requiring Zhdanov to spend only ten days per month in Moscow.) A 27 November 1938 Politburo resolution dividing up areas of responsibility among Central Committee secretaries put Zhdanov in charge of "supervision and oversight of the operation of Komsomol organizations," as well as "supervision and oversight of publishing bodies and conveying necessary instructions to editors."[56] Since he was often in Moscow, Zhdanov began playing a more active role in the Orgburo and Politburo and often visited Stalin's office.[57] Meeting protocols indicate that during Stalin's absences Zhdanov essentially took his place within the Politburo. In any event, his signature comes first on many Politburo decisions adopted in Stalin's absence.[58]

Stalin himself, as in the past, showed Zhdanov special favor. As a rule, the Politburo granted Zhdanov every request he submitted in his capacity as head of the Leningrad party organization. On 4 April 1939 the Politburo considered a decree by the presidium of the Supreme Soviet to confer awards on outstanding agricultural workers in Leningrad Province. Stalin personally entered Zhdanov's name in the list of those to receive the Red Banner of Labor award.[59] Not long before the war, on 10 June 1941, the Politburo considered a memorandum from the head of the Kremlin health service urging that Zhdanov be given a monthlong vacation in Sochi owing to his poor health and "extreme overexhaustion." Such memorandums on high-ranking officials were no rarity, and the Politburo generally followed doctors' recommendations. But in this case Zhdanov was given more than the doctors were asking. The Politburo adopted a decision in accordance with the note Stalin had written on the request: "Give Com. Zhdanov a one and one-half month vacation in Sochi."[60]

From the earliest days of the terror, Yezhov had come first among the youngest group of up-and-coming leaders, having been given control over several key party-state structures at once. As Yezhov's influence waned, Beria and Malenkov, both of whose careers had advanced at a meteoric pace, were brought in to fill his shoes. Thirty-nine-year-old Beria, who had been brought to Moscow from Georgia to serve as deputy commissar of internal affairs in August 1938, had become commissar of internal affairs by the end of the year and was made a candidate member in the Politburo the next March.[61] Meeting protocols indicate that he did not play a very active role in the Politburo itself. He did, however, visit Stalin's office regularly, submitted many decisions on organizational and personnel changes within the NKVD to the Politburo for approval, and fought for the interests of his commissariat.[62]

Beria had favorably impressed Stalin back in the early 1930s, and Stalin had promoted his gradual ascendance to the leadership of the Transcaucasian Federation. In a letter to Kaganovich dated 12 August 1932, Stalin proposed appointing Beria first secretary of the party's Transcaucasian territorial committee. "Beria makes a good impression. He is a good organizer, an efficient, capable functionary."[63] Beria himself skillfully exploited Stalin's interest in the Caucasus, subtly reminding him from time to time of their common roots. In letters to Stalin, Beria called him "dear Comrade Koba."[64] The book about the history of Bolshevik organizations in the Caucasus that Beria arranged for placed Stalin among the most important leaders of the revolutionary movement in the Russian empire. Energetic and ruthless, Beria enthusiastically followed the general line and proved to be a master of repression in the Caucasus.

Stalin liked the antagonism between Beria and the former party leadership in the Caucasus, the old guard that had allied itself with Ordzhonikidze. Distinguished Caucasian Bolsheviks who traveled in top Kremlin circles did not have nice things to say about Beria and particularly enjoyed bringing up his ties with Musavat intelligence. We see evidence of this in Beria's letters to Ordzhonikidze in the 1930s, preserved in Ordzhonikidze's archive in the Russian State Archive of Social and Political History (RGASPI). According to these letters, Beria was forced to make a show of strong admiration for Ordzhonikidze and refute the slander of his foes. Here is an example, from a letter that Beria wrote to Ordzhonikidze on 2 March 1933: "Levon Gogoberidze is vacationing in Sukhumi. According to Com. Lakoba and a number of other comrades, Com. Gogoberidze is spreading the most awful rumors about me and about the new Caucasian leadership in general. In particular, he is saying that the party didn't know about my past work in Musavat counterintelligence and does not know about it. By the way, you know well that I was sent to Musavat counterintelligence by the party and that this question was settled by the Azerbaijan Central Committee in 1920 in your presence."[65] Stalin was also pleased to have compromising materials on Beria. The matter of his ties to a hostile intelligence agency (ties that were purposely never investigated) hung over Beria for the rest of his life. In 1953 Khrushchev used the rumor of these ties as a pretext in one of the charges that led to Beria's execution.

In 1937, Georgy Maksimilianovich Malenkov was only thirty-five years old, but he already had extensive bureaucratic experience in various sectors of the party: from 1925 to 1930 in the Central Committee apparatus, from 1930 to 1934 in the Moscow party committee, and, starting in late 1934, in the Central Committee's party personnel department, of which he was head. The party personnel department, ORPO, was created in 1934 to directly supervise the secretaries of republican, territorial, and provincial party organizations. As vast numbers of party officials needed to be expeditiously replaced over the course of the terror, the department took on increasing importance. For this reason, in 1937 and 1938 Malenkov, who was not yet even an official member of the Politburo, had regular access to Stalin. In the course of his duties, Malenkov was constantly submitting proposals about appointments of party-state officials to the Politburo for approval. In some cases, Malenkov himself took the initiative in reassigning personnel and submitted memorandums on these reshufflings directly to Stalin.[66]

His successful management of the purge of the party apparatus earned Malenkov Stalin's growing support and favor. Stalin chose Malenkov to give the main speech during the January 1938 Central Committee plenum, even though Malenkov was not even a Central Committee member.[67] Soon afterward Stalin proposed that the ORPO be expanded to include ninety-three new positions in order to create an apparatus of responsible organizers for every provincial party organization.[68] After the 18th Party Congress, at which Malenkov gave one of the speeches, he became a Central Committee member, a Central Committee secretary, and a member of the Orgburo. At the very end of March 1939, Malenkov was put in charge of a new Central Committee structure—the huge Central Committee Administration of Cadres, which consisted of forty-five departments (broken down by sectors), an administrator's inspection group directly reporting to Malenkov, and an archive of files on party officials.[69] The log of visits to Stalin's office indicates that during the months leading up to the war, Malenkov was among those working most closely with Stalin.[70]

Stalin kept a file of compromising materials on Malenkov, as he did on all of his underlings. As we can see from a letter found among Stalin's papers that Malenkov wrote to him on 28 January 1939, some sort of investigation into the ORPO and Malenkov himself was being conducted at the time. Malenkov complained to Stalin about the bias of the Moscow party collegium in charge of the case. "I want to say to you, Comrade Stalin," Malenkov wrote, "that some of the facts you have about me (having to do with personal morality) date from a time long before I started to have direct access to you. Ever since the first time I was personally in your office, I, being really worried, as any party member would be, about this first visit, made a firm promise to myself to be a model party member in every way in your eyes. I am sticking by that solidly."[71] A new threat hung over Malenkov after the arrest of Yezhov, with whom he had worked closely for many years. Yezhov gave some testimony against Malenkov. Although Stalin never took action on the allegations, Malenkov always knew they were there.[72]

During the 18th Party Congress in 1939, another party official who was rapidly advancing under Stalin's aegis was given Central Committee membership: the thirty-six-year-old economist and new chairman of Gosplan, Nikolai Alekseevich Voznesensky.[73] Beginning in May 1937, before being promoted to his new post in Moscow, Voznesensky had served under Zhdanov in Leningrad. It is possible that Zhdanov himself recommended Voznesensky to Stalin. There are many indications that Stalin valued Voznesensky as a highly qualified and dedicated administrator.

This fits with the overall image of Voznesensky, who, according to those who knew him, was not a pleasant person to be around. As Yakov Chadaev, chief of administration at the Council of People's Commissars, recalls, "Nikolai Alekseevich was an exceptionally energetic worker who solved whatever problems arose quickly and effectively. But he was unable to conceal his mood and was too short-tempered. What's more, his bad moods took the form of extreme irritability, haughtiness, and arrogance. But when Voznesensky was in a good mood he was witty, exuberant, cheerful, and amiable. The way he comported himself generally and in discussions—there was an erudition, a breadth of knowledge, high culture. But such moments were rather rare. They were over in a flash, and then Voznesensky again became sullen, unrestrained, and thorny."[74] Mikoyan, who felt sympathy for Voznesensky, nonetheless wrote, "As a person, Voznesensky had obvious flaws. For example, ambition, arrogance. Within the close inner circle of the Politburo this was obvious to everyone. As was his chauvinism."[75]

Malenkov and Voznesensky delivered the main speeches at the 18th party conference, which took place in January and February 1941.[76] During the Central Committee plenum convened soon after the conference, on 21 February 1941, Malenkov, Voznesensky, and the new first secretary of the Moscow party organization, Aleksandr Shcherbakov (Khrushchev had been sent to head the Ukrainian party) were made candidate members of the Politburo. In proposing these new candidacies to the plenum, Stalin repeated the arguments he had made during the February–March 1937 plenum.

> We have come together here, Politburo members and some TsK members, we have come to the conclusion that it would be good to expand the makeup at least of the candidate members of the Politburo. Now we have quite a few old men in the Politburo, people who will be retiring, and somebody else who's younger should be selected, so they can start learning and, in case something happens, be ready to take their place. What I'm talking about is that it's necessary to expand the circle of people working in the Politburo.
>
> Specifically, this has boiled down to the fact that we are of the opinion that it would be good to make additions now. Now we have two candidate members. The first candidate is Beria and the second is Shvernik. It would be good to bring this number to five, to add three more, so they would help the Politburo members work. Let's say, it wouldn't be bad to bring in Com. Voznesensky as a candidate member, he has earned that,

and Shcherbakov, the first secretary of Moscow Province, and Malenkov, third. I think it would be good to incorporate them.[77]

Subsequent events showed that Stalin did not make these proposals lightly. Those elevated to the position of candidate members during this era of repression—Beria, Voznesensky, and Malenkov—really did go on to hold key posts in the postwar years. After Stalin's death it was the people promoted during the late 1930s—Beria, Malenkov, and Khrushchev—who were the main contenders in the struggle for succession.

THE POLITBURO AND THE COUNCIL OF PEOPLE'S COMMISSARS

The final consolidation of Stalin's personal dictatorship was reflected not only in cardinal changes in his relationship with his comrades-in-arms but also in the breakdown of the old decision-making system and the creation of a new one. The virtual liquidation of the Politburo as an instrument of collective power reached its logical conclusion during the years of the Great Terror. On 14 April 1937, soon after the February–March Central Committee plenum, on Stalin's initiative the Politburo membership was polled on and approved a very important decision entitled "On Preparing Issues for the Politburo of the TsK VKP(b)." It was resolved:

1. For the purposes of preparing [issues] for the Politburo and, in cases of particular urgency, also for resolving problems of a secret nature, including questions of foreign policy, to create a permanent TsK VKP(b) Politburo commission made up of Comrades Stalin, Molotov, Voroshilov, L. Kaganovich, and Yezhov.
2. For the purposes of preparing for the Politburo urgent current issues of an economic nature, to create a permanent TsK VKP(b) Politburo commission made up of Comrades Molotov, Stalin, Chubar, Mikoyan, and L. Kaganovich.[78]

This decision was of fundamental importance. Basically, it legalized something that was already an actuality—it limited the rights of the Politburo in favor of an exclusive group consisting of Stalin and his closest comrades-in-arms. Stalin felt compelled to explain the reasons behind his proposal to members of the Politburo. He dictated this explanation of his motivations to Poskrebyshev.

>Questions of a secret nature, including foreign policy questions, must be addressed by the Politburo in accordance with the rules of the TsK VKP(b) secretariat. Since TsK secretaries, with the exception of Com. Stalin, usually either work outside Moscow (Zhdanov) or in other agencies, where they are seriously overburdened with work (Kaganovich, Yezhov), and TsK secretary Com. Andreev is often forced to travel out of town, at the same time that the number of secret questions is constantly increasing, the TsK secretariat overall is not able to carry out the abovementioned tasks. Furthermore, it is self-evident that secret foreign-policy questions absolutely cannot be dealt with without the participation of Comrades Molotov and Voroshilov, who are not members of the TsK secretariat.[79]

Stalin thus tried to create an impression that the change meant using commissions instead of the Central Committee Secretariat only at the stage of preparing issues. In fact, the right not only to prepare but also to resolve issues ("in cases of particular urgency") meant that the commissions would supplant both the Secretariat and the Politburo.

For the time being, there is insufficient evidence to determine the extent to which these commissions carried out the functions entrusted to them, the frequency with which they met, or the questions they considered. It is, however, possible to assert that a Politburo governing commission did function. For example, an encoded telegram from the head of the political department of the Far Eastern Railroad dated 18 October 1937 bears a typewritten proposal addressed to the "secret five." Since the original document has not been found, it is hard to say with certainty who appended this proposal. Its style indicates that it came from Stalin. It was signed by the members of the first commission that had been established in April—Stalin, Molotov, Voroshilov, Kaganovich, and Yezhov. The decision resolving the matter raised in this telegram was drafted as a Politburo special-folder decision dated 20 October.[80] As the log of visitors to Stalin's office shows, on 18 and 19 October no meetings took place there, but on 20 October there was a brief meeting with Central Committee secretary Andreev and first secretary of the Central Committee of the Communist Party of Uzbekistan, U. Yu. Yusupov.[81] Meanwhile, the protocol for the 20 October 1937 session of the Politburo records forty-five decisions, including thirteen secret-folder decisions.[82] Most likely, the Five got together on 20 October in the Politburo meeting hall in the Kremlin.

Two years later, on a report from M. V. Danchenko, head of the

Council of People's Commissars' Administration of State Reserves, stating that large quantities of nonferrous metal and rubber had been released from mobilization stockpiles and proposing the import of additional quantities of these materials, Stalin placed the following comment: "*To members of the PB (the Five)*—I propose prohibiting the release of nonferrous metals and rubber from state stockpiles *without the permission of the TsK VKP(b) Politburo.* A copy of the Politburo decision, if it is adopted, should be given to Comrades Danchenko and Voznesensky, *assigning the latter control over this matter.*"[83] The corresponding decision (which was entirely consistent with Stalin's proposal) became a Politburo resolution dated 16 December 1939.[84] Below Stalin's note on the report stand the signatures of Molotov, Voroshilov, Mikoyan, and Kaganovich. An entry in the log of visitors to Stalin's office for 16 December 1939 shows that only this foursome met with him in his office that day.[85] Evidently, the decision on the state stockpiles was made during this meeting in Stalin's office, as were other decisions later recorded as Politburo resolutions. In his comments on Danchenko's report, Stalin fully equated the Politburo and the Five, which undoubtedly reflected the true state of affairs.

All this suggests that on the eve of the war, an exclusive governing group of five people had largely supplanted the Politburo. By 1939 it appears to have become a merged form of the two commissions created in April 1937. After Chubar was destroyed, then Yezhov, Mikoyan became a part of the "secret five" (the first of the two commissions). The other four members (Stalin, Molotov, Voroshilov, and Kaganovich) had initially been members of both commissions. In 1939, Molotov, Voroshilov, Kaganovich, and Mikoyan visited Stalin's office much more often than other members of the Soviet leadership. Stalin's office is probably where the meetings of this fivesome took place.[86] It was also these Politburo members who most often signed Politburo decisions. At some point, the makeup of the Five may have changed. As Anastas Mikoyan testifies in his memoirs, before the war the Five consisted of Stalin, Molotov, Malenkov, Beria, and Mikoyan.[87] It is plausible that Kaganovich and Voroshilov, who had lost status during the prewar years, were replaced by the up-and-coming Malenkov and Beria, but archival evidence to confirm Mikoyan's assertion has yet to be found.

That the full, official Politburo had ceased to function as it had in the past is also reflected in the meeting protocols. Between June 1937 and the beginning of the war in June 1941, Politburo protocols show only ten regular sessions of the Politburo attended by the majority of members and candidate members, plus a group of Central Committee members. Most of the resolutions included in the Politburo protocols were designated "decisions of the Politburo," and beginning in 1939, after the 18th Party Congress, all decisions in Politburo protocols were given this designation. Undoubtedly, the new way protocols were put together reflected the true state of affairs: regular Politburo meetings of various sorts had been supplanted by meetings of smaller, more exclusive groups. Decisions were taken by the Five, and many other issues were decided collaboratively between Stalin and whatever members of the Politburo he felt needed to be brought into the particular discussion. As the visitor log shows, many of these meetings took place in Stalin's office. In some instances they took place in the Politburo meeting hall or at Stalin's dacha. Molotov's published notes, compiled before his trip to Berlin in November 1940, which essentially constituted Stalin's directives on how negotiations should be conducted, include the following: "If they ask about our relations with the English, reply in accordance with the exchange of opinions at St[alin's] dacha."[88] By no means all decisions adopted during such meetings were even officially recorded. No Politburo protocols contain any decisions about a pact with Germany in August 1939 or Molotov's negotiation directives, or many other decisions that must have been made in a variety of areas.

As a result of changes to the way the Politburo operated, there were significantly fewer official Politburo decisions in 1938–1940 compared with the number in the beginning of the 1930s. Protocols during the prewar years were primarily filled with Politburo approvals of decisions by the Orgburo and the Central Committee Secretariat on personnel issues, as well as ideological pronouncements. A reorganization of the Central Committee apparatus underscored the Politburo's specialization in these areas—personnel and ideology. In 1939 two key Central Committee administrations were established to be responsible for cadres and propaganda. The departments that had been in charge of these areas were abolished. Malenkov headed the Administration of Cadres, and Zhdanov was put in charge of propaganda. It was these two offices and, correspondingly, Malenkov and Zhdanov, who prepared decisions having to do with party and personnel issues. The decisions were submitted to Stalin for approval and issued in the name of the Politburo. On 17 January 1941, during a rare Politburo meeting, Stalin himself explained the essence of the new, simplified decision-making procedures: "It's been four–five months since we in the TsK have convened the Politburo. All questions are prepared by Zhdanov, Malenkov, and others in separate meetings with comrades who have the necessary expertise, and the business of governing has not suffered as a result, but has gotten better."[89]

Another significant portion of decisions seen in the protocols of Politburo meetings comprised approvals of Council of People's Commissars resolutions and of resolutions issued jointly by the Central Committee and the council, which it had become customary for the Politburo to approve back in the 1930s. As usual, these Council of People's Commissars resolutions dealt primarily with economic and defense issues. In the past, however, Politburo commissions had been created to develop council resolutions; now the resolutions were prepared within the government apparatus. The functions and structure of the Council of People's Commissars apparatus became more complex.

On 27 April 1937, immediately after the establishment of the two Politburo commissions, the Politburo adopted a decision to establish a Defense Committee under the Council of People's Commissars. The new committee replaced both the Labor and Defense Council (which was abolished by the same 27 April decision) and the joint Politburo–Council of People's Commissars defense commission, which had functioned since 1930. The new Defense Committee was composed of seven full members—Molotov (chairman), Stalin, Kaganovich, Voroshilov, Chubar, Moisey Rukhimovich, and Valery Mezhlauk—as well as four candidate members, Yan Gamarnik, Mikoyan, Zhdanov, and Yezhov.[90] It had a more substantial support apparatus than the previous defense commission. In December 1937 a special Defense Committee decision concerning this apparatus was adopted and subsequently confirmed by the Politburo. The decisions stipulated that the apparatus of the Defense Committee should prepare for the committee's review issues related to mobilizing for war, equipping the army, and preparing the economy for mobilization and that it should verify that Defense Committee decisions were properly implemented. A special Defense Committee inspectorate was created and given broad rights, including those that had previously been enjoyed by the now-abolished defense department of Gosplan and the military oversight groups under the Party Control Commission and the Soviet Control Commission.[91]

Another sign that government structures were expanding was the November 1937 creation of the Economic Council of the Council of People's Commissars, which had the status of a permanent commission. The chairman of this Economic Council, according to its statute, was the chairman of the Council of People's Commissars, and its membership included the Council of People's Commissars deputy chairmen as well as a labor union representative. The Economic Council was in charge of a broad range of economic matters and issued resolutions and orders pertaining to them. A special apparatus was created to prepare these decisions.

On 10 September 1939 the Politburo approved a resolution of the Council of People's Commissars and the Central Committee that delineated the functions of the Defense Committee and the Economic Council, primarily in the area of defense. The Economic Council was charged with "supplying the army and navy with food, clothing and footwear, as well as their medical, veterinary, and fuel provisions and necessary political-educational materials." Responsibility for "supplying the army and navy with armaments, equipment, transport, as well as meeting the army's railway and water transport needs," was assigned to the Defense Committee. The deputy chairman of the Council of People's Commissars, Mikoyan, was appointed chairman of the Economic Council, and Nikolai Bulganin, who was assigned to "prepare questions and observations pertaining to the implementation of decisions by the council," was appointed to serve as his permanent deputy chairman. The same resolution appointed Nikolai Voznesensky to serve under Molotov as permanent deputy chairman of the Defense Committee. Voznesensky was charged with preparing "questions and observations pertaining to the implementation of decisions" by the Defense Committee. The resolution mandated that the Defense Committee and the Economic Council each meet daily.[92]

In early 1940, on Stalin's initiative, the Economic Council was reorganized yet again. In accordance with a 28 March 1940 resolution officially attributed to the Politburo (the corresponding resolution of the Council of People's Commissars is dated 3 April), separate economic councils were established for six sectors: metallurgy and chemistry, machine building, the defense industry, fuel, consumer goods, and agriculture and procurement. Each of the councils, all under the Council of People's Commissars, would be headed by one of the deputy chairmen of the Council of People's Commissars, who would be directly in charge of the corresponding commissariat. The council heads were made members of the Economic Council, which was again to be headed by Molotov as chairman of the Council of People's Commissars. Mikoyan was moved into the position of Economic Council deputy chairman (Stalin himself wrote the item on Molotov's and Mikoyan's appointments, which he added in the draft resolution).[93] This reorganization was apparently conceived to increase efficiency within the commissariats.

Such intense activity within the government, along with the assignment of most Politburo members to either the Defense Committee or the Economic Council (or both) largely explains the change in how the Politburo dealt with economic and defense questions.[94] Resolutions pertaining to these areas were developed and coordinated within the apparatus of the Council of People's Commissars with the active involvement of Politburo members. This led to a sort of de facto Politburo approval of resolutions of the council, the Economic Council, and the Defense Committee and made it possible to do without special commissions made up of Politburo members to conduct further work on questions that arose.

This system, which was created on Stalin's initiative and with his direct involvement, became the object of his harsh criticism in early 1941. On 17 January 1941, in connection with a discussion of the economic plan for 1941 at a session of the Politburo, Stalin raised the question of the Economic Council's activities. As usual, no stenographic record of the meeting was kept; however, one of the meeting participants recorded a brief account of Stalin's remarks in his diary. According to V. A. Malyshev, deputy chairman of the Council of People's Commissars, Stalin severely criticized the Economic Council for its "parliamentarism"—its frequent meetings, at which attempts were made to decide long lists of questions. He demanded that work on specific problems be handed over to the sector-specific councils and that the Economic Council be convened just "once per month to discuss two–three fundamental questions and steer policy."[95]

Stalin's complaints were hardly fair. The 10 September 1939 resolution mandated daily meetings. Nonetheless, Stalin's comments instigated preparations for another reorganization of the Council of People's Commissars apparatus, one that culminated in the adoption of two joint council–Central Committee resolutions, dated 20 March 1941. The resolution entitled "On Organization of the Work of the USSR Sovnarkom" called for an increase in the number of deputy chairmen so that each of them would be responsible for two or three commissariats. The deputy chairmen were given the right (within the framework of economic plans) to unilaterally decide operational questions related to the commissariats under their jurisdiction. Furthermore, all decisions by the deputy chairmen were to be published as council orders. These new powers—the authority to approve quarterly plans for the distribution of funds, credit plans, and cash budgets, and monthly plans for production and shipping, all with Council of People's Commissars authority— were also bestowed on the chairman of the Council of People's Commissars and his first deputy. The resolution abolished the economic councils under the Council of People's Commissars, which had created, in the words of the document, "partitions between the people's commissars and the Sovnarkom of the USSR."[96]

The second resolution approved by the Politburo on 20 March mandated the creation of a Bureau of the Council of People's Commissars, a new agency of government that, while not stipulated in the USSR constitution, would nonetheless be vested, as stated in the resolution, "with all the powers of the USSR Sovnarkom."[97] The Bureau was entrusted with a wide range of functions relating to management of the economy. Bureau meetings were to take place once a week (or more often if needed); the Council of People's Commissars itself was supposed to convene only once per month. Bureau decisions were published as council resolutions. Molotov (council chairman), Voznesensky (first deputy chairman), Mikoyan, Bulganin, Beria, Kaganovich, and Andreev were appointed to the Bureau.

The Bureau took on a significant portion of the responsibilities previously carried out by the Defense Committee and the Economic Council—which is why the resolution that established the Bureau abolished the Economic Council and reduced the Defense Committee to five members. The functions of the Defense Committee were limited to questions of adopting new military technologies, the review of military and naval procurement orders, and the development of mobilization plans to be approved by the Central Committee and Council of People's Commis- ·

sars. The management of the economy was now largely carried out by means of orders from the council leadership. In April 1941 just the council chairman and his deputies published 4,589 orders (almost a third of them—1,516—were signed by Voznesensky).[98] In comparison, for the entire year of 1936 there had been only 4,486 such orders, and over a ten-month period in 1937 there had been 7,506.[99]

As can be seen from the original protocols of Politburo meetings, the initial draft resolution establishing the Bureau stipulated the creation of a "Lesser Sovnarkom" endowed with the authority of a permanent commission. As proposed, the Lesser Sovnarkom seemed to represent a return to the traditions of the Leninist Sovnarkom created in 1918. In fact, the idea behind this body was quite different. The Lesser Sovnarkom of the Leninist period truly was a commission intended to free the Council of People's Commissars from decisions on minor questions (the precursor to the original Lesser Sovnarkom had been created in December 1917 as the "macaroni commission," charged with reviewing petty matters).[100] The new government body created in March 1941 was in essence the ruling group of the Council of People's Commissars, organized along the same principle as the Politburo's ruling group was. Stalin's corrections to the draft resolution underscored the parallel. He replaced the vague statement that the new body would be endowed with the authority of a permanent commission with the key provision that it would "be endowed with the full authority of the USSR SNK."[101]

There is documentary evidence that Nikolai Voznesensky drafted the March decision to reorganize the government.[102] The decision to create the Bureau made him first deputy to Molotov, council chairman. This appointment was at the center of the political intrigue behind Stalin's reorganization of the government. Promoting Voznesensky into such an important post over the heads of more senior members of the Politburo (Mikoyan and Kaganovich) raised tensions within Stalin's inner circle. In memoirs written many decades later, Mikoyan, for example, was still unable to hide the sense of injury he had felt: "But what struck us most of all about the composition of the Bureau leadership was that Voznesensky became first deputy chairman of the Sovnarkom. [. . .] Stalin's motives in this whole leapfrog were still not clear. And Voznesensky, being naive, was very pleased with his appointment."[103] According to Yakov Chadaev, who, as chief of the council's administration, was able to observe the intrigues from the inside, Stalin was clearly pitting Voznesensky and Molotov against one another and openly demonstrating his displeasure with the latter. From this perspective, the reorganization of the Council of People's Commissars and the personnel reshuffling within the leadership of the government may well have been designed to lay the groundwork for the coup de grâce—Stalin's appointment as chairman of the Council of Ministers.

As we saw in chapter 1, the Politburo had seriously considered this idea in 1930, when Rykov was removed as head of the Council of People's Commissars. For a number of reasons, Stalin had preferred to appoint Molotov to this post, but he was apparently not rejecting the idea that he might head the government at some point in the future. The intense attacks against Molotov and the reorganization of the Council of People's Commissars in 1940 and early 1941 could well be viewed as preparations for removing Molotov as council head. Stalin may have decided to finally make this move for a variety of reasons. First and foremost was the political and propaganda context; taking that step would formally consolidate Stalin's position as leader and heir to Lenin. Nor should Stalin's personal qualities be discounted—the hunger for power, the urge to not only be in control but to have all the trappings of power, and his jealousy of his comrades-in-arms. Purely administrative considerations may have played a role, too—a desire to delineate the functions of the party and state apparatuses and expand the role of the latter.

On 28 April 1941, just over a month after the Bureau had been established, Stalin sent a memorandum to its members. It said that the reason the Bureau had been created was to straighten out government operations and put an end to the "chaos" in the management of the economy, where the practice of "deciding important questions related to the building of the economy through so-called 'polling'" continued. In fact, Stalin wrote, this approach to decision making had become even more prevalent. "The question arises: What exactly is the SNK Bureau doing if serious questions related to the building of the economy get past it as a management *collective*?" Stalin underscored under the word "collective." As an example of an issue that had been decided through the inappropriate use of "polling," Stalin brought up a draft resolution, submitted by Beria, about construction of an oil pipeline in the Sakhalin region. Stalin wrote indignantly that Molotov had signed the document even though it had not been discussed at a Bureau meeting. This practice

Stalin called "bureaucratic paper-pushing and scribbling." and he issued an ultimatum: "I think 'management' of this sort can't go on. I propose discussing this question in the TsK Politburo. And for now, I feel
compelled to say that I refuse to participate in voting through polling on
any draft resolution whatsoever on economic questions of any consequence at all if I don't see the signatures of the SNK Bureau indicating
that the draft has been discussed and approved by the Bureau of the
USSR SNK."[104]

Stalin's complaints must have come as a total surprise to Molotov. In
January 1941, Stalin had condemned the Council of People's Commissars leaders for parliamentarism. Their tendency to raise too many matters during meetings was the complaint that led ultimately to the creation of the Bureau. In the resolutions of 20 March nothing had been
said about the evils of polling. Rather, a number of key points in these
resolutions had suggested a move toward simplifying decision-making
procedures. It was also rather suspicious that Stalin based his criticism
on a single example of polling, especially since Stalin's memorandum
did not make it clear whether or not construction of the Sakhalin oil
pipeline did indeed demand an in-depth discussion by the Bureau.

Overall, the attacks against Molotov in Stalin's 28 April memorandum were hard to take seriously. Molotov himself and other members of
the Politburo doubtless understood that something else was behind
Stalin's complaints, something that he did not want to say outright. Indeed, the discussions of Stalin's memorandum had a different outcome
than its contents might have suggested. Stalin's memorandum is among
the papers associated with Politburo protocols; it is appended to the
resulting 4 May 1941 Politburo resolution, which is entitled "On
Strengthening the Work of Soviet Central and Local Bodies."[105] In the
text of the resolution it says:

> I. In the interests of full coordination between Soviet and party organi-
> zations and the unconditional assurance of unity in their work as lead-
> ers, as well as to further enhance the authority of Soviet bodies given the
> current tense international situation, which demands every possible ef-
> fort by Soviet agencies in the defense of the country, the PB TsK VKP(b)
> unanimously resolves:
> 1. To appoint Com. I. V. Stalin Chairman of the Council of People's
>   Commissars of the USSR.

2. To appoint Com. V. M. Molotov Deputy Chairman of the USSR SNK and to place him in charge of the foreign policy of the USSR, leaving him in the post of People's Commissar of Foreign Affairs.

3. To appoint Com. A. A. Zhdanov Com. Stalin's deputy in the TsK Secretariat and relieve him of his duties of overseeing the TsK VKP(b) Administration for Propaganda and Agitation, inasmuch as Com. Stalin, who on the insistence of the PB TsK retains the position of first secretary of the TsK VKP(b), will not be able to allot sufficient time to work in the TsK Secretariat.

4. To appoint Com. A. S. Shcherbakov TsK VKP(b) secretary and head of the Administration for Propaganda and Agitation, leaving him in the post of First Secretary of the Moscow Province Committee and City Committee of the VKP(b).[106]

This resolution revealed Stalin's true motives in attacking Molotov and the Bureau. On the surface, the reshufflings at the highest echelons of power looked like a return to the Leninist model of party-state leadership. In fact, top Soviet leaders had never before been in a position of such dependence on the leader of the party. One sign of this dependence was the very way Stalin took over the post of chairman of the Council of People's Commissars. Unlike in 1930, when Stalin had conducted lengthy correspondence and negotiations with his comrades-in-arms—and in the end turned down the position of head of the government—in 1941 he finally ascended to that position with no more than a reprimand and an expression of his dissatisfaction with the state of affairs at the council.

Stalin's appointment as council chairman prompted changes to the council's Bureau. On 7 May the Politburo approved its new composition: council's chairman Stalin, council's first deputy chairman Voznesensky, council's deputy chairmen Molotov, Mikoyan, Bulganin, Beria, Kaganovich, Mekhlis, and Andreev, who was a Central Committee secretary and chairman of the Party Control Commission.[107] This decision was most likely adopted at a meeting in Stalin's office attended by Beria, Bulganin, Voznesensky, Molotov, Kaganovich, and Mikoyan—in other words, by most of the leaders making up the Bureau.[108] Members of the Central Committee's Special Sector, which was in charge of formalizing the decision as a Politburo resolution, polled the remaining Politburo members—Kalinin, Zhdanov, Andreev, Shvernik, Shcherbakov—by telephone.[109] On Stalin's orders (as we can see from a note he made on the document), the resolution on the Bureau was also submitted to people's commissars and the council's committee chairmen for approval by poll.[110] The first resolution of the new Bureau, which concerned the distribution of responsibilities among the council's chairman and his deputies, was processed in the same way. This document was also most likely put together at the 7 May meeting in Stalin's office.[111] It listed the new chairman's fifteen deputies: Voznesensky, Molotov, Voroshilov, Kaganovich, Mikoyan, Andreev, Beria, Bulganin, Mekhlis, Vyshinsky, Rozaliia Zemliachika, Malyshev, Mikhail Pervukhin, Kosygin, and Maxim Saburov.

In May 1941 the majority of Politburo members held high-ranking posts within the Council of People's Commissars. On 15 May, Voroshilov, deputy chairman of the council and chairman of the Defense Committee, and Shvernik, first secretary of the All-Union Central Council of Labor Unions, were appointed to the Bureau, followed on 30 May by Central Committee secretaries Zhdanov and Malenkov.[112] When all was said and done, almost all members of the Politburo, with the exception of Kalinin, Khrushchev, and Shcherbakov, were included in the Bureau, and only two members of the Bureau were not Politburo members: Mekhlis and Bulganin. Out of fourteen members and candidate members of the Politburo, eight were chairmen or deputy chairmen in the Council of People's Commissars.

Once the highest-level party and state bodies were both under Stalin's direct control, their formal union did indeed lead to a certain orderliness in their functioning. During the final weeks before the war, meetings of the highest party and governmental groups—the Bureau and the Politburo—took place on a regular basis. It was initially decided that the Bureau would meet twice weekly (on Tuesdays and Fridays) at six in the evening. This schedule was followed for a while; meetings took place on 9, 13, 16, and 20 May. On 20 May a decision was made to reduce the frequency of meetings to once weekly (on Thursdays), so meetings were held on 29 May and 5, 12, and 19 June. The Bureau conducted its work with notable rigor. At each meeting the main agenda for the next meeting was set, which allowed the corresponding draft resolutions and background materials to be prepared and circulated in advance. In addition to the main questions—in general, ten to fourteen were covered—Bureau members approved several dozen resolutions on so-called current issues presented by the deputy chairmen of the Council of

People's Commissars for preliminary consideration by Voznesensky, the first deputy chairman of the council. The Bureau used commissions to draft decisions. In submitting a draft resolution entitled "On Procurement Contracts for the Kolkhoz Sugar Beet Crop of 1941," for example, Anastas Mikoyan reported in an accompanying note addressed to Stalin that the document had been edited by a commission of the Bureau "in accordance with the exchange of opinions that took place during the meeting of the Bureau of the Sovnarkom."[113] In addition to temporary commissions created to work on specific questions, the Bureau sprouted permanent commissions, as had also happened in the Politburo. On 30 May 1941 the Defense Committee was abolished and replaced with a permanent Bureau Commission on Military and Naval Matters consisting of Stalin (chairman), Voznesensky (deputy chairman), Voroshilov, Zhdanov, and Malenkov.[114]

Stalin was actively involved in the Bureau's work. He chaired almost every meeting and spoke out on almost all issues. His participation in meetings affected the way the Politburo functioned. Since almost all Politburo members belonged to the Bureau, it became customary to conduct Politburo meetings immediately after Bureau meetings—and with broader participation than just the Five.[115]

After the disruptions of the terror, on the eve of the war a system of institutions of supreme power that followed relatively orderly procedures and divisions of responsibility took shape. The apparatus of the Central Committee, which was responsible for ideological and personnel questions, was almost completely removed from decision making on economic matters. The apparatus of the Council of People's Commissars, which was focused on the economic sphere, including the defense industry, notably increased in importance. A sort of division of labor at the highest level occurred. Party personnel matters were handled primarily by the Politburo. The majority of the resolutions related to the economic sphere were issued by the council (or, in fact, the Bureau). While the past practice of having the Politburo approve the most important council resolutions was still adhered to, this procedure became more of a formality. During the previous period, council resolutions were, as a rule, submitted to the Politburo with a cover note, signed by Molotov or a deputy, that briefly explained the matter at hand and proposed approving the given decision. The council proposal was voted on at a Politburo meeting or by polling the membership. After Stalin was appointed chairman of the council, most council resolutions submitted to the Central Committee included a record of their approval by the Bureau, made by the chief of administration of the Council of People's Commissars, Yakov Chadaev. When such a record was included, the Central Committee's Special Sector clerks polled only the few members of the Politburo who were not also members of the Bureau. When the Bureau was established, Kalinin, Voroshilov, Zhdanov, Shcherbakov, and Malenkov were polled.[116] When almost all members of the Politburo had joined the Bureau, only Kalinin had to be consulted before the Special Sector formalized Politburo decisions confirming council decrees.[117] In other words, the procedure of having the Politburo approve resolutions of the Council of People's Commissars had lost its relevance. It was reduced to a formality carried out by a clerk.

In the final analysis, both the Politburo and the Bureau functioned as consultative structures under Stalin, who himself constituted the supreme authority. Decisions on key questions of military strategy and foreign policy were his exclusive domain. He also involved himself in countless secondary problems. Younger, recently promoted leaders acted as Stalin's deputies—Malenkov within the Central Committee apparatus (Zhdanov, who had been officially given this title by the 4 May 1941 resolution, spent a significant portion of his time in Leningrad), and Voznesensky within the Council of People's Commissars apparatus. The administrative influence of the older Politburo members diminished commensurately, and Stalin demonstrated his displeasure with the older members whenever possible. At the second meeting of the newly constituted Bureau, on 9 May 1941, Stalin sharply attacked Viacheslav Molotov, who was delivering a report on awarding bonuses to leading engineers and technicians. Yakov Chadaev, who acted as recording secretary at the meeting, recalled the following.

> Stalin did not hide his disapproving attitude toward Molotov. He listened with great impatience to Molotov's lengthy responses to every remark made by Bureau members about the draft resolution. [. . .] It could be sensed that Stalin was launching into Molotov the way someone with the upper hand deals with his opponent. [. . .] Molotov's breathing was heavy, and every now and then he would let out a loud sigh. He squirmed in his chair and muttered something to himself. Finally, Molotov could stand it no longer:

"It's all very well to talk," Molotov said bitterly, but quietly. But Stalin heard these words.

"It's long been known," Stalin commented, "that he who is afraid of criticism is a coward."

Molotov winced, but fell silent. [. . .] The remaining members of the Bureau sat quietly, bent over their papers [. . .] At this meeting I once again saw the majesty and strength of Stalin. His closest comrades-in-arms feared him like fire. They agreed with him on every point.

Launching such attacks against Molotov, who in the unofficial hierarchy of the top leadership was second only to Stalin, was a good way for Stalin to instill fear in those around him. The top Soviet leaders were constantly aware of their total dependence on the will and whims of the Leader. Such dependence undermined the effectiveness of the administrative system, but it was an important element of the dictatorship.

The mass purges of the nomenklatura and the destruction of a significant portion of Politburo members in 1937 and 1938 cleared the way for the consolidation of Stalin's dictatorship. Even the top Soviet leaders, to say nothing of lower-level officials, found themselves totally dependent on Stalin and lived under the constant threat of losing not only their jobs but their lives. An important consequence of the slavish dependency was the total breakdown of the institution and procedures of collective leadership. The Politburo no longer functioned as it had in the past. An exclusive ruling group of five supplanted it, and its composition was determined by the dictator. Decisions of any importance were made, as a rule, by Stalin alone.

The new political reality led to numerous administrative reorganizations, over the course of which Stalin attempted to find the optimal lines of authority between the various institutions of party and state. The most notable among these reorganizations involved the delineation of functions of the apparatuses of the Central Committee and the Council of People's Commissars. The former focused on the administration of personnel decisions and ideological questions, the latter on managing the economy. Concomitant changes were made to the apparatuses of these bodies, and responsibilities were redistributed among the members of the Politburo. Stalin's comrades-in-arms were fully transformed into high-level bureaucrats assigned purely executive functions. Stalin determined their spheres of competence. They sought his approval for even relatively minor decisions and gave him a thorough accounting of their activities.

Having grasped not only the levers of power but also all the official trappings of political leadership and operational management (the titles of General Secretary of the Central Committee, Chairman of the Council of People's Commissars), Stalin created a distinct system of "administrative dictatorship" by the time war came. Its most notable feature was the total control that Stalin exercised over not only questions of military strategy and foreign policy but also a disproportionate share of routine administrative functions. After redistributing roles among the members of the Politburo and promoting new, young assistants, Stalin nevertheless tried to stay maximally involved in administrative routines. Living with constant pressure and scrutiny from Stalin (who, beginning in 1937, did not leave Moscow even to vacation in the south), his comrades-in-arms shed their last traces of independence, even in deciding operational questions. This ultra-centralization was one of the main reasons for the catastrophic failures at the beginning of the war.

Conclusion
Master of the House

BY 1941, STALIN had consolidated his dictatorship and established one of the most brutal regimes that has ever existed in Russia or the world. The factors contributing to Stalin's successful takeover of power that are often cited by historians and political scientists—the authoritarian traditions of Russian history and the fractured state of Russian society after years of war and revolution—do nothing to change the fact that Stalin's dictatorship was imposed from above, even if it did have fertile ground on which to grow. Every dictator must carry out a revolution from above. Without this, he (or she) cannot become a dictator. The limits and nature of the Stalinist revolution from above were largely determined by the struggle within the Bolshevik party, the balance of power between Stalin and the other party leaders, and the dictator's own ideas, his misconceptions, and the extent of his criminality.

Although numerous distinct stages can be identified in Soviet history, in terms of the structure of supreme authority there are only two periods: oligarchy and dictatorship. The latter existed only under Stalin. The fundamental difference between these two stages—a difference that to a great extent determined all the other distinctions between stages of Soviet history—was the extent to which the leader had power over officialdom, especially at its highest levels. In the oligarchy, the leader, while exercising significant power, was surrounded by influential comrades-in-arms and a strong nomenklatura. He may have shaped important state decisions, but the decisions were enacted collectively. Reconciling the interests of various institutions and groups was an important aspect of the decision-making process. Networks of clients from the mid-level bureaucracy (the administrators of regions and government agencies), which constituted the backbone of the party's Central Committee, formed around the more influential members of the Politburo. The collective bodies of power functioned regularly, which partly limited the actions of the leader and provided for a degree of political predictability.

By crippling this oligarchic system, Stalin achieved his dictatorship. Limitless power over the fates of every Soviet official, including the top leaders—the members of the Politburo—was its foundation. Stalin acquired the exclusive right to initiate and approve decisions at any level, even if he did not always exercise this right. Growing out of the chaos of revolution and the forced reshaping of every aspect of the country's way of life, the dictatorship relied primarily on violence, and the dictator strove (in many cases under false pretenses) to run the political system and mobilize society as if the country were in a permanent state of emergency. This led to the enormous influence, especially during the Great Terror, of the secret police—the agents of state security. Firm personal control over the secret police was Stalin's highest priority. Using periodic purges of party functionaries at the hands of chekists and of chekists at the hands of party functionaries, Stalin achieved total control over these two fulcrums of power.

This way of viewing Soviet history has informed much of the historical literature investigating the political mechanisms of Stalin's dictatorship. The voluminous archival sources that have become available since the early 1990s tend to support the soundness of this approach. At the same time, historians, in keeping with the imperatives of their calling, have tried to present a fuller, more detailed picture of how Stalin's dictatorship functioned, to look beyond official documents and the regime's self-representation in order to define the true nature of Stalin's power. The quest for deeper understanding has been launched from many points, extending to two extremes. Seen from one viewpoint, Stalin was a totalitarian leader with unlimited power. On a variety of pretexts, those looking from the other viewpoint reject this conclusion, emphasizing instead signs of political weakness in the dictatorship and Stalin himself. The most radical adherents of this approach have even written that Stalin lost hold of power during various periods of his rule and that his role in such events as the Great Terror was insignificant.

Among the many approaches to analyzing the politics of the Stalin period, the theory that factions existed within the Politburo holds a special place. According to this theory, approximately until the mid-1930s, at the highest echelons of power adherents of hard-line measures faced off against adherents of more moderate policies. Different historians construct different hypotheses about the makeup of these factions and Stalin's relation to them. In most cases, the moderates are purported to include Kirov, Ordzhonikidze, and Kuibyshev. Those Politburo members who perished during the years of terror are also suspected of liberalism (the logic here is simple: these particular members must have been victimized for a reason). Kaganovich, Molotov, and Yezhov are usually included among the radical leaders who advocated a policy of terror and an escalation of the class struggle. As many historians see it, Stalin, who is generally supposed to have sympathized with the radicals, wavered between the two camps (or at least was forced to contend with the presence of opponents of the hard-line policies within his inner circle) until the mid-1930s, at which point he finally took a firm stand with the advocates of terror.

Such ideas are fundamental in shaping how we view this period. They allow the mechanisms operating at the highest levels of party-state power in the Soviet Union to be clearly and consistently delineated. Most important, the confrontation between two factions explains the fluctuations in the general line of the 1930s between escalations of state terror and reforms. When the hardliners were on top, repression intensified and extreme policies predominated; when the moderates held the upper hand, attempts at reform ensued. The lead-up to the Great Terror and the 1937–1938 terror itself also become easier to explain: The presence of moderates had constrained Stalin and his radical supporters. Exploiting a weakening of the moderates' position after Kirov's murder and the death of Kuibyshev, Stalin, with support from the radicals, made his choice in favor of mass repression. The moderate members of the Politburo were the first targets of the terror. Their destruction paved the way for completion of Stalin's "revolution from above"—the consolidation of Stalin's dictatorship.

A number of sources and facts have always supported this picture.

Contemporaries could see a certain wavering in the policies of the top Soviet leadership. In the economic sphere, there was alternation between accelerated industrialization and reductions in industrial growth targets; between forced collectivization coupled with dekulakization and promotion of the development of private plots; between attempts to scale down commerce and eliminate currency in favor of direct commodity exchange and a "rehabilitation" of commodity-money relations. In the area of ideology, exhortations to follow "revolutionary asceticism" gave way to slogans extolling a "prosperous life." In foreign policy, the unmasking of social democrats was replaced with support for "people's fronts." Even within the policy of state terror, which proved to be a persistent element, there were fluctuations between extreme brutality and relative moderation.

Nevertheless, as I argue in this book, archival materials that became accessible ten years ago do not support the theory that there were factions within the Politburo. Documents show that the relationships among Politburo members tended to be defined by the roles they played within the government. Personal connections were also important. For example, Ordzhonikidze (who is usually counted among the moderates) and Kaganovich (who came to be viewed as a leader of the hardliners) were close friends. This personal tie had a substantial impact on the decisions these men made in their jobs. Archival evidence shows that when Kaganovich was left in charge of the Politburo during Stalin's summer vacations, he tried, whenever possible, to satisfy Ordzhonikidze's requests and demands. After Kaganovich moved to the Transport Commissariat, his bonds of friendship with Ordzhonikidze were strengthened by their common institutional interests: both were often in a state of conflict with Gosplan and the heads of the government over the allocation of capital funds, and both tried to prevent out-of-control purges from affecting their commissariats.

There is clear archival evidence of another pairing—Kuibyshev and Molotov. Working together from 1930 to 1935, when Kuibyshev was Molotov's deputy in the Council of People's Commissars, they held similar views and supported each other when conflict arose between the government and its agencies. Correspondence between Molotov and Kuibyshev shows that they would discuss all important matters together before unveiling initiatives. The notion that Kuibyshev and Molotov had such a relationship does not fit into the moderate versus radical scheme of things, either: Kuibyshev is consistently placed among the moderates, and Molotov is considered by historians to be one of the main leaders of the hardliners.

It is often hard to decide just where to place individual leaders within the moderate versus radical spectrum. One and the same Politburo member might appear moderate or radical, depending on the circumstances. Historians have long noted that Ordzhonikidze, for example, was one of the most stalwart advocates of forced industrialization and an ardent foe of wreckers when he was serving as chairman of the Central Control Commission during the late 1920s. After he became chairman of the Supreme Economic Council (and later commissar of heavy industry), he came to adopt a different point of view, fighting for a more balanced pace of industrial growth and demanding a halt to actions against specialists and limits on the interference of the secret police in the management of enterprises. Kaganovich appears to have undergone a similar metamorphosis after taking up the post of transport commissar. Yezhov, who came to the defense of economic managers a number of times in the early 1930s when he headed the Central Committee's industrial department, is famous for organizing the brutal terror of 1937–1938. Molotov was a consistent advocate for reducing funding for industry, which would have promoted a more balanced economic policy. At the same time, Ordzhonikidze demanded increased investment in heavy industry, which corresponded to the interests of his own commissariat but undermined economic stability and promoted the use of extreme methods of economic management. There are many more such examples.

The case of Kirov deserves particular attention. Many historians have traditionally viewed him as something akin to a leader of a supposed moderate faction. At this point it appears that the main reason he is suspected of having had reformist tendencies is his tragic death. A flimsy logical construct appears to be at work here. After Kirov's murder the relatively moderate policies of 1934 were followed by the onset of terror, so Kirov must have been one of the pillars of moderation. That is the argument, but there is no significant evidence to support it. Available documents fail to demonstrate that Kirov had any separate political agenda whatsoever or that he supported policies that differed in any significant way from those supported by Stalin. Politburo records show that Kirov had a minimal role in the highest bodies of the party. His visits to Moscow were extremely infrequent. Only in rare cases can his name be seen on Politburo decisions, even those taken by polling. The initiatives and proposals that Kirov did make were typical of those by other secretaries of major regional party organizations. He asked for additional resources for Leningrad, took the side of his constituents in various disputes, and defended his subordinates.

What available documents do show is that the initiator of key decisions determining the overall political course was, in most cases, Stalin. The conduct of both large-scale repressive measures and reforms was based on his proposals (or, in most cases, on his orders). At this point there is no sign of a single important decision taken in the 1930s that did not belong to Stalin and certainly no sign of any that were taken against his will. In this sense, Stalin represented both the radical and the moderate factions of the Politburo to which historians have attributed decisions that initiated some change in policy.

The decisions that were adopted on Stalin's initiative and that reflected his personal predilections left a mark, in many cases, a lasting mark, on the development of the country and the development of government policy. Whatever was most important to Stalin became most important to the state. Stalin's commitment to using repression to solve any problem probably had the most significant impact. This tendency was not at all remarkable considering the political traditions of Bolshevism and the emergence of the new government out of revolution and civil war. Under Stalin, however, this tendency was undoubtedly exaggerated and imbued with particular brutality and intolerance. There is much evidence to support the viewpoint of Alec Nove that true Stalinism exhibited an exceptional reliance on terror and gave birth to extreme measures and excesses. These measures were at times so radical, even within the context of the Soviet system's laws and Stalinist policy, that they actually weakened the system rather than strengthening it.[1] The most obvious example is the Great Terror. The destructive consequences of the mass repressions were so obvious that in the end it seems that even Stalin recognized them. In any event, he never again undertook repressive measures of such scope and brutality.

Like other dictators, Stalin lay great store by his own insights and infallibility. In political practice, this manifested itself in the form of exceptional stubbornness and a refusal to compromise. Unlike his handling of foreign affairs, into which he injected a notable dose of realism, in domestic policy realism was not a priority. His approach might be described as "crisis pragmatism." Stalin agreed to insignificant and inconsequential concessions only when he had run out of other options and crisis was imminent. While some fluctuation in Stalin's policies should be recognized, its significance should not be exaggerated.

Even if there is no evidence of factions, this does not mean that Stalin's comrades-in-arms did not play active political roles. In the early 1930s, Politburo members enjoyed relative independence and the Politburo itself could still be seen as a collective body. Several things explain this. First of all, traditions of party governance established earlier could not be transformed overnight. As the first among equals, the leader had to contend both with his closest associates and with a wider circle of party functionaries: the members of the Central Committee, who enjoyed relative freedom of action in their own domains, whether in Moscow or elsewhere in the Soviet Union. Even after Stalin had achieved victory in his lengthy struggle with oppositionists (Trotsky, Zinoviev, Kamenev, Bukharin, Rykov, and the rest), his position was not yet so strong that he could openly disregard the principles of collective leadership. Furthermore, while the country was facing severe crises resulting from the leftward policy shifts of the late 1920s, Stalin himself wanted to maintain traditions of shared responsibility among the top leaders.

During the early 1930s, the Politburo still followed the formal procedures that made it a collective body. Individual Politburo members continued to enjoy some independence in the running of their own agencies. Archival documents suggest the existence of informal networks among the upper- and middle-level nomenklatura, linking regional leaders and their particular patrons in the Politburo. Even though Politburo members enjoyed power and influence over their own fiefdoms, every one of them pledged unconditional allegiance to their supreme arbiter and "master." Stalin himself, while he considered himself to be the leader, had to contend with his fellow Politburo members having their own patrimonies. In practice, this meant that Politburo members actively and persistently fought for the interests of the institutions of government for which they were responsible and the people who helped them run those institutions. As a rule, in their attempts to get what they wanted for their domains, especially in times of crisis, Politburo members would resort to all kinds of tactics, including threats to resign. In the early 1930s, Stalin was still fairly tolerant of such démarches.

The special position of the commissariats became evident during the development of economic policy at the start of the Second Five-Year Plan. The crisis toward the end of the First Five-Year Plan had occasioned an awakening and brought a growing tendency toward dissidence in various quarters of the party-state apparatus. Under the pressures created by socioeconomic realities, pragmatic institutional interests were expressed with a candor that had been unthinkable when the country's unquestioning "unified will" had been marshaled to fulfill the ambitious plans set out for the first five years. Corrections to the general line allowing greater flexibility resulted from give and take among the government institutions involved: the economic commissariats, Gosplan, the Finance Commissariat, and the heads of the government. How much weight the desires of each of these parties was given depended both on the priority allotted to that particular area and the influence of its leaders.

Stalin played two primary roles within the collective leadership of the early 1930s. He acted as supreme arbiter of inter-institutional disputes and served as the initiator of the most important decisions affecting the country. These two roles were often hard to delineate. As arbitrator in disputes among branches of the government, Stalin generally defended "state interests." In every way possible he emphasized his role as an opponent of the harmful force of institutional parochialism. In practice, this often allied him with the leadership of the Council of People's Commissars, Gosplan, and the Commissariat of Finance, but not always. As a strong advocate of forced (accelerated) industrial development, he encouraged the ambitions of the economic commissariats. Overall, Stalin played an integral role within the system of competing institutional interests.

From a political perspective, the interests of government agencies, interests that were often supported by a particular member of the Politburo, constituted one of the last obstacles in the way of Stalin's dictatorship. The strong positions of individual Soviet leaders and the real influence of various party-state structures might have contributed to the gradual formation of a system that was more predictable, balanced, and free of violent extremes—a kinder, gentler Stalinism. But the struggle over institutional interests never led to the formation of factions uniting several members of the Politburo. Even those commissariats that were headed by Politburo members were not able to serve as a serious counterbalance to the sole authority of the leader. When the time came, Stalin was able to tilt the balance of power in his direction with ease. In early 1935, after the deaths of Kirov and Kuibyshev, Stalin initiated what amounted to the abolition of the post of second secretary of the Central Committee, Stalin's deputy within the party. Until late 1930 this post had been held by Molotov, who was succeeded by Kaganovich. The duties of the second secretary were now divided among several members of the top leadership. Stalin's young protégés—Zhdanov and Yezhov— gained in stature. Despite their official standing (Zhdanov was only a candidate Politburo member and Yezhov was not a member at all), they handled many of the most important matters, taking their orders directly from Stalin. The Politburo ceased to function as it had traditionally—official sessions were held less frequently and most questions were voted on by polling the membership. Repressive measures that had in the past affected only rank-and-file citizens began to impinge on many highly placed party members who were within the spheres of influence of individual Politburo members. Politburo members found it harder and harder to fight for the "rights" of their people.

None of the Politburo members could have liked this turn of events. Regarding the repression of party-state officials, all of the members of the Politburo had every reason to be on the side of moderation. Undoubtedly they all understood perfectly well the dangers inherent in mass arrests within the nomenklatura. Testimony that the NKVD extracted from officials with personal and professional ties to members of the Politburo not only limited the power and influence of Stalin's comrades-in-arms but compromised their personal security. Given the choice, however, most members of the Politburo failed to resist Stalin's actions in any significant way; indeed, they raced to express their support of the new policies, eager to show their heightened vigilance and loyalty to the leader. Ordzhonikidze was an exception. As numerous documents testify, conflicts arose between Stalin and Ordzhonikidze over arrests in the Commissariat of Heavy Industry and among Ordzhonikidze's loyal followers. Ordzhonikidze fought for the right to rule over his own domain, to decide the fates of his people. The personal qualities of the impulsive and unrestrained Ordzhonikidze intensified the conflict—which ended in his death.

Scholars debate just how far Ordzhonikidze was prepared to go in opposing Stalin. Archival evidence suggests that Ordzhonikidze was probably not willing to engage in an outright fight. He was too dependent on Stalin to engage him in head-to-head conflict. The facts at hand suggest that Ordzhonikidze simply attempted to convince Stalin to temper repressive measures, arguing his case forcefully and, it could be said, fearlessly. In essence, Ordzhonikidze was fighting for the traditions of collective leadership that had existed in the early 1930s, which had provided, among other things, for relative stability in the party-state nomenklatura. Other Politburo members must have shared Ordzhonikidze's feelings and also been concerned about preserving the stability of the nomenklatura. But they were not prepared to confront Stalin.

Ordzhonikidze's death heralded a change in the relationship between Stalin and his closest comrades-in-arms. In terms of the number of Politburo members directly affected by the terror, the Politburo fared better than other party-state structures. Eight out of the fifteen full and candidate members elected to the Politburo after the 17th Party Congress (and surviving until 1937) got through the Great Terror—more than half. But almost all of the older Politburo members were persecuted in some way during these years. Some of them suffered under the constant threat of political accusations. Others had relatives or close associates who were caught up in the terror. Zhdanov, Beria, and Malenkov—the up-and-coming younger members of the ruling circle who, unlike the older Politburo members, had not earned their seats through distinguished service during the revolution but were beholden to Stalin himself for their high positions—began to play ever more significant roles in the Politburo. The top Soviet leadership was now fully dependent on Stalin.

With the start of the Great Terror, the Politburo no longer played the same role it had in the past. Meetings of the full membership became extremely rare. The most important decisions were made by Stalin, who let only a select few Politburo members in on his plans. In 1937 this new way of doing things was made official through the creation of two Politburo commissions acting with its full authority. Later, these commissions evolved into the Politburo's ruling group—the Five. The appointment of Stalin as chairman of the USSR Council of People's Commissars in May 1941 not only politically sealed his personal dictatorship (even making Stalin the official heir of Lenin, who had chaired the council from its 1917 inception) but facilitated a transfer of the most significant administrative functions to the council's apparatus.

After a lengthy period of reorganization, one and a half months before the war started, the system of supreme power had developed a clear structure. Almost all key Soviet leaders, while maintaining their membership in the Politburo, became a part of the highest state body—the Bureau of the USSR Council of People's Commissars. Meetings of the Bureau (usually chaired by Stalin and with his active participation) were held on a regular basis, at least once a week. In most cases Bureau meetings flowed seamlessly into Politburo meetings, inasmuch as these bodies were largely composed of the same people. The decisions that were adopted were officially issued as either Politburo decisions or council decrees—the matter was purely technical, depending on their content. The preparation of draft resolutions was carried out within the apparatuses of the Central Committee and the council, whose functions came to be clearly delineated. The Central Committee dealt primarily with personnel and ideological issues, the state apparatus with economic issues. Two of Stalin's aides, members of the new generation, oversaw this work. Georgy Malenkov administered the Central Committee apparatus for the most part. (Zhdanov, Stalin's official deputy within the party, was unable to carry out these duties because he continued to serve as head of the Leningrad party organization.) Nikolai Voznesensky was appointed first deputy to the chairman of the Council of People's Commissars (first Molotov, then Stalin). As a result of this division of labor, the old Stalinist guard was placed in a weakened position.

In the final analysis, while they adopted numerous and varied decisions, both the Politburo and the Bureau ultimately acted as consultative commissions for Stalin. This was a direct result of Stalin's purposeful effort to take over complete control of decision making not only in the critical realm of military-strategic and international problems but also for a broad range of matters having to do with the day-to-day running of the country.

Stalin's model of ultra-centralized power revealed its fatal flaws within the first days of the war. Catastrophic military defeats, which stemmed to a large degree from Stalin's criminally inept strategic blunders, led to another reorganization at the highest level of government. The most notable aspect of the reorganization was the return of the old Politburo members, Molotov first and foremost, to the top of the administrative structure. On 30 June 1941 a supreme wartime authority was founded, the State Defense Committee, which included Stalin (chairman), Molotov (deputy chairman), Voroshilov, Malenkov, and

Beria. Half a year later, in February 1942, Mikoyan, Voznesensky, and Kaganovich also joined.[2] Since a majority of Politburo members and Council of People's Commissars leaders were members of the committee, in many cases the State Defense Committee, the Politburo, and the Bureau wound up acting as if they were one body. As contemporary witnesses attest, it was not always possible to tell which separate body they were dealing with. Decisions, depending on their nature, were issued in the name of any of the three.[3]

Wartime centralization paradoxically went hand in hand with increased independence in operation matters at all levels. The main criterion for evaluating performance was the attainment of specific results. A blind eye was turned to slight deviations from orders or regulations. This tendency could also be observed at the highest echelons of power. Stalin's comrades-in-arms, who were carrying out critical functions under extreme conditions, were actually given great administrative independence. To a certain extent, the war years saw a rebirth of the early 1930s system of collective leadership, or at least elements of it. As Mikoyan reflected, "During the war we had a certain cohesion amongst the leadership. [. . .] Stalin, having understood that in hard times fervent work was needed, created conditions of trust, and each of us, the members of the Politburo, carried a tremendous load."[4] This did not mean that a system of oligarchic rule by the Politburo replaced Stalin's dictatorship during the war. Stalin continued to hold the main levers of power firmly in his hands. From time to time he would remind his comrades-in-arms of their vulnerability.

On 1 April 1942 the Politburo adopted a resolution entitled "On the Work of Com. Voroshilov" in which Stalin's comrade-in-arms, who had been serving on the State Defense Committee, was harshly criticized. The resolution enumerated Voroshilov's mistakes: poor preparations for the war with Finland when he was in charge of the Defense Commissariat and failed actions at the front in the war with Germany. The resolution stated that Voroshilov had refused to take over command of the Volkhov Front, "citing the fact that the Volkhov Front was a difficult front, and he did not want to fail in that endeavor." The Politburo therefore recognized that "Com. Voroshilov had not acquitted himself in the work assigned to him at the front," and resolved to send him to conduct "military work in the rear."[5] The resolution was circulated among all members of the Central Committee and the Party Control

Commission and thus was publicized among the nomenklatura. In November 1944, Voroshilov was removed from the State Defense Committee.[6] Another Politburo member targeted by Stalin during the war was Mikoyan. In September 1944, Stalin rejected Mikoyan's proposal to allocate seeds for sowing crops in the liberated regions of Ukraine. On 17 September, Stalin wrote the following comment on Mikoyan's proposal: "Molotov and Mikoyan. I vote against. Mikoyan is behaving in an anti-state manner, tailing along behind provincial committees and corrupting them [. . .]. He must be removed from the Procurement Commissariat and it must be given, for example, to Malenkov."[7] The next day, 18 September, the Politburo passed a resolution to that effect.[8]

Such attacks against members of the Politburo had various outcomes. When Voroshilov was essentially removed from the top leadership, Mikoyan continued as one of the Five—the exclusive ruling group existed until the conclusion of the war.[9] The other members, besides Stalin himself, were Molotov, Malenkov, and Beria. The Five therefore included both Stalin's longtime comrades-in-arms and those who had risen to power during the terror. The Leningraders Zhdanov and Voznesensky, who had played significant roles right before the war, receded into the background.

Of all the Politburo members, Molotov enjoyed the greatest improvement in status. Soon after he was appointed deputy chairman of the State Defense Committee, on 16 August 1942, he was reinstated as first deputy chairman of the Council of People's Commissars.[10] In keeping with his new appointment, Molotov ran the council until the end of the war, heading the Bureau's Commission on Current Issues and later the Bureau itself.[11] He took over these positions and functions from Voznesensky. At the same time, Molotov maintained important positions within the State Defense Committee and was a member of its Operational Bureau, created in December 1942 to manage the industrial commissariats that were critical to the war effort.[12] During the final stage of the war, Molotov was somewhat superseded by Beria. On 15 May 1944, Beria took over the Operational Bureau of the State Defense Committee, and Molotov was removed from this organ, focusing his efforts within the Council of People's Commissars.[13] Malenkov carried out many vital functions, both within the Central Committee and the Council of People's Commissars and the State Defense Committee. Mikoyan, as a member of the ruling Politburo group, the Council of People's Commissars (and council's Bureau), and the State Defense Committee (the Operational Bureau), oversaw a significant portion of the economy.

A long-term strengthening of the positions of Politburo members did not fit in with Stalin's plans, however. Immediately after the war he conducted a sort of demobilization of the top leadership, intended to restore the prewar balance of power.[14] By late 1945, Stalin had provoked a sharp conflict with Molotov, which heralded numerous analogous conflicts that would plague Stalin's comrades-in-arms until his death. Over several months, from the end of 1945 and to the beginning of 1946, Stalin changed the makeup of his inner circle, promoting Zhdanov to first place within the leadership of the party apparatus and incorporating Voznesensky into the Politburo leadership group. Those who had made up the wartime Five were subject to numerous attacks and dismissed from some of their posts. The balance of power that resulted from these reshufflings remained in place until mid-1948, when, as a result of Zhdanov's illness and death (it is possible that other factors were involved, although they have yet to be established), Malenkov returned to the leadership of the party apparatus. The Leningrad affair of 1949, an extension of this top-level shakeup, ended in the physical destruction of one member of the leadership group, Nikolai Voznesensky, along with Central Committee secretary Aleksei Kuznetsov. At the same time, unrelated to the Leningrad affair, Molotov and Mikoyan were subject to further attacks.

Objectively speaking, these actions against members of the top leadership strengthened the positions of Malenkov and Beria. To counterbalance their power, Stalin advanced Nikita Khrushchev and Nikolai Bulganin within the party and state leadership. Historians are unanimous in believing that the purges in Georgia in 1952 (the Mingrelian affair) mainly targeted Beria. Stalin initiated a new reorganization at the highest levels half a year before his death. This reorganization marked the feeble dictator's effort to forestall even the hypothetical possibility that the members of the Politburo could make a joint move against him. As Lenin had done when in failing health, Stalin undertook two measures. First, he diluted the makeup of the party's ruling bodies with new faces, guiding a resolution through the 19th Party Congress to create a more-numerous Central Committee Presidium to replace the Politburo. Second, like Lenin in his famous Testament, Stalin publicly discredited the senior and most distinguished among his comrades-in-arms: Molotov and Mikoyan. In October 1952, at the first plenum of the new Central Committee, Stalin gave a speech in which he subjected these men to extremely harsh criticism and announced their immediate exclusion from any role in ruling the country.

While Stalin controlled the main levers of power right up until his death, extensive evidence suggests that within the depths of the dictatorship, the grounds were being laid for a rebirth of political oligarchy. Although Stalin's comrades-in-arms may have lost their political independence, they still possessed a degree of institutional autonomy and could decide operational questions within their purview. This independence grew as Stalin himself was inevitably forced to reduce his role in the everyday running of the country. Hand in hand with institutional autonomy came the formation of client networks among members of the top leadership.[15] Evidence for the existence of such networks can be seen in the reshuffling of cadres after Stalin's death, when members of the top leadership tried to place their people in key posts.

One factor that may have limited the dictatorship (and created conditions for power sharing among an oligarchy) was the formation of semi-collective decision-making mechanisms over the final years of Stalin's life. During Stalin's lengthy 1950–1952 absences from Moscow, the ruling group within the Politburo, the Seven—Molotov, Mikoyan, Kaganovich, Malenkov, Beria, Bulganin, and Khrushchev—met regularly. Meeting protocols indicate that this group acted as a collective body, dealing with issues the way the Politburo had dealt with them in the 1920s and early 1930s—through discussion and through the formation of commissions to investigate various problems and draft resolutions.[16] When Stalin was in Moscow, such collaborative activities disappeared almost entirely from the Politburo protocols. Although decisions by the Seven were sent to Stalin for approval or were discussed with him on the telephone (whether all decisions or just the most important is still unclear), this return to some of the formal aspects of collective leadership provided experience that would prove important after Stalin's death.[17] The ruling bodies of government held regular and frequent meetings, which was important for the reemergence of elements of collective leadership. The Bureau of the Presidium of the Council of Ministers, created in April 1950, had the same membership as the Politburo's ruling group: Stalin, Bulganin, Beria, Kaganovich, Khrushchev, Malenkov, Mikoyan, and Molotov. Although meetings of the Politburo group were usually chaired by Stalin, the Presidium Bureau meetings always took place without him.[18] It was on such government bodies that the main burden of managing the country fell.

Institutional independence, patron-client connections, and experience in collective leadership helped lay the groundwork for the oligarchization of supreme authority. Stalin's comrades-in-arms, in their roles as the executors of critical functions within the party-state system, had real administrative influence, if not political power, making them just as essential to the dictatorship as Stalin himself. Available evidence, therefore, allows us to see Stalin's dictatorship as a system of power founded on the standard model of authoritarian oligarchy, functioning in accordance with the principle of competition and coordination between interest groups (different organs of government and different regions of the country). The dictator served as an active superstructure for this system. He both took part (often the part of arbiter) in inter-institutional conflict and served as the force behind initiatives that had a critical, even defining effect on the development of the country. First among these initiatives were the various acts of state terror perpetrated by his regime. It was the brutal policies of terror that serve as the best example of how Stalin's political ambition, personal predilections, mistakes, and crimes changed the nature of the system, making it extraordinarily repressive, even by the standards of dictatorship.

The two-tiered organization of the system that exercised authority and made decisions constantly generated elements of oligarchization within the depths of dictatorship, a tendency that Stalin expended effort on suppressing. This two-tiered system set objective limitations to Stalin's personal power. Immediately after Stalin's death, the institutional autonomy of members of the top Soviet leadership and their shared desire to oppose the emergence of a new dictatorship were manifested when, in the absence of dictatorial control, institutional influence was naturally transformed into political influence.

Although both levels of authority that existed during Stalin's dictatorship were intertwined, the system of oligarchical institutional self-interest certainly had the potential to exist without a dictator. This explains the smooth transition from dictatorship back to collective leadership after Stalin's death in 1953. The elimination of the extreme aspects of brutal state repression that had originated with Stalin meant that as early as 1953, the character of the regime changed significantly, making it less bloody, more predictable, and capable of reform, even though many of the fundamental principles of the system remained untouched and Stalin's heirs acted within a narrow authoritarian framework.

Appendix 1
Politburo Membership

According to party rules in effect during the 1930s, the Politburo was elected by each newly constituted Central Committee at the conclusion of each party congress. There were four Politburos over the course of the 1930s. Individual members could be elected between congresses.

Full members: N. I. Bukharin, M. I. Kalinin, V. V. Kuibyshev, V. M. Molotov, Ya. E. Rudzutak, A. I. Rykov, I. V. Stalin, M. P. Tomsky, K. Ye. Voroshilov

Candidate members: A. A. Andreev, V. Ya. Chubar, L. M. Kaganovich, S. M. Kirov, S. V. Kosior, A. I. Mikoyan, G. I. Petrovsky, N. A. Uglanov

On 29 April 1929 a Central Committee plenum relieved candidate member N. A. Uglanov of his duties and elected K. Ya. Bauman in his place.

On 21 June 1929 a Central Committee plenum elected S. I. Syrtsov as a candidate member of the Politburo.

On 17 November 1929 a Central Committee plenum removed N. I. Bukharin from the Politburo.

Full members: L. M. Kaganovich, M. I. Kalinin, S. M. Kirov, S. V. Kosior, V. V. Kuibyshev, V. M. Molotov, Ya. E. Rudzutak, A. I. Rykov, I. V. Stalin, K. Ye. Voroshilov
Candidate members: A. A. Andreev, V. Ya. Chubar, A. I. Mikoyan, G. I. Petrovsky, S. I. Syrtsov

On 1 December 1930 a Central Committee plenum voted by polling to expel S. I. Syrtsov from the Politburo.
On 21 December 1930 a joint session of the Central Committee and the Central Control Commission relieved A. I. Rykov of his duties as a member of the Politburo and A. A. Andreev of his duties as a candidate member. It elected G. K. Ordzhonikidze to membership in the Politburo.
On 4 February 1932 a Central Committee plenum expelled Ya. E. Rudzutak from the Politburo. It made A. A. Andreev a full member of the Politburo.

Full members: A. A. Andreev, L. M. Kaganovich, M. I. Kalinin, S. M. Kirov, S. V. Kosior, V. V. Kuibyshev, V. M. Molotov, G. K. Ordzhonikidze, I. V. Stalin, K. Ye. Voroshilov
Candidate members: V. Ya. Chubar, A. I. Mikoyan, G. I. Petrovsky, P. P. Postyshev, Ya. E. Rudzutak

On 1 December 1934, S. M. Kirov was killed.
On 25 January 1935, V. V. Kuibyshev died.
On 1 February 1935 a Central Committee plenum confirmed A. I. Mikoyan and V. Ya. Chubar as members of the Politburo and A. A. Zhdanov and R. I. Eikhe as candidate members.
On 18 February 1937, G. K. Ordzhonikidze committed suicide.
On 26 May 1937, Ya. E. Rudzutak was expelled from the Central Committee.
On 12 October 1937 a Central Committee plenum made N. I. Yezhov a candidate member of the Politburo.
On 14 January 1938 a Central Committee plenum relieved P. P. Postyshev of his duties as a candidate member of the Politburo and elected N. S. Khrushchev a candidate member.
On 16 June 1938, V. Ya. Chubar was expelled from the Politburo by decision of its members.
On 29 April 1938, R. I. Eikhe was arrested.
On 26 February 1939, S. V. Kosior was shot.

Politburo Elected after the 18th Party Congress, 22 March 1939

Full members: A. A. Andreev, L. M. Kaganovich, M. I. Kalinin, N. S. Khrushchev, A. I. Mikoyan, V. M. Molotov, I. V. Stalin, K. Ye. Voroshilov, A. A. Zhdanov
Candidate members: L. P. Beria, N. M. Shvernik

On 21 February 1941 a Central Committee plenum confirmed N. A. Voznesensky, G. M. Malenkov, and A. S. Shcherbakov as candidate members of the Politburo.

Appendix 2
Visits to Stalin's Office by Politburo Members and Central Committee Secretaries

Visitors received by the general secretary were logged in notebooks, and the tables here, based on those logs, show the number of visits by Politburo members and Central Committee secretaries and the amount of time they spent with him. The logs were published in the journal *Istoricheskii arkhiv*, no. 6 (1994); nos. 2–6 (1995), and S. G. Wheatcroft compiled and systematized the data in "From Team-Stalin to Degenerate Tyranny," in E. A. Rees (ed.), *The Nature of Stalin's Dictatorship: The Politburo, 1924–1953* (Basingstoke, UK, 2004), pp. 79–107.

The logs contain several errors and omissions. A number of entries do not include how much time a given visitor spent in Stalin's office or provide obviously mistaken data about the time of arrival or departure. In such cases, the length of visit is calculated based on the average visit time for that particular person for that year.

Beginning in the late 1930s the pattern of visits changes. It is possible that many of Stalin's meetings after this point took place at his dacha rather than in his office. This is reflected in the journals.

At certain points, especially in 1939, it became common for Politburo members to visit Stalin twice daily (in the afternoon and the evening). Such instances are counted as two visits.

The first column of figures for each year indicates the total number of visits made by a particular official for that year. The second column shows the percentage this number of visits represents in proportion to all visits by Politburo members and Central Committee secretaries for the year. The third column represents the total time (in hours and minutes) spent by a given official in Stalin's office for the year (an entry of zero indicates that the journal does not show a single visit to Stalin's office by this official). The fourth column shows the total time for this official as a percentage of the total time all these visitors combined spent in Stalin's office.

| | Visits to Stalin's Office | | Time in Stalin's Office | | Visits to Stalin's Office | | Time in Stalin's Office | | Visits to Stalin's Office | | Time in Stalin's Office | |
	Number	Percent	Total	Percent	Number	Percent	Total	Percent	Number	Percent	Total	Percent
	1931				1932				1933[a]			
Andreev	20	5.49	41:10	5.07	15	2.81	28:15	2.18	20	3.89	53:45	3.66
Chubar	2	0.55	0:45	0.09	2	0.38	1:25	0.11	3	0.58	8:15	0.56
Kaganovich[b]	73	20.05	168:48	20.81	126	23.64	283:05	21.86	125	24.32	384:35	26.16
Kalinin	11	3.02	21:40	2.67	10	1.88	22:30	1.74	22	4.28	46:25	3.16
Kirov	12	3.30	22:05	2.72	10	1.88	30:25	2.35	5	0.97	9:50	0.67
Kosior	7	1.92	15:25	1.90	5	0.94	6:05	0.47	11	2.14	29:15	1.99
Kuibyshev	15	4.12	32:55	4.06	49	9.19	114:05	8.81	24	4.67	73:30	5.00
Mikoyan	16	4.40	33:40	4.15	35	6.57	84:00	6.49	40	7.78	84:40	5.76
Molotov[c]	100	27.47	224:40	27.69	119	22.33	295:45	22.84	143	27.82	447:30	30.44
Ordzhonikidze[d]	24	6.59	60:57	7.51	48	9.01	124:15	9.59	35	6.81	99:55	6.80
Petrovsky	0	0	0	0	0	0	0	0	0	0	0	0
Postyshev[e]	51	14.01	114:40	14.13	56	10.51	166:08	12.83	13	2.53	37:05	2.52
Rudzutak	4	1.10	12:05	1.49	16	3.00	39:15	3.03	6	1.17	23:20	1.59
Voroshilov[f]	29	7.97	62:29	7.70	42	7.88	99:55	7.71	67	13.04	171:50	11.69
Total	364	100	811:19	100	533	100	1,295:08	100	514	100	1,469:55	100

[a]Visits to Stalin's office were also recorded in the logs during Stalin's vacation from 16 August 1933 to 4 November 1933, when Kaganovich was left in charge of the Politburo. These visits are not included in this compilation.

[b]Time of exit not indicated for 16 January 1931 or 23 and 24 February 1931.

[c]Time of exit not indicated for 4 January 1931, 16 January 1931, 24 February 1931, 4 March 1931, or 15 April 1931.

[d]Time of exit not indicated for 24 February 1931.

[e]Time of exit not indicated for 23 and 24 February 1931, 4 March 1931, or 25 January 1932.

[f]On 15 April 1931 no exit time is given. On 27 February 1932 the exit time is not given, either, but since Molotov and Kaganovich, who left Stalin's office at 18:05 visited Stalin along with Voroshilov, the time of Voroshilov's exit was presumed to be 18:05.

| | 1934 | | | | 1935 | | | | 1936 | | | |
| | Visits to Stalin's Office | | Time in Stalin's Office | | Visits to Stalin's Office | | Time in Stalin's Office | | Visits to Stalin's Office | | Time in Stalin's Office | |
	Number	Percent	Total	Percent	Number	Percent	Total	Percent	Number	Percent	Total	Percent
Andreev	28	3.85	75:45	3.55	24	4.15	73:10	4.62	21	4.29	55:10	4.32
Chubar	22	3.03	66:40	3.13	24	4.15	62:30	3.94	28	5.71	68:30	5.31
Eikhe	4	0.55	3:45	0.18	3	0.52	6:40	0.42	2	0.41	4:20	0.34
Kaganovich	104	14.31	330:20	15.49	91	15.72	257:48	16.27	58	11.84	161:50	12.64
Kalinin	31	4.26	82:30	3.87	36	6.22	76:41	4.84	18	3.67	48:10	3.76
Kirov[g]	18	2.48	62:15	2.92	—	—	—	—	—	—	—	—
Kosior	11	1.51	25:50	1.21	8	1.38	23:55	1.51	6	1.22	13:25	1.05
Kuibyshev[h]	50	6.88	162:10	7.60	6	1.04	15:25	0.97	—	—	—	—
Mikoyan	43	5.91	102:35	4.81	30	5.18	73:18	4.63	31	6.33	66:21	5.17
Molotov[i]	98	13.48	343:45	16.12	102	17.62	317:36	20.05	110	22.45	302:07	23.52
Ordzhonikidze	60	8.25	189:45	8.90	77	13.30	224:45	14.19	68	13.88	179:00	13.93
Petrovsky	6	0.83	15:10	0.71	0	0	0	0	1	0.20	4:25	0.34
Postyshev	8	1.10	18:35	0.87	11	1.90	25:10	1.59	1	0.20	2:30	0.19
Rudzutak	9	1.24	31:15	1.47	4	0.69	14:25	0.91	2	0.41	6:00	0.47
Voroshilov	79	10.87	241:00	11.30	72	12.44	206:28	13.03	76	15.51	218:01	17.07
Yagoda	52	7.15	77:20	3.63	37	6.39	56:00	3.53	20	4.08	31:20	2.43
Yezhov	16	2.20	20:10	0.95	33	5.70	91:50	5.80	32	6.53	77:35	6.06
Zhdanov	88	12.10	285:45	13.31	21	3.63	58:45	3.71	16	3.27	37:35	2.94
Total	727	100	2,132:35	100	579	100	1,584:26	100	490	100	1,276:19	100

[g]Killed 1 December 1934.

[h]Died 25 January 1935.

[i]Time of exit not indicated for 27 February 1935

	1937				1938				1939			
	Visits to Stalin's Office		Time in Stalin's Office		Visits to Stalin's Office		Time in Stalin's Office		Visits to Stalin's Office		Time in Stalin's Office	
	Number	Percent	Total	Percent	Number	Percent	Total	Percent	Number	Percent	Total	Percent
Andreev	53	5.04	139:35	4.83	33	4.33	68:45	3.64	35	3.39	82:50	3.27
Beria	2	0.19	1:30	0.05	33	4.33	45:35	2.39	106	10.26	170:33	6.73
Chubar[j]	31	2.95	74:30	2.58	6	0.79	10:45	0.56	—	—	—	—
Eikhe[k]	4	0.38	7:40	0.27	2	0.26	2:40	0.14	—	—	—	—
Kaganovich[l]	126	11.99	404:46	14.00	77	10.10	213:04	11.19	96	9.29	245:01	9.66
Kalinin	20	1.90	34:35	1.20	11	1.44	20:15	1.06	9	0.87	15:45	0.62
Khrushchev	21	2.00	30:00	1.04	18	2.36	42:00	2.21	24	2.32	77:40	3.06
Kosior[m]	19	1.81	32:55	1.14	5	0.66	7:45	0.41	—	—	—	—
Malenkov	68	6.47	77:00	2.66	72	9.45	95:35	5.02	52	5.03	81:56	3.23
Mikoyan	58	5.52	134:50	4.66	48	6.30	99:10	5.21	143	13.84	306:35	12.09
Molotov[n]	225	21.41	726:01	25.10	171	22.44	512:45	26.93	282	27.30	793:32	31.29
Ordzhonikidze[o]	22	2.09	71:55	2.49	—	—	—	—	—	—	—	—
Petrovsky[p]	0	0	0	0	3	0.39	2:50	0.15	—	—	—	—
Postyshev[q]	8	0.76	11:20	0.39	—	—	—	—	—	—	—	—
Voroshilov	147	13.99	450:01	15.56	97	12.73	261:22	13.72	187	18.10	524:14	20.67
Yezhov[r]	185	17.60	542:40	18.76	103	13.52	312:40	16.42	—	—	—	—
Zhdanov[s]	62	5.90	152:40	5.28	83	10.89	209:10	10.98	99	9.58	237:46	9.38
Total	1,051	100	2,891:58	100	762	100	1,904:21	100	1,033	100	2,535:52	100

[j] Expelled from the Politburo on 16 June 1938.

[k] Arrested on 29 April 1938.

[l] Time of exit not indicated for 4 April 1938.

[m] Arrested in May 1938.

[n] Time of exit not indicated for 10 September 1938 or 3 October 1938.

[o] Committed suicide on 18 February 1937.

[p] Not reelected to the Politburo in 1939.

[q] Expelled from the Politburo on 14 January 1938.

[r] Not reelected to the Politburo in 1939.

[s] Time of entry not indicated for 8 January 1938. Time of exit not indicated for 10 September 1938.

| | 1940 | | | | 1941 (through 22 June) | | | |
| | Visits to Stalin's Office | | Time in Stalin's Office | | Visits to Stalin's Office | | Time in Stalin's Office | |
	Number	Percent	Total	Percent	Number	Percent	Total	Percent
Andreev	15	1.84	24:45	1.31	3	0.86	5:30	0.65
Beria[t]	96	11.76	159:50	8.48	42	12.07	70:10	8.22
Kaganovich	51	6.25	100:20	5.32	17	4.89	51:55	6.08
Kalinin	5	0.61	16:00	0.85	1	0.29	2:30	0.29
Khrushchev	34	4.17	77:42	4.12	23	6.61	44:40	5.23
Malenkov[u]	51	6.25	105:00	5.57	62	17.82	145:10	17.00
Mikoyan	85	10.42	145:00	7.69	28	8.05	70:31	8.26
Molotov[v]	235	28.80	602:10	31.94	87	25.00	240:28	28.16
Shvernik	4	0.49	5:40	0.30	1	0.29	2:15	0.26
Shcherbakov[w]	8	0.98	11:15	0.60	3	0.86	5:20	0.62
Voroshilov	125	15.32	397:13	21.07	26	7.47	87:12	10.21
Voznesensky[x]	32	3.92	58:45	3.12	22	6.32	51:25	6.02
Zhdanov	75	9.19	181:40	9.64	33	9.48	76:45	8.99
Total	816	100	1,885:20	100	348	100	853:51	100

[t] Time of exit not indicated for 18 May 1941.

[u] Politburo member beginning 21 February 1941.

[v] Time of exit not indicated for 22 March 1940 or 8 May 1941.

[w] Politburo member beginning 21 February 1941.

[x] Politburo member beginning 21 February 1941.

Notes

Introduction

1. Lars T. Lih, Oleg V. Naumov, and Oleg Khlevniuk (eds.), *Stalin's Letters to Molotov, 1925–1936* (New Haven, 1995), pp. 184–185.

2. Russian State Archive of Social and Political History (RGASPI), f. 558, op. 11, d. 99. l. 95; d. 771, ll. 15–16; O. V. Khlevniuk et al. (eds.), *Politbiuro TsK VKP(b) i Sovet Ministrov SSSR 1945–1953* (Moscow, 2002), p. 198.

3. RGASPI, f. 558, op. 11, d. 99, l. 120; d. 771, l. 17; Khlevniuk et al. (eds.), *Politbiuro TsK VKP(b) i Sovet Ministrov SSSR*, p. 209.

4. For a more detailed examination of the relationship between Stalin and Molotov during the postwar period, see Yoram Gorlizki and Oleg Khlevniuk, *Cold Peace: Stalin and the Soviet Ruling Circle, 1945–1953* (New York, 2004).

5. The most comprehensive analysis of these efforts is provided in Stephen F. Cohen, *Bukharin and the Bolshevik Revolution: A Political Biography, 1888–1938* (New York, 1973). For fresh archival material relating to the struggle within the Politburo from 1928 to 1929, see V. P. Danilov and O. V. Khlevniuk (eds.), *Kak lomali nep. Stenogrammy plenumov TsK VKP(b) 1928–1929* (Moscow, 2000), vols. 1–5.

6. According to one point of view, Stalin possessed dictatorial power as early as the start of the 1930s and was transformed into a despot by the wave of repression in 1936–1938 (E. A. Rees [ed.], *The Nature of Stalin's Dictatorship: The Politburo, 1924–1953* [New York, 2004], pp. 39–42, 205–207). This opinion is not necessarily incompatible with the idea that the models of power that were in place at the highest levels during the first and second halves of the 1930s differed from each other.

7. *Sotsialisticheskii vestnik*, nos. 23–24 (1936), pp. 20–23; nos. 1–2 (1937), pp. 17–24.

8. Boris I. Nikolaevsky (1887–1966) was a well-known figure in the Russian so-cial-democratic movement and a Menshevik. In 1922 he was expelled from the So-viet Union by the Bolshevik authorities. After emigration he devoted himself to scholarly research, collecting materials relating to the political history of Russia and the Soviet Union. In 1936 he played a consultative role in negotiations over the sale of the Marx and Engels archives (which belonged to the German Social Democratic Party) to the Soviet Union. These negotiations brought him together with Nikolai Bukharin, who was a member of the Soviet delegation. Nikolaevsky's 1937 article has been published in English as *Letter of an Old Bolshevik: The Key to the Moscow Trials* (New York, 1937).

9. A. M. Larina (Bukharina), *Nezabyvaemoe* (Moscow, 1989), pp. 243–286. This work has also been published in English under the title *This I Cannot Forget: The Memoirs of Nikolai Bukharin's Widow* (New York, 1993).

10. André Liebich, "I Am the Last: Memories of Bukharin in Paris," *Slavic Review*, 51, no. 4 (winter 1992), pp. 767–778; Yu. G. Fel'shtinskii, *Razgovory s Bukharinym. Kommentarii k vospominaniiam A. M. Larinoi (Bukharinoi) "Nez-abyvaemoe" s prilozheniiami* (Moscow, 1993).

11. Alexander Orlov, *The Secret History of Stalin's Crimes* (New York, 1953). For a more detailed assessment of Orlov as a source, see O. Khlevniuk, "Istoriia *Tainoi istorii*," *Svobodnaia mysl'*, no. 3 (1996); M. A. Tumshis and A. A. Pachin-skii, "Pravda i lozh' A. Orlova," *Otechestvennaia istoriia*, no. 6 (1999), pp. 179–182.

12. See, for example, Robert C. Tucker, *Stalin in Power: The Revolution from Above, 1928–1941* (New York, 1992).

13. Hiroaki Kuromiya, *Stalin's Industrial Revolution: Politics and Workers, 1928–1932* (New York, 1988); E. A. Rees (ed.), *Decision-Making in the Stalinist Command Economy, 1932–1937* (New York, 1997); Paul R. Gregory, *The Political Economy of Stalinism: Evidence from the Soviet Secret Archives* (Cambridge, UK, 2004).

14. R. W. Davies, "Some Soviet Economic Controllers. III," *Soviet Studies*, 12, no. 1 (July 1960); Sheila Fitzpatrick, "Ordzhonikidze's Takeover of Vesenkha: A Case Study in Soviet Bureaucratic Politics," *Soviet Studies*, 37, no. 2 (April 1985); Francesco Benvenuti, "A Stalinist Victim of Stalinism: 'Sergo' Ordzhonikidze," in *Soviet History, 1917–53: Essays in Honour of R. W. Davies* (Basingstoke, UK, 1995); Oleg V. Khlevniuk, *In Stalin's Shadow: The Career of "Sergo" Ordzhoni-kidze* (New York, 1995).

15. Derek Watson, "Molotov and Soviet Government: Sovnarkom, 1930–1941" (Basingstoke, UK, 1996); Derek Watson, *Molotov: A Biography* (Basingstoke, UK, 2005).

16. See, for example, the comprehensive collection of documents and research: *Istoriia stalinskogo Gulaga. Konets 1920-kh–pervaia polovina 1950-kh godov. Sobranie dokumentov v semi tomakh* (Moscow, 2004); Barry McLoughlin and Kevin McDermott (eds.), *Stalin's Terror: High Politics and Mass Repression in the Soviet Union* (Basingstoke, UK, 2003); Oleg V. Khlevniuk, *The History of the Gu-lag: From Collectivization to the Great Terror* (New Haven, 2004).

17. Robert Conquest, *The Great Terror: A Reassessment* (New York, 1991), p. 33.

18. References to research that supports this perspective are provided in chapter 5. One of the most important recent works on this topic that attempts to reconcile a priori formulations of the terror's spontaneous nature with archival evidence that obviously contradicts them is J. Arch Getty, "Excesses Are Not Permitted: Mass Terror and Stalinist Governance in the Late 1930s," *Russian Review,* 61, no. 1 (2002), pp. 113–138.

19. See Paul Gregory and Eugenia Belova, "'Hang Them All': The Economics of Crime and Punishment under Stalin," presented at the Annual Meetings of the American Economic Association, Boston, Mass., 5–7 January 2005.

20. For numerous instructions from Stalin concerning the fabrication of cases and the destruction of officials, see V. N. Khaustov et al. (comps.), *Lubianka. Stalin i Glavnoe upravlenie gosbezopasnosti NKVD. 1937–1938* (Moscow, 2004); S. A. Mel'chin et al. (comps.), *Stalinskie passtrel'nye spiski* (Moscow, 2002). The lists of those executed have been jointly published electronically by the Presidential Archive of the Russian Federation (ARPF, which holds the lists) and the Memorial Society, at http://www.memo.ru/history/vkvs/.

21. For a fuller description of the archival holdings of the highest bodies of the Soviet government, see Jana Howlett, Oleg Khlevniuk, Ludmila Kosheleva, and Larisa Rogovaia, "The CPSU's Top Bodies under Stalin: Their Operational Records and Structure of Command," The Stalin-Era Research and Archives Project, CREES. University of Toronto, Working Paper no. 1; Andrea Graziosi, "The New Soviet Archival Sources: Hypotheses for a Critical Assessment," *Cahiers du Monde Russe,* 40, nos. 1–2 (1999), pp. 13–64.

22. For a catalogue of Politburo resolutions based on reference protocols, see G. M. Adibekov et al. (eds.), *Politbiuro TsK RKP(b)-VKP(b). Povestki dnia zasedanii. 1919–1952* (Moscow, 2000–2001), vols. 1–3.

23. G. M. Adibekov et al. (eds.), *Politbiuro TsK RKP(b)-VKP(b) i Evropa. Resheniia "Osoboi papki." 1923–1939* (Moscow, 2001); V. N. Khaustov et al. (comps.), *Lubianka. Stalin i VChK-GPU-OGPU-NKVD. Ianvar' 1922–dekabr' 1936* (Moscow, 2003), and others.

24. *Istoricheskii arkhiv,* no. 6 (2001), p. 3.

25. Among collected materials of this sort the following, for example, is worthy of note: N. N. Pokrovskii et al. (eds.), *Politbiuro i krest'ianstvo: vysylka, spetsposelenie. 1930–1940* (Moscow, 2005), book 1. Five thematic files from the Presidential Archive of the Russian Federation (APRF) under the heading "On kulaks (special settlements and labor settlements)" are reproduced in their entirety and provided with detailed commentary.

26. RGASPI, f. 17, op. 3, d. 360, l. 12.

27. Publication of this important collection (Politburo stenograms and the many documents and materials associated with them) is being undertaken jointly by RGASPI and the Hoover Institution on War, Revolution and Peace. See *Stenograms of the TsK RKP(b)-VKP(b) Politburo Meetings, 1923–1938* (Moscow, 2007), vols. 1–3.

28. Danilov and Khlevniuk, *Kak lomali nep,* pp. 577–601, 604–633.

29. The only significant personal journal we have is the intermittent but very rich (attesting to the value of diaries as sources) prewar reflections of the commissar of heavy machinery, V. A. Malyshev (*Istochnik,* no. 5 [1997], pp. 104–116). Anastas Mikoyan's memoir is entitled *Tak bylo. Razmyshleniia o minuvshem* (Moscow, 1999). Chuev's accounts have been published as *Sto sorok besed s Molotovym: Iz dnevnika F. Chuev* (Moscow, 1991); *Kaganovich. Shepilov* (Moscow, 2001).

30. Lazar Kaganovich, *Pamiatnye zapiski* (Moscow, 1996).

31. Lih, Naumov, and Khlevniuk, *Stalin's Letters to Molotov;* O. V. Khlevniuk et al. (eds.), *Stalinskoe Politbiuro v 30-e gody* (Moscow, 1995); A. V. Kvashonkin et al. (comps.), *Sovetskoe rukovodstvo. Perepiska. 1928–1941* (Moscow, 1999); R. W. Davies et al. (eds.) *The Stalin-Kaganovich Correspondence, 1931–36* (New Haven, 2003).

32. RGASPI, f. 85, recent acquisitions; f. 74, op. 2, d. 37, l. 49.

CHAPTER 1. THE STALINIZATION OF THE POLITBURO, 1928–1930

1. RGASPI, f. 558. op. 11, d. 767, ll. 35–39, 45–48, 56–60.

2. Ibid., l. 35–39, 45–48; RGASPI, f. 558, op. 11, d. 71, ll. 11, 13–14.

3. Ibid., d. 767, ll. 56–60.

4. RGASPI, f. 82, op. 2, d. 1420, ll. 200, 220.

5. Ibid., f. 558, op. 11, d. 777, ll. 75–78.

6. A. V. Kvashonkin et al. (comps.), *Sovetskoe rukovodstvo. Perepiska. 1928–1941* (Moscow, 1999), pp. 58–59.

7. Lars T. Lih, Oleg V. Naumov, and Oleg Khlevniuk (eds.), *Stalin's Letters to Molotov, 1925–1936* (New Haven, 1995), p. 149.

8. Stephen F. Cohen, *Bukharin and the Bolshevik Revolution: A Political Biography, 1888–1938* (Oxford, 1980), p. 329.

9. RGASPI, f. 85, recent acquisitions, d. 2, ll. 1–11, 28–30.

10. V. P. Danilov, R. Manning, and L. Viola (eds.), *Tragediia sovetskoi derevni. Kollektivizatsiia i raskulachivanie* (Moscow, 2000), vol. 2, p. 789.

11. Ibid., p. 703. For more detail on mass uprisings in the countryside during this period, see Lynne Viola, *Peasant Rebels under Stalin: Collectivization and the Culture of Peasant Resistance* (New York, 1996); V. Vasiliev and L. Viola, *Kollektivizatsiia i krestianskoe sprotivlenie na Ukraine (noiabr' 1929–mart 1930 g.g.)* (Vinnitsa, 1997); I. E. Plotnikov, "Krest'ianskie volneniia i vystupleniia na Urale v kontse 20-x-nachale 30-x godov," *Otechestvennaia istoriia,* no. 2 (1998), pp. 74–92.

12. Kvashonkin et al., *Sovetskoe rukovodstvo,* p. 118.

13. This is undoubtedly a reference to Lenin's "Letter to the Congress," in which, critically ill, he harshly characterized his comrades-in-arms and warned about Stalin's brutality. During the early 1930s, this letter was still widely known throughout the party and often served as a basis for criticizing Stalin (see O. Khlevniuk, *1937: Stalin, NKVD i sovetskoe obshchestvo* [Moscow, 1992], pp. 15, 53–54). Later, the mere mention of "Lenin's testament" would be fatal.

14. *Istoricheskii arkhiv,* no. 1 (1997), pp. 136–137.

15. Kvashonkin et al., *Sovetskoe rukovodstvo,* p. 135.

16. Oleg V. Khlevniuk, *The History of the Gulag: From Collectivization to the Great Terror* (New Haven, 2004), pp. 16, 288; State Archive of the Russian Federation (GARF), f. R-9401, op. 1, d. 4157, l. 202.

17. RGASPI, f. 17, op. 117, d. 873, l. 23.

18. A. S. Senin, *Rykov. Stranitsy zhizni* (Moscow, 1993), pp. 108–109.

19. GARF, f. R-5446, op. 55, d. 2055, l. 10.

20. Ibid., l. 6.

21. GARF, f. R-5446, op. 55, d. 2051, ll. 37–38.

22. Ibid., d. 2051, ll. 29–33.

23. RGASPI, f. 17, op. 3, d. 561, l. 11.

24. GARF, f. R-5446, op. 55, d. 2037, ll. 52–54.

25. Ibid., op. 11a, d. 656, ll. 1–3.

26. Ibid., op. 55, d. 1986, l. 26; d. 1945, ll. 51–52.

27. RGASPI, f. 17, op. 162, d. 9, l. 4.

28. See, for example, *Pravda,* 26 July 1930, p. 5; 2 August 1930, p. 5.

29. Lih, Naumov, and Khlevniuk, *Stalin's Letters to Molotov,* p. 190.

30. Ibid.

31. Ibid., p. 200.

32. RGASPI, f. 17, op. 162, d. 9, l. 16.

33. Ibid., op. 3, d. 800, ll. 7–8.

34. This work has been published in English as *The Russian Revolution, 1917: A Personal Record.*

35. Lih, Naumov, and Khlevniuk, *Stalin's Letters to Molotov,* pp. 199–200.

36. RGASPI, f. 558, op. 11, d. 769, ll. 5–11.

37. Lih, Naumov, and Khlevniuk, *Stalin's Letters to Molotov,* p. 203.

38. Ibid., p. 210.

39. RGASPI, f. 17, op. 3, d. 795, l. 6.

40. *Voennye arkhivy Rossii,* no. 1 (1993), p. 103.

41. Ibid., p. 104.

42. Ibid., pp. 104–105

43. RGASPI, f. 17, op. 163, d. 1002, ll. 174–175.

44. A. N. Yakovlev (ed.), *Reabilitatsiia. Politicheskie protsessy 30–50-x godov* (Moscow, 1990), pp. 242, 244.

45. RGASPI, f. 17, op. 3, d. 801, l. 12.

46. *Stenograms of the TsK RKP(b)-VKP(b) Politburo Meetings, 1923–1938* (Moscow, 2007), vol. 3, p. 285.

47. Ibid., p. 211.

48. RGASPI, f. 17, op. 162, d. 9, l. 54.

49. Ibid., op. 3, d. 745, l. 4.

50. A. V. Kvashonkin et al. (eds.), *Bolshevitskoe rukovodstvo, 1912–1927* (Moscow, 1996), pp. 344–345.

51. RGASPI, f. 669, op. 1, d. 30, ll. 192–193.

52. For a more detailed description of Syrtsov's views and for more on the Syrtsov-Lominadze affair, see R. W. Davies, "The Syrtsov-Lominadze Affair," *So-*

viet Studies, 33, no. 1 (January 1981); S. A. Kislitsyn, *Variant Syrtsova (Iz istorii formirovaniia antistaliskogo soprotivleniia v sovetskom obshchestve v 20–30 gg.*) (Rostov-on-the-Don, 1992); James Hughes, "Patrimonialism and the Stalinist System: The Case of S. I. Syrtsov," *Europe-Asia Studies,* 48, no. 4 (1996), pp. 551–568.

53. Lih, Naumov, and Khlevniuk, *Stalin's Letters to Molotov,* p. 64.

54. RGASPI, f. 558, op. 11, d. 769, ll. 37–38. Molotov also spoke about this session of the Politburo and the alliance between Rykov and Syrtsov at the joint session of the Politburo and the presidium of the Central Control Commission on 4 November 1930, during which the Syrtsov-Lominadze affair was discussed (ibid., f. 17, op. 163, d. 1002, l. 127).

55. RGASPI, f. 17, op. 3, d. 800, l. 7.

56. O. V. Khlevniuk et al. (eds.), *Stalinskoe Politbiuro v 30-e gody* (Moscow, 1995), p. 97. A Thermidorian is someone who betrays a revolution.

57. RGASPI, f. 85, op. 1, d. 130, ll. 15–33. Later, when editing the stenographic record, Ordzhonikidze deleted the phrase "and allowed him to follow that path."

58. Khlevniuk et al., *Stalinskoe Politbiuro,* pp. 99–100.

59. *Stenograms of the TsK RKP(b)-VKP(b) Politburo Meetings,* vol. 3, p. 178. The first to point out this aspect of Stalin's speech was S. A. Kislitsyn (*Kentavr,* no. 1 [1991], p. 118).

60. *Stenograms of the TsK RKP(b)-VKP(b) Politburo Meetings,* vol. 3, p. 185.

61. RGASPI, f. 17, op. 162, d., 9, l. 57.

62. Along these lines, as the 4 November joint session of the Politburo and Central Control Commission presidium came to a close, Stalin unexpectedly proposed softening the decision that had been taken: rather than expel Syrtsov and Lominadze from the Central Committee, change their membership status to that of candidate. Understanding Stalin's game perfectly well, the Politburo members "firmly" rejected this proposal (*Stenograms of the TsK RKP(b)-VKP(b) Politburo Meetings,* vol. 3, p. 193).

63. Lih, Naumov, and Khlevniuk, *Stalin's Letters to Molotov,* p. 214.

64. Ibid., pp. 217–218

65. "We agreed that each of us would write his own thoughts," Kaganovich wrote in his letter (RGASPI, f. 558, op. 11, d. 738, l. 110).

66. Kvashonkin et al., *Sovetskoe rukovodstvo,* pp. 144–145. For further details, see Benno Ennker, "Struggling for Stalin's Soul: The Leader Cult and the Balance of Social Power in Stalin's Inner Circle," in Klaus Heller and Jan Plamper (eds.), *Personality Cults in Stalinism* (Göttingen, 2004), pp. 172–175; O. Khlevniuk, "Stalin i Molotov. Edinolichnaia diktatura i predposylki 'oligarkhizatsii,'" in B. S. Ilizarov et al. (eds.), *Stalin. Stalinizm. Sovetskoe obshchestvo* (Moscow, 2000), pp. 273–276.

67. RGASPI, f. 558, op. 11, d. 765, l. 68a.

68. Ibid., d. 769, ll. 55–58.

69. Ibid., d. 738, ll. 110–111.

70. Ibid., d. 778, l. 43.

71. Ibid.

72. Ibid., d. 769, ll. 57–58.

73. RGASPI, f. 17, op. 2, d. 735, ll. 9–10.

74. *Stenograms of the TsK RKP(b)-VKP(b) Politburo Meetings,* vol. 3, p. 187.

75. Ibid., p. 157.

76. RGASPI, f. 17, op. 2, d. 735, ll. 12–13.

77. Ibid., op. 162, d. 9, ll. 88–92.

78. Ibid., op. 2, d. 735, ll. 14–15.

79. Ibid., l. 15.

80. Ibid., d. 460, ll. 61–64.

81. Ibid., ll. 81–83.

82. Ibid., l. 87.

CHAPTER 2. POWER IN CRISIS, 1931–1933

1. V. N. Zemskov's chapter in Yu. A. Poliakov (ed.), *Naselenie Rossii v XX veke, Istoricheskie ocherki* (Moscow, 2000), vol. 1, p. 277. There are other figures cited in the literature, but overall they differ very little.

2. V. P. Danilov and N. A. Ivnitskii, *Dokumenty svidetel'stvuiut* (Moscow, 1989), pp. 46–47.

3. For a detailed discussion of this, see R. W. Davies, *The Soviet Economy in Turmoil, 1929–1930* (London, 1989).

4. R. W. Davies, *Crisis and Progress in the Soviet Economy, 1931–1933* (Basingstoke, UK, 1996), pp. 77–103.

5. O. V. Khlevniuk et al. (eds.), *Stalinskoe Politbiuro v 30-e gody* (Moscow, 1995), p. 60. The resolution was initially a special-folder resolution, therefore not subject to wide dissemination (RGASPI, f. 17, op. 162, d. 11, l. 108), but later it was given a less secret classification and was circulated.

6. RGASPI, f. 17, op. 162, d. 11, l. 109.

7. Ibid., op. 3, d. 835, l. 25.

8. V. N. Khaustov et al. (comps.), *Lubianka. Stalin i VChK-GPU-OGPU-NKVD. Ianvar' 1922–dekabr' 1936* (Moscow, 2003), pp. 287–288.

9. I. E. Zelenin, "Byl li 'kolkhoznyi neonep'?" *Otechestvennaia istoriia,* no. 2 (1994), p. 106.

10. I. E. Zelenin et al. (eds.), *Tragediia sovetskoi derevni. Kollektivizatsiia i raskulachivanie* (Moscow, 2001), vol. 3, p. 350.

11. GARF, f. R-5446, op. 82, d. 11, ll. 8–12.

12. RGASPI, f. 17, op. 42, d. 26, l. 1–6.

13. For more on the events in Ivanovo Province, see N. Werth and G. Moullec, *Rapports secrets soviétiques* (Paris, 1994), pp. 209–216; J. Rossman, "The Teikovo Cotton Workers' Strike of April 1932: Class, Gender and Identity Politics in Stalin's Russia," *Russian Review,* 56 (January 1997), pp. 44–69; Rossman, "The Worker's Strike in Stalin's Russia: The Vichuga Uprising of April 1932," in Lynne Viola (ed.), *Contending with Stalinism: Soviet Power and Popular Resistance in the 1930s* (Ithaca, NY, 2002), pp. 44–83; RGASPI, f. 81, op. 3, d. 213, ll. 3–7, 64–65, 77–78, 93.

14. RGASPI, f. 17, op. 20, d. 109, l. 1060b.

15. Other evidence indicated that one demonstrator had been wounded and one had been killed (ibid., f. 81, op. 3, d. 213, l. 4).

16. APRF, f. 3, op. 22, d. 39, ll. 6–7.

17. RGASPI, f. 17, op. 42, d. 33, l. 5.

18. Ibid., op. 20, d. 121, l. 226.

19. Ibid., d. 106, l. 36.

20. *XVII s'ezd Vsesoiuznoi kommunisticheskoi partii. Stenograficheskii otchet* (Moscow, 1934), p. 165.

21. E. A. Rees (ed.), *Decision-Making in the Stalinist Command Economy, 1932–1937* (New York, 1997), pp. 43–44.

22. R. W. Davies and S. G. Wheatcroft, *The Years of Hunger: Soviet Agriculture, 1931–1933* (Basingstoke, UK, 2004), p. 411. There is extensive literature on the famine. Historians in Ukraine, which suffered from the famine more than many other parts of the Soviet Union, have investigated it with particular energy. See, for example, the overview provided in a collaborative work by Ukrainian historians: *Golod 1932–1933 pokiv v Ukraini: Prichini ta naslidki* (Kyiv, 2003).

23. Davies and Wheatcroft, *Years of Hunger,* pp. 412–415.

24. RGASPI, f. 17, op. 42, d. 38, l. 80.

25. GARF, f. R-5446, op. 26/5, d. 1, ll. 109, 115.

26. RGASPI, f. 558, op. 11, d. 155, ll. 71, 73.

27. RGASPI, f. 17, op. 3, d. 921, l. 67.

28. Poliakov, *Naselenie Rossii v XX veke,* pp. 279, 311.

29. A. V. Kvashonkin et al. (eds.), *Sovetskoe rukovodstvo. Perepiska. 1928–1941* (Moscow, 1999), p. 313.

30. A. N. Yakovlev (ed.), *Reabilitatsiia. Politicheskie protsessy 30–50-kh godov* (Moscow, 1990), pp. 94–95.

31. RGASPI, f. 17, op. 117, d. 873, ll. 23–24.

32. Khlevniuk et al., *Stalinskoe Politbiuro,* pp. 30–31.

33. Ibid., pp. 31–33. For a detailed account of the reorganization of the Council of People's Commissars during this period, see Derek Watson, *Molotov and Soviet Government: Sovnarkom, 1930–1941* (Basingstoke, UK, 1996).

34. Khlevniuk et al., *Stalinskoe Politbiuro,* pp. 180–181.

35. Ibid., p. 24.

36. Ibid., p. 181.

37. Ibid., p. 25.

38. Ibid.

39. Ibid.

40. Ibid., p. 181.

41. See Appendix 2.

42. Khlevniuk et al., *Stalinskoe Politbiuro,* p. 14.

43. *Istochnik,* nos. 5–6 (1993), p. 94.

44. Khlevniuk et al., *Stalinskoe Politbiuro,* p. 14.

45. Ibid., p. 27. This decision was drafted by Central Committee secretary P. P. Postyshev.

46. See Appendix 1.

47. Khlevniuk et al., *Stalinskoe Politbiuro,* pp. 112–113.

48. Lars T. Lih, Oleg V. Naumov, and Oleg Khlevniuk (eds.), *Stalin's Letters to Molotov, 1925–1936* (New Haven, 1995); RGASPI, f. 558, op. 11, d. 767–769.

49. R. W. Davies et al. (eds.), *The Stalin-Kaganovich Correspondence, 1931–36* (New Haven, 2003).

50. RGASPI, f. 17, op. 163, d. 945, l. 121.

51. Ibid., op. 162, d. 10, l. 165.

52. Ibid., d. 12, l. 154.

53. RGASPI, f. 17, op. 3, d. 911, l. 12.

54. Khlevniuk et al., *Stalinskoe Politbiuro*, pp. 69–70.

55. Ibid., p. 138.

56. See Appendix 2.

57. G. K. Ordzhonikidze, *Stat'i i rechi* (Moscow, 1957), vol. 2, pp. 268–269, 277–281.

58. K. E. Bailes, *Technology and Society under Lenin and Stalin: Origins of the Soviet Technical Intelligentsia, 1917–1941* (Princeton, NJ, 1978).

59. Hiroaki Kuromiya, *Stalin's Industrial Revolution: Politics and Workers, 1928–1932* (Cambridge, UK, 1988), pp. 275–276.

60. RGASPI, f. 17, op. 3, d. 803, l. 15; d. 804, l. 13.

61. Ibid., op. 163, d. 857, ll. 115–116.

62. RGASPI, f. 558, op. 1, d. 5243, l. 4.

63. Ibid., l. 1.

64. RGASPI, f. 17, op. 3, d. 811, l. 9.

65. Ibid., f. 558, op. 1, d. 2960, ll. 7, 9, 23.

66. APRF, f. 3, op. 45, d. 38, ll. 20–22.

67. RGASPI, f. 17, op. 163, d. 880, l. 3.

68. Ibid., op. 162, d. 11, l. 119 (Politburo special-folder resolution dated 15 July 1931).

69. RGASPI, f. 85, op. 28, d. 8, ll. 160, 192.

70. Ibid., d. 7, ll. 122–139.

71. RGASPI, f. 17, op. 163, d. 895, ll. 68–69.

72. N. A. Ivnitskii, *Kollektivizatsiia i raskulachivanie (nachalo 30-x godov)* (Moscow, 1994), p. 191.

73. Ibid.; RGASPI, f. 17, op. 3, d. 876, l. 1; R. Ya. Pyrig (ed.), *Golod 1932–1933 rokiv na Ukraini* (Kyiv, 1990), p. 129.

74. RGASPI, f. 17, op. 162, d. 12, l. 108; V. Vasil'ev and Yu. Shapoval (eds.), *Komandyry velykogo golodu: Poizdki V. Molotova i L. Kaganovicha v Ukrainu ta Pivnichnyi Kavkaz. 1932–1933* (Kyiv, 2001), p. 86.

75. N. N. Pokrovskii (ed.), *Politbiuro i krestianstvo: Vysylka, spetsposelenie. 1930–1940* (Moscow, 2005), bk. 1, pp. 23–24, 518–519, 536.

76. Ibid., p. 24.

77. Ibid., p. 23.

78. *Sotsialisticheskii vestnik*, nos. 23–24 (1936), pp. 20–21.

79. B. Starkov, "Delo Riutina," in *Oni ne molchali* (Moscow, 1991), p. 170.

80. Yakovlev, *Reabilitatsiia*, pp. 92–104.

81. *Pravda*, 11 October 1932.

82. RGASPI, f. 17, op. 163, d. 960, l. 64.

83. See Stalin's office visitation log in *Istoricheskii arkhiv,* no. 2 (1995), pp. 150–153.

84. *Voenno-istoricheskii arkhiv,* no. 11 (2004), pp. 158–159.

85. E. A. Osokina, "Zhertvy goloda 1933 goda," *Istoriia SSSR,* no. 5 (1991), p. 23.

86. RGASPI, f. 17, op. 42, d. 38, l. 48.

87. Ibid., op. 163, d. 1010, l. 281. When editing the stenographic record, Kirov softened his wording, replacing "punch in the snout" with "punch politically."

88. Sheila Fitzpatrick, "Ordzhonikidze's Takeover of Vesenkha: A Case Study in Soviet Bureaucratic Politics," *Soviet Studies,* 37, no. 2 (April 1985); Oleg V. Khlevniuk, *In Stalin's Shadow: The Career of "Sergo" Ordzhonikidze* (New York, 1995).

89. For a study of the practice and a description of the model of the Soviet system of economic management in the 1930s, as well as the relationship between Stalin and the managers of the economic agencies, see Paul R. Gregory, *The Political Economy of Stalinism: Evidence from the Soviet Secret Archives* (Cambridge, UK, 2004).

90. RGASPI, f. 17, op. 3, d. 818, l. 1.

91. Ibid., op. 163, d. 890, l. 24.

92. Ibid., d. 891, l. 21.

93. RGASPI, f. 17, op. 3, d. 838, l. 1.

94. Ibid., op. 114, d. 251, l. 4.

95. RGASPI, f. 84, op. 2, d. 135, ll. 5–50b.

96. Lih, Naumov, and Khlevniuk, *Stalin's Letters to Molotov,* p. 205.

97. Ibid., p. 206.

98. Davies et al., *Stalin-Kaganovich Correspondence,* p. 374.

99. Ibid., p. 54.

100. Khlevniuk et al., *Stalinskoe Politbiuro,* p. 121; Davies et al., *Stalin-Kaganovich Correspondence,* p. 45.

101. Davies et al., *Stalin-Kaganovich Correspondence,* p. 79.

102. RGASPI, f. 558, op. 11, d. 779, ll. 7–20, 29–31.

103. Davies et al., *Stalin-Kaganovich Correspondence,* pp. 374–375; RGASPI, f. 558, op. 11, d. 779, ll. 21–23, 32–33.

104. Davies et al., *Stalin-Kaganovich Correspondence,* pp. 47–48; RGASPI, f. 558, op. 11, d. 765, ll. 72–73; f. 84, op. 2, d. 134, l. 5.

105. Khlevniuk et al., *Stalinskoe Politbiuro,* p. 123.

106. For several illustrative statements by Ordzhonikidze, see ibid., pp. 120–121, 124.

107. Davies et al., *Stalin-Kaganovich Correspondence,* p. 54.

108. RGASPI, f. 558, op. 11, d. 779, ll. 21–23 (letter from Stalin to Ordzhonikidze after 11 September 1931).

109. Ibid., ll. 32–33 (letter from Stalin to Ordzhonikidze dated 4 October 1931).

110. The following note from Ordzhonikidze has been preserved among Kuibyshev's papers: "I have heard about these little talks, but personally I think that this is incorrect. Separate branches of industry are so closely tied with one another that their immediate inclusion in STO should seriously complicate and confuse the situation. I am decidedly opposed." On the first page of the note, Kuibyshev wrote,

"Note from Sergo dated 11 October [1931] concerning the liquidation of VSNKh." (Khlevniuk et al., *Stalinskoe Politbiuro*, p. 124).

111. Ibid., pp. 123–124.

112. RGASPI, f. 17, op. 3, d. 867, ll. 11–12.

113. Ibid., d. 946, l. 17.

114. Khlevniuk et al., *Stalinskoe Politbiuro*, p. 140.

115. Ibid., pp. 25–26.

116. Ibid., p. 26.

117. GARF, f. R-5446, op. 27, d. 6, ll. 349–352.

118. Khlevniuk et al., *Stalinskoe Politbiuro*, p. 26.

119. RGASPI, f. 17, op. 163, d. 989, l. 221. Analogous conflicts between Voroshilov and Ordzhonikidze, resolved in compromise decisions by the Politburo, occurred during subsequent years as well. For example, in August–September 1936, the Politburo twice considered disagreements between the Heavy Industry Commissariat and the Defense Commissariat concerning the call-up of workers in the aviation industry and mining to serve in the army. Both times, as in the 1933 case described, an intermediate number of deferments was approved, despite demands by Ordzhonikidze and the categorical objections of Voroshilov (ibid., d. 1120, l. 24; d. 1122, l. 95.)

120. Besides the September 1931 conflict over imported equipment for the Supreme Economic Council, another conflict, this one tied to a reduction in capital investment, was a significant source of tension in 1932. See Rees, *Decision-Making in the Stalinist Command Economy*, pp. 42–43.

121. GARF, f. R-5446, op. 82, d. 26, ll. 34–36.

122. Ibid., l. 37.

123. Ibid., ll. 18–20.

124. Ibid., ll. 21–22.

125. *Pravda*, 23 August 1933.

126. RGASPI, f. 17, op. 163, d. 989, l. 165.

127. Ibid., d. 990, l. 70; RGASPI, f. 558, op. 11, d. 80, l. 49.

128. Ibid., d. 990, l. 70.

129. Davies et al., *Stalin-Kaganovich Correspondence*, p. 199.

130. Lih, Naumov, and Khlevniuk, *Stalin's Letters to Molotov*, p. 233.

131. Davies et al., *Stalin-Kaganovich Correspondence*, pp. 204–205.

132. RGASPI, f. 558, op. 11, d. 766, ll. 127–128.

133. Lih, Naumov, and Khlevniuk, *Stalin's Letters to Molotov*, p. 234.

134. Khlevniuk et al., *Stalinskoe Politbiuro*, p. 125 (letter from Kaganovich to Ordzhonikidze dated 2 August 1932); Andrea Graziosi, *A New, Peculiar State: Explorations in Soviet History* (London, 2000), p. 28. Kaganovich used the term *glavny drug*.

135. Davies et al., *Stalin-Kaganovich Correspondence*, p. 375 (letter to Ordzhonikidze dated 9 September 1931).

136. Ibid., p. 71 (letter to Kaganovich dated 4 September 1931).

137. Ibid., pp. 169–170 (letter to Kaganovich dated 26 July 1932).

138. RGASPI, f. 82, op. 2, d. 1421, ll. 258–260 (letter to Molotov dated 8 August 1932).

139. Davies et al., *Stalin-Kaganovich Correspondance*, pp. 225–226.

140. Lih, Naumov, and Khlevniuk, *Stalin's Letters to Molotov*, p. 231.

141. Khlevniuk et al., *Stalinskoe Politbiuro*, p. 126.

CHAPTER 3. A FACADE OF LIBERALIZATION, 1934

1. M. Ia. Gefter, *Iz tekh i etikh let* (Moscow, 1991), pp. 260–261.

2. RGASPI, f. 17, op. 162, d. 15, ll. 154–155; G. M. Adibekov et al. (eds.), *Politbiuro TsK RKP(b)-VKP(b) i Evropa. Resheniia "osoboi papki"* (Moscow, 2001), pp. 305–306.

3. According to recent estimates, the grain harvest of 1933 yielded 70–77 million metric tons, as compared to 55–60 million metric tons in 1932 (R. W. Davies and S. G. Wheatcroft, *The Years of Hunger: Soviet Agriculture, 1931–1933* [Basingstoke, UK, 2004], pp. 448–449).

4. RGASPI, f. 17, op. 3, d. 917, l. 7.

5. These instructions were first published by Merle Fainsod based on a copy preserved within the Smolensk archive: Merle Fainsod, *Smolensk under Soviet Rule* (Cambridge, MA, 1958), pp. 185–188; RGASPI, f. 17, op. 3, d. 922, ll. 58–58ob.

6. GARF, f. R-5446, op. 15a, d. 1073, l. 35.

7. *XVII s'ezd Vsesoiuznoi Kommunisticheskoi partii. Stenograficheskii otchet* (Moscow, 1934), p. 67.

8. RGASPI, f. 17, op. 3, d. 936, ll. 5, 15.

9. *XVII s'ezd Vsesoiuznoi Kommunisticheskoi partii*, p. 259.

10. Ibid.

11. RGASPI, f. 17, op. 3, d. 939, l. 2.

12. Ibid., d. 941, l. 20.

13. RGASPI, f. 17, op. 163, d. 1016, l. 143.

14. Ibid., op. 3, d. 944, l. 17.

15. Ibid., ll. 15, 42.

16. RGASPI, f. 17, op. 163, d. 1033, l. 20.

17. Ibid., op. 86, d. 231, ll. 49–51.

18. *Sotsialisticheskii vestnik*, no. 19 (1934), p. 14.

19. GARF, f. R-9401, op. 1, d. 4157, l. 202; J. Arch Getty and Oleg V. Naumov (eds.), *The Road to Terror: Stalin and the Self-Destruction of the Bolsheviks, 1932–1939* (New Haven, 1999), p. 588.

20. For the essential elements of this reorganization, see Francesco Benvenuti, "The 'Reform' of the NKVD, 1934," *Europe-Asia Studies*, 49, no. 6 (1997), pp. 1037–1056.

21. RGASPI, f. 17, op. 3, d. 948, ll. 95–100. For greater detail, see Peter H. Solomon, Jr., *Soviet Criminal Justice under Stalin* (New York, 1996), pp. 153–195.

22. O. V. Khlevniuk et al. (eds.), *Stalinskoe Politbiuro v 30-e gody* (Moscow, 1995), p. 70.

23. RGASPI, f. 17, op. 3, d. 941, l. 14.

24. In accordance with a new party statute adopted during the 17th Party Congress in early 1934, the secret department of the Central Committee was transformed into the Special Sector of the Central Committee. The Special Sector took

over the functions of the secret department, which had been reorganized at the end of 1933. On 10 March 1934 the Politburo appointed Aleksandr Poskrebyshev as head of the Special Sector (RGASPI, f. 17, op. 3, d. 941, l. 14).

25. Khlevniuk et al., *Stalinskoe Politbiuro*, pp. 141–142. The draft resolution on distributing responsibility among Central Committee secretaries was written by Stalin himself (RGASPI, f. 17, op. 163, d. 1026, l. 19).

26. RGASPI, f. 17, op. 3, d. 948, l. 31.

27. M. V. Rosliakov, *Ubiistvo Kirova. Politicheskie i ugolovnye prestupleniia v 1930-kh godakh* (Leningrad, 1991), pp. 28–29.

28. A. A. Kirilina, *Rikoshet* (St. Petersburg, 1993), p. 75.

29. See RGASPI, f. 17, op. 163, d. 1039.

30. For more on this, see Oleg V. Khlevniuk, *In Stalin's Shadow: The Career of "Sergo" Ordzhonikidze* (New York, 1995), p. 22–24.

31. See Appendix 2.

32. See Appendix 2.

33. N. A. Zen'kovich, *Tainy kremlevskikh smertei* (Moscow, 1995), pp. 322–323.

34. *Moskovskie novosti*, 22–29 January 1995, p. 14.

35. *Istoricheskii arkhiv*, no. 3 (1995), p. 141; R. W. Davies et al. (eds.), *The Stalin-Kaganovich Correspondence, 1931–36* (New Haven, 2003), pp. 236–288.

36. GARF, f. R-5446, op. 27, d. 92, ll. 34–35.

37. Ibid., l. 39.

38. Lars T. Lih, Oleg V. Naumov, and Oleg Khlevniuk (eds.), *Stalin's Letters to Molotov, 1925–1936* (New Haven, 1995), p. 234.

39. See Appendix 2.

40. See, for example, RGASPI, f 17, op. 163, d. 1012, ll. 87–89, 94.

41. See ibid., d. 1038.

42. The following material is taken from: R. W. Davies and O. Khlevnyuk, "Gosplan," in E. A. Rees (ed.), *Decision-Making in the Stalinist Command Economy, 1932–1937* (New York, 1997), pp. 32–66.

43. This perspective is most thoroughly presented in J. A. Getty, *Origins of the Great Purges: The Soviet Communist Party Reconsidered, 1933–1938* (New York, 1985), pp. 12–25.

44. Rees, *Decision-Making in the Stalinist Command Economy*, pp. 42–44.

45. RGASPI, f. 17, op. 2, d. 750, l. 52.

46. Ibid., op. 3, d. 913, l. 9.

47. Ibid., op. 2, d. 750, ll. 54–56.

48. Russian State Archive of the Economy (RGAE), f. 4372, op. 92, d. 14, ll. 62–65. The First Five-Year Plan provided for smelting 17 million metric tons of iron in 1932–1933. Adjusted annual growth targets for industrial production during the First Five-Year Plan were: 1929–21.4 percent; 1930–32.0 percent; 1931–45.0 percent; 1932–36.0 percent.

49. Ibid., d. 13, ll. 98–103.

50. Ibid., d. 18, ll. 1–2.

51. Ibid., d. 17, l. 366.

52. Ibid., d. 16, ll. 149–150; d. 17, ll. 213–214.

53. Ibid., d. 17, ll. 367, 434–442.

54. Ibid., d. 18, ll. 76–78.

55. RGASPI, f. 558, op. 11, d. 769, l. 123.

56. Ibid., f. 17, op. 3, d. 933, l. 5.

57. Ibid., f. 558, op. 1, d. 3109; f. 79, op. 1, d. 563, ll. 1–23.

58. GARF, f. R-5446, op. 27, d. 24, ll. 114–1140b.

59. *XVII s'ezd Vsesoiuznoi kommunisticheskoi partii,* p. 435.

60. Ibid., p. 523.

61. Ibid.

62. Robert C. Tucker, *Stalin in Power: The Revolution from Above, 1928–1941* (New York, 1992), pp. 238–242; Robert Conquest, *Stalin and the Kirov Murder* (New York, 1989).

63. Francesco Benvenuti, "Kirov in Soviet Politics, 1933–1934," SIPS, no. 8, CREES, University of Birmingham (1977).

64. Getty, *Origins of the Great Purges,* pp. 92–136.

65. R. A. Medvedev, *O Staline i stalinizme* (Moscow, 1990), pp. 294–296; A. V. Antonov-Ovseenko, "Stalin i ego vremia," *Voprosy istorii,* no. 4 (1989), pp. 93–94.

66. The most detailed refutation of the idea that there was an oppositionist bloc of delegates at the 17th Party Congress is found in Alla Kirilina's book *Rikoshet,* pp. 76–80.

67. In keeping with the subject of this book, the question of Kirov's activities and the legitimacy of seeing a political line separate from Stalin's will be examined further. The question of Kirov's murder and whether or not Stalin was involved in it will not be explored here. It should be noted, however, that documents and research published in recent years refute the idea that Stalin was working to eliminate his potential rival and instead support the idea of a murderer acting alone. Extensive evidence suggests that the man who shot Kirov, L. V. Nikolaev, was the husband of Kirov's lover and that he had reason to seek revenge. There is even evidence suggesting that the murder was committed during a liaison between Kirov and Nikolaev's wife, who worked at party headquarters in Smolny. All of this, of course, does not change the well-established fact that Stalin fully exploited Kirov's murder to intensify repression and deal with former oppositionists. Among the most significant works on this subject are A. Artizov et al. (comp.), *Reabilitatsiia: Kak eto bylo,* vol. 3, *Seredina 80-kh godov — 1991* (Moscow, 2004); A. Kirilina, *Neizvestnyi Kirov* (Moscow, 2001); "Gibel' Kirova. Fakty i versii," *Rodina,* no. 3 (2005), pp. 57–65.

68. N. A. Efimov, "Sergei Mironovich Kirov," *Voprosy istorii,* nos. 11–12 (1995), pp. 51–53.

69. RGASPI, f. 17, op. 162, d. 8, ll. 24–25. For greater detail, see Khlevniuk, *In Stalin's Shadow,* pp. 26–29.

70. A. N. Yakovlev (ed.), *Reabilitatsiia. Politicheskie protsessy 30–50-kh godov* (Moscow, 1990), pp. 362–363. The reference to Serebrovsky's being a "former loyal servant of capitalists" recalls his employment before the revolution as an engineer for private companies.

71. Ibid., p. 421.

72. *Voprosy istorii,* no. 3 (1990), pp. 74–75.

73. A. Orlov, *Tainaia istoriia stalinskikh prestuplenii* (New York, 1983), pp. 24–25.

74. RGASPI, f. 17, op. 163, d. 999, l. 63.

75. Ibid., l. 65. The decision to open a department store in Leningrad was adopted a few months later, on 16 March 1934, after Mikoyan again brought up the matter in the Politburo, where he reported that there was a sufficient supply of goods (ibid., d. 1016, l. 64).

76. GARF, f. R-5446, op. 15a, d. 337, l. 7.

77. Ibid., ll. 8, 9. The text of the telegram also preserves Kuibyshev's comment, "Correct."

78. Ibid., l. 10.

79. Ibid., l. 4.

80. Ibid., l. 2.

81. RGASPI, f. 17, op. 2, d. 484, l. 42.

82. *XVII c'ezd Vsesoiuznoi kommunisticheskoi partii*, p. 26.

83. Davies, *Stalin-Kaganovich Correspondence*, pp. 284–285.

84. O. V. Khlevnyuk and R. W. Davies, "The End of Rationing in the Soviet Union, 1934–1935," *Europe-Asia Studies*, 51, no. 4 (1999).

85. RGASPI., f. 17, op. 2, d. 530, l. 78–98.

86. *Sotsialisticheskii vestnik*, nos. 23–24 (1936), p. 23.

87. RGASPI, f. 80, op. 18, d. 171, ll. 5, 7.

88. Ibid., f. 17, op. 163, d. 1012, ll. 1, 4.

89. Ibid., d. 1015, l. 70.

90. Ibid., ll. 61–62 (emphasis added).

91. Ibid., f. 81, op. 3, d. 164, ll. 39, 48.

92. V. K. Vinogradov et al. (eds.), *Genrikh Iagoda. Sbornik dokumentov* (Kazan, 1997), pp. 405–423. The publishers of this document do not provide an exact date for the conference, but the document content suggests that the conference must have taken place after the creation of the USSR NKVD but before Kirov's murder—in other words, between July and December 1934.

93. RGASPI, f. 558, op. 11, d. 174, l. 137.

94. Robert Sharlet, "Stalinism and Soviet Legal Culture," in Robert C. Tucker (ed.), *Stalinism* (New York, 1974); Eugene Huskey,"Vyshinskii, Krylenko, and the Shaping of the Soviet Legal Order," *Slavic Review*, 46, nos. 3–4 (1987), pp. 414–428; Peter H. Solomon, Jr., *Soviet Criminal Justice under Stalin* (Cambridge, UK, 1996), pp. 153–195.

95. On the activities of the NKVD in 1934, see V. N. Khaustov et al. (comps.), *Lubianka. Stalin i VChK-GPU-OGPU-NKVD. Ianvar' 1922–dekabr' 1936* (Moscow, 2003), pp. 477–576.

96. APRF, f. 3, op. 58, d. 71, ll. 11–31.

97. RGASPI, f. 17, op. 162, d. 16, ll. 88–89. Seliavkin's subsequent life turned out rather well. He survived 1937–1938 and fought in the war, holding the rank of colonel by the time it was over. In the early 1980s he even managed to publish his memoirs (A. I. Seliavkin, *V trekh voinakh na bronevikakh i tankakh* [Kharkov, 1981]), which under the Soviet system signaled a comfortable position within society.

98. Ibid., op. 163, d. 1043, l. 35.

99. Ibid., ll. 38–39.

100. Ibid., l. 37.

101. Ibid., l. 36.

102. Ibid., l. 34.

103. RGASPI, f. 17, op. 163, d. 1045, ll. 136–137.

104. B. A. Viktorov, *Bez grifa "sekretno." Zapiski voennogo prokurora* (Moscow, 1990), pp. 136–138.

105. APRF, f. 3, op. 58, d. 72, ll. 180–187; RGASPI, f. 671, op. 1, d. 80, ll. 33–40.

106. APRF, f. 3, op. 58, d. 72, ll. 4, 91.

107. Ibid., ll. 2–3; Viktorov, *Bez grifa "sekretno,"* p. 139.

108. RGASPI, f. 17, op. 162, d. 17, l. 42.

109. Ibid., l. 57.

110. Viktorov, *Bez grifa "sekretno,"* p. 140.

111. GARF, f. R-5446, op. 27, d. 81, ll. 428–429.

112. RGASPI, f. 17, op. 163, d. 1046, ll. 21–23.

113. Viktorov, *Bez grifa "sekretno,"* p. 140. For the commission's draft conclusions, see APRF, f. 3, op. 58, d. 72, ll. 253–254.

114. APRF, f. 3, op. 58, d. 72, l. 270; Viktorov, *Bez grifa "sekretno,"* p. 140.

115. GARF, f. R-9401, op. 1, d. 4157, l. 202; N. Vert and S. Mironenko (eds.), *Istoriia Stalinskogo Gulaga,* vol. 1, *Massovye repressii v SSSR* (Moscow, 2004), p. 609.

116. RGASPI, f. 17, op. 162, d. 17, l. 31; Khaustov et al., *Lubianka,* p. 566.

117. For more detail, see Khlevniuk et al., *Stalinskoe Politbiuro,* pp. 19, 58–66.

118. Ibid., p. 65.

119. RGASPI, f. 17, op. 162, d. 17, l. 74.

120. GARF, f. R-5446, op. 27, d. 73, l. 3.

121. RGASPI, f. 17, op. 162, d. 17, ll. 80, 82, 86.

CHAPTER 4. TERROR AND CONCILIATION, 1935–1936

1. RGASPI, f. 17, op. 162, d. 17. l. 87.

2. A. N. Yakovlev (ed.), *Reabilitatsiia. Politicheskie protsessy 30–50-kh godov* (Moscow, 1990), pp. 123–147.

3. Ibid., pp. 147–170.

4. Ibid., pp. 191–195.

5. RGASPI, f. 17, op. 162, d. 17, l. 124; op. 42, d. 171, l. 14.

6. Yakovlev, *Reabilitatsiia,* pp. 104–122.

7. V. N. Khaustov et al. (comps.), *Lubianka. Stalin i VChK-GPU-OGPU-NKVD. Ianvar' 1922–dekabr' 1936* (Moscow, 2003), pp. 654–655.

8. RGASPI, f. 17, op. 162, d. 17, ll. 94, 101, 149.

9. O. V. Khlevniuk, *1937-i. Stalin, NKVD i sovetskoe obshchestvo* (Moscow, 1992), pp. 56–57.

10. RGASPI, f. 17, op. 120, d. 184, l. 63; d. 183, ll. 60, 92.

11. Ibid., d. 177, l. 22.

12. The text of the decree has been published several times. See Khaustov et al., *Lubianka,* pp. 676–677.

13. RGASPI, f. 17, op. 3, d. 969, l. 21. This Politburo decision was issued as a decree of the Council of People's Commissars and the Central Executive Committee dated 29 July.

14. Ibid., op. 163, d. 1090, l. 57.

15. Ibid., d. 1106, ll. 135–137.

16. RGASPI, f. 17, op. 163, d. 1091, l. 8.

17. GARF, f. R-5446, op. 18a, d. 896, l. 52.

18. GARF, f. R-8131, op. 37, d. 58, ll. 76–77.

19. For more on this, see Golfo Alexopoulos, *Stalin's Outcasts: Aliens, Citizens, and the Soviet State, 1926–1936* (Ithaca, NY, 2003).

20. V. N. Zemskov, *Spetposelentsy v SSSR, 1930–1960* (Moscow, 2003), p. 21.

21. Oleg V. Khlevniuk, *The History of the Gulag: From Collectivization to the Great Terror* (New Haven, 2004), pp. 129–139.

22. *Pravda,* 2 December 1935. The Politburo decision of 29 March 1936 concerning the case of kolkhoz worker L. A. Oboznaya, the daughter of a kulak, represented a continuation of this campaign (RGASPI, f. 17, op. 163, d. 1102, l. 61). The local authorities had refused to enroll her in courses to become a tractor operator because of her family background. In the Politburo resolution, which was widely published in newspapers, this refusal was characterized as a "violation of the instructions of the party and the government."

23. RGASPI, f. 17, op. 163, d. 1089, ll. 67–68. The initials on the resolution indicate that it was drafted by Vyshinsky.

24. GARF, f. R-8131, op. 37, d. 70, l. 165.

25. Ibid., l. 53.

26. RGASPI, f. 17, op. 163, d. 1098, l. 7.

27. GARF, f. R-8131, op. 37, d. 70, l. 231.

28. Khlevniuk, *History of the Gulag,* pp. 135–137.

29. I. E. Zelenin, "Byl li 'kolkhoznyi neonep'?" *Otechestvennaia istoriia,* no. 2 (1994), p. 118.

30. RGASPI, f. 17, op. 163, d. 1052, l. 153. For the complete text of Stalin's note, see ibid., f. 71, op. 10, d. 130, ll. 13–15.

31. J. Arch Getty, *Origins of the Great Purges: The Soviet Communist Party Reconsidered, 1933–1938* (New York, 1985), chaps. 4, 6, 7; J. Arch Getty and Roberta T. Manning (eds.), *Stalinist Terror: New Perspectives* (New York, 1993), p. 5.

32. O. V. Khlevniuk et al. (eds.), *Stalinskoe Politbiuro v 30-e gody* (Moscow, 1995), p. 142.

33. RGASPI, f. 17, op. 163, d. 1056, ll. 35–36.

34. Khlevniuk et al., *Stalinskoe Politbiuro,* p. 143.

35. Ibid.

36. RGASPI, f. 17, op. 3, d. 961, l. 58.

37. Ibid., d. 963, l. 3.

38. *Izvestiia TsK KPSS,* no. 7 (1989), pp. 86–93.

39. Khaustov et al., *Lubianka,* pp. 599, 601–612, 618–619, 626–637, 638–650, 663–669.

40. RGASPI, f. 17, op. 3, d. 960, l. 14. The same day Ivan Akulov, who held the post of USSR procurator, was appointed Central Executive Committee secretary. Andrei Vyshinsky, Akulov's first deputy, was named to succeed him.

41. Ibid., op. 163, d. 1057, ll. 128–135.

42. A. V. Kvashonkin et al. (comps.), *Sovetskoe rukovodstvo. Perepiska. 1928–1941* (Moscow, 1999), p. 305.

43. RGASPI, f. 17, op. 163, d. 1058, ll. 69, 70.

44. Ibid., d. 1062, ll. 164–169; Yu. N. Zhukov, "Tainy 'kremlovskogo dela' 1935 goda i sud'ba Avelia Enukidze," *Voprosy istorii,* no. 9 (2000), pp. 97–98. "Mineralnye Vody group" was the name given to the numerous resorts located near the town of Mineralnye Vody. In addition to ordinary Soviet vacationers, many top-level officials made it a favorite vacation spot.

45. For greater detail, see Zhukov, "Tainy 'kremlovskogo dela,'" pp. 98–104.

46. O. V. Khlevniuk et al. (comps.), *Stalin i Kaganovich. Perepiska. 1931–1936 gg.* (Moscow, 2001), pp. 557–558.

47. R. W. Davies et al. (eds.), *The Stalin-Kaganovich Correspondence, 1931–36* (New Haven, 2003), p. 307.

48. RGASPI, f. 17, op. 3, d. 971, l. 30.

49. Khlevniuk et al., *Stalin i Kaganovich,* pp. 580, 583.

50. RGASPI, f. 17, op. 2, d. 571, ll. 205–206.

51. V. Tikhanova, *Rasstrel'nye spiski,* vol. 1, *Donskoe kladbishche. 1934–1940* (Moscow, 1993), p. 150.

52. RGASPI, f. 17, op. 163, d. 1081, l. 22; d. 1082, ll. 155, 160, etc.

53. Ibid., d. 1079, l. 140.

54. Ibid., d. 1081, ll. 88, 92; d. 1079, l. 63.

55. Khlevniuk et al. (eds.), *Stalinskoe Politbiuro,* pp. 146 (letter to Ordzhonikidze dated 4 September 1935), 148 (letter to Ordzhonikidze dated 30 September 1936), 149 (letter to Ordzhonikidze dated 30 September 1936), 151 (letter to Ordzhonikidze dated 12 October 1936).

56. See Appendix 2.

57. Khlevniuk et al., *Stalinskoe Politbiuro,* p. 146. "Annual expenditures" is a reference to capital investment in the People's Commissariat of Heavy Industry.

58. RGASPI, f. 17, op. 163, d. 1077, l. 107.

59. Davies et al., *Stalin-Kaganovich Correspondence,* pp. 359–360.

60. RGASPI, f. 17, op. 3, d. 981, ll. 49, 50.

61. Ibid., f. 17, op. 163, d. 1123, ll. 146–147.

62. Yakovlev, *Reabilitatsiia,* p. 200.

63. An actual incident was used to support this accusation. During a September 1934 visit to Prokopevsk, Molotov was involved in a minor automobile accident. The passenger-side wheels of the car driving him from the train station became caught in a ditch. No injuries were sustained.

64. *Sotsialisticheskii vestnik,* nos. 1–2 (1937), p. 24.

65. Aleksandr Orlov, *Tainaia istoriia stalinskikh prestuplenii* (New York, 1983),

pp. 154–159. Based on Orlov's evidence, Robert Conquest believes that Molotov possibly wavered regarding plans to destroy the old Bolsheviks (Robert Conquest, *The Great Terror: A Reassessment* [New York, 1991], pp. 90–91).

66. F. Chuev, *Sto sorok besed s Molotovym* (Moscow, 1990), pp. 414–415.

67. Ibid., pp. 338–339, 416.

68. For more on this, see Oleg V. Khlevniuk, *In Stalin's Shadow: The Career of "Sergo" Ordzhonikidze* (New York, 1995), pp. 40–61.

69. *Voprosy istorii*, nos. 11–12 (1995), pp. 16–17.

70. RGASPI, f. 17, op. 163, d. 988, l. 167.

71. Khlevniuk, *In Stalin's Shadow*, pp. 76–77.

72. GARF, f. R-5446, op. 1, d. 101, l. 170.

73. Davies et al., *Stalin-Kaganovich Correspondence*, p. 182.

74. V. F. Nekrasov (ed.), *Beriia: Konets kar'ery* (Moscow, 1991), p. 378.

75. APRF, f. 3, op. 22, d. 150, l. 129.

76. Davies et al., *Stalin-Kaganovich Correspondence*, pp. 344–345.

77. RGASPI, f. 17, op. 3, d. 980, l. 79.

78. Ibid., l. 75.

79. RGASPI, f. 558, op. 11, d. 779, ll. 98–100. Ordzhonikidze sent Stalin another letter with analogous warnings about mass arrests of former oppositionists in early October (ibid., ll. 119–120).

80. E. A. Rees, *Stalinism and Soviet Rail Transport* (Basingstoke, UK, 1995), pp. 147, 148, 150, 158, 159.

81. RGASPI, f. 558, op. 11, d. 779, l. 100.

82. Ibid., f. 17, op. 2, d. 573, l. 33. The first scholar to take note of this document is J. Arch Getty: J. Arch Getty and Roberta T. Manning (eds.), *Stalinist Terror: New Perspectives* (New York, 1993), p. 55; J. Arch Getty and Oleg V. Naumov (eds.), *The Road to Terror: Stalin and the Self-Destruction of the Bolsheviks, 1932–1939* (New Haven, 1999), pp. 290–291.

83. Quoted in Nekrasov, *Beriia: Konets kar'ery*, p. 368. Bagirov's testimony reflected the position of the party leadership in 1953, after Beria was arrested. Khrushchev laid primary blame on Beria both for the arrest of Papulia Ordzhonikidze and for the death of Sergo Ordzhonikidze himself. But in fact Beria had acted on Stalin's orders, and Ordzhonikidze seems to have understood this perfectly well: Amy Knight, *Beria: Stalin's First Lieutenant* (Princeton, NJ, 1993), pp. 73–74; Khlevniuk, *In Stalin's Shadow*, pp. 103–110.

84. RGASPI, f. 671, op. 1, d. 52, l. 199 (a cover letter accompanying the protocols of NKVD interrogations, which were dated 8 October 1936, sent by Stalin to Yezhov).

85. *O Sergo Ordzhonikidze: Vospominaniia, ocherki, stat'i sovremennikov* (Moscow, 1981), p. 272.

86. *Voprosy istorii*, nos. 11–12 (1995), p. 14.

87. RGASPI, f. 558, op. 11, d. 132, l. 132.

88. Ibid., op. 1, d. 3350, l. 1; *Kommunist*, no. 13 (1991), pp. 59–60.

89. *Voprosy istorii KPSS*, no. 3 (1991), pp. 91–92.

90. RGASPI, f. 558, op. 1, d. 3350, l. 1; *Kommunist*, no. 13 (1991), p. 60.

91. *O Sergo Ordzhonikidze*, p. 275.

92. For the report prepared by Ordzhonikidze's secretary, see RGASPI, f. 85, op. 1, d. 143, l. 1.

93. *Za industrializatsiiu,* 21 February 1937, p. 6.

94. I. Dubinskii-Mukhadze, *Ordzhonikidze* (Moscow, 1963), p. 6.

95. Francesco Benvenuti, "Industry and Purge in the Donbass, 1936–37," *Europe-Asia Studies,* 45, no. 1 (1993), pp. 61–63.

96. S. Z. Ginzburg, *O proshlom — dlia budushchego* (Moscow, 1984), p. 195.

97. RGASPI, f. 17, op. 3, d. 983, l. 1.

98. Ibid., op. 163, d. 1131, ll. 77–79.

99. *O Sergo Ordzhonikidze,* p. 274.

100. *Za industrializatsiiu,* 21 February 1937, p. 8.

101. Ibid., p. 7.

102. *O Sergo Ordzhonikidze,* pp. 278–279.

103. Robert C. Tucker, *Stalin in Power: The Revolution from Above* (New York, 1992), p. 418.

104. See Appendix 2.

105. For more on this, see Khlevniuk, *In Stalin's Shadow,* pp. 150–162.

CHAPTER 5. STALIN AND THE GREAT TERROR, 1937–1938

1. J. Arch Getty, *Origins of the Great Purges: The Soviet Communist Party Reconsidered, 1933–1938* (New York, 1985); G. T. Rittersporn, *Stalinist Simplifications and Soviet Complications: Social Tensions and Political Conflicts in the USSR, 1933–1953* (Philadelphia, 1991); J. Arch Getty and Roberta T. Manning (eds.), *Stalinist Terror: New Perspectives* (New York, 1993); Robert W. Thurston, *Life and Terror in Stalin's Russia, 1934–1941* (New Haven, 1996). Getty reaffirmed his commitment to his long-held views (albeit in a less categorical form) in J. Arch Getty and Oleg V. Naumov (eds.), *The Road to Terror: Stalin and the Self-Destruction of the Bolsheviks, 1932–1939* (New Haven, 1999).

2. A. E. Gur'ianov (ed.), *Repressii protiv poliakov i pol'skikh grazhdan* (Moscow, 1997); I. L. Shcherbakova (ed.), *Repressii protiv rossiiskikh nemtsev. Nakazannyi narod* (Moscow, 1999); Marc Jansen and Nikita Petrov, *Stalin's Loyal Executioner: People's Commissar Nikolai Ezhov, 1895–1940* (Stanford, CA, 2002); M. Yunge and R. Binner, *Kak terror stal "bol'shim." Sekretnyi prikaz No. 00447 i tekhnologiia ego ispolneniia* (Moscow, 2003); J. Baberowski, *Der rote Terror: Die Geschichte des Stalinismus* (Munich, 2004); Oleg V. Khlevniuk, *The History of the Gulag: From Collectivization to the Great Terror* (New Haven, 2004).

3. RGASPI, f. 17, op. 71, d. 43, 44, 45.

4. *Voprosy istorii,* nos. 11–12 (1995), p. 13.

5. Ibid., no. 3 (1995), p. 8.

6. Ibid., p. 9.

7. Ibid., no. 7 (1995), pp. 12–15.

8. Sheila Fitzpatrick, *The Cultural Front: Power and Culture in Revolutionary Russia* (Ithaca, NY, 1992), p. 180. In her book, Fitzpatrick defines *vydvizhentsy* as "workers and peasants 'promoted' to white-collar, professional, and managerial

work, especially the cohort selected for higher education during the Cultural Revolution." Ibid., p. xx.

9. *Voprosy istorii*, no. 3 (1995), p. 14.

10. *Istochnik*, no. 0 (1993), p. 23; no. 4, p. 18.

11. Joseph E. Davies, *Mission to Moscow* (London, 1942). I am grateful to Professor E. A. Rees for pointing this out to me.

12. Isaac Deutscher, *Stalin: A Political Biography* (London, 1949), pp. 376–377.

13. Mark Harrison and R. W. Davies, "The Soviet Military-Economic Effort during the Second Five-Year Plan (1933–1937)," *Europe-Asia Studies*, 49, no. 3 (1997), pp. 369–406.

14. APRF, f. 3, op. 65, d. 223, ll. 90, 141–142, 146. For a closer look at this, see O. V. Khlevniuk, "The Reasons for the 'Great Terror': The Foreign-Political Aspect," in S. Pons and A. Romano (eds.), *Russia in the Age of Wars, 1914–1945* (Milan, 2000), pp. 159–170.

15. *Belaia kniga o deportatsii koreiskogo naseleniia Rossii v 30-kh godakh. Kn. 1*, (Moscow, 1992), pp. 68–69.

16. F. Chuev, *Sto sorok besed s Molotovym* (Moscow, 1990), pp. 390, 391, 416.

17. L. M. Kaganovich, *Pamiatnye zapiski* (Moscow, 1996), pp. 549, 558.

18. RGASPI, f. 558, op. 11, d. 772, l. 14.

19. Ibid., l. 88.

20. *Voprosy istorii*, no. 3 (1995), pp. 13–14.

21. RGASPI, f. 558, op. 11, d. 203, ll. 62, 77–78.

22. Between 1930 and 1936 alone, according to estimates, approximately one-sixth of the adult population were subject to some form of repression and persecution: arrest, conviction, expulsion from the party, exile, dekulakization, etc. (Khlevniuk, *History of the Gulag*, p. 304).

23. Vladimir N. Khaustov, "Razvitie sovetskikh organov gosudarstvennoi bezopasnosti: 1917–1953 gg.," *Cahiers du monde russe*, 42, nos. 2–4 (2001), p. 370. Khaustov points out that by March 1941 approximately 1,263,000 people were registered as "anti-Soviet elements." It can be presumed that in 1937, before the mass operations, the figure was higher.

24. Recent research in this area has shown that the government's struggle against growing criminality was fed into the policy of mass repression: D. Shearer, "Social Disorder, Mass Repression and the NKVD during the 1930s," in Barry McLoughlin and Kevin McDermott (eds.), *Stalin's Terror: High Politics and Mass Repression in the Soviet Union* (Basingstoke, UK, 2003), pp. 85–117; Paul Hagenloh, "'Socially Harmful Elements' and the Great Terror," in Sheila Fitzpatrick (ed.), *Stalinism: New Directions* (London, 2000), pp. 286–308.

25. RGASPI, f. 17, op. 2, d. 773, l. 115.

26. *Voprosy istorii*, nos. 11–12 (1995), pp. 21–22.

27. Sheila Fitzpatrick, *Stalin's Peasants: Resistance and Survival in the Russian Village after Collectivization* (Oxford, 1994), pp. 238–254.

28. *Voprosy istorii*, no. 6 (1993), p. 6.

29. Ibid., p. 27.

30. Ibid., p. 25.

31. The census results showed that 57 percent of those sixteen and older were re-

ligious (more than fifty-five million people), even though many believers, fearing repercussions, hid their true attitude toward religion (B. V. Zhiromskaia, I. N. Kiselev, and Iu. A. Poliakov, *Polveka pod grifom "sekretno": Vsesoiuznaia perepis' naseleniia 1937 goda* [Moscow 1996], pp. 98, 100).

32. *Voprosy istorii*, no. 6 (1993), pp. 14–15.

33. Ibid., nos. 5–6 (1995), pp. 10–11. The Dashnaks were members of the Armenian Dashnaktsutiun (Union) Party, founded in the late nineteenth century. The Musavat (Equality) Party emerged in Azerbaijan in 1911 as the Islamic Democratic Musavat Party.

34. Ibid., no. 8 (1995), p. 16.

35. Ibid., p. 22.

36. To be officially registered, a religious society had to have no fewer than twenty founding members. This is the origin for the common name used for registered societies—*dvadtsatki* (*dvadtsat'* is Russian for "twenty"). Many more than that number of religious believers could be organized around the twenty activists who wrote the application registering the society.

37. APRF, f. 3, op. 60, d. 5, ll. 34–37.

38. L. P. Rasskazov, *Karatel'nye organy v protsesse formirovaniia i funktsionirovaniia administrativno-komandnoi sistemy v sovetskom gosudarstve (1917–1941 gg.)* (Ufa, 1994), p. 316.

39. RGASPI, f. 17, op. 162, d. 21, l. 9.

40. V. N. Khaustov et al. (comps.), *Lubianka. Stalin i Glavnoe upravlenie gosbezopasnosti NKVD. 1937–1938* (Moscow, 2004), pp. 189–190.

41. Ibid., p. 642.

42. For a more detailed look at the lead-up to and implementation of large-scale operations, see Khlevniuk, *History of the Gulag*, pp. 140–170.

43. This document was first published in the newspaper *Trud* (4 June 1992). Taken from this source, it has been published in English in Getty and Naumov, *Road to Terror*, pp. 470–471 (the Politburo decision is mistakenly given as 3 July instead of 2 July).

44. This order has been widely published. Its English translation can be found in Getty and Naumov, *Road to Terror*, pp. 473–478.

45. The text of this order is available in numerous publications. See, for example, *Butovskii polygon, 1937–1938 gg.: Kniga pamiati zhertv politicheskikh represii* (Moscow, 1997), pp. 353–354.

46. N. V. Petrov and A. B. Roginskii, "'Pol'skaia operatsiia' NKVD 1937–1938 gg.," in A. E. Gur'ianov (ed.), *Repressii protiv poliakov i pol'skikh grazhdan*, pp. 22–43; N. Okhotin and A. Roginskii, "Iz istorii 'nemetskoi operatsii' NKVD 1937–1938," in Shcherbakova, *Repressii protiv sovetskikh nemtsev*, pp. 35–75.

47. It was this requirement that not just individual "enemies" but "counterrevolutionary groups" be identified that was a main reason the chekists had to obtain confessions from those arrested.

48. N. F. Bugai, "Vyselenie sovetskikh koreitsev s Dal'nego Vostoka," *Voprosy istorii*, no. 5 (1994), pp. 141–148.

49. There were several ways to have a quota raised: through Politburo decisions,

by receiving permission personally from Stalin, or by receiving permission from Stalin through Yezhov. Permission from Stalin did not have to be formally entered in Politburo protocols (Jansen and Petrov, *Stalin's Loyal Executioner,* pp. 90–91).

50. Petrov and Roginskii, "'Pol'skaia operatsiia' NKVD," p. 30.

51. RGASPI, f. 17, op. 3, d. 994, l. 56. This decision was issued as a USSR Council of People's Commissars decree dated 10 January 1938 (GARF, f. R-5446, op. 1, d. 498, l. 27).

52. Peter H. Solomon, Jr., "Soviet Criminal Justice and Great Terror," *Slavic Review,* 46, no. 3 (1987), pp. 405–406.

53. The decrees were published in *Moskovskie novosti,* 21 June 1992, p. 19, and in *Izvestiia,* 3 April 1996.

54. RGASPI, f. 558, op. 11, d. 729, ll. 94–95; Khaustov et al., *Lubianka,* p. 463; Khlevniuk, *History of the Gulag,* p. 163.

55. GARF, f. 9401, op. 1, d. 4157, ll. 201–205. These figures have been cited in a number of sources. See, for example, J. Arch Getty and Oleg V. Naumov, *Road to Terror,* p. 588. The difference of more than 200,000 between arrests and convictions could have a variety of explanations. Some of those arrested in 1937–1938 were convicted in later years. Some of them died while their cases were under investigation. A small number of those arrested were released.

56. Jansen and Petrov, *Stalin's Loyal Executioner,* pp. 103–104.

57. For the text of the directive on banning troikas, see *Moskovskie novosti,* 21 June 1992, p. 19.

58. *Istoricheskii arkhiv,* no. 1 (1992), pp. 125–128.

59. A. N. Yakovlev (ed.), *Reabilitatsiia. Politicheskie protsessy 30–50-kh godov* (Moscow, 1990), p. 39.

60. *Stalinskie rasstrel'nye spiski* (Moscow, 2002), available at http://www.memo .ru/history/vkvs/.

61. A number of documents on such trips are published in A. V. Kvashonkin et al. (comps.), *Sovetskoe rukovodstvo. Perepiska. 1928–1941* (Moscow, 1999).

62. Robert Conquest, *The Great Terror: A Reassessment* (New York, 1991), p. 14.

63. B. Sultanbekov, "Nikolai Ezhov," *Tatarstan,* no. 1 (1992), p. 30.

64. *Literaturnaia gazeta,* 22 August 1990, p. 6.

65. A. M. Larina (Bukharina), *Nezabyvaemoe* (Moscow, 1989), p. 270. Similar testimonials have recently been published in a new, otherwise uninteresting book about Yezhov: A. Polianskii, *A. Ezhov. Istoriia "zheleznogo" stalinskogo narkoma* (Moscow, 2001), pp. 29–30.

66. RGASPI, f. 17, op. 3, d. 805, l. 16.

67. See R. A. Medvedev, *O Staline i stalinizme* (Moscow, 1990), p. 320.

68. Robert Thurston, "The Stakhanovite Movement: The Background to the Great Terror in the Factories, 1935–1938," in Getty and Manning, *Stalinist Terror,* pp. 159–160.

69. RGASPI, f. 17, op. 114, d. 332, ll. 150–151.

70. Ibid., ll. 4, 20.

71. Ibid., d. 353, l. 37; d. 351, l. 14.

72. *Voprosy istorii,* no. 2 (1995), pp. 16–17.

73. RGASPI, f. 671, op. 1, d. 52, l. 48.

74. Ibid., ll. 72–76. On 19 September 1935 the Politburo adopted a decision to grant Yezhov a two-month vacation beginning 1 October and a directive that he go abroad with his wife for treatment. Three thousand rubles in foreign currency were allocated for this purpose. When circulating the resolution for voting, Kaganovich made the following note on the draft: "To Politburo Members. Com. Stalin, in a letter to Com. Yezhov, indicated the necessity of his going on vacation" (RGASPI, f. 17, op. 163, d. 1079, l. 63).

75. Yakovlev, *Reabilitatsiia,* pp. 178–180.

76. Ibid., pp. 244–245.

77. *Rodina,* no. 2 (1996), pp. 92–93.

78. RGASPI, f. 671, op. 1, d. 52, ll. 186–194.

79. Ibid., f. 558, op. 11, d. 729, ll. 90–92.

80. On 14 September 1936 Yezhov sent Stalin yet another letter with information that the NKVD apparatus was intentionally "glossing over" the case against Trotskyites (ibid., ll. 86–89).

81. RGASPI, f. 671, op. 1, d. 52, ll. 191–193.

82. Larina (Bukharina), *Nezabyvaemoe,* pp. 269–270.

83. V. F. Nekrasov, *Trinadtsat' "zheleznykh" narkomov. Istoriia NKVD-MVD ot A. I. Rykova do Shchelokova. 1917–1982* (Moscow, 1995), p. 211.

84. RGASPI, f. 17, op. 163, d. 1163, l. 71 (the decision to appoint Gribov and Timoshenko was approved by the Politburo the next day, 3 September).

85. Numerous examples of such interrogation transcripts with notes and comments by Stalin are published in Khaustov et al., *Lubianka.*

86. Yakovlev, *Reabilitatsiia,* p. 291.

87. See Appendix 2.

88. Many of these directives are published in Getty and Naumov, *Road to Terror.*

89. RGASPI, f. 558, op. 11, d. 57, l. 57. Other telegrams from Stalin of a similar nature have been published. See *Izvestia,* 10 June 1992, p. 7.

90. RGASPI, f. 17, op. 3, d. 998, l. 21.

91. Ibid., ll. 37, 40, 41.

92. RGASPI, f. 671, op. 1, d. 265, l. 19.

93. Ibid., l. 22.

94. Ibid., ll. 22–25.

95. RGASPI, f. 17, op. 3, d. 1002, l. 37; op. 163, d. 1200, l. 1.

96. Ibid., op. 3, d. 1002, l. 51; d. 1003, ll. 11, 13, 17.

97. *Voprosy istorii,* nos. 2–3 (1992), p. 87.

98. *Istoricheskii arkhiv,* no. 1 (1992), pp. 125–128.

99. Ibid., nos. 5–6 (1995), p. 25.

100. Ibid., no. 1 (1992), pp. 129–130.

101. Ibid., p. 131.

102. RGASPI, f. 671, op. 1, d. 265, l. 220b.

103. *Voenno-istoricheskii zhurnal,* no. 7 (1993), p. 50.

CHAPTER 6. ON THE EVE OF WAR: THE NEW STRUCTURE OF STALIN'S GOVERNMENT

1. RGASPI, f. 17, op. 3, d. 983, ll. 110–112; J. Arch Getty and Oleg V. Naumov (eds.), *The Road to Terror: Stalin and the Self-Destruction of the Bolsheviks, 1932–1939* (New Haven, 1999), pp. 353–357.

2. *Voprosy istorii*, no. 7 (1995), p. 19.

3. Ibid.

4. *Bolshevik*, no. 7 (1937), p. 24.

5. Despite her moment in the sun, Nikolaenko did not manage to have a successful career. The new leadership in Kiev also tried to get rid of Nikolaenko, who did not abandon her denunciatory ways. On 17 September 1937, Nikolaenko wrote a new letter to the "Leader of the party and the people, the Great Stalin," complaining that she was being victimized. Acting expeditiously, Stalin forwarded the letter on 27 September to S. A. Kudriavtsev, second secretary of the Ukrainian Communist Party's Central Committee, with the following note: "Com. Kudriavtsev! Please take note of Com. Nikolaenko (see her letter below). Is it really so hard to protect her from hooliganistic types? . . ." (RGASPI, f. 558, op. 11, d. 132, l. 136). Some time later, Nikita Khrushchev was forced to deal with Nikolaenko's complaints when he was appointed first secretary of the Ukrainian Central Committee. In February 1939, Stalin was prompted by a letter from Nikolaenko to assign him the following task: "Com. Khrushchev. A request to take measures so that Com. Nikolaenko can work productively and in peace" (ibid., l. 141). As Khrushchev writes in his memoirs, he had to meet several times with Nikolaenko and finally was forced to conclude that she was not psychologically normal. Soon Nikolaenko moved to Moscow and then to Tashkent. According to Khrushchev, Stalin eventually lost interest in her (*Voprosy istorii*, no. 4 [1990], pp. 70–72).

6. A. N. Yakovlev (ed.), *Reabilitatsiia. Politicheskie protsessy 30–50-kh godov* (Moscow, 1990), p. 34.

7. Ibid., pp. 63–64.

8. *Voprosy istorii*, nos. 5–6 (1995), p. 4.

9. RGASPI, f. 17, op. 3, d. 989, l. 9; Getty and Naumov, *Road to Terror*, p. 363 (Politburo resolution dated 14 July 1937).

10. RGASPI, f. 17, op. 163, d. 1180, ll. 57–59.

11. Ibid., op. 3, d. 994, l. 55.

12. Ignatov played his part well and, having earned Stalin's approval, went on to have a successful career. For many years he headed a series of provincial and territorial party organizations, and during the last year of Stalin's life he was made a secretary of the Central Committee of the Communist Party of the Soviet Union. Under Khrushchev, Ignatov held high-level government posts, but feeling that he had been passed over, he recalled the years of his political youth and became actively involved in the plot against Khrushchev, which led to his removal from power in October 1964.

13. O. V. Khlevniuk et al. (eds.), *Stalinskoe Politbiuro v 30-e gody* (Moscow, 1995), p. 166.

14. Ibid., pp. 166–167; Getty and Naumov, *Road to Terror*, p. 510.

15. Khlevniuk et al., *Stalinskoe Politbiuro*, p. 167; Getty and Naumov, *Road to Terror*, p. 512.

16. RGASPI, f. 17, op. 3, d. 996, ll. 17–18; Getty and Naumov, *Road to Terror,* p. 514.

17. Lars T. Lih, Oleg V. Naumov, and Oleg Khlevniuk (eds.), *Stalin's Letters to Molotov, 1925–1936* (New Haven, 1995), pp. 202–203.

18. Yakovlev, *Reabilitatsiia,* pp. 35–37.

19. Khlevniuk et al., *Stalinskoe Politbiuro,* p. 167.

20. Ibid., p. 168.

21. For greater detail, see T. H. Rigby, *Political Elites in the USSR: Central Leaders and Local Cadres from Lenin to Gorbachev* (Aldershot, UK, 1990), pp. 138–143.

22. R. W. Davies et al. (eds.), *The Stalin-Kaganovich Correspondence, 1931–36* (New Haven, 2003), pp. 152, 180–181.

23. G. Kumanev, *Riadom so Stalinym* (Smolensk, 2001), p. 94; F. Chuev, *Sto sorok besed s Molotovym* (Moscow, 1990), pp. 413–414.

24. GARF, f. R-5446, op. 37, d. 1, ll. 27–28.

25. RGASPI, f. 17, op. 162, d. 19, ll. 193, 201.

26. Chuev, *Sto sorok besed s Molotovym,* pp. 411–412.

27. RGASPI, f. 17, op. 3, d. 995, l. 17.

28. This view received its fullest expression in articles by Boris Starkov and J. Arch Getty published in J. Arch Getty and Roberta T. Manning (eds.), *Stalinist Terror: New Perspectives* (New York, 1993). However, as I have already written, the sensational data reported by Starkov do not hold up to verification (O. Khlevniuk, "Upravlenie gosudarstvennym terrorom," *Svobodnaia mysl',* nos. 7–8 [1994], pp. 123–127; O. Hlevnjuk, "L'Historien et le document. Remarques sur l'utilisation des archives," *Cahiers du monde russe,* 40, nos. 1–2, pp. 101–112).

29. RGASPI, f. 671, op. 1, d. 52, l. 122.

30. F. Chuev, *Kaganovich. Shepilov* (Moscow, 2001), pp. 53–54, 103–105.

31. *Voprosy istorii,* no. 8 (1990), p. 65.

32. Ibid., p. 71.

33. K. M. Simonov, *Glazami cheloveka moego pokoleniia. Razmyshleniia o I. V. Staline* (Moscow, 1988), p. 347.

34. RGASPI, f. 17, op. 3, d. 990, ll. 54, 72.

35. Khlevniuk et al., *Stalinskoe Politbiuro,* p. 171.

36. Ibid., p. 172; RGASPI, f. 17, op. 163, d. 1237, ll. 223–224. On 21 November 1939 the Politburo approved Zhemchuzhina's appointment as head of the Textile and Notions Industry Administration of the RSFSR Commissariat of Light Industry (Khlevniuk et al., *Stalinskoe Politbiuro,* p. 172).

37. G. V. Kostyrchenko, *Tainaia politika Stalina. Vlast' i antisemitizm* (Moscow, 2001), pp. 445–450.

38. RGASPI, f. 17, op. 163, d. 1135, l. 13.

39. Ibid., d. 1173, l. 41.

40. Ibid., l. 17.

41. See, for example, Khlevniuk et al., *Stalinskoe Politbiuro,* pp. 38–39.

42. RGASPI, f. 17, op. 163, d. 1216, l. 194.

43. *XVIII s'ezd Vsesoiuznoi kommunisticheskoi partii (b). 10–21 marta 1939 g. Stenograficheskii otchet* (Moscow, 1939), p. 493.

44. Lih, Naumov, and Khlevniuk, *Stalin's Letters to Molotov,* p. 131.

45. Ibid., p. 232.

46. Ibid., p. 238.

47. Ibid., p. 228.

48. N. G. Kuznetsov, "Krutye povoroty. Iz zapisok admirala," *Voenno-istoricheskii zhurnal,* no. 7 (1993), p. 48.

49. *Izvestiia TsK KPSS,* no. 1 (1990), pp. 193–209.

50. *Voprosy istorii,* no. 7 (1990), p. 104.

51. *Desiatyi s'ezd RKP(b). Stenograficheskii otchet. Mart 1921 g.* (Moscow, 1963), pp. 381–383, 674–685; *Istochnik,* no. 3 (1994), p. 74.

52. R. A. Medvedev, *Oni okruzhali Stalina* (Moscow, 1990), p. 183. Anastas Mikoyan's son, Sergo Mikoyan, believes that the story of this threat is apocryphal. In his opinion, Mikoyan could not have been shot along with the Baku commissars since he was not one of them (*A. I. Mikoian. K 100-letiiu so dnia rozhdeniia. Materialy 'kruglogo stola' v Gorbachev-Fonde 15 dekabria 1995* [Moscow, 1996], pp. 84, 85). This argument, however, does not preclude the possibility of a case having been fabricated against Mikoyan.

53. Moshe Lewin, *Russia—USSR—Russia* (New York, 1995), p. 90.

54. J. Arch Getty, "Stalin as Prime Minister: Power and the Politburo," in Sarah Davies and James Harris (eds.), *Stalin: A New History* (New York, 2005), p. 99.

55. RGASPI, f. 17, op. 3, d. 986, ll. 1–2.

56. Khlevniuk et al., *Stalinskoe Politbiuro,* p. 171.

57. See Appendix 2.

58. RGASPI, f. 17, op. 163, d. 1179, ll. 144, 146, 154, 160, 164, 166; d. 1180, l. 21, etc.

59. Ibid., d. 1221, l. 36.

60. Ibid., d. 1315, ll. 152–153.

61. For more on this period in Beria's career, see Amy Knight, *Beria: Stalin's First Lieutenant* (Princeton, NJ, 1993), pp. 90–109.

62. See Oleg V. Khlevniuk, *The History of the Gulag: From Collectivization to the Great Terror* (New Haven, 2004), pp. 186–227.

63. Davies et al., *Stalin-Kaganovich Correspondence,* p. 182.

64. See, for example, GARF, f. R-5446, op. 27, d. 67, l. 16.

65. A. V. Kvashonkin et al. (comps.), *Sovetskoe rukovodstvo. Perepiska. 1928–1941* (Moscow, 1999), p. 204; Knight, *Beria,* pp. 50–51.

66. RGASPI, f. 17, op. 163, d. 1161, ll. 11, 60; d. 1195, ll. 76–77, etc.

67. See Medvedev, *Oni okruzhali Stalina,* p. 281.

68. RGASPI, f. 17, op. 163, d. 1185, ll. 235–236.

69. Ibid., d. 1220, ll. 106–107.

70. See Appendix 2.

71. RGASPI, f. 558, op. 11, d. 762, ll. 1–2.

72. In 1953, after Beria was arrested and sent to Malenkov, the transcript of the interrogation during which Yezhov gave evidence against Malenkov was found in

Beria's safe. Malenkov destroyed it (O. V. Khlevniuk et al. [comps.], *Politbiuro TsK VKP(b) i Sovet Ministrov SSSR. 1945–1953* [Moscow, 2002], p. 203).

73. For information about Voznesensky's activities during the prewar years, see Mark Harrison, *Soviet Planning in Peace and War, 1938–1945* (New York, 1985), pp. 13–27.

74. Kumanev, *Riadom so Stalinym,* p. 496.

75. A. I. Mikoian, *Tak bylo. Razmyshleniia o minuvshem* (Moscow, 1999), p. 559.

76. For greater detail, see S. S. Khizhniakov and O. V. Khlevniuk, *XVIII partkonferentsiia: Vremia, problemy, resheniia* (Moscow, 1990).

77. Khlevniuk et al., *Stalinskoe Politbiuro,* pp. 172–173.

78. Ibid., p. 55.

79. RGASPI, f. 17, op. 163, d. 1145, l. 63.

80. V. N. Khaustov et al. (comps.), *Lubianka. Stalin i Glavnoe upravlenie gosbezopasnosti NKVD. 1937–1938* (Moscow, 2004), pp. 400, 651.

81. *Istoricheskii arkhiv,* no. 4 (1995), p. 67.

82. G. M. Adibekov et al. (eds.), *Politbiuro TsK RKP(b)-VKP(b). Povestki dnia zasedanii,* vol. 2, *1930–1939* (Moscow, 2001), pp. 916–917.

83. RGASPI, f. 17, op. 163, d. 1242, l. 69.

84. Khlevniuk et al., *Stalinskoe Politbiuro,* p. 44.

85. *Istoricheskii arkhiv,* nos. 5–6 (1995), pp. 62–63.

86. See Appendix 2.

87. L. E. Reshin et al. (comps.), *1941 god. Kn. 2* (Moscow, 1998), p. 499.

88. L. E. Reshin et al. (comps.), *1941 god. Kn. 1* (Moscow, 1998), p. 350.

89. *Istochnik,* no. 5 (1997), p. 114.

90. Khlevniuk et al., *Stalinskoe Politbiuro,* p. 33.

91. Ibid., p. 34.

92. RGASPI, f. 17, op. 162, d. 26, ll. 3–4.

93. RGASPI, f. 82, op. 2, d. 393, ll. 63–70; GARF, f. R-5446, op. 1, d. 164, ll. 269–272; Mikoian, *Tak bylo,* pp. 344–345.

94. Zhdanov, Mikoyan, and Beria were appointed to the Defense Committee by a Politburo resolution dated 10 September 1939.

95. *Istochnik,* no. 5 (1997), p. 114.

96. It was issued as a USSR SNK and TsK VKP(b) resolution dated 21 March 1941 (GARF, f. R-5446, op. 1, d. 183, ll. 315–317).

97. It was issued as a USSR SNK and TsK VKP(b) resolution dated 21 March 1941 (GARF, f. R-5446, op. 1, d. 183, ll. 323–324).

98. GARF, f. R-5446, op. 70, d. 4, l. 221.

99. Ibid., op. 34, d. 1, l. 39.

100. T. P. Korzhikhina, *Sovetskoe gosudarstvo i ego uchrezhdeniia. Noiabr' 1917 g.-dekabr' 1991 g.* (Moscow, 1994), p. 47.

101. RGASPI, f. 17, op. 163, d. 1304, ll. 150–151.

102. APRF, f. 3, op. 52, d. 251, l. 50.

103. Mikoian, *Tak bylo,* p. 346.

104. RGASPI, f. 558, op. 11, d. 769, ll. 176–176ob.

105. APRF, f. 3, op. 52, d. 251, ll. 58–60.

106. Khlevniuk et al., *Stalinskoe Politbiuro*, pp. 34–35; *Istoricheskii arkhiv*, no. 5 (1994), p. 222.

107. Khlevniuk et al., *Stalinskoe Politbiuro*, p. 35.

108. *Istoricheskii arkhiv*, no. 2 (1996), p. 46.

109. RGASPI, f. 17, op. 163, d. 1313, l. 128.

110. Ibid., ll. 128–130. The decision on the new composition of the Bureau was recorded as a Council of People's Commissars decree dated 7 May 1941 (GARF, f. R-5446, op. 1, d. 190, l. 253).

111. GARF, f. R-5446, op. 1, d. 190, ll. 254, 259–260; RGASPI, f. 17, op. 163, d. 1313, ll. 131–133.

112. GARF, f. R-5446, op. 1, d. 192, ll. 100, 435.

113. GARF, f. R-5446, op. 1, d. 192, l. 111. (The decree was approved on 19 May 1941.)

114. Khlevniuk et al., *Stalinskoe Politbiuro*, pp. 35–36.

115. The chief of administration of the Council of People's Commissars, Ya. E. Chadaev, attested to this. He was present during meetings of the council and the Bureau and, in a number of cases, at Politburo meetings.

116. RGASPI, f. 17, op. 163, d. 1314, ll. 1, 18, 152, 153, etc.

117. Ibid., l. 171; RGASPI, f. 17, op. 163, d. 1315, ll. 57, 58, 60, 183; d. 1316, ll. 15, 105, 107, etc.

CONCLUSION: MASTER OF THE HOUSE

1. Alec Nove (ed.), *The Stalin Phenomenon* (New York, 1993), pp. 24–29.

2. Iu. A. Gor'kov, *Gosudarstvennyi Komitet Oborony postanovliaet (1941–1945). Tsifry. Dokumenty* (Moscow, 2002), pp. 30–31.

3. A. A. Pechenkin, "Gosudarstvennyi Komitet Oborony v 1941 godu," *Otechestvennaia istoriia*, nos. 4–5 (1994), p. 130; ibid., no. 3 (2003), p. 70 (interview by G. A. Kumanev with I. T. Peresypkin, former head of the Main Communications Administration of the Red Army); A. I. Mikoian, *Tak bylo. Razmyshleniia o minuvshem* (Moscow, 1999) pp. 463–464.

4. Mikoian, *Tak bylo*, p. 465.

5. RGASPI, f. 17, op. 163, d. 1335, ll. 42–45.

6. Gor'kov, *Gosudarstvennyi Komitet Oborony*, p. 31.

7. Mikoian, *Tak bylo*, p. 466.

8. RGASPI, f. 17, op. 163, d. 1420, l. 136.

9. O. V. Khlevniuk et al. (eds.), *Politbiuro TsK VKP(b) i Sovet Ministrov SSSR. 1945–1953* (Moscow, 2002), pp. 195–202.

10. RGASPI, f. 17, op. 163, d. 1349, l. 5.

11. Ibid., d. 1350, l. 40; d. 1356, ll. 120–121; d. 1406, l. 27.

12. Ibid., d. 1356, ll. 120–121.

13. Ibid., d. 1406, l. 27.

14. The following description of the system of leadership and the relationships between Stalin and his comrades-in-arms during the postwar years is based on materials from Yoram Gorlizki and Oleg Khlevniuk, *Cold Peace: Stalin and the Soviet Ruling Circle, 1945–1953* (New York, 2004).

15. The opinion has been expressed in scholarly literature that under Stalin the patron-client relationship played a special role, even greater than after his death (Charles H. Fairbanks, Jr., "Clientelism and the Roots of Post-Soviet Disorder," in Ronald Grigor Suny [ed.], *Transcaucasia, Nationalism, and Social Change* [Ann Arbor, 1996], p. 347).

16. RGASPI, f. 17, op. 163, d. 1598, l. 60; d. 1604, l. 186; d. 1611, l. 140, etc.

17. Khlevniuk et al., *Politbiuro TsK VKP(b) i Sovet Ministrov SSSR*, pp. 113–114, 116. According to M. A. Menshikov, who served as minister for foreign trade from 1949 to 1951 and was often present at meetings of the Politburo or the Bureau of the Council of People's Commissars, there was a telephone booth behind the chairman's seat equipped with a direct line for talking with Stalin or his aides. "The walls and door of the booth were well soundproofed, so those sitting in the hall could not hear a thing" (M. A. Men'shikov, *S vintovkoi i vo frake* [Moscow, 1996], p. 148).

18. Khlevniuk et al., *Politbiuro TsK VKP(b) i Sovet Ministrov SSSR*, pp. 438–564.

Index

Administrative cadres, Stalin's attacks on, 81–82, 169–172

Agranov, Yakov Saulovich, 191

Agriculture: collectivization, 8, 37, 42; dekulakization, 10, 39–40; grain collection policy, 42, 45–46, 47, 48–49, 62, 87; minireforms in, 45–46, 62–63; moderate policies in, 87, 91. *See also* Peasants

Akulov, Ivan Alekseevich, 35, 42, 77, 119, 121, 122, 123, 290n40

All-Union Conference of Workers of Socialist Industry, 57–58

Andreev, Andrei Andreevich, xxiii, 49, 68, 78, 230; in Bureau of Council of People's Commissars, 236, 240, 241; in interagency conflict, 75; Politburo appointment of, 54; and Postyshev's dismissal, 209; responsibilities of, 139, 140; and Trotskyites, 223; visits to Stalin's office, 230, 268–271

Antipov Nikolai Kirillovich, 216

Archival sources: correspondence, xxiv–xxv; memoirs and journals, xxiv; for Politburo meetings, xxi–xxiv

Army: Cossacks in, 136; expenditures, 173; interagency conflicts over deferments, 76; modernization, 97–98; purge of, 166, 174, 180, 222; and rightist plot, 17–18

Arrest procedures of NKVD, 131, 198, 199

Bagirov, Mir Dzhafar Abbasovich, 155–156, 291n83

Baltimore Sun (newspaper), 91

Barter transactions, 9, 113

Belenky, Mark Natanovich, 114

Benvenuti, Francesco, 108

Beria, Lavrenty Pavlovich: xiii–xiv; arrest of, 291n83, 299n72; in "bad" cohort of Politburo, xvii; black mark against, 110; in Bureau of Council of People's Commissars, 236, 240, 241; in group of Five, 231; Molotov on, 149; NKVD under, 225; and Ordzhonikidze, 226, 291n83; Ordzhonikidze on, 155–156; Politburo appointment of, 224, 229; in postwar leadership, 259, 260; and Stalin, 225–226; on subversive elements, 178–179; visits to Stalin's office, 225, 240; in wartime leadership, 257, 258; as Yezhov's deputy, 197–198, 225

Bezymensky, Aleksandr Ilich, 69–70

Bilik, Pavel Borisovich, 75–76

Bolshevik (journal), 90

Briukhanov, Nikolai Pavlovich, 14, 15

Brodov, Evel' L'vovich, 164

Bukharin, Nikolai Ivanovich, xv, xvi, 173; editorship of *Izvestia*, 89, 93; rehabilitation of, 89; removal from Politburo, 10;